Remember "Hever"
5. 6. '97

THE DUKE

and

THE EMPEROR

Wellington and Napoleon

———— ✳ ————

JOHN STRAWSON

Constable · London

First published in Great Britain 1994
by Constable and Company Limited
3 The Lanchesters, 162 Fulham Palace Road
London W6 9ER
Copyright © John Strawson 1994
The right of John Strawson to be
identified as the author of this work
has been asserted by him in accordance
with the Copyright, Designs and Patents Act 1988
ISBN 0 09 472930 1
Set in Linotron Ehrhardt 11 on 13 pt by
Rowland Phototypesetting Limited
Bury St Edmunds, Suffolk
Printed in Great Britain by
St Edmundsbury Press Limited
Bury St Edmunds, Suffolk

A CIP catalogue record for this book
is available from the British Library

An English army led by an Irish general; that might be a match for a French army led by an Italian general.

George Bernard Shaw

Contents

Illustrations

between pages 128 and 129

Arthur Wesley as Lieutenant-Colonel of the 33rd Foot, by John Hoppner
Napoleon crossing the St Bernard Pass, by David
Bonaparte at Rivoli, 1797, by Felix Philippoteaux
Kitty Packenham, by Slater
William Pit the Younger, by John Hoppner
Talleyrand, from a portrait of Gérard
Napoleon at Jena, 1806, by Horace Vernet
Wellesley in India, by John Hoppner
Nelson, by Lemuel Abbott
Marie Walewska, by Robert Lefevre
Czar Alexander I
The Passage of the Bidassoa, 1813, from a painting by James Prinsep Beadle
Hougoumont, by J. Crofts
Ney, by Flameng
Wellington at Waterloo, 18 June 1815, by Sir William Allan
Napoleon at Waterloo, 18 June 1815, by Sir William Allan
Murat, by Gérard
Wellington's funeral procession

MAPS

Acknowledgements

In *Napoleon and his Marshals* – still to my mind of all books about the Emperor the most enjoyable – A. G. Macdonnell makes 'the simple statement that every detail of this book has been taken from one or other work of history, reference, reminiscence or biography'. He made this statement because of his profound suspicion of all bibliographies, which he maintained tend 'to persuade the non-suspecting that the author is a monument of erudition and laboriousness'. At the recommendation of my publisher, however, a bibliography *is* included. I must complement it by acknowledging a very special debt to the following works: first and foremost A. G. Macdonnell's own (which Macmillan Publishers have kindly granted permission to quote from) and then also Sir Arthur Bryant's ever readable and enjoyable trilogy about the Revolutionary and Napoleonic wars together with his separate tribute to Neptune's General, *The Great Duke*; Vincent Cronin's masterly biography of the Emperor; A. P. Herbert's delightful portrait of Napoleon on the island of Elba; Lady Longford's incomparable account of Wellington's life and times; Gilbert Martineau's moving and colourful description of *Napoleon's Last Journey*; Lord Rosebery's eloquent, well-judged and convincing picture of the Emperor's unhappy sojourn at St Helena; and, a great favourite of mine for many years, *Wellingtonian Studies*, which gives such excellent summaries of the Great Duke as man, general, statesman and diplomatist. I have drawn heavily on all these works in preparing my own presentation of the Duke and the Emperor. I have drawn on many other works in my own presentation of the Duke and the Emperor – which the reader will find listed in the bibliography – and of these I owe a particular debt to: the Marquess of Anglesey's *The Capel Letters, 1814–1817*; Correlli Barnett's *Bonaparte*; Sir Winston Churchill's *A History of the English-Speaking Peoples*; Sir John Fortescue's *A History of the British Army; Wellingtonian Studies* (edited by Michael Howard); Victor Hugo's *The Battle of Waterloo*; Sir William Napier's *History of the War in the Peninsula*; Nigel Nicolson's *Napoleon 1812*; Sir Charles Oman's *A History of the Peninsular War*; Sir Charles Petrie's *When Britain Saved Europe*; Tom Pocock's *Horatio Nelson*; Susan Sontag's *The Volcano Lover*; the Earl of Stanhope's *Conversations with Wellington*; Leo Tolstoy's *War and Peace*; J. Steven Watson's *The Reign of George III, 1760–1815*.

The author and publisher are also very grateful to the following for their permission to reproduce pictures in this book, the Trustees of the Cavalry & Guards Club and the Queen's Royal Hussars.

My thanks go to Mr R. Tubb, Mrs J. Blacklaw and Mrs M. J. Menhinick of the Ministry of Defence library for their help in letting me see various works of reference.

I wish to thank my wife and my daughters, Viola Lambert and Carolin Strawson (especially the latter), for their invaluable support during the preparation and production of this book.

CHAPTER 1

Two Men of Destiny

Why then the world's mine oyster,
Which I with sword will open.

Pistol, *The Merry Wives of Windsor*

WELLINGTON AND NAPOLEON, two men born in the same
year, both destined to make use of the sword for effective
oyster-opening, yet utterly different in upbringing and
character: the one an aristocratic reactionary who was able to reconcile
himself to change only reluctantly; the other an ardent revolutionary
who tried to change everything by seizing and exercising tyrannical
power. Wellington was the third son of a careless, pleasure-loving Irish
peer, Napoleon the second son of a Corsican patriot with pretensions
to nobility. Had it not been for the soaring genius and insatiable ambition
of the latter, it may be doubted whether the commonsensical genius
and devotion to public service of the former would have been fully
developed. They met but once on the field of battle, and on this historic
occasion – Europe's future depended on their encounter – they had
some unkind things to say about each other. The Emperor dismissed
the warnings and advice of his subordinates who had fought in the
Peninsula, telling them that Wellington was a bad general, that the
English were bad soldiers and that the whole thing would be a walkover.
In his turn the Iron Duke was surprised, even disappointed, that Napoleon made no effort to manoeuvre against him, but relied on heavy
artillery bombardment and frontal assault, and made the laconic comment that 'the fellow was a mere pounder after all'. At Waterloo Wellington had just passed and Napoleon not quite reached his forty-sixth
birthday. They had both made their entry into the world in 1769.
    What a year to be born in, for as each of them approached manhood,

13

Europe was to be turned upside down by the actions of a revolutionary Parisian mob, graced with the title of citizens' militia, actions which gave rise to some twenty-five years of more or less continuous warfare and whose consequences were to echo menacingly throughout most of the nineteenth century. Such circumstances spelled infinite opportunity for those possessing courage, imagination and perseverance. It was a time when *la carrière ouverte aux talents*[1] was there for the taking. Our two men took it. One was to finish up as the virtual master of Europe. Indeed, had he but seen when it was time to call a halt to his game, he might have remained master of France for the rest of his life and founded a dynasty of Bonapartism. It was because he could not see it that the other made an indispensable contribution to bringing him down. As a result of this contribution Wellington became the keystone of Toryism, achieving the rare distinction of holding the highest political and military posts in the land, at once major-domo of England and a kind of supreme oracle whom everyone consulted for advice. 'Better ask the Duke' became a household dictum. Fortunately the Duke liked it. 'The Duke of Wellington is amazingly sensible to attention,' observed Lord Melbourne, Whig Prime Minister in 1834 and again from 1835 to 1841: 'Nothing pleases him so much as when one asks his opinion about anything.' There was therefore much pleasure in store for him.

It was less common for the men around Napoleon to ask for his opinion. He was more wont to give it without a request. He did, however, seek the opinion of others, and from time to time accepted it, notably during his first campaign as Commander of the Army of Italy in 1796. When the whole outcome of the campaign hung in the balance, when 50,000 Austrians under Marshal Wurmser were advancing over the Brenner to attack him, with Mantua still holding out behind him, Napoleon hesitated. Most of his subordinate generals were for retreating to Milan, but Augereau, the huge, boastful, urchin-like former cavalry trooper, urged bolder measures, and as a result the battle of Castiglione, five furious days of fire and movement, soundly defeated the Austrian columns, and Napoleon's lightning advance continued. Its astonishing success demonstrated to the world what revolutionary spirit harnessed to willpower of genius could achieve.

[1] Napoleon's own phrase.

What a contrast there was between these two men in their attitudes to and conduct of war! Napoleon, as Wellington himself pointed out, was always seeking to fight a great battle, and by winning it determine the shape of things to come. Wellington on the other hand, notably in the Peninsula, tried to avoid fighting a great battle in order to keep the contest going. 'Britain has but one army,' he observed after executing one of his strategic withdrawals, 'so we had better look after it.' Unlike Napoleon, he never gloried in war. Three weeks after Waterloo, he told Lady Shelley that he hoped he had fought his last battle. It was a bad thing to be always fighting. It was quite impossible to think of glory: 'I am wretched even at the moment of victory and I always say that, next to a battle lost, the greater misery is a battle gained.' Not only did you lose those dear friends with whom you had been serving, but you were forced to leave the wounded behind. Napoleon thought otherwise. He revelled in war. He recalled emotionally the sun of Austerlitz, long after such victories evaded him. His last words were: '*Tête d'Armée.*' In order to have good soldiers, he maintained, a nation must be always at war. Metternich, the Austrian Chancellor, understood this obsession of Napoleon's, and during negotiations for peace after the Russian campaign, when Metternich put forward proposals which were impossible for him to accept, the Emperor not only lost his temper. He shouted at Metternich that 'a man such as I am does not concern himself much about the lives of a million men,' and flung his hat into the corner of the room. Before this outburst, Napoleon had reminded Metternich that unlike himself, brought up in the field, the Austrian Chancellor had no idea what went on in the mind of a soldier. But Metternich did know that what went on in Napoleon's mind were unending thoughts of further battles and further victories. Yet all his arguments were in vain. 'Misfortune like success,' he observed despairingly to the Emperor, 'hurries you to war.' And before leaving, he murmured to Berthier, Napoleon's Chief of Staff: '*C'est un homme perdu.*'

Although Wellington acknowledged Napoleon's greatness, the compliment was not returned. In a memorandum written in 1836 Wellington wrote: 'Napoleon was a *grand homme de guerre*, possibly the greatest that ever appeared at the head of a French army.' He went on to explain what he meant. Napoleon was not only the sovereign, but also Commander-in-Chief of the army. The whole of France had a military structure, organized to create and support its armies with a view to conquering other countries. Moreover, the great offices of state and numerous favours in the Sovereign's gift were mainly awarded to the army. To be a successful general under Napoleon could bring with this success the ultimate reward: a kingdom of your own, however humble might be your origins – a cavalry trooper, an innkeeper's son or a peasant. After all, every French soldier carried the baton of a marshal of France in his cartridge-pouch.[2] For these reasons, argued Wellington, the presence of Napoleon with the army greatly stimulated its soldiers' exertions.

Yet Napoleon was well aware that 'men are never attached to you by favours'. Despite this cynical observation, he showered favours on his subordinates. As with Mark Antony, crowns and coronets walked in his livery, realms and islands dropped as plates from his pocket. Of course, he made sure that in general he dropped them into the right hands. The Bonaparte family did uncommonly well for crowns and coronets. The marshals had little to complain of with their batons, their dukedoms, principalities and – in a few cases – kingdoms. Even professional turn-coats like the reptilian Talleyrand and the sinister Fouché did not go unrewarded. There was no shortage of favours under Bonaparte. And as long as his star was shining, men were attached to him. But when the game went wrong, the men went too.

That they went so far and so fast was due in large measure to the efforts of Wellington. Yet he was the first to recognize the magical effect that Napoleon had on his soldiers by merely being present on the battlefield; he even went so far as to say that because the Emperor was able to exercise absolute power and a united command – putting paid to the marshals' disputes and jealousies – his presence 'was equal to a reinforcement of 40,000 men'. Although Wellington sub-sequently admitted that this was a very loose way of talking, what he meant was that the balance of opposing armies was greatly enhanced in the French army's favour simply by virtue of Napoleon's being there.

Napoleon was far from acknowledging any such greatness in Welling-ton. He dismissed him as a 'sepoy general' and when in 1809 Wellington arrived in the Peninsula with his army for the second time, Napoleon, as Elizabeth Longford puts it, 'hit upon a particularly offensive name

---

[2] *Tout soldat français porte dans sa giberne le bâton de maréchal de France.* Napoleon.

for his opponent – not a British lion, kings of beasts, but an emaciated leopard, hideous and heraldic.' We may note that Wellington himself regarded his days of being a sepoy general as profoundly significant. When, long after his campaign was over, he was asked by George Chad what was the best thing he had ever done in the way of fighting, he answered without hesitation: 'Assaye.' Of course, as Arthur Bryant points out, if we look at the two men in 1804, the year after Assaye, the difference in their positions is striking: 'Compared with that man of genius and destiny – born in the same year as himself and now Emperor of the French and the self-proclaimed successor of Charlemagne – Arthur Wellesley was still very small beer.' But Bryant also reminds us that Wellesley, still only thirty-five in 1804, had commanded an army of more than 50,000 men, had manoeuvred, supplied and directed it over huge distances of wholly inhospitable desert and jungle, had shown infinite daring in attacking enemies vastly superior in number, and by his tactical skill had won victory after victory. Wellesley himself observed later that at that time he understood military affairs as much as he ever did.

While Wellington may have admired Napoleon's generalship, he had no such regard for his character. In 1811 he wrote of Napoleon's 'fraudulent and disgusting tyranny', and to Croker[3] he said that Napoleon cared nothing for what was right or wrong, just or unjust, honourable or dishonourable – although he acknowledged that the huge stakes Napoleon played for 'threw the knavery into the shade'. The fact is that, as Wellington is alleged to have said of the Emperor, 'the feller wasn't quite a gentleman'. Wellington most assuredly was. This contrast in character was absolute. Wellington was honest, loyal, magnanimous, truthful, honourable and kindly. Napoleon was treacherous, disloyal, amoral, a cheat, a liar and a bully – 'fit for treasons, stratagems and spoils'. His only limits were his own will-power, egotism and ambition. No doubt this explains why each in his separate way and separate sphere was such a success. Talleyrand observed to Czar Alexander I that Napoleon was not civilized, and on the occasion that Napoleon called him, Talleyrand, 'so much dung in a silk stocking', Talleyrand's only

---

[3] John Wilson Croker (1780–1857), Tory MP and writer. Friend and confidant of Wellington and like him opposed to the Reform Bill. Renowned for his brutal criticism of Keats's *Endymion*.

reaction as he left the disagreeable scene was to say quietly to one of those present: 'What a pity that such a great man should be so ill-bred.'

This difference in breeding was to some extent reflected in the armies the two men commanded. The Grande Armée was full of first-class soldiers, but not many of them were gentlemen – although Napoleon had tried to enlist some;[4] the British Army on the other hand was largely officered by gentlemen and many of them were also excellent soldiers. The behaviour of each side was well illustrated in the autumn of 1813 when Wellington pursued Soult into France. Soult's retiring troops 'after twenty years of pillage, rape and arson abroad could not deny themselves these pleasures in their homeland'. Wellington, however, forbade all offences against people or property and enforced this ban with the most rigid discipline. He would not allow the bulk of the Spanish troops into France at all, for he knew that without pay or supplies of food, they would plunder – 'and if they plunder, they will ruin us all.' To the great astonishment of the French, therefore, they found that the British Army actually paid for what they had. 'Having long repudiated the idea of gentility, the people of south-western France found themselves quartering an army of gentlemen.'

So we have two men of destiny, the Duke and the Emperor – however diverse in character and method, both great generals. There have been many estimates of what does or does not constitute a great soldier – not the least interesting or relevant being that of Walter Bagehot.[5] Having rejected the idea of a soldier being a romantic creature, dashing at forlorn hopes, full of fancies as to lady-love or a sovereign, he depicted him as quiet and grave, surrounded by maps and charts, exact in calculations, a master tactician immersed in detail, eschewing all forms of eloquence and grand gestures, thinking 'as the Duke of Wellington was said to do, *most* of the shoes of his soldiers'. How exactly Bagehot hits the target in relation to our two men in some respects, and how widely he misses it in others! While we may wonder what British soldier

---

[4] After Austerlitz, when members of the *ancien régime* returned to France, it was places at court they sought, not on the field of battle. 'I opened my armies to them,' Napoleon said bitterly, 'and not one came forward. I opened my ante-chambers and they crowded in.'

[5] *The English Constitution*, 1867.

Bagehot could have had in mind, it is no puzzle to see that he was a disciple of the Jomini school.[6]

Jomini, it will be recalled, laid down, as a result of studying the campaigns of Frederick and Napoleon, certain principles for the conduct of war, many of which held good for most of the nineteenth century and some of which still hold good today. They were mainly concerned with concentration of force at a decisive time and place, and with the disruption of the enemy's communications while preserving one's own. A striking example of these principles was given by Napoleon himself in February 1814 – after Jomini had deserted him – when, with his game going wrong on all fronts, he once more pulled on his long boots and in six swift encounters with the Russian, Prussian and Austrian armies at Champaubert, Montmirail, Château-Thierry, Vauchamp, Nangis and Montereau, displayed all his old gifts of speed and decision in bringing superior numbers to bear on his enemies' columns and struck dismay into his fellow sovereigns' hearts. Wellington's comment on it was that he knew 'how very exact a man must be in his calculations and how very skilful in his manoeuvres to be able to do that'. His own experience and his own practice had left him in no doubt about the absolute necessity of being, in Bagehot's words, which echo Wellington's, 'exact in calculations'.

Thus far, therefore, Bagehot is on target, as he is with his reference to the need for tactical expertise and being busy with charts and maps. Napoleon constantly pored over maps with Berthier. The masterpiece of moving the Grande Armée from the Pas-de-Calais camps and across the roads of France, Holland and Germany to the spectacular triumphs of Ulm and Austerlitz is a model of strategic prescience. In a comparable respect Wellington's meticulous attention to detail, his study of ground, his insistence on a proper commissariat and supply system, confirm what Bagehot wrote. Indeed, as Bagehot suggests, he *was* concerned that the soldiers should have shoes. Before undertaking his final decisive Peninsular advance of 1813, he ensured that every soldier had three pairs of shoes with a spare pair of soles and heels in his knapsack – and he was bitterly angry with the Spanish General Murillo for his lack of

---

[6] Baron Antoine Jomini, a Swiss mercenary soldier and historian, punctilious and orderly. Chief of Staff in Ney's 6th Corps, he accompanied Napoleon on the Russian campaign.

such care: 'How could he have the heart to make his unfortunate troops march without shoes or bread?'

But administrative and tactical skills are by themselves not enough for successful command. There is also the question, as Antony Macdonnell put it, 'of playing upon that stormy harp whose strings are the hearts of men'. Lord Macaulay gives us the proper recipe to redress the notion of too much reliance on the theory as opposed to the practice of military command:

> An unlearned person might be inclined to suspect that the military art is no very profound mystery, that its principles are the principles of good plain sense, and that a quick eye, a cool head and a stout heart will do more to make a general than all the diagrams of Jomini.

In talking of good plain sense, Macaulay puts his finger on one of Wellington's greatest qualities. 'When one is strongly intent on an object,' he told Stanhope,[7] 'common sense will usually direct one to the right means.' Yet how many of us, in situations when common sense is above all else required, lose sight of it? Wellington's common sense was inspired, never more so than when in action. Crisis seemed to increase his calm. Then, his transcendent common sense assumed the nature of genius. Napoleon's genius was of a different sort. It was almost sublime and enabled him to reach such fantastic heights of power and achievement that, when his star began to wane, he was able to say more than once: *'Du sublime au ridicule il n'y a qu'un pas.'*

But what on earth could Bagehot have been thinking of when he wrote that the great soldier was not a romantic animal, not animated by frantic sentiment, nor full of fancies as to a lady-love? Listen first to Napoleon, then to Wellington.

From the beginning of his success in command of the Armies of Italy Napoleon looked on war as a great romantic adventure and on himself as the hero of it. 'Fortune is a woman,' he told Marmont[8] in May 1796,

---

[7] Philip Henry 5th Earl of Stanhope was Under-Secretary to Wellington when the Duke was Foreign Secretary. His *Conversations with Wellington* was first published in 1888.

[8] Marmont, Napoleon's friend, was with him in Italy, made a crucial contribution at Marengo and commanded in Spain. A marshal and Duke of Ragusa, he failed Napoleon in 1814, and the French language acquired a new verb, *raguser* – to betray.

'and the more she does for me, the more I shall demand from her.' By this time Napoleon was married to Josephine and he wrote such letters to her as to leave no doubt about his being full of fancies for a lady-love. Here is part of his plea for her to return with an aide-de-camp, Junot (later a general):

> Unhappiness without cure, inconsolable anguish, sorrow without end, should I be unhappy enough to see him [Junot] to return alone. My adorable sweetheart . . . you are coming aren't you? You are going to be here by my side, on my heart, in my arms, on my mouth . . . A kiss on your heart, and then one a little lower down, much lower down!

Even before they married – in fact the morning after he first made love to her – he was writing in a similar strain:

> I have woken up full of you. Your portrait and the memory of yesterday's intoxicating evening have given my senses no rest. Sweet and incomparable Josephine, what an odd effect you have on my heart . . . I cannot rest when I yield to the deep feeling that overpowers me and I draw from your lips and heart a flame that burns me . . . in three hours I shall see you. Until then, mio dolce amor, thousands of kisses . . .

It was not only to Josephine that he wrote such letters. No sooner had Napoleon met Marie Walewska in 1807 than he was pouring out his passion:

> *Je n'ai vu que vous, je n'ai admiré que vous, je ne désire que vous. Une réponse bien prompte pour calmer l'impatiente ardeur de*   N

and later:

> Marie, my sweet Marie, my first thoughts are of you, my only wish is to see you again. You will come, won't you. You promised. If you failed, the eagle would fly to you! . . . When I put my hand on my heart you will know that it beats for you alone . . .

Marie Walewska was to prove truer to him than many others.

Wellington may have been more honest, more matter of fact, less emotional, more scrupulous than Napoleon; more concerned with duty and service than with honour and glory – he was not called the Iron Duke for nothing – but he was just as susceptible to the ladies. Here he is in 1847 at the age of seventy-eight writing to Angela Burdett-Coutts:[9]

> My dearest Angela, I have passed every moment of the Evening and Night since I quitted you in reflecting upon our conversation of yesterday, Every Word of which I have considered repeatedly. My first Duty towards you is that of Friend, Guardian, Protector. You are Young, My Dearest. You have before you the prospect of at least twenty years of employment of Happiness in Life. I entreat you again in this way, not to throw yourself away upon a man old enough to be your Grandfather . . . I cannot too often and too urgently entreat you to consider this well. I urge it . . . But I must add, as I have frequently, that my own happiness depends on it. My last days would be embittered by the reflection that your Life was uncomfortable and hopeless. God Bless you My Dearest! Believe me Ever Yours
>
> Wn

Hardly the words of one who was not a romantic animal or fanciful as to a lady-love. There were many others – whom we shall meet later – who could testify similarly, among them Mrs Arbuthnot, Harriete Wilson and Frances Webster.

The attitude of both Napoleon and Wellington to a sovereign varied with the sovereign. For the most part Napoleon regarded his fellow sovereigns with contempt; his own sovereignty, however, was in his eyes sublime. As Correlli Barnett puts it: 'There could be only one answer to these combined yearnings of the romantic and the egoist – that he should be Caesar, be Charlemagne, and yet more glorious than either.' Wellington took a more prosaic view of royalty. His pronouncement on George IV was blunt – 'the worst man that ever lived'. His comment

[9] Angela Burdett-Coutts (1814–1906), heiress and philanthropist, friend of Disraeli, Gladstone and Dickens. In love with Wellington and proposed marriage – declined, as letter above shows. In *Flashman's Lady*, George MacDonald Fraser's eponymous hero has this to say: 'I, too, had admired little Angie, though not for her enlightened opinions – more for the fact that she had a superb complexion, tits like footballs and two million in the bank.' In 1881, when Angela was nearly 67, she married William Ashmead Bartlett, aged 30.

on George and his brothers, the royal princes, was equally so – 'the damnedest millstones about the neck of any Government that can be imagined'. But he came to admire and respect Queen Victoria.

We have seen that there was no eschewing eloquence by either of our two men when it came to writing love letters. What about their eloquence when exercising military command? Napoleon always maintained that one of the attributes of a great commander was eloquence such as appeals to soldiers. He certainly gave endless instances of his own eloquence. In recalling and recording at St Helena his order of the day issued to the Army of Italy in 1796, he showed how his first triumphs were heralded with characteristically extravagant language:

> Soldiers, you are naked, ill-fed; though the Government owes you much, it can give you nothing. Your patience, the courage you have shown amidst these rocks, are admirable; but they procure you no glory, no fame shines upon you. I want to lead you into the most fertile plains in the world. Rich provinces, great cities will be in your power; you will find there honour, glory and riches. Soldiers of the Army of Italy, will you lack courage or steadfastness?

They did not, and Correlli Barnett pointed out that it was this very order of the day which served to stimulate the grand and romantic drama of Napoleon's Italian campaign and the magical legend of the man. Two years later in Egypt he is at it again: '*Soldats, songez que, du haut de ces pyramides, quarante siècles vous contemplent.*' The battle of the Pyramids was a walk-over. The Marmaluke horsemen, no matter how brilliantly attired or courageously led, could not prevail against the disciplined squares of French soldiers with their accurate musketry and devastating cannonades. Yet for all Napoleon's grandiloquence the whole Egyptian campaign was, as we shall see later, a strategic failure, leading to the destruction of the French fleet by Nelson and the cutting off of Napoleon's army from France after his repulse at Acre by another British admiral, Sir Sidney Smith.

Napoleon's strategic idea had been as magnificently bold and imaginative as his oratory. Egypt would become a French colony. Its conquest would be a preliminary move to the further aim of striking at India. All these ideas were crushed by Nelson and Sidney Smith – and Smith's chivalry in sending his opponent a package with the latest newspapers

from Europe convinced Napoleon that events in France made it necessary for him to abandon the Army of Egypt and make all speed for
Paris. There would be no expedition to India for him now. Had there
been he might have crossed swords there and then with Wellington who
was winning some modest laurels in the Deccan. *His* eloquence was
quite unlike Napoleon's. It was plain, blunt, simple, honest, clear and
accurate. *He* inspired confidence, not by emotional, theatrical gestures
(so beloved by the French Emperor), but by an absolute commitment
to his soldiers' health and sustenance and by a conscientious frugality
with their lives. His pronouncements proclaim the man. Before the
battle of Salamanca his orders to his brother-in-law Edward Pakenham,
commanding the 3rd Division, were a model of brevity and clarity: 'Ned,
d'ye see those fellows on the hill?', pointing to the French left. 'Throw
your division into column; at them! and drive them to the devil.' Or
when he reinforced Hougoumont – an absolute key to the successful
defensive action at Waterloo – with four extra companies of Foot
Guards: 'There, my lads, in with you, let me see no more of you.' He
could be cutting too, as when he told Sir Thomas Picton: 'I sent for
you to hear my orders, not to receive yours.' The inestimable value of
his orders was that they were invariably clear. On one occasion Napoleon
told Talleyrand: 'Your letter is too clever. Cleverness is not needed in
war. What is needed is accuracy, simplicity and character.' In naming
these three elements, the Emperor might have been summarizing
Wellington's principal virtues both as a man and as a soldier.

Both men, of course, pass with flying colours Macaulay's prescription
for a quick eye, a cool head and a stout heart. Both were indifferent to
danger on the battlefield. Both possessed that degree of physical courage
which in those days was indispensable for a general to reach great heights.
This was perhaps the reason for its being insufficiently recognized – it
was simply taken for granted. Wellington's coolness at Waterloo echoed
Napoleon's at Austerlitz. The quick eye of each was never better illustrated than by Wellington in attacking Marmont at Salamanca or by Napoleon in turning to destroy Sir John Moore's army when he heard that
thousands of British redcoats were pursuing Soult in Old Castile.

So we have seen that Bagehot's capricious description of the great
soldier is badly flawed in regard to romantic notions, the petticoat allure,
ideas about royal loyalties and martial eloquence, while wholly sound
as to the need for exact calculations, mastery of maps, charts and tactics,

and provision of shoes for soldiers. Yet the question persists – who on earth could Bagehot have been thinking of? The Duke of Wellington's successors in command of British armies – with the exception of the generals of the Crimean War, Raglan, Lucan and Cardigan, who distinguished themselves for only one thing: blundering – were concerned with the fighting of Imperial wars. 'Bobs', Napier, Gordon, Hope-Grant – none of these answers the description, they were all too flamboyant and colourful. Perhaps it was Wolseley whom Bagehot had in mind, with his flair for organization, his intense interest in the theory of war, his meticulous attention to detail, victor of so many of Queen Victoria's little wars, Gilbert and Sullivan's 'very model of a modern major-general', who had given the phrase 'All Sir Garnet' to the nation as a universal recipe for getting things right, and whom Disraeli called an 'egoist and a braggart'. The only objection to selecting Wolseley as Bagehot's choice of a great soldier is that *The English Constitution* was published in 1867 – before Wolseley's greatest achievements had occurred. Yet he had by then shown himself in the Crimea, the Indian Mutiny and China to be pious, brave, studious and thorough, constantly in action and a worthy candidate. Perhaps Bagehot anticipated him. The main point that Bagehot was making was that by the time he was writing there had grown upon the world a certain matter-of-factness, foreign to former affairs. A hundred years earlier things were otherwise. There was too much turmoil then, too many new ideas and a number of remarkable men and women whose acquisition of power and subsequent use of it for the promotion of their own and their country's position produced an ever-changing set of war-like circumstances. The one common factor in fluctuating alliances seemed to be that France and Britain were nearly always at odds. In 1763, six years before Napoleon and Wellington were born, there had been an end of one such struggle; in 1775, six years after their birth, there began another. In the first of these, the Seven Years War, the brilliant, inspiring leadership of Pitt the Elder had rewarded England with spectacular victory; in the second, the American War of Independence, rejection of Pitt's warnings and advice had brought England ignominious defeat. Now was to come a third, prolonged and final struggle between France and England in which our two men of destiny would play principal roles, and at length be pitted one against the other. But first, of course, each of them was required to serve an apprenticeship to fit them for making their entry upon the world stage.

CHAPTER 2

Learning the Trade

Napoleon, for whom I had brought a drum and a wooden
sword, painted nothing but soldiers drawn up on parade.

Letizia Bonaparte

I vow to God I don't know what I shall do with my awkward
son Arthur . . . [he is] food for powder and nothing else.

Lady Mornington

T HE early careers of Wellington and Napoleon were in marked
contrast. Origins, upbringing, education, political circumstances, social position, military experience – all were widely
different. Napoleon's turbulent childhood in Ajaccio and in the Corsican
countryside, his remarkable intelligence, his defiant courage, his egotism
and aggression, his mastery of mathematics, his determination to excel,
his boundless self-confidence – these influences and qualities needed
only one thing to find expression in action: opportunity. And opportunity
came with Revolution. Arthur Wesley meanwhile seemed very mild in
comparison. After attending schools at Trim and Chelsea, he went to
Eton in 1781. At this time little of the future soldier was evident, whereas
Napoleon had already spent three years at a military academy. Wesley
was 'dreamy, idle and shy'; his sole accomplishment was that he could
play the violin. At Eton he spent little time on the playing fields – to
which he later attributed his Waterloo victory – but he did display plenty
of spirit and had some stand-up fights. There was little sign of academic
distinction. Indeed had it not been for the French Revolution there
might have been no distinction at all.

England's initial reaction to the French Revolution – at least for those
entitled to an opinion which might be listened to – was generally one

of satisfaction. There was satisfaction in the reflection that France, which had tried so hard to damage British interests in two recent wars, was now in trouble; there was satisfaction to be had from the notion that the present head of the Bourbon dynasty – descending directly from two of Britain's most implacable enemies, Louis XIV and Louis XV – should have difficulties of his own; there was even satisfaction in the idea that the upheaval in Paris and elsewhere would result in the establishment in France of a monarchy limited by parliamentary authority, on the lines of our own system born of the Glorious Revolution of 1688. Fox went further and hailed the fall of the Bastille as 'the greatest event that ever happened in the world and the best'.[1] The British Ambassador in Paris reported that 'the greatest revolution that we know anything of has been effected with the loss of a very few lives; from this moment we may consider France a free country.' Others were more circumspect, notably Burke[2] and Pitt.[3] Burke regarded it not as a copy of the 1688 Revolution, but as its direct opposite. Believing as he did that 'good order is the foundation of all good things', he saw that by destroying the past, human rights would themselves be destroyed, and that the result of the Revolution would be ruthless dictatorship and bloody war. Pitt, however, refused to see it. He more or less reserved his judgement and awaited events. He did not have long to wait. While he is waiting, Napoleon is immersing himself in Corsican revolutionary politics and Wellington is having a quiet time in Ireland as ADC to the Lord Lieutenant. Soon their two nations will be at war and they will both be in action.

It was not until late in 1792 that Pitt became convinced that war with France was necessary – not, mind you, on ideological, but on strategic grounds. From the British Army's point of view the timing could hardly have been worse, for the Army Estimates had reduced each regiment by seventy men so that the entire force in the British Isles was little more than 13,000 strong. Indeed Pitt's economies had done the British

---

[1] Charles James Fox (1749–1806), Whig MP, welcomed the French Revolution. He was Foreign Secretary in 1806. His three great interests were, it was said, gambling, women and politics – in that order.
[2] Edmund Burke (1729–97), statesman and writer, Whig MP, friend of Fox, until his *Reflections on the Revolution in France* denounced it. Opposed democracy, believed in good order.
[3] William Pitt, the Younger (1759–1806), Prime Minister 1783–1801 and 1804–6, saviour of Europe.

Army great harm, while France's armies were to be measured in hundreds of thousands. When introducing the budget earlier that year Pitt made the astonishing statement that 'unquestionably there was never a time in the history of this country, when from the situation of Europe, we might reasonably expect fifteen years of peace than at the present moment'. He would have been much nearer the mark if he had expected twenty years of war.

Nevertheless in December 1792, Pitt called out two-thirds of the militia and recalled Parliament.[4] Despite a characteristically capricious attack by Fox on the government's proposal to strengthen the armed forces, the House of Commons approved measures which would add 17,000 soldiers to the army and 9,000 seamen to the Royal Navy. Moreover, the Aliens' Bill authorized the means of closely supervising the activities of foreign refugees. The French Ambassador, Chauvelin, protested against this last measure and demanded its repeal. His request was rejected. In France itself Napoleon had witnessed the Paris mob's attack on the Tuileries, which caused the death of some 800 nobles and Swiss guards. He was disgusted by it, and by the failure of those in authority to quell the rising. 'If Louis XVI had mounted his horse,' he wrote to his brother Joseph, 'the victory would have been his.' But Louis XVI's part in all these affairs was shortly coming to an end. Also soon to end for the time being would be Arthur Wesley's courting of Kitty Pakenham in Ireland – her brother Tom did not regard a mere captain of the 18th Light Dragoons as a sufficient catch, and Wesley's offer was rejected.

Meanwhile, France was exporting terror and violence. Her revolutionary army had already repulsed the Duke of Brunswick's forces at Valmy. Now her armies invaded the Austrian Netherlands and the Rhineland. The purpose was not to spread revolutionary ideas, but to acquire anything that could be turned into hard cash. France's invasion of the Netherlands was bound to antagonize England, and Pitt vainly tried to get Russia and the other European powers to mediate with France. If France would withdraw her armies and abandon her conquests, Pitt declared, the Great Powers would undertake to leave France alone. His

[4] In addition to the Regular Army, Britain was able to call on the militia (raised by ballot); the volunteers (one way of avoiding militia service); the fencibles, for home defence only, like the militia; and the yeomanry.

ideas were treated with contempt. Of the Great Powers, Russia and Prussia were more interested in aggrandizing themselves than re-straining France, while Austria wanted the Bourbons restored. The French themselves were ardently embracing further conflict and con-quest. On 21 January 1793 Louis XVI was executed.[5] Three days later Danton boasted to the Convention that France would throw Louis's head at the feet of those kings who were combining against her. Belgium must be annexed, he bellowed, and a week later, on 1 February, the French Republic declared war on Great Britain and Holland.

For the British Army, war could not have come at a more inconvenient time. Macaulay was not kind in writing about the army under Pitt's direction. He called it the laughing-stock of Europe, without a single successful campaign to its credit. It only had to show itself on the Continent to be defeated, pursued, obliged to surrender or reduced to running away. 'To take some sugar island in the West Indies, to scatter some mob of half-naked Irish peasants, such were the splendid victories won by British troops under Pitt's auspices.' It was an army which had been neglected for years, contemptibly small, poorly paid, ill-trained and badly equipped and supported. And this was the army in which Lieutenant-Colonel Arthur Wesley was about to make his début in command of troops.

France's revolutionary armies, on the other hand, did not lack numbers. Danton's *levée en masse* took care of this. The entire nation would be prepared for total war. Every man and woman in France would be mobilized to perform some duty – either as soldier, arms manufacturer, nurse, tailor, recruiter or storeman. There would be no shortage of men at arms or arms for them. What is more, the architect of victory, Carnot, had introduced new devastating tactics. In front of the main columns, a flood of *tirailleurs*, swift sharp-shooting skirmishers, would advance, reconnoitring enemy dispositions and disrupting them. Then would follow the powerful, compact main columns, whose sheer weight and revolutionary ardour would penetrate the enemy's defences which usually lacked the depth needed to slow and stop them. Carnot's strategic notion of immense concentration on a narrow front against extended and thus inadequate defensive positions was exactly suited to

---

[5] He told the onlookers: 'I pray God that the blood you are going to shed may never be visited on France.' Seldom can a prayer have been more in vain.

the spirit of the revolutionary armies and overcame France's enemies time after time. Moreover, Carnot understood, as did Napoleon, that the cardinal principles of war – singleness of aim and concentration of force, to achieve one objective after another, but always one at a time – were the key to success. This was the raw material which Napoleon was to forge into a seemingly invincible Grande Armée at whose head he was to ride in triumph through most of the capital cities of Europe and some even further afield.

Thus it may be seen at once that as far as armies went, the balance of power between England and France was heavily weighted in the latter's favour. Happily for the former there was still the Royal Navy. Even Pitt's economies had not robbed it of two priceless assets – a large number of battleships and matchless seamen[6] to sail in them. And in the end it was the Royal Navy that put paid to Napoleon's ambition. After the declaration of war by France, there were some further declarations by eminent men of the day. Gaspard Monge, a mathematician, who did very well under Napoleon, becoming a count and acquiring a rich estate in Westphalia, was, like many of his countrymen, not lacking in flamboyant challenges – although he misjudged the English people. Would the English republicans, he demanded, allow George III and his Parliament to make war upon France? Rather the French would fly to succour their brothers in arms. 'We will lodge there 50,000 caps of liberty.' Before long, he prophesied, the tyranny of the British would be destroyed. Pitt's pronouncements were more restrained:

> We have, in every instance, observed the strictest neutrality with respect to the French: we have pushed, to its utmost extent, the system of temperance and moderation: we have waited until the last moment for satisfactory explanation . . . They have now, at last, come to an actual aggression, by seizing our vessels in our very ports, without any provocation given on our part; without any preparations having been adopted but those of necessary precaution, they have declared and are now waging war . . .

Moreover, Pitt told the House of Commons, there could be no compromise with what seemed to be the voracious territorial ambitions of

---

[6] Of whom the brightest star was, of course, Nelson.

France. The French government, it seemed, would not tolerate any form of administration in other countries that did not conform to their own ideas of liberty. Yet this idea of liberty was best described as denying liberty to those who opposed them. England must therefore set its face against France's aggression, for in the long run what France was after was the subjugation of England. If France should want friendship and peace with England, she would have to renounce aggrandizement and confine herself to her own frontiers, without violating the rights and upsetting the tranquillity of other countries. Unless this came about, 'the final issue must be war'.

What is more, warned Burke, it would be the most dangerous war England had ever been engaged in, one of a very peculiar nature. It was not against an ordinary state, which might be swayed by interest or passion. England was to be at war with 'a system . . . inimical to all other governments' – a system determined to subvert all other nations. 'It is with an armed doctrine that we are at war.'

There can have been few wars between England and France when each side was totally confident of speedily triumphing over the other. To British ministers it was clear that France was enfeebled by internal conflicts and that the weight and number of allies against her would soon bear fruit. 'That these allies would prove a liability rather than an asset; that they would be overthrown until the whole mainland of Europe lay prostrate at the feet of France; and that the enemy would produce one of the greatest generals of all time; these events could not be foreseen.'[7] England's misplaced confidence in speedy victory over France was matched by France's assurance that her traditional enemy, Britain, would soon be overcome. Successful invasion, which had eluded them in the past, would be a very different matter now Holland was in their possession with its numerous and nearby ports and estuaries from which to launch it. England in the view of many Jacobins was vulnerable because of Scots and Irish discontent and longing for independence, while England's reliance on foreign trade could be undermined by a naval offensive. This last idea was emphasized by one of the speakers in the Convention, Kersaint, formerly a naval officer, who accurately forecast some of Napoleon's later adventures, when he recommended an attack on the main source of British wealth, her seaborne trade.

---

[7] *When Britain Saved Europe*, Sir Charles Petrie.

'Asia, Portugal and Spain are the best markets for the produce of her industry. We must close them by opening them to all. We must attack Lisbon and Brazil, and send an army to help Tippoo Sultan [against whom Wellington would soon be campaigning] . . . If you know how to direct the naval war it will pay the costs of the land war, and perhaps France will owe to her naval victories the strengthening of her liberty.'

French naval victories, however, were hard to come by. The only success enjoyed by the French over the Royal Navy in the opening stages of the war was directed not by the French navy but, as we shall shortly see, by an artillery officer, Captain Napoleon Bonaparte. It came about as a result of Pitt's so-called blue-water policy – a strategy which he had inherited from his father. For it to be successful, it was necessary to have abundant resources – and at this time in the war, they were not to be had. Pitt was only able to contemplate such a policy at all because of the existence of the Royal Navy, which could boast a total of 113 ships, although at the beginning of the war less than half this number, some fifty battleships, were provisioned, manned and in commission. However, another forty required only crews to ready them for service. This rapid mobilization of British sea-power was possible because during the ten years of financial economy since the end of the American war, Pitt had not neglected the Royal Navy, as he had the army. Repair of existing ships, building of new ones, mobilization of crews, accumulation of naval stores in properly maintained dockyards – all these measures made it possible for plans to be effected which quickly put the Royal Navy on a war footing. There was thus an instant advantage over the French navy, whose deterioration – removal of competent royalist officers, neglect of ports and magazines, disbandment of crews, decay of ships – had accompanied revolution. So, Pitt believed, the employment of the British fleet, together with limited numbers of troops, would enable Britain to rob France of her colonies and, by even more profitable trade, finance his allies, Austria and Prussia, to engage the enemy's main armies on the Continent. There was nothing wrong with the concept. The strategic conditions of the time were those familiar to the British when waging war on a Continental power which was embarked on European domination and the dismantling of Britain's world position. It had traditionally been Britain's aim under such circumstances to acquire allies enjoying the advantages of large armies and extensive territories, who would take on the bulk of the enemy's land forces and slowly but surely knock the stuffing out of them, thus leaving the British free to deploy their sea-power at will, gaining more trade and overseas possessions, and provided there was not too much risk, fiddling about on an open flank in Europe. The trouble was that those directing policy – a triumvirate of the King, Pitt and Dundas[8] – did not know how to deploy and employ their military resources properly. In any event the army was at this time far too small. Pitt altogether overlooked the two cardinal strategic rules – singleness of aim and concentration of force. Instead he chose diversity of aim and dissipation of force. So that in framing his military policy, he tried to do too much with too little. He failed to select his primary objective and then deploy his forces in such a way as to guarantee this objective's achievement. A whole bunch of ventures was devised – seizure of Haiti from French colonists, despatch of an army to Flanders, raids on the French coast to rouse Royalists there, an expedition to the eastern Mediterranean. Yet the strength to undertake all these enterprises did not exist. The British Army could muster no more than 20,000 effectives. So instead of striking one powerful blow and winning one battle, Pitt supervised a series of ineffectual blows, widely dispersed, and came off worst in them all. In two such encounters Napoleon and Wellington were engaged, first at Toulon, and then in Flanders.

At Toulon another great hero of English history makes his appearance on the stage in a leading role – Horatio Nelson. Early in 1793 Captain Nelson took command of a ship of the line, the *Agamemnon*, at Chatham, and in the spring of that year sailed from Spithead to join Lord Hood's Mediterranean fleet. On passage to Gibraltar he visited Cadiz (Spain was at this time neutral), where, surprised by the slackness of the Spanish naval crews, he made one of his celebrated pronouncements: 'The Dons may make fine ships; they cannot make men.' The task of Hood's fleet with fourteen sail of the line was to blockade French ships and trade at Toulon and Marseilles. Toulon was especially important. Not only was it a fortified base, but it was believed that some twenty French battleships were positioned there.

After a month of this blockade, something quite remarkable and unexpected occurred. On 27 August 1793 the Royalists in Toulon

---

[8] Henry Dundas, Pitt's colleague and tippling crony. He was Secretary of State for War, Treasurer of the Navy, First Commissioner for India. Totally ignorant of military affairs, he nonetheless became a kind of Defence Minister in the Churchill style.

declared for Louis XVII, the Dauphin imprisoned in Paris; they ran up the white flag and invited Hood to enter its strongly defended harbour. 'What an event this has been for Lord Hood,' wrote Nelson to his wife. 'Such a one as History cannot produce its equal. That the strongest place in Europe and twenty-two sail of the line should be given up without firing a shot; it is not to be credited.' Thereupon Hood sent his Royal Marines ashore. The city's defences, although strong, would need about 50,000 troops to man them effectively. Hood urgently needed reinforcements and one of the measures he took was to despatch Nelson to enlist support from the Kingdom of the Two Sicilies, ruled by Ferdinand IV – the bulbous-nosed, uxorious Bourbon monarch, passionately addicted to hunting of most four-legged beasts, and husband of Marie-Antoinette's sister, Maria-Carolina. Nelson's mission was successful and reinforcements for Toulon were forthcoming. Of even greater significance for Nelson was that when he went ashore with despatches for the British Ambassador at Naples, Sir William Hamilton, he encountered for the first time the beautiful, plump, stimulating and desirable Emma. What an unlikely pair of lovers they were. In *The Volcano Lover*, Susan Sontag has this to tell us:

> He was often described as little. Certainly he was short, a good bit shorter than the Cavaliere [Hamilton] and his young wife, and thin, with an arresting tanned face set low on his large squarish head, thick brows, heavy-lidded eyes, a deep philtrum below his bold nose, full lips, a wide mouth . . . he had the look, the hungry look that evinces the power to concentrate utterly on something, of one destined to go far . . . he will be the bravest hero England has ever produced . . . A star is always a star . . . and the thirty-five-year-old Captain was undoubtedly a star – like the Cavaliere's wife.

Nelson was to prove an even greater stumbling block to Napoleon's realization of his overriding strategic objective – the conquest of Britain. And the object of Nelson's all-consuming passion? Again Susan Sontag and the Cavaliere's reaction when Emma arrives in Naples:

> He hadn't remembered she was that beautiful. Stupendously beautiful. He must have seen how beautiful she was last year, since when he had possessed this beauty in the form of an image, as the Bacchante

in Romney's picture hanging in the hall to his study, which he sees every day. But she is much more beautiful than the painting.

While Nelson is raising reinforcements in the Mediterranean, Lord Hood is appealing to Pitt for more British troops to garrison Toulon. But, manacled by their strategy of diversity and dispersion of effort, what are Pitt and his advisers to do? Reinforce Toulon by withdrawing the British Army from Flanders and eschewing any military ventures elsewhere? Or continue with the blue-water policy of seizing French colonies overseas, so pandering to London's city merchants, and being obliged to forget about European commitments? In any event, even if the whole available strength of the British Army had been mustered and despatched to Toulon – in the most unlikely circumstances that it could be done with sufficient celerity – it still would not have been enough effectively to have guaranteed the defence of the town.

Meanwhile Carnot, the architect of victory, was preparing to restore Toulon to the revolutionary cause. Unlike Pitt, who took on too many objectives simultaneously, Carnot concentrated on threats to the Republic one by one. First he blocked an attempt by Austrian troops to cross the Alps; then in October 1793 he turned again on Flanders, defeating the Austrians at Wattignies, and by driving through Ypres and Nieuport, obliging the Duke of York's army to retire on Ostend; next he turned his attention to the Vendée, suppressing the rebels there with such ferocity that innumerable villages were burnt to the ground and thousands of corpses strewed the fields. Then he was able to turn his attention to Toulon – where an artillery captain called Bonaparte was already serving.

In September 1793, the French commander of the revolutionary forces besieging Toulon had been General Carteaux, whose only military distinction was the impressive black moustache favoured by the French light cavalry. He and his staff were equally incompetent and when Bonaparte arrived at the headquarters that same month, he lost no time in impressing on everyone there that, however perplexed they might be as to what should now be done, he, Bonaparte, was in no doubt. He saw at once that the key to taking Toulon was to force the British fleet to withdraw, and that to do this the Jacobin army must capture the Le Caire peninsula with its two forts: this would enable them to bring direct artillery fire on the Royal Navy's warships. Once the British left, Bonaparte insisted, the Royalists' position would collapse. The first attempt to capture Le Caire failed because Carteaux provided inadequate assaulting troops. But Bonaparte, from 18 October a major, persisted. He dismissed conventional assault plans for taking Toulon, sent from Paris by the Committee of Public Safety, and made it plain to the Minister of War that *his* plan was the right one – emphasizing constantly all that *he* had done and denouncing Carteaux as useless. His boundless energy and forceful eloquence had their effect. Carteaux was replaced by Dugommier, who accepted Bonaparte's insistence that Fort l'Aiguilette, commanding the harbour entrance, was the crucial objective. 'There is Toulon,' he said, and on 17 December 1793 a successful assault against the fort, led by Bonaparte himself, who sustained a bayonet wound in the thigh, proved him to be wholly right. On the morning following the fort's capture, the British fleet departed. It was the end of Toulon's defiance. The defences collapsed; hurried evacuation of those lucky enough to get away followed. Such was the haste of all that only nine of twenty-seven French warships were burnt, thus leaving a French Mediterranean fleet in being. Even in Toulon British strategy had failed. Worse was to come. But for Major Napoleon Bonaparte, it was the beginning of great things. Robespierre and the Committee of Public Safety wanted to know more about the young artillery officer who had not only put his finger on the military solution to a problem, but had also instinctively understood the political significance of removing the Royal Navy's support for Toulon's Royalist forces. Napoleon's star was now in the ascendant and would continue to shine dazzlingly for the next fifteen years. On 22 December he was promoted to *général de brigade*. He was only twenty-four. Moreover he had been noticed by up-and-coming Citizen Barras – shortly to be Commander-in-Chief of the Army of the Interior, and at this time, incidentally, protector of Josephine, the widowed Vicomtesse de Beauharnais.

While all these exhilarating events were presenting Napoleon with unending activity and unlimited opportunity, Arthur Wesley was having a rather poor time of it. In 1794 he had taken his regiment, the 33rd Foot, to Flanders. The Flanders campaign of 1793 to 1795 was a model of how not to combat France's new revolutionary armies. It might have served very well for besieging and reducing fortified towns in the day of Louis XIV, but against the swift and reckless manoeuvring of ardent, revolutionary masses, it would not do. The Duke of York, who later proved himself to be a brilliant army reformer and administrator, did not shine as a commander of troops in the Flanders campaign. He had an endless struggle to control both his troops and his allies. The troops were lacking in almost everything that was required: adequate numbers, sound equipment and support, discipline and leadership. The allies were not to be trusted or relied on – except to be in the wrong place at the wrong time. The goings-on in 1794 were about as unfortunate as could be. While vainly trying to come to the Austrians' support at Tourcoing, the Duke only narrowly escaped capture because of the speed and staying power of his horse. In July of that year the French victory at Fleurus led to their pursuit of the Allied armies and their recapture of all the frontier fortresses. There was nothing for the Duke of York's army to do but retreat and go on retreating, a process which was accompanied by the most disgraceful ill discipline. The campaign ended humiliatingly when a mere 6,000 British soldiers were obliged to retire through Germany to Bremen from where they were evacuated to England.

The future Duke of Wellington, at this time Lieutenant-Colonel Arthur Wesley, commanding the 33rd Foot, savoured his first taste of war during this disastrous campaign. He may have been disappointed in love – his offer for Kitty Pakenham's hand having been rejected – yet once he got command of a regiment he was able to prove that he possessed a powerful coalition of intellect and resolution. He threw himself whole-heartedly into the essence of proper management of men, care for their health, their food, their uniform and equipment, their training and discipline, above all their pride in regiment. It took him only a year to turn the 33rd Foot into the finest regiment in Ireland. He was now displaying some of the very qualities which Bagehot admired: 'thoroughness, exactitude, and a capacity for accurately weighing up facts and figures and putting them to practical, common-sense use'. It only remained to pass the test of action on the battlefield and this was not long in coming. He himself later made it clear that he owed his success in the direction of divisions and command of an army to his sound understanding of the capabilities of individual soldiers and the tactical skills demanded of a regimental officer. He learned it all the hard way – during the defeat and retreat of a British army.

In June 1794 he and his regiment were part of a force which joined the Duke of York's army as it withdrew towards Holland. It was in September of that year that Wesley was first in action, and he saw at first hand all that could go wrong. Command was divided, there was no proper supply organization for food or clothing, the whole system was rotten. 'I learnt more by seeing our own faults and the defects of our system in the campaign of Holland,' he subsequently remembered, 'than anywhere else.' His regiment acquitted itself admirably when the French attacked the Duke of York's army at Boxtel on 15 September. Wesley's coolness and tactical skill, the discipline he had instilled into the 33rd and their accurate musketry, when each company fired volley after volley at the advancing French columns, checked the enemy advance. It was an admirable instance of keeping your head when all about you are losing theirs. It also taught Wesley that there was nothing wrong with the British soldier if he were properly directed and supported. It was the system itself – organization, administration and command – that was at fault. Later, when the army had withdrawn behind the Waal, Wesley noted that he and his regiment were not once visited by the Commander-in-Chief, an omission he was at pains not to allow when he himself was in command of an army. Then he would always see everything for himself and do things himself – which, he believed, explained his own future success.

He further distinguished himself during the retreat across Holland when temporarily in command of a brigade acting as a covering force. 'He was always on the spot,' writes Bryant; 'saw everything for himself, did everything.' That something was rotten in the state of the army was made startlingly clear by Sir John Fortescue in his great history, showing to what depths and degradation a defeated, disintegrating army could descend:

Far as the eye could reach over the whitened plain were scattered gun-limbers, wagons full of baggage, stores or sick men, sutler's carts and private carriages. Beside them lay the horses, dead; here a straggler who had staggered to the bivouac and dropped to sleep in the arms of the frost; there a group of British and Germans round an empty rum cask; here forty English Guardsmen huddled together about a plundered wagon; there a pack-horse with a woman lying alongside it, and a baby swaddled in rags peering out of the pack with its mother's milk turned to ice upon its lips – one and all stark, frozen dead. Had the retreat lasted but three or four days longer, not a man would have escaped.

Wellington was to conduct some retreats of his own in years to come, but they would not be like this one. Here in Holland he learned 'what one ought not to do, and that is always something'. Back in England in April 1795, Wesley found himself so despondent and disillusioned that he had thoughts of leaving the army altogether. Happily for Great Britain he could find no other employment and that autumn sailed with his regiment under Abercombie to another abortive expedition, intended for the Caribbean, but destined to battle only against the elements at sea. He would not see action again until 1799, and this time it would be in India. He sailed there in June 1796, still in command of the 33rd Foot.

Meanwhile Brigadier Bonaparte had another stroke of luck. He had been appointed by Barras as military adviser to the government in August 1795; only two months later the Paris mob rose again and Barras gave him the task of suppressing it. His renowned 'whiff of grapeshot' did the trick, and also gained him an ADC who became both his brother-in-law and the most celebrated cavalry commander of all time, Joachim Murat. When Bonaparte, charged with suppressing the revolt of October 1795 – 13 Vendémiaire – remembered that forty National Guard guns were at Les Sablons, it was Murat, commanding the 21st Chasseurs, who galloped through the night to fetch them and so enabled Bonaparte to blow away the new revolution. 'From that moment,' wrote A. G. Macdonnell, 'the Master-Gunner never forgot the young cavalryman who sharked up the tools of his trade for him in that October darkness, and when, in 1796, Captain Murat gasconaded up to Bonaparte on the eve of his departure to command the Army of Italy, and said: "General, you have no Colonel ADC. I propose to accompany you in that capacity," Bonaparte smiled and accepted the audacious offer.'

Bonaparte's association with Barras led to a more intimate association with Barras's discarded mistress, Josephine. So powerful was her spell that Napoleon did some discarding of his own – Désirée Clary (who did pretty well for herself by marrying Bernadotte, future King of Sweden, instead) – and in March 1796 he married Josephine. He was twenty-six, the lady thirty-two. Two days after the wedding, he set off for Nice to take command of the Army of Italy. Thus it was that, by the year 1796, Napoleon had made conquests both on the battlefield and in the bedchamber. Wellington had done neither.

CHAPTER 3

Conquest

The campaign of '96 shook Europe to its foundations. A twenty-seven-year-old gunner had opened a campaign at Nice and closed it within sixty-five miles of Vienna, and the world understood vaguely that a portent had arrived, and that though the Revolution was over in the streets of Paris, the Three Colours might yet be seen upon the battlefields of Europe and Asia and Africa.

A. G. Macdonnell

AN eagle is ascendant in spirit, swift in flight, sudden in decision and ruthless in deed. How apt a symbol then was the eagle for Napoleon! His descent on Italy and his conduct of war there illustrated to the letter the way in which he combined all these characteristics. However true, this is, of course, what Wellington would have called a loose way of speaking. There are more pertinent grounds for Napoleon's astonishing success, both in conceiving and conducting warfare as he did and in the effect he had on his subordinates. When the diminutive gunner general arrived at Nice on 27 March 1796 to take command of the Army of Italy, the four veterans awaiting him, Schérer (from whom Bonaparte was taking over), Sérurier, Augereau and Masséna, did not think much of the appointment, which they regarded as having been secured largely by intrigues of political counsels and the bedchamber. They were soon to change their minds. The new Commander-in-Chief had brought with him four associates, who in their separate ways were to serve the Napoleonic legend with great distinction: Berthier, the brilliant Chief of Staff, originally a royalist engineer officer who had survived the Terror, whose mastery of detail and ability to work without sleep appeared limitless and whose displeasing appearance

40

and brusque manners were more than redeemed by his always knowing with absolute exactitude the whereabouts, strengths and command arrangements of every unit deployed in the army (in short, a staff officer *par excellence*); Murat, an innkeeper's son who had joined the cavalry as a trooper two years before the Revolution, an arrogant, philandering and unscrupulous braggart, who became nevertheless an outstandingly brave and successful cavalry leader; Marmont, a close friend of Bonaparte and like him an artilleryman, who commanded a French army against Wellington in Spain and later was made Duke of Ragusa; and Junot, another cavalryman, who was Bonaparte's aide-de-camp and who led several pursuits during the Italian campaign, on one occasion sabring six Austrian Uhlans in a single encounter. Of these eight men, having hitched themselves to Bonaparte's star, all except two – Schérer and Junot – were to become Marshals of the Empire.

When we reflect that after three years of indecisive playing at warfare, which the French had been indulging in against their Austrian and Piedmontese enemies, Bonaparte was suddenly by his whirlwind tactics of rapid marching and concentration of force to turn the whole concept of warfare upside down, we may also concede that an extraordinary talent was on parade. So extraordinary indeed that even those two veterans, Masséna and Augereau, initially most sceptical about the capabilities of the ridiculous little Tom Thumb of a gunner general who had been hoisted on them, were not slow to be impressed. Masséna – the stern, obstinate, silent, eagle-featured general, who on the field of battle was fired with activity and decision, and whose two great obsessions were money and women – and Augereau – 'a buffoon, a brute and a *bonhomme*' as Macdonnell put it, but a brilliant divisional commander, whose troops were always on time and up to strength and were so cared for by him that they adored him – these two veteran fighters were to recognize Napoleon's genius: his iron will-power, his soaring vision, his tactical brilliance, his driving ambition, his stern discipline. 'That little bugger makes me afraid,' Augereau told Masséna. 'I can't understand it.' The qualities of the man were exactly what was required to conduct a lightning, remorseless series of battles. Napoleon had an iron constitution which permitted superhuman activity; an ability to go without sleep which enabled him to maintain this activity for weeks on end; and an eye for country (as every aspiring military commander should have) which he owed to his upbringing in the savage, undeveloped hills and mountains of Corsica, and with which he could gauge (as Wellington was always trying to do) what lay on the other side of the hill. Lastly, as a gunner, he knew how important it was to concentrate fire-power on to a single objective, and then, having taken that one, to switch his fire-power rapidly to the next.[1] These qualities do not in themselves tell us how it came about that Bonaparte, beginning his campaign in April 1796 at Nice, and ending it just over a year later 65 miles from Vienna, obliged his principal enemy, Emperor Francis II of Austria, to make peace with France and hand over the Duchy of Milan. It was not that Napoleon had created or inherited a new army. What he had inherited was the spirit of attack, the tradition of glory, the solid inexorable column of infantry, preceded by a cloud of skirmishing *tirailleurs*, the sheer individualistic *élan* of the French; and on it all he had imposed his own concentration of effort, will-power of genius, clarity of purpose and furious speed of movement. He also brought an incentive to bravery and a unity of command that had not previously been known in the revolutionary armies. What was the Army of Italy like when he took command? What sort of opposition was he facing? And what did he do?

Materially the army was in a deplorable state. It was penurious, hungry, ragged, badly shod, unpaid, and ill disciplined. Of his 41,000-odd effectives, Napoleon had some 3,300 cavalry and 1,700 gunners and sappers; the rest were infantry. The first things required were bread and boots. He instructed the government commissioner who accompanied his army, Saliceti, to provide them. Saliceti bought 18,000 pairs of boots and corn to last for three months. Next Napoleon had both to establish his own authority and to prepare his army for rapid offensive action. There seemed now to be little doubt about his fitness to command. His old friend Marmont conceded that there was a certain gaucheness about him, some lack of dignity. Yet 'he had the quality of command in his attitude, his gaze, his manner of talking; and everyone sensing this found himself ready to obey.'

Napoleon's army faced two enemies – Piedmont and Austria, whose rulers were both dedicated to a Bourbon restoration. Victor Amadeus III of Piedmont, father-in-law of the Comte de Provence (later Louis XVIII), was a bigoted, self-opinionated tyrant, always falling asleep (his nickname was King of the Dormice). Francis II of Austria, nephew of

---

[1] For this analysis I am indebted to Vincent Cronin's *Napoleon*, Collins, 1971.

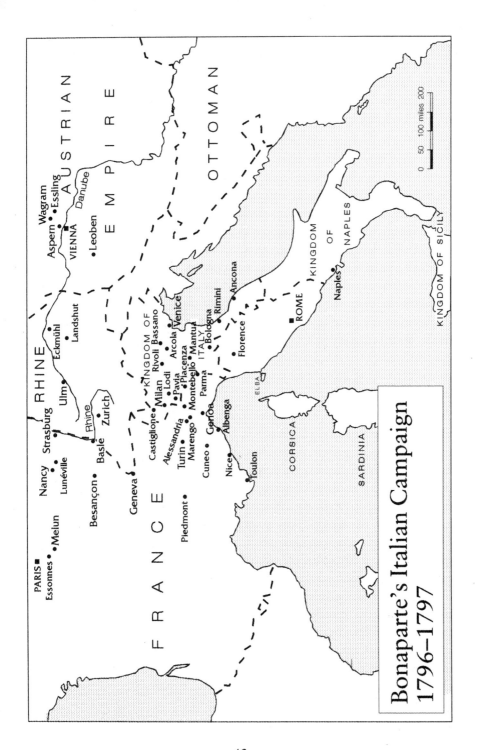

Bonaparte's Italian Campaign 1796–1797

43

Marie-Antoinette, was weak, ordinary and respectable. Between them they mustered some 47,000 soldiers – 22,000 Austrians, 25,000 Piedmontese – deployed between Genoa and Cuneo to protect the Alpine and Apennine passes into Piedmont. The junction point of their two armies was north of the Cadibona Pass. By 6 April 1796 Bonaparte's headquarters was at Albenga on the coast. His orders from the Directory were to attack and eliminate the Piedmontese first, capture Turin and then move east against the Austrians.

In the past French attempts to cross the Maritime Alps into Piedmont by breaking through the narrow, well-defended passes had failed. Napoleon's idea was different. His plan was to feint along the coast towards Genoa with the aim of drawing the Austrians down from their base at Alessandria, some 40 miles north of Genoa, and then, when the enemy forces were extended, to strike rapidly through the Cadibona–Carcase gap and so, by turning the whole enemy position, pour into Piedmont. Thus by a combination of deception, speed and concentration of force, he would defeat his enemies in detail. In order to be able to adapt speedily to changing situations and give himself the greatest possible mobility, he divided his army into three divisions, under Augereau, Masséna and Sérurier respectively, organized his cavalry into two divisions and created a small reserve of artillery. Then having set in train his deception plan, first by asking neutral Genoa – whose government, he knew, would tell the Austrian generals – for their agreement for him to advance through their country and second by despatching a small force under La Harpe to Voltri, west of Genoa, he prepared to strike. The Austrians fell for it, and while one of their generals, Beaulieu, descended from Alessandria with 10,000 soldiers to drive the French out of Voltri, another general, Argenteau, advanced by a different route in an attempt to trap La Harpe's force. The conditions for Napoleon's offensive had now been created and on 11 April the eagle struck.

A. G. Macdonnell summed up what immediately followed in a memorable passage: 'On April 11th, 1796, the Army of Italy was flung at the point of the wedge, the junction of the Austrian and Sardinian [Piedmont was a province of the Kingdom of Sardinia] armies. In ninety-six hours of marching and fighting the wedge was split, the armies driven apart, and the line of the Alps had been turned. Nine days later the Sardinians threw up the sponge and the tattered, shoeless, passionately uplifted Army of France was in full cry for Milan and Mantua, and

North Italy was ablaze with welcome for the liberators . . . the great campaign was all Bonaparte's.' To be more exact what happened was this. During these ninety-six hours Napoleon first defeated the Austrians at Montenotte on 11 and 12 April, and the Piedmontese at Millesimo on 13 and 14 April, then the Austrians again at Dego. Thus already he had departed from his instructions to deal with the Piedmontese first, before turning on the Austrian army.

Correlli Barnett's book about Napoleon, whose title, *Bonaparte*, at once reveals the author's sentiments, has some hard things to say about the creation and nurturing of the Napoleonic legend. From the very outset of this Italian campaign, he argues, Bonaparte deliberately set out to advertise, exaggerate and glorify his achievements. He 'began propagating his own legend just as soon as the Army of Italy marched, feeding Paris with grandiloquent accounts of his successes, exaggerating enemy losses and defeats.' Barnett goes on to say that history tended to accept and endorse the brilliance of Napoleon's victories both because the sheer romance of heroic geniuses appealed to nineteenth-century opinion and because Napoleon was illustrating and practising the Comte de Guibert's theory of warfare, which was essentially that armies should live off the country, thus totally liberating themselves from the laborious system of wagon-train supply, and also should eschew the tedious business of fortress sieges. Both these measures would enable armies to move fast and freely. Napoleon certainly showed how it was to be done. After his victory at Millesimo, he broke through the Allied lines then attacked the Piedmontese at Ceva, whose defences the enemy abandoned. Next, on 21 April, he routed the Piedmontese at Vico, entering Mondovi – whose municipality was ordered to provide nearly 40,000 rations of biscuit, 16,000 rations of meat, 8,000 of bread and 8,000 bottles of wine, all within twenty-four hours. This was living off the country indeed. When the Piedmontese army fell back on Cherasco, a mere 30 miles from Turin, the capital, Napoleon pursued them and declared what his peace terms were. They included the surrender of Cuneo – crucial to the Piedmontese Alpine positions – and at first King Victor Amadeus's envoys were reluctant to comply. Napoleon simply gave them one hour to agree. If not he would order his army to resume the attack. The envoys agreed to sign. Thus with the Cherasco armistice of 28 April Piedmont was out of the war, and Napoleon, before turning on the Austrians again, was able to give vent to some more highly coloured and dramatic pronouncements. He told his soldiers: 'You have won six victories in five days, taken twenty-one colours, fifty-five pieces of cannon, several fortresses, conquered the richest part of Pied-mont . . .', and in preparing them for their next task – defeat of the Austrian army under General Beaulieu – he spurred them on to fresh triumphs: 'You have accomplished nothing unless you finish what remains to be done. Are there any among you whose courage is flagging? No. Every one of you, on returning to his village, would like to be able to say with pride: "I was with the Army of Italy." '[2] To the Italians themselves he was no less eloquent. He had come not just to fight the Austrians, but to liberate the Italians. The French army would break their chains, respect their property, their religion, their customs. He and his soldiers made war with generous hearts and fought only against tyrants seeking to enslave others.

After the Piedmontese surrender, the Austrians retired east into Lom-bardy. To get at them and at Milan, Napoleon had to cross the River Po. He did not choose the shortest route, at Pavia – Beaulieu had strongly defended the crossing there – but raced for Piacenza, whose neutrality, as part of the Duchy of Parma, he ignored. He then called on Lannes, the gallant Gascon *général de brigade* who specialized in leading infantry attacks and was later a Marshal of the Empire, to cross the 500-yards-wide river and establish a bridgehead. Against all likeli-hood and the expectations of his men, Napoleon had his entire army across the Po in two days, and then, having completely outflanked Beaulieu's main force, rushed on towards Milan. On the way there was another river, the Adda; the bridge over it was at Lodi, where Beaulieu's rearguard was positioned to argue the toss. Here another Napoleonic legend was born, when the Commander-in-Chief reinforced his repu-tation both for courage and leadership by personally directing the assault on the bridge 'even in the cannon's mouth'. While his infantry under the close command of Lannes, Berthier and Masséna stormed across the bridge and the river itself only to be met by devastating artillery and musket fire from the defending Austrians, his cavalry had galloped upstream to find a crossing and then attack the Austrian right flank. Despite French losses – about 200 were killed – the plan succeeded.

---

[2] Which Churchill no doubt recalled when he observed that when history came to be written, it would be enough to say: 'I marched with the 8th Army.'

The Austrian guns were silenced, allowing more French infantry to cross and drive away the enemy, who lost sixteen guns, more than 300 dead and wounded and 1,700 prisoners. Five days later Bonaparte triumphantly entered Milan. He had 'taught the world', wrote Stendhal, 'that Caesar and Alexander had a successor.' By securing peace with Piedmont and conquering the Duchy of Milan, he had completed the first two phases of his campaign. There still remained the third – the most important, most difficult and most prolonged: to bring to battle and defeat the Austrian army.

Having invested Mantua, Napoleon's army was at first obliged to stand on the strategic defensive. While doing so, he informed the Directors that 'the tricolour was now flying over Milan, Pavia, Como and all Lombardy'. The Directors however were not at first willing to leave Napoleon in sole command of what they now called the Army of the Alps, proposing instead a kind of combined command, with Kellermann, heroic victor of the crucial battle at Valmy in 1792, responsible for dealing with Austrian forces in the north, while Napoleon dealt with the Papal States and Tuscany. It was in his reply to the Directors that Napoleon, objecting so strongly to their proposal that it constituted a refusal to serve with Kellermann, also produced one of his maxims which has found its way into the *Faber Book of Aphorisms*. 'One bad general does better than two good ones.' He not only added the somewhat curious comment that war was a question of tact, but went on later to demand the Directors' entire and absolute confidence. Without it he could not give France the service it so badly needed. In other words, if he did not get his way, he would resign. The Directors gave in. There would be no joint command. Napoleon would remain sole Commander-in-Chief in Italy and was required to subdue the Papal States and Tuscany *and* beat the Austrians in the north. Once more he set about a lightning campaign. In less than six weeks between the beginning of June and mid-July 1796, he had marched his army 300 miles, swept aside the Papal forces, entered Florence, captured the valuable commercial port of Leghorn and taken possession of some 40 million francs' worth of bullion. He was back in Milan by mid-July, having successfully carried out the first of the two tasks set him by the Directors.

In achieving the second one it was first necessary to defeat repeated Austrian attempts to relieve Mantua. It was during the first of these attempts that Napoleon accepted Augereau's staunch insistence that of search and destroy. To start with, Nelson had no luck. While his squadron was watching and waiting off Toulon, a terrible storm struck and dispersed his ships, yet carried the French fleet out of Toulon and over the horizon before Nelson could reassemble his squadron and resume the search. By mid-June Bonaparte had forced the capitulation of Malta and sailed on towards Egypt, while Nelson was writing to Lord Spencer, First Lord of the Admiralty:

> The last account I had of the French fleet was from a Tunisian courier, who saw them on the 4th [June] off Trapani in Sicily, steering to the eastward. If they pass Sicily, I shall believe they are going on their scheme of possessing Alexandria and getting troops to India – a plan concocted with Tippoo Sahib, by no means so difficult as might at first view be imagined; but be they bound for the Antipodes, your Lordship may rely that I shall not lose a moment in bringing them to action.

He was as good as his word. He paused at Naples for supplies and fresh water and – the petticoat influence was strong in these heroic days – to send a letter to Lady Hamilton in which he assured her that as soon as he had fought the French fleet, he would do himself the honour of paying his respects and hoped to be congratulated on a victory. Her reply was equally fervent. She asked for God to bless him, send him back victorious – with Bonaparte a prisoner. 'I shall be in a fever of anxiety' – she could not say how glad she would be to see him or even describe her feelings at his proximity. On he went, out-sailing the French fleet so that when he reached Alexandria, there was no sign of them. Nelson was, however, convinced that the French had gone east. If Bonaparte landed in Egypt, he reasoned, the French could march an army to the Red Sea, embark in vessels provided by Tippoo Sultan and three weeks later threaten British possessions in India. On 28 June, Nelson's squadron was at Alexandria, but the French were not there. 'The Devil's children have the Devil's luck,' he observed. Now his main concern was that Napoleon might have descended on Sicily. He at once sailed back, and on 19 July learnt at Syracuse that the French were not there either. Lack of frigates, he wrote to St Vincent, the Commander-in-Chief Mediterranean, had handicapped him. If he had been wrong, he should be superseded. But it was his intention to head east once attack was the best form of defence. With Mantua still holding out and the Austrian Marshal Wurmser streaming across the Brenner with 50,000 men, even Napoleon, who later called himself the boldest general who ever lived, was given pause and was inclined to accept the advice of his council of war, to raise the siege of Mantua and retire on Milan. But Augereau spoke up to the effect that only if they were beaten should they think of retreat. Attack first and support the right wing with bayonets. Even he, Augereau, might be a little worried, but not by the enemy's proximity; he would simply like to see more calmness in his fellow generals. 'Fight here', he concluded, 'and I will answer for victory.' So another furious five days of marching and shooting transpired, Augereau's division itself storming the final objective at Castiglione. Time after time the enemy had been defeated in detail. So once more Napoleon's recipe of rapid movement and concentration of force at the crucial time and place paid great dividends, and the Austrians were repulsed. Wurmser made another attempt in September, only to be checked and thrown back.

The next Austrian general to test his luck against Napoleon was Alvinzi, who like Wurmser tried to relieve Mantua in November 1796, swarming down into Italy with a new Austro-Hungarian army and meeting Napoleon's army east of Verona at Arcola, where a bridge over the Adige was the key to the battle. Once more in the thick of things, the Commander-in-Chief's horse was hit, then bolted and threw Napoleon into a swamp, from which he was rescued by Louis Bonaparte, his brother, and Marmont. Lannes once again distinguished himself by his front-line courage in leading an attack. After the day was won Napoleon sent him a captured flag to honour him, accompanied by a message in appropriately high-flown language about Lannes's utmost bravery saving a desperate situation and his resolution to conquer or die. It was all part of the game of winning and keeping the affection, respect, indeed devotion of his subordinate commanders. Napoleon's star was riding high, and was to wax still more with a further victory at Rivoli early in 1797.

The French strategic position this time was even more dangerous, for while Mantua was holding out with 20,000 Austrians, no fewer than 45,000 were advancing to their relief – 28,000 under Alvinzi moving down the Adige valley while 17,000 more commanded by General Provera were directed at Verona. Napoleon had but 20,000; the rest of his army was either garrisoning captured towns, watching Mantua or sick. Yet once more the tactically brilliant, fast-marching little gunner general was more than a match for his enemies. Choosing the vitally important plateau at Rivoli, on the east bank of the Adige north of Verona, as his battleground, Napoleon occupied it with Joubert's 10,000 men, arriving there himself very early on the morning of 14 January. Masséna with a further 8,000 men was to arrive by dawn, with another 4,000 men under Rey to come later that day. Seeing that Alvinzi's army was dispersed round the plateau, Napoleon proceeded to attack each of Alvinzi's five corps in turn. It was again a desperate struggle, Masséna reinforcing the main army in the nick of time and Rey coming up to thwart and capture an entire Austrian corps which was counter-attacking Napoleon's main body. It was yet one more example of the way in which speed, fire and movement, concentration and tactical dexterity enabled inferior numbers to outmanoeuvre and crush a numerically superior force. Masséna, whose timely arrival at a critical moment ensured success, was greeted by Napoleon as '*l'enfant chéri de la Victoire*'. And as if all this were not enough, on his return towards Mantua, Napoleon defeated Provera, capturing most of his army and finally forcing Mantua to surrender in February 1797. Napoleon now set his sights on Vienna itself, but first the Directory gave him another task – to chastize the Pope for lending his moral and material aid to the Austrians.

So Napoleon pulled on his long boots once more and at the beginning of February his army rushed along the Via Emilia taking Bologna, Rimini and Ancona. It was near Ancona that the irrepressible Lannes with a handful of troopers suddenly encountered several hundred cavalry of the Papal States, and by sheer bluff and bravado persuaded them to disarm, dismount and lead their horses into captivity. Such ineffectual opposition simply ensured that Napoleon overran the Papal States and made terms with the Pope's envoy at Tolentino. Napoleon was wary of the danger from the Bourbon régime in Naples (we have already met, with Nelson, King Ferdinand and his neurotic wife Maria-Carolina, sister of Marie-Antoinette) which, were the Pope rendered powerless, might take control of central Italy, so his terms in the treaty of Tolentino were moderate – to remove from Papal control Bologna, Ferrara, Romagna and 30 millions of gold. The whole thing had taken less than three weeks. Despatching this treaty to the Directory, Napoleon then hurried north again. It was to be a triumphant conclusion to the whole campaign.

While Joubert guarded his left flank in the Tyrol, Napoleon himself set out from Bassano on 10 March 1797 with four divisions – one commanded by another future marshal, the Gascon Bernadotte – to invade Austria with Masséna's division leading and heading for the ultimate prize, Vienna, capital city of the Austrian, indeed the Holy Roman, Emperor, Francis II. By 7 April he and his veterans had reached Leoben, some 25 miles north of Graz, and only 65 miles from Vienna itself. There he dictated terms and on 18 April the treaty of Leoben was signed: Austria was to cede the Duchy of Milan and end the five-year war with France. It was all formally concluded at the Peace of Campo Formio in October 1797. Austria gave up Belgium and Lombardy to France, and accepted French control of the Rhine's west bank and of the Cisalpine Republic in Italy. In compensation Austria was awarded Venice. Republican France had made peace with Continental Europe – although war with England went on. Napoleon had done all he had so far set out to do. His star was shining more brightly than ever. How was this astonishing success to be explained?

It was not that he had invented a new sort of army, manufactured a whole new range of weapons or created a completely new set of leaders. He simply took what was there – the spirit, pride, vivacity, tactical methods, toughness, intelligence of the Revolutionary soldiers, with their traditional sense of glory, their indomitable belief in victory and their rich nuggets of brave, dashing young officers – and by his own will-power, discipline, imagination, unity of command and action (so that one man was in co-ordinated control of the whole army's many actions), above all by his astonishing speed of thought and deed, welded it into an irresistible instrument of conquest. We have seen how time and time again he was able to feint at, outflank and deceive a dispersed, slow-moving, slow-thinking enemy, and then by sheer rapidity of movement and concentration of effort shatter a numerically superior enemy force by defeating it in detail, one part after another. Napoleon himself put the whole thing in a nutshell when he told the Directors that he had won battles over superior forces because his troops, knowing that the Directors trusted him, 'moved as rapidly as my own thoughts'. It looked as if Catherine the Great's prediction about a future French soldier-statesman – 'a superior, clever, courageous man, well above his contemporaries, the man of the century perhaps' – was about to come true.

Napoleon's own thoughts, when not concentrating on how to defeat his enemies, were much taken up with his wife, Josephine, who, although reluctant to leave the salons, the gaiety, flirtations and gossip of Paris, had eventually been persuaded to join her husband in Italy. In July 1796 she came to Milan, accompanied, however, by a dashing young Hussar officer, Lieutenant Hippolyte Charles, with whom she had been having a liaison. It was not only Napoleon who was having petticoat trouble. Arthur Wesley had told Kitty Pakenham that in spite of her family's rejection of him as a suitor for her hand, if something in the future were to change their minds, 'my mind will still remain the same'. It was a characteristically honourable gesture and led to a move on his part which he was most heartily to regret. In June 1796, while Napoleon was tasting the first fruits of his victory, Wesley sailed for India, where before long he would be winning some victories of his own. Bonaparte too was shortly to have his eye on India. 'He now saw as his next step,' wrote Churchill,[3] 'nothing less than a conquest of the Orient after the fashion of Alexander the Great. He planned the invasion of Egypt as a preliminary to the capture of Constantinople and all that lay in Asia.' Thus again we see what a contrast there is in the careers of our two men at this point. 'If Napoleon Bonaparte's star was in the dazzling ascendant,' wrote Bryant, 'Arthur Wesley's seemed anything but bright. He was now in his twenty-eighth year, heavily troubled with debt and bound on a six-months' voyage to a remote land far from the scene of the great struggle in which his country was engaged ... When he sailed from Portsmouth that June it cannot have seemed to him that the future had much to offer.'

[3] *A History of the English-Speaking Peoples*, Vol. III, Cassell, 1957.

CHAPTER 4

The Gorgeous East

In order to destroy England utterly, we must get possession
of Egypt.

Napoleon

[When asked to explain his remarkable endurance on the field
of Waterloo.] Ah, that is all India.

Wellington

I N February 1797, while Napoleon was putting the finishing touches
to his Italian campaign, Wesley landed at Calcutta. His first feelings
about India were far from being favourable. In a letter to his brother
he described it as a miserable country and the native people, whether
Hindu or Musselman, without any good qualities. Not only were they
devoid of mildness, but they would take advantage of their disproportionate numbers to turn on and destroy Europeans when they could, besides
being atrociously cruel to one another. Still in command of the 33rd
Foot at this time, Wesley took his share of the social round in Calcutta,
but with his customary common sense, was determined not to over-
indulge in India's pleasures. Rather, if he were to make his mark as a
military man, he would keep himself fit for the campaigning by taking
plenty of exercise, eating sparingly and plainly, and drinking spirits or
wine hardly at all. Yet his fellow officers found him lively and spirited,
always speaking rapidly and physically notable for his long sharp nose
and clear blue eyes. One of his first sightseeing visits was to a battlefield
some 100 miles north of Calcutta – Plassey, where Robert Clive in June
1757 with a mere 3,000 soldiers, only one-third of whom were British,
had thrashed Nawab Surajah Dowlah's host of 60,000. So complete
was the victory that Clive had made himself master of Bengal. It would

not have been lost upon Wesley that whereas the Nawab of Bengal's army was incomparably superior in numbers, Clive's was markedly superior in discipline and valour. Before long Wesley was to win some victories of his own against vastly greater enemy strength. Meanwhile in the same month that Wesley had landed at Calcutta, far away off the coast of Portugal the man who was to prove such a thorn in Napoleon's flesh, who was so implacably opposed to him in all his thoughts and actions, whose courage, audacity, humanity and strategic vision and whose spectacular victories and unswerving devotion to duty won both the huzzas and hearts of the British people – Commodore Horatio Nelson – was in action.

The battle of Cape St Vincent was fought on 14 February 1797 by Sir John Jervis's fleet, fifteen sail of the line, including Nelson's *Captain*, against the Spanish fleet – Spain had changed sides in October 1796 after Bonaparte's successes in Italy.[1] Jervis, later Earl St Vincent, was made of stern stuff. He had declared on the day before the battle that a victory was essential to England at this time, for everything was going wrong elsewhere. Europe was dominated by France, Ireland was as usual rebellious, the Royal Navy was abandoning the Mediterranean, there was even talk of mutiny in the British fleet. Clearly some striking success for Britain was needed. Jervis and Nelson were just the men to deliver just such a success.

The engagement at St Vincent was remarkable for two things – first Jervis's admirable indifference to the daunting size of his enemy's fleet. When the captain of his flagship, *Victory*, reported twenty Spanish sail of the line, Jervis replied: 'Very well, sir.' Then on the next report's being of twenty-seven enemy ships, nearly double their own strength, Jervis retorted: 'Enough, sir, no more of that. The die is cast and if there are fifty sail of the line, I will go through them.' This splendid spirit was matched by an enthusiastic endorsement of Jervis's defiance by a huge Canadian, Captain Hallowell, standing near him. 'That's right, Sir John, and a damned good licking we'll give them.' That they did so was due in large measure to the tactical brilliance of Nelson. When Nelson saw that his admiral's orders to the fleet might allow the

---

[1] Ten years later, when Napoleon made the fatal mistake of sending his armies across the Pyrenees, Spain changed sides again, so giving Britain – and Wellington – a great opportunity.

two Spanish divisions to join up and present greatly superior fire-power to bear on the British, he acted with what Arthur Bryant has called the 'instinct of genius' and contrary to order, indeed contravening a cardinal rule of naval warfare, he bore out of the line of battle, and headed straight for the main Spanish division. By bringing them to action, he sought to prevent their reunion with the other Spanish vessels. It was an act of the utmost daring to take on five enemy ships of the line. But the tactic succeeded. Nelson was supported by Collingwood in *Excellent* and he in turn was followed by Troubridge's *Culloden* and Frederick's *Blenheim*. What transpired was what Nelson always aimed at – a pell-mell battle in which British seamanship and gunnery would triumph. Nelson even went so far as personally to board a Spanish first-rate, the 112-gun *San Josef*, via the 80-gun *San Nicolas*, which Nelson, as always eager for closer action, had rammed with his own ship, *Captain*.

This further act of cool courage appealed to the British fleet and his use of the *San Nicolas* became famous as Nelson's Patent Bridge for boarding first-rates. The outcome of the battle was eminently satisfactory. Four Spanish battleships were captured; the rest of the enemy fleet, still outnumbering the British, limped back to Cadiz; the junction of the Spanish and French fleets had been prevented; the threat of England's invasion was removed. Nelson himself, longing for recognition and fame, was made a Knight of the Bath and a rear-admiral. 'His sudden exploit', says Arthur Bryant, 'caught England's imagination . . . For all men knew him now for what he was. That knowledge was the measure of his opportunity. The years of testing and obscurity were over, the sunrise gates of fulfilment opening before him.' Nelson's next great task and triumph would be against the endeavours and ambitions of Napoleon himself.

In India Wesley did not hear about the victory off Cape St Vincent until early in 1798. At about the same time he learnt that his brother, Richard, Lord Mornington, was to be Governor-General of India. Mornington had decided that his former family name, Wellesley, should now be revived (he later became Marquis Wellesley), and this meant that Arthur too had to change his name. As another brother, Henry, was Richard's secretary, there were now to be no fewer than three of them engaged in directing India's destiny. Between them they made a remarkable job of it. From May 1798 when Mornington arrived in Calcutta to take up his duties as Governor-General, Arthur Wellesley's entire position and prospects changed. When it became clear that Tippoo Sultan, the Tiger of Mysore, was in league with the French, Mornington determined to teach Tippoo a lesson, and as it fell out, the officer to help administer this instruction was to be Colonel Arthur Wellesley.

But before we follow his fortunes in Mysore, we must turn to another event which occurred in May 1798. Napoleon, having at first been appointed to the Army of England, and not thinking much of the idea of an invasion when the British navy enjoyed absolute command of the seas, summed up the situation like this: 'Too chancy. I don't intend to risk *la belle France* on the throw of a dice.' He writes to Barras and the other Directors: 'Even with our best efforts, it will take us several years to get the upper hand at sea. The invasion of England would be a desperate venture; it will only be possible if we take the islanders by surprise . . .we shall need long nights, so it must be in winter. Consequently we cannot make the attempt till next year. Before then it is likely enough that hindrances will have arisen on the Continent. Perhaps the great moment has been lost forever.'[2] Instead he turns his thoughts once more to Egypt, with a view in the end to striking a blow at India itself, the richest jewel of the British Empire, where an ally – the very Tippoo Sultan whom Arthur Wellesley was soon to engage in combat – would be ready to co-operate with him in ejecting the British from India once and for all. In March 1798, General Bonaparte was appointed Commander-in-Chief, Army of the East. Emil Ludwig's[3] highly coloured account of Napoleon's life makes it clear that the Directors welcomed renewing the idea of an Egyptian expedition. Talleyrand, Minister of Foreign Affairs, had long been in favour of it, and there existed between him and Napoleon a tacit understanding that he, Talleyrand, would go to Constantinople as French Ambassador, and there reconcile the Turks to the conquest of Egypt, Palestine, Syria and Asia Minor, which the newly appointed Commander-in-Chief, Army of the East, would by then have conquered. Together they would establish a new Empire of the East. 'However wild and fantastic the dreams of Napoleon at this time may have been,' writes Duff Cooper in his masterly *Talleyrand*, 'they were hardly wilder or more fantastic than

[2] Napoleon did not think so in 1803.
[3] Emil Ludwig, German biographer of Napoleon, Goethe, Bismarck, Wilhelm II, Hindenburg, Roosevelt. His study of Napoleon was first published in 1924.

what he subsequently accomplished.' Whether Talleyrand himself believed in these dreams was another matter. His coolness, clarity and cynicism may have given him pause, although like many another, he was conscious of Napoleon's magic, had responded to his boundless vision, had even confided in him. Yet there was always the notion that it would be expedient to remove from the shifting scenes of the French revolutionary power-game so disturbingly brilliant and dangerous an element. In any event Talleyrand supported the scheme and we therefore find Napoleon writing to his brother: 'I am going to the East with all the means to ensure success. Should France need me . . . should war break out and take an unfavourable turn, I shall come home, and public opinion will be more solidly on my side than it is now.' It was a remarkably prophetic observation.

So on 19 May 1798 Napoleon Bonaparte, not yet twenty-nine years old, set sail from Toulon, he himself in the huge 120-gun flagship *L'Orient*, taking with him his army of soldiers, scientists, artists and philosophers. With him too went nearly 200 ships, 1,000 guns, plentiful ammunition, 700 horses and some 20,000 men – later this force was more than doubled by another fleet sailing from Italian ports. The purpose of the expedition was threefold: first, to make Egypt a French colony – militarily this would be a picnic compared to the invasion of England; second, to be a preliminary move in the ultimate aim to strike at India; third (and this was essentially Napoleon's own idea), 'to improve the lot of the natives of Egypt' by bringing them the latest benefits of civilization – medicine, science and technology. Whether conquering Egypt would actually improve the lot of the people was, of course, another consideration. All these grandiose enterprises deserved, indeed demanded, some appropriate Napoleonic rhetoric and as usual he was not slow to come up with something. His order of the day on 19 May appealed to his soldiers: 'You are one of the wings of the Army of England. You have waged war in the mountains, in the plains . . . it remains for you to wage war at sea . . . Soldiers, Europe has its eyes on you.'

Meanwhile someone who did understand the business of waging war at sea was scanning the distant horizons for a glimpse of the French armada. Rear-Admiral Sir Horatio Nelson, having recovered from the loss of his right arm at Tenerife, had re-entered the Mediterranean in May 1798 with a powerful squadron, traditionally intent on a mission

more to search for the French off Greece, the Levant and again Egypt. He knew that by this time the French would have been able to land their army and harbour their fleet. But still he persevered. To the Hamiltons he had written that they must have a victory: 'We shall sail by the first breeze and be assured I will return either covered with laurels, or covered with cypress.' At last he was to be rewarded for his vigilance. At two o'clock in the afternoon of 1 August 1798, having already sighted French transports at Alexandria, and pushed on east-wards, two ships in the van of Nelson's squadron, Hood's *Zealous* and Foley's *Goliath*, sighted Admiral Bruey's line of battle at anchor in Aboukir Bay. The signal 'Enemy in Sight' had its expected effect. Captain Berry of Nelson's flagship *Vanguard* noted that 'the utmost joy seemed to animate every breast'. Nelson had been right all along. Now it would be a peerage or Westminster Abbey. Before we see how he gained the peerage, we must look at what Bonaparte had been up to by virtue of Nelson's earlier misfortune in not catching his expedition while still at sea.

Having had the Devil's own luck in getting his army to Egypt at all, once there Bonaparte lost no time in making his presence felt. Disembarking on 1 July at Marabout, to the west of Alexandria, his veterans quickly overcame the inadequate defences of this renowned city. Then there followed, as was his style, a proclamation to the people of Egypt in his customary high-flown language and already printed in Arabic during the passage east. God, his prophet and the Koran would be respected. The Egyptian people's misfortunes were laid solely at the door of their rulers, the Marmalukes, who owned everything, the land, houses, horses and slaves.[4] Those who supported the French would be happy and would prosper. 'But woe, three times woe, to those who take up arms for the Marmalukes and fight against us! There will be no hope for them; they will perish.' In short, soft talk plus the big stick, a recipe not unlike Charles Napier's in dealing with Sind – a good thrashing followed by kindness.

Next came the frightful march from Alexandria to Cairo – across the rocky desert, burning by day, cold at night, no supplies to be looted,

---

[4] The Marmalukes were not Egyptian, but Albanian or Circassian. Dedicated from childhood to the military profession, they were as richly attired themselves as were their scimitars, their pistols and their horse furniture.

short of water, myriads of flies, that unpleasant disorder known by the British Tommy as Gyppy tummy. It was all very different from the lush plains of Lombardy, but did not alter the result. In two battles, one at Shubra Kit on 13 July, the other at the Giza Pyramids eight days later, Napoleon destroyed the 24,000-strong Turkish-Egyptian army. The élite part of it consisted of the courageous, splendidly attired, but ill-organized Marmaluke cavalry, 8,000 of them, who charged with the utmost gallantry. At the decisive battle of the Pyramids – '*Soldats, songez que, du haut de ces pyramides, quarante siècles vous contemplent*' – Napoleon, who was short of cavalry, had simply formed up his divisions in squares, with guns at the corners, and when the Marmalukes charged, blew them to pieces with case-shot and musket fire. The *coup de grâce* was delivered by Napoleon himself; he led the reserve division to the rear of the Marmalukes, and in the space of two hours, using his artillery to maximum effect and losing only 200 men, he eliminated the entire enemy force – either killed or surrendered. Lower Egypt and Cairo were now in his hands. Eleven days later Nelson destroyed the French battle fleet at Aboukir, and Napoleon's army of some 40,000 men was cut off from its homeland.

If Napoleon vindicated, time without number, his own description of himself as the boldest general who ever lived, Nelson was certainly the boldest admiral who ever trod the quarterdeck of a British man-of-war. His tactic at Aboukir was a masterpiece of quick thinking, indomitable courage, brilliant seamanship and devastating gunnery. Two of his four aces of leadership were imagination and the offensive spirit, and at the battle of the Nile he played them both to full effect. By concentrating against Admiral Bruey's battleships *on either side of them*, that is by means of sailing some of his own ships between the French line and the shore, Nelson's band of brothers rapidly overcame the French ships. Nelson himself was wounded by a splinter, Bruey directing his own operations from his flagship *L'Orient* with both legs shot away – in those days generals and admirals alike were in the thick of things. At ten o'clock in the evening of 1 August 1798, *L'Orient* blew up, a detonation heard 15 miles away in Alexandria, where General Kléber was in command – soon to report the destruction of the French battle fleet to Napoleon in Cairo. At the end of it all, of Bruey's thirteen sail of the line, ten had been taken by the British, one blown up, two escaped. 'Victory', said Nelson, 'is not a name strong enough for such a scene.' His despatch was couched in suitable terms: 'Almighty God has blessed His Majesty's Arms in the late Battle by a great Victory over the Fleet of the Enemy, whom I attacked at sunset on the 1st August, off the mouth of the Nile.'

One of the most enthusiastic recipients of this news was, of course, Emma Hamilton, who wrote to Nelson that she was delirious with joy: 'I fainted when I heard the joyful news and fell on my side and am hurt, but what of that . . . I should feel it a glory to die in such a cause. No, I would not like to die until I see and embrace the *Victor of the Nile.*' Embrace him she did, in the days to come – completely, with total abandon, unbridled passion, and absolute devotion.

So the British fleet once more had command of the Mediterranean sea. The destruction of Admiral Bruey's line of battle had effectively marooned Napoleon's army in Egypt. 'His generals', writes A. G. Macdonnell, 'were flung instantly into despair, for France, the gentle land of their homes, seemed cut off for ever . . . But though they despaired, which was bad, they learnt, which was good, for the first time that they were serving under a commander who never despaired.' Bonaparte's tireless activity took innumerable forms: the baking of bread, the brewing of beer, water or windmills, gunpowder for the army – how were all these things to be organized in Egypt? And then the study of ancient tombs, the mystery of the Sphinx, the interpretation of hieroglyphics, improvement of agricultural methods – these matters no doubt intrigued the Commander-in-Chief, as did his attempted reconciliation of the religious leaders to his government. His decrees included setting up a lighting system for principal cities, a postal system, a stage-coach service, even a mint, but none of these measures could prevent an insurrection in Cairo, which he put down with the same blood-spilling ruthlessness he had employed in Paris in 1795 and was to have repeated by Murat in Madrid some ten years later. Yet there was still the question of what to do next. Without sea-power he could not proceed to India. It was beginning to look as if the whole Egyptian game had been a failure. Turkey's declaration of war in September 1798 provided the catalyst for further action. Preparations for further campaigns were pushed ahead, and Napoleon determined to advance into Syria to destroy a Turkish army assembling there under Djezar Pasha. In February 1799 he marched, took Jaffa by storm in March,[5] and pushed on to Acre.

---

[5] 4,000 Turkish prisoners were taken. Napoleon had to choose between feeding them, freeing them for further action against him or shooting them. He chose the last.

Although he annihilated a Turkish army at Mount Tabor in April, he failed to capture Acre, largely because of the efforts of Captain Sidney Smith RN and his squadron, who not only captured Napoleon's siege-train but so bolstered the Turks and Acre's fortress defences with his seamen that Napoleon abandoned the siege and returned to Egypt. Once more, as he later declared, wherever there was water to float a ship, the English would be in the way. 'Had it not been for the English Navy, I should have been Emperor of the East.' There would be no going to India for him now. Had he done so at this time, he might have crossed swords with Wellesley, who was doing great things there and whose fortunes we will shortly follow.

But before doing so, we had better catch up with the petticoats. Josephine no doubt was misbehaving in Paris with Hippolyte Charles, the handsome young Hussar lieutenant, and Napoleon's rage and humiliation were redoubled by the publication in London's *Morning Chronicle* of letters to Josephine from her son, Eugène, and to his brother Joseph from Napoleon himself. However, consolation was at hand. Pauline, the pretty young wife of Lieutenant Fourès, became what the troops called their general's 'favourite mistress'. It was not only by dropping realms, islands, crowns and coronets from his pocket that Napoleon was to resemble Antony. He had found a Cleopatra too. 'Love rules the camp, the court, the grove,' wrote Byron,[6] and if it were so with the Commander-in-Chief, it was equally so with his Chief of Staff, Berthier, who hated Egypt, was longing to see his adored lady-love, Madame de Visconti, and bitterly reflected that Masséna had not only taken over Berthier's command in Rome – with all its extravagant lootability – but, being near the de Visconti, was probably practising his celebrated successes in the boudoir as well.

In July 1799 the Turks were unwise enough to land nearly 10,000 men at Aboukir, where Napoleon with some 8,000 took them on and utterly routed them, Lannes leading the infantry right wing against the Turks, while Murat with the cavalry turned the flanks. Both men were wounded, Murat flamboyant as ever leading both a cavalry and a dromedary charge, brandishing a sabre engraved with the words *L'honneur et les dames* and receiving a bullet in the jaw for his pains. This only encouraged him to write home with a message for *les dames*

---

[6] *Don Juan*, Canto XII.

to the effect that Murat might have lost some of his good looks, but none of his dash in the art of love. Lannes, on the other hand, learnt that his wife, whom he had not seen for more than a year, had just given birth to a fine baby son.

Sidney Smith had not only thwarted Napoleon at Acre. He now sent to the enemy Commander-in-Chief a packet of back numbers of the *Gazette Française de Francfort*. From these he discovered that everything was going wrong for the French Republic. She was at war not only with England and Turkey, but with Russia, Austria and Naples. Corfu had been lost, Zurich taken by Austro-Russian forces, northern Italy had been invaded, the Cisalpine Republic was no more, there was fighting in Holland. France itself was in economic turmoil. There was but one course of action for him – to return to France. Leaving the Egyptian command to Kléber, he embarked in a frigate, *Muiron*, on the night of 22 August 1799 and with three other vessels sailed for France. He took with him Berthier, Murat, Marmont, Bessières and Lannes. He was never to return to Egypt. Indeed the whole Egyptian campaign had been futile. Nor would he ever go to India now. But we must.

It was one of Wellington's great qualities as a military commander that he was able to foresee and state the difficulties of any campaign he undertook, and having done so, then get on with finding solutions to these difficulties, thus enabling him to carry out the task in hand. He gave the soundest advice to his brother Richard, the Governor-General, about how to remove the threat to the British position in India. The most serious danger, he argued, was that French officers in the service of Indian princes should train their armies in the revolutionary tactics of heavy artillery bombardments followed by thickly packed columns of infantry concentrating against the relatively small forces of the East India Company. To increase the size of the Company's armies would be self-defeating in that the cost of doing so would be disproportionate to the Company's revenue from other sources. In undertaking a campaign against Tippoo Sultan, therefore, it would be necessary to anticipate the problems and plan meticulously in overcoming them – not to rush in unprepared, only to be confronted by seemingly irremovable obstacles. In August 1798 he and his regiment sailed from Calcutta for Madras instantly to encounter the very sort of corrupt carelessness that so irritated him. 'Too much of water hast thou, poor Ophelia,' mourns Hamlet's mother, and the same might be said of Wellesley and his regiment, for first they narrowly escaped drowning when their ship ran on to a reef, and then by drinking contaminated water supplied by an idle contractor all went down with dysentery. Death struck down 'fifteen as fine men as any we had'. On arrival in Madras Wellesley found himself in an awkward situation. He had the dual task of not antagonizing the new Governor of Madras, Lord Clive (son of the great Robert Clive), who believed that Mornington wished to precipitate war with Mysore, and at the same time preparing for war with Tippoo should it become necessary. He advised his brother to be moderate in his dealings with Tippoo in such a way that if war could with honour be avoided, it should be. At the same time his calm good sense and agreeable firmness won Wellesley both Clive's confidence and the co-operation of General Harris, Commander-in-Chief, Madras Presidency, in organizing lines of communication and supply bases between Madras and Mysore. In his later years of the sword Wellington was sometimes criticized for being too commissariat-minded. This tendency should have been praised, not condemned. He never forgot the lessons of campaigning in desert and jungle, instantly grasping that to mount an invasion of Mysore and to reach Tippoo's remote headquarters at the fort of Seringapatam with 50,000 soldiers, a siege-train and 100,000 camp followers, after negotiating some 200 miles of trackless wild country, would demand exact calculation and an unfailing supply of rations, forage and ammunition. There would therefore need to be untold numbers of bullocks – which the various District administrators would be required to collect at a variety of bases on the line of advance. 'It is impossible', he declared, 'to carry on a war in India without bullocks.' So throughout the latter months of 1798, preparations continued. One of the negotiations crucial to conducting a successful campaign was to gain support from the Nizam of Hyderabad, which was to the north of Mysore. This support was gained by the British Resident, and Wellesley himself was given command of the Hyderabad army, reinforced by 6,000 sepoys and his own 33rd Foot. In all he would have a force of 16,000 soldiers, consisting, apart from the 33rd, of 'six excellent battalions of the Company's Sepoys, four rapscallion battalions of the Nizam's . . . and about 10,000 cavalry of all nations.' Small-scale stuff when we compare it with Bonaparte's commands of the Armies of Italy and the Orient, but not the less effective for all that.

With the news of Nelson's Nile victory, it became clear to the

Governor-General that Tippoo would be getting no reinforcement from Egypt and, in the light of Tippoo's continued unwillingness to come to terms, he gave orders early in February 1799 that the general advance on Seringapatam should get under way. It took more than two months for this vast assembly of soldiers, tents, bullocks, elephants, camels, siege guns and camp followers to reach Seringapatam, having fought a short action with Tippoo's cavalry and infantry *en route*, when the disciplined fire-power of Wellesley's sepoys and the 33rd's brave work with bayonets drove off the enemy. 'We are here,' Wellesley sent word to the Governor-General, 'with a strong, healthy and brave army, with plenty of stores, guns, etc.', and he promised that they would soon be masters of Tippoo's fortifications. That the army had got there at all in such good order owed much to Wellesley's foresight, planning and calculated preparations. His initial attempt to take the place, however, failed, and in this failure he underwent a most chastening experience.

The approach to Seringapatam was screened by numerous thickets, called 'topes', and Wellesley was required to clear the Sultanpettah Tope, which had the additional hazard of being criss-crossed by irrigation canals. There had been no time to reconnoitre in daylight, and when Wellesley with his 33rd Foot tried to push through the enemy outposts in darkness, he and his men were unable to locate them, suffering casualties from musket and rocket fire. So confused did the situation become that he lost all control of the operation and was obliged to withdraw and to report failure to General Harris. There and then he determined that he would never again allow an attack to be made on a strongly fortified enemy position without properly reconnoitring it in daylight beforehand. At his next attempt to deal with the Sultanpettah Tope delivered the following day, Wellesley carried all before him – 'done in high style and without loss,' Colonel Close reported – and now the proper business of laying siege to the fortress could proceed. On 4 May 1799, the assault went in. The preparatory bombardment most satisfactorily blew up the magazine in Tippoo's fort, clearing a breach for the 4,000 storming troops, gallantly led by Major-General David Baird (who had been imprisoned by Tippoo's father, Hyder Ali, and kept in chains for three years) with these stirring words: 'Now, my brave fellows, follow *me* and prove yourself worthy of the name of British soldiers!' Indeed they did and rapidly reached the breach's summit. Reinforcements poured in, Tippoo's soldiers fled and Tippoo himself was killed, fighting to the last as became the Tiger of Mysore. 'When news of the Allies' victory reached the Governor-General', writes Elizabeth Longford, 'it drew from him an avalanche of congratulatory eloquence: consummate judgement, unequalled rapidity, animation, skill, humanity, honour, splendour, glory and lustre – all were theirs. In England it seemed as if the days of the Great Clive had returned.'[7] Colonel Wellesley was appointed Governor of Seringapatam, much to the disgust of Baird, who was twelve years older, a major-general and very experienced in the affairs of India.

We will return shortly to Wellesley's Mysore command and his dalliance with the memsahibs, but first we will accompany Napoleon to Paris, looking in briefly at the Kingdom of the Two Sicilies where Nelson has finally succumbed – not to French men-of-war, but to the voluptuous charms and stifling exhausting embraces of an English three-decked cruiser, Emma Hamilton. In November 1798 Nelson's initiative in stirring up the Neapolitans to make war on France was as calamitous a failure as his attack on the French fleet three months earlier had been a triumphant success. Although the Austrian General von Mack pronounced the Neapolitan force *'la plus belle Armée d'Europe'* on account of their dazzling uniforms and although Mack and King Ferdinand absolutely led this army into Rome, while Nelson landed a force at Leghorn, as soon as the French counter-attacked a month later, the splendid Neapolitan army was routed and melted away. Dress them in blue, red or any other colour, was the contemporary comment, and they'll run away just the same. The French advanced on Naples and there was nothing for it but that Nelson had to embark King Ferdinand, Queen Carolina, their children, courtiers and the Hamiltons in his own flagship and sail for Palermo. It was here that Nelson and Emma became lovers. For Nelson it was the very ecstasy of love and Emma was no longer obliged to simulate pleasure for he yielded to her as much as she yielded to him. They both embarked on the adventure of pleasure with the same slight anxiety about their ability to please or be pleased, and the same ease, the same trust. They were equals in pleasure, because equals in love. Was not this love indeed? None but the brave deserve the fair, they say. If ever a man of heroic stature deserved the kind

---

[7] Elizabeth Longford, wife of Lord Longford, and by marriage the great-great-niece of Kitty Pakenham. Her two-volume biography of Wellington is unsurpassed.

of love he longed for and Emma gave him, that man was Nelson.

Although the French regained Rome and Naples in 1798, 1799 was a bad year for the Republic. Shortly before Napoleon was starting his voyage from Egypt back to France, militarily the Republic itself was in a perilous condition. In March 1799, Austria had declared war and its army was advancing under the ablest of its generals, the Archduke Charles, bundling the Republicans back through the Black Forest to the Rhine. The Russian armies, subsidized by Pitt's gold, were active everywhere: one force under Korsakov was supporting the Archduke Charles; another under the dreaded Suvorov was ranging through Italy taking Mantua – whose capture had cost Napoleon so much time and effort – then Milan and Turin. Republican general after Republican general was defeated – Moreau, Joubert, Grouchy (who was to play such a vitally *inactive* role at Waterloo), Pérignon and Macdonald, who abandoned Naples only to be crushed by Suvorov on the River Trebbia. By July 1799, the French Republic had its back to the wall: the Army of the Rhine had been pushed beyond that river, Italy was lost and even the British – with Russians paid for by Britain – were about to land in Flanders once more. You would have thought that the former British experiences in Flanders might have dissuaded them from trying again there, but no, Pitt was so impatient to be doing something that he even moved to Walmer Castle to supervise the expedition. What is more, for want of anyone more qualified or acceptable to the government, the Duke of York was appointed to command. It was just as well that the government also named that brave, distinguished veteran General Abercromby as the Duke's deputy and principal adviser, for if anyone could see the risks involved, it was he.

In England there was great enthusiasm for the idea of the redcoats having a crack at the enemy. Confidence in their ability to take on and beat the despised French was widespread – but this confidence was largely confined to those who knew very little of the matter. King George III may have swelled with pride as he watched the London volunteers and militia marching past in Hyde Park, even giving the Inns of Court Regiment a nickname, 'The Devil's Own', which has survived to this day. But Abercromby, who had little faith in the expedition, raised constant objections to what was proposed – to the intense irritation of Pitt. The Prime Minister could not seem to grasp that no matter how desirable a political objective might be, it could not be achieved by military means if these means were impracticable. Thus when Abercromby told him that 'an Army is not a machine that can move of itself; it must have the means of moving', in other words it required transport for guns, stores and the wounded, Pitt dismissed such reasonable arguments as quibble – 'the ill-timed pedantry of an old woman in a red coat'. He deluded himself that Abercromby took pleasure in opposing whatever was proposed. However, before the expedition got under way, he had relented sufficiently to agree that a royal wagon-train should hurriedly be put together. This instance of Pitt's refusal to comprehend the practical business of waging war enables us to endorse Macaulay's condemnation of Pitt's military administration as that of a mere driveller.

In this particular case Pitt's political touch was equally amiss. He had brought himself to believe, because he wished to do so, that the Foreign Office and Dutch refugees sympathetic to the House of Orange were correct in alleging that the peoples of the Netherlands would assist the Allied armies by rising in opposition to the French and so help turn out the hated invader. Nothing like it happened at all. On 27 August 1799 (four days after Bonaparte sailed from Egypt) Admiral Mitchell with the British fleet landed Abercromby's army of 10,000 men at Den Helder. The defending French and Dutch troops were quickly disposed of, and the Allied armies were free to advance. The whole campaign strikingly illustrated how to break the principles of war. There was no proper co-ordination between the army and the Royal Navy, although the latter under Mitchell captured the entire Dutch fleet at anchor. There was no proper co-operation between the British and Russian armies, no attempt either to concentrate in order to win a telling victory or to make use of sea-power to outflank and turn the French defences; as usual artillery supplies and transport were totally inadequate. It was a repetition of all that Arthur Wesley had seen go wrong in the previous expedition of 1793–95. There were perhaps two redeeming features from the British Army's point of view. Abercromby's second-in-command, Major-General Sir John Moore, who was badly wounded at the battle of Egmont, had observed how effective were the French *tirailleurs*, their skirmishing sharp-shooters, in causing heavy casualties to and disrupting the advance of British redcoats. It was a lesson he never forgot and later turned to great advantage when training another British army. There were also the exploits of that great cavalryman Lord Henry Paget (later Earl of Uxbridge and Marquess of Anglesey) in conducting one of those brilliant charges for which he became famous, and rescuing the Allied line from disruption when Brune, the French commander, counter-attacked a Russian column in the last serious engagement of the whole affair. In his *The Reign of George III*, J. Steven Watson summed up the campaign by saying simply that the Allied armies had advanced in drenching rain from Den Helder to the line of the Zype Canal, where they stuck fast in the mud, while the Dutch people did not lift even a finger to support their supposed liberators. After much dithering and recrimination, the British Army withdrew again and was evacuated. One more expedition to the Netherlands had ended in failure. It was all very well for Pitt to be comforted by reflecting that the army had been returned to England. The fact was that the country was losing confidence in the army. It would be for Sir John Moore and Sir Arthur Wellesley – each of whom would campaign against Bonaparte – to restore this confidence.

While Bonaparte was making his way to Paris, Flanders was not the only theatre of war in which the French armies were defying their enemies. There was also Switzerland, where the brilliant and stubborn Masséna was plucking the flower, safety, from the nettle, danger. The great strategic value of Masséna's army, spread out on the frontiers of Switzerland, was this. If either Archduke Charles or Suvorov attempted to invade France, the former by crossing the Rhine, the latter by advancing along the coast to Nice, Masséna would be able to emerge from his Alpine bastion, pounce on their communications and sever them from their supply columns. As A. G. Macdonnell has reminded us, Masséna's army 'was blazing with military talent'. Among his subordinates were numbered no fewer than five men who subsequently became Marshals of the Empire – Oudinot, Mortier, Suchet, Ney and Soult. Yet it was Masséna himself who made the all-important decision not to abandon his mountain bastion when faced with a simultaneous attack from three sides, but rather to concentrate his force outside Zurich and await events. As it turned out events went his way. The allies, believing Masséna to be trapped, did not concentrate all their forces against him. Archduke Charles with 50,000 men went off towards the Netherlands to lend support to the expected Anglo-Russian landings there, leaving Masséna to Korsakov, reputed lover of Catherine the Great and a celebrated bon viveur, commanding the Austro-Russian army at Zurich, and Suvorov, the hideous butcher, whose military doctrine was simply to go bull-headed at the enemy, whom Byron called half demon and half dirt and whose army was coming up from Italy, having already thrashed the French army under Macdonald. But even Suvorov could not fight without supplies of some sort and it had been agreed that Korsakov would send supplies to Schwyz, some 20 miles south of Zurich. But by the time Suvorov – harassed and delayed by French forces under Lecombe and further slowed by snow and furious winds – had reached Schwyz on 28 September, Masséna, observing Korsakov's dangerous extension of his position to the west of Zurich, had attacked him with his whole army and driven him out of Switzerland altogether, causing Catherine's paramour to leave 8,000 men, all his guns, money and supplies in Masséna's hands. Simultaneously, to the south, Soult had ejected the Austrians under Hotze and Molitor had mauled one of Suvorov's corps. Without either supplies or support, there was nothing for it but for Suvorov to abandon his offensive and march the remnants of his cold, hungry and ill-clad army, some 15,000 of them, across the mountains and away. Masséna's cold, crafty, calculating waiting game, a game played with infinite patience and perseverance, yet ever-ready for the controlled pounce on opportunity, had saved the Republic from invasion. By the time it was next threatened, Napoleon would not merely be once more in command of the army. He would be the political leader of France.

General Bonaparte had landed at Fréjus on 13 October and was in Paris three days later. One of his first comments – a cynical one at that – was in the petticoat line. On finding that Josephine was not at home, he suggested that the warriors of Egypt resembled those of Troy: their wives were comparably faithful. But Napoleon forgave her dalliance with Lieutenant Charles and they began to deal more comfortably together. There was in any case more serious work at hand. While Bonaparte had still been in Egypt, the Directory, a government of lawyers, had fallen from favour, and every sort of intrigue was under way to make a change. It was no wonder that a change was sought, for everything was going wrong. The armies, except for Masséna's, had been defeated, Napoleon's glorious conquests forfeited, the Treasury was empty, widespread disorder was matched by widespread discontent. So the Abbé Siéyès, one of the Directors, hit upon the idea that he himself would be an excellent replacement for the Directory. But others would need to be similarly persuaded, among them that great survivor, Talleyrand,

and the Chief of Police, Fouché; there would also need to be a soldier to wield the sword for Siéyès. At first Siéyès thought of Bernadotte, Minister of War, but Bernadotte was too circumspect; Moreau might do, but he was too timid. It was, however, Moreau who made the crucial suggestion when he heard on 13 October 1799 that Bonaparte had landed at Fréjus. Bonaparte, Moreau told Siéyès, was the man to manage a *coup d'état*. And manage it he did.

There was a lot of manoeuvring to be done first, and between 16 October and the end of that month, Josephine's salon was crowded with politicians and soldiers, while Bonaparte gauged the situation and made his plans. After two weeks of deliberation, he threw in his lot with Siéyès and Ducos, another Director, and made sure that he could rely on some of the key soldiers whose support would be vital if it came to fighting. These were the men who had been with him in Italy and Egypt – Berthier, Murat, Lannes and Marmont. Sérurier and Moreau also pledged their support. There was still Lefèbvre, Military Governor of Paris, to get on their side, and if possible Bernadotte. Poor, bluff, naïve, manipulable Lefèbvre fell for the blandishments of Josephine and the smooth reassurances of Bonaparte, but Bernadotte continued to sit on the fence. The conspiracy would have to proceed without him. The first step was to get the soldiers in position; on 9 November, Bonaparte's men took a firm grip on key places and deployed their troops in readiness. Marmont, as became an artilleryman, had the guns; Murat took the cavalry to the Palais Bourbon; Lannes was in command of the Tuileries; Macdonald was at Versailles, Sérurier at St Cloud. By the end of that day all the Directors were rendered impotent and it only remained for Bonaparte to confront next day the Council of the Ancients and the Deputies at St Cloud for the whole *coup d'état* to be complete.

There were few things that daunted Bonaparte, but one of those few things was a hostile mob. It was precisely this that he had to face in the Council Chamber at St Cloud outside Paris on 10 November. When he addressed the Council of the Ancients, he struck quite the wrong chord, talking to them not as the statesman they expected, but as a soldier, bragging that with him marched the god of victory and the god of fortune. He was greeted with angry shouts. Worse was to come when he entered the orangery to address the Five Hundred Deputies. At once he was accused of violating the law; angry deputies crowded round him, clawing and striking at him, shouting that he was a dictator and should be outlawed. Napoleon was rescued by four stalwart soldiers and led outside. Lucien Bonaparte, his brother, who was President of the Five Hundred, then tried to restore order and quickly sent a note to Napoleon telling him to act at once. After appealing to the soldiers – 'I led you to victory, can I count on you?', an appeal reinforced by Lucien, who swore to run his own brother through if he should jeopardize the freedom of Frenchmen – Napoleon instructed General Leclerc (a comrade in arms at Toulon and married to Pauline, Napoleon's sister) and Murat to clear the Orangery. Murat, with his customary blend of eloquent bravado and practical action, invited his grenadiers to chuck the deputies – 'these blighters' – out of the Orangery window. This effectively ended all opposition and early next morning on 11 November 1799, still at the Orangery, the new government formally took office.

There were to be three Consuls – Bonaparte, Ducos and Siéyès. They swore to serve the Republic loyally, and to uphold the principles of Liberty, Equality and the Representative System. None of this counted for much when about a month later Bonaparte became First Consul and virtual ruler of France. He was only thirty years old. He moved to the Tuileries in February 1800, telling the 'little Creole', Josephine, to 'sleep in the bed of your masters'. It would not be long, however, before he found himself once more confronting France's enemies at the head of another army. He would have preferred to concentrate on matters of peace, but neither Austria nor Great Britain was prepared to make peace. As it was, he both made war successfully – we shall shortly accompany him to Marengo – and at the same time set about the gigantic task of completely overhauling the organization and conduct of affairs in France. That Bonaparte wished for peace was made clear by his declaration to the people on becoming First Consul that he knew they wanted peace and that the government wanted it even more. He went so far as to send a message to King George III proposing just that and asking 'why the two most enlightened nations of Europe should go on sacrificing their trade, their prosperity, and their domestic happiness to false ideas of grandeur?' He got a dusty answer.

At the beginning of 1800, George told Grenville, Foreign Secretary, to write to Talleyrand rejecting any idea of treating with the First Consul. Grenville did so with irrational, tactless pomposity, demanding the restoration of the Bourbons and the pre-revolutionary frontiers.[8] Pitt justified his dismissal of Bonaparte's peace offer on the grounds of security. When challenged in the House of Commons as to the object of the war, which was becoming increasingly unpopular in the country, Pitt replied that it was 'security; security against a danger, the greatest that ever threatened the world ... against a danger which has been resisted by all the nations of Europe, and resisted by none with such success as by this nation ...' Jacobinism, which had manifested itself in the persons of Robespierre and Barras, the Terror and the Directory, had not disappeared 'because it has all been centred and condensed into one man, who was reared and nursed in its bosom, whose celebrity was gained under its auspices, who was at once child and champion of all its atrocities and horrors'. Bonaparte would not bring England security. Peace, far from affording a prospect of security, would threaten all the evils they had been struggling to avoid. The prosecution of war, on the other hand, particularly if accompanied by increased resources, commerce and prosperity, *would* attain security. Therefore 'it is prudent in us not to negotiate at the present moment'. It was all very eloquent and effective no doubt. Underlying this insistence on security was fear of an enlarged, powerful and stable France, spreading revolutionary ideas and undertakings to the *émigré* French families. It was not the enmity of France, Burke noted, that was most to be feared, but her friendship and her doctrines.

One of those facing and countering the enmity of France, while maintaining and enhancing the security, prosperity and commerce of Britain, was of course Colonel Arthur Wellesley who in India was learning more and more about how to command armies in the field and how to govern great tracts of country where disorder was endemic. His recipe for proper rule was very different from Bonaparte's. 'It depends', he declared, 'on justice, freedom from corruption and unswerving truth to one's word and to every obligation that is undertaken.' There were two ways in which Wellesley distinguished himself during his years in command at Mysore. Firstly, he was determined to establish and maintain law and order, so that the customary methods of creating wealth –

[8] At this time France enjoyed by right of conquest natural frontiers – the Rhine, the Alps and the Pyrenees – and had established friendly republics in Switzerland and Holland.

farming, commerce, craftsmanship – could thrive, and also so that the authority of the native princes should be preserved, with all this meant for local employment. He was strongly opposed to an extension of British rule, arguing that it was beyond the Company's means, and simply added to the number of their enemies. 'Wherever we spread ourselves, we increase this evil. We throw out of employment and means of subsistence all who have hitherto managed the revenue, commanded or served in the armies or have plundered the country. These people become additional enemies at the same time that, by the extension of our territory, our means of supporting our government and of defending ourselves are proportionally decreased.' Yet, and this brings us to the second point of distinction, Wellesley was equally determined to stamp out the bands of plunderers which ravaged the country. One of his principal targets here was a Mahratta freebooter, Dhoondiah Waugh, who had escaped from Seringapatam after its storming by Wellesley, and who had now collected a band of former soldiers to terrorize and plunder the Deccan. Wellesley, in command of the troops in Mysore and south-west India, set out to chase and destroy Dhoondiah. He was soon to find that the advantage initially lay with his enemy who, without the need for cumbersome supply lines, living off the country and enjoying intelligence from the villages, was able to move much more quickly. Nonetheless Wellesley marched to, attacked and captured Dhoondiah's stronghold at Chitteldroog, dispersing his band of followers. Dhoondiah, however, escaped; during the winter months of 1799–1800 he put together another army and returned with it in April 1800. Wellesley took the field once more, dividing his force and so harrying Dhoondiah from one end of the Deccan to the other than when he caught up with his enemy in September 1800, trapping him between his two contingents, he utterly routed the bandit army. Wellesley himself absolutely led the cavalry chase which finished off the business. Dhoondiah Waugh was killed. It was Wellesley's first victory in sole command, writes Bryant, and it brought him the recognition he so much deserved. It was another example of careful planning and organization of supplies, and demonstrated what had previously been thought impossible – that a regular disciplined military force, even though dependent on supply lines, could catch and destroy a rapidly moving irregular body of troops living off the country. Despite this triumph, Wellesley was then to suffer the disappointment of being offered by his brother command of an expedition to Mauritius, only to find the offer withdrawn again. The summer of 1801 found him back at Mysore in his former command. How well he had justified his subsequent comment on his service in India: 'I am not afraid of responsibility, God knows!'

By this time Pitt was out of office, Egypt had been retaken by the British, Nelson had won another glorious victory at Copenhagen and Napoleon, having smashed the Austrians at Marengo, had dealt with all his enemies in Europe and was shortly to conclude a peace treaty with England. We will look at these events as they occurred. During the early months of 1800 the First Consul had to interrupt the furious work of organizing France's finances, its judicial system, its Civil Code, its religion, its educational structure, its roads, ports, canals, and its countrywide administration, in order to raise another army to beat off enemies who were gathering again to overthrow the Revolution once and for all. France was being threatened on two fronts – the Rhine and from Italy. Napoleon positioned his army of the Reserve at Dijon from where he could reinforce either front. In the end it was to Italy that he marched for, whereas the Army of the Rhine succeeded in checking the Austrians at Biberach, south of Ulm, the position in Italy was potentially much more dangerous. It all depended on that old fox Masséna, who was defending Genoa, boxed in by the Austrian army on land and the Royal Navy at sea. Masséna defied all the odds – starvation, disease, a mutinous army, a rebellious population, hanging on at all costs – for the Austrians dared not advance beyond Genoa leaving albeit weak French forces astride their communications. Towards the end of May 1800, Masséna heard at last that the First Consul had crossed the Great St Bernard with the Reserve army, and was in Lombardy at Marengo, positioned between Vienna and the Austrian army under Melas. Masséna could now march out of Genoa with his bedraggled remains of an army, and leave the contest to Napoleon.

It was much further on in his career that Napoleon cried: 'Give me lucky generals.' At Marengo in June 1800, making mistakes as he did, he needed luck himself – and got it! Having dispersed his forces too widely (a mistake he was dramatically and fatally to repeat twelve years later when he strung out the Grande Armée between Cadiz and Moscow) and not giving the Austrian commander credit for being able to mount a concentrated attack on him, the First Consul was dismayed to find his divisions being pushed back and his whole position in danger of cracking. Only a counter-attack could save the situation. It was fortunate that three of his subordinate commanders came to the rescue. His desperate plea to Desaix, 'For God's sake come back,' was instantly acted upon, and back came Desaix with his 5,000 infantry. Marmont, in charge of the guns, had been fighting all day, and was down to five pieces of artillery, which were promptly made up to a battery of eighteen by the arrival of five from the reserve and eight with Desaix. Thus Marmont was able to deliver an effective bombardment while Desaix prepared to go forward. On the flank, waiting, was young Kellermann with some cavalrymen. The field of Marengo then witnessed how the combined action of horse, foot and guns could transform the fortunes of battle. The description given by A. G. Macdonnell of this crucial action cannot be bettered:

> The French counter-attack was, by chance, one of the most perfectly timed tactical operations by combined infantry, artillery and cavalry in the whole history of warfare . . . For twenty minutes Marmont's battery of eighteen kept up the bombardment . . . and then Desaix went forward. Marmont managed to limber up four of his guns and went up in support. Suddenly, through the dense smoke he saw, not fifty yards in front, a battalion of Austrian grenadiers advancing in perfect formation to counter the counter-attack, and some of Desaix's men were tumbling back in confusion. Marmont, whatever his faults might be, was a quick thinker, and he unlimbered his four guns and fired four rounds of canister at point-blank range into the compact battalion, and at that precise moment, while the Austrians were staggering under the blow, and an Austrian ammunition-wagon was exploding with a monstrous detonation, Desaix[9] went forward with a shout, and young Kellermann came thundering down on the flank, through the mulberry-trees and the tall luxuriant vines, with a handful of heavy cavalry. A minute earlier, or three minutes later, and the thing could not have succeeded, but the timing was perfect, and North Italy was recovered in that moment for the French Republic.

Napoleon's own part in the battle had not been particularly distinguished yet the victory confirmed his position as First Consul and enabled him

---

[9] Desaix was killed in the attack – a bullet in the head.

to make peace. When, however, Berthier consoled an Austrian officer after the battle by pointing out that the Austrians had been defeated by the greatest general in the world, the reply was that it was what had been done at Genoa by the iron hand of Masséna that had won the battle of Marengo.

Napoleon had had his share of luck on this occasion. Moreover the French Army of the Rhine had not merely defeated the Austrians near Ulm. They had occupied Munich. At this point in their long struggle against France, the Austrians had distinguished themselves only by failure. It was hardly kind of Grenville, Pitt's Foreign Secretary, in commenting on the performance of the British Army, to say of it that it could hardly have done worse than the Austrians. Yet the British redcoats were about to rebuild their reputation for valour and initiative. To see how, we must return to the Egyptian desert. Bonaparte had had few qualms about abandoning his army there, when he felt that both for his own future and for that of France his presence would be of more use in Paris. But the French army was still there – now under command of Menou, who, despite being an ardent Bonapartist, had rather let the revolutionary side down when he became a Mohammedan and married the elderly and ill-favoured daughter of the Shireef. Trouble with the petticoats was not confined to the very great. The British Army would shortly be administering another sharp lesson to Menou.

One of the few players in the game *not* to have petticoat trouble was, of course, the man whom George Canning later called 'the pilot that weathered the storm' – William Pitt. He may have had a *tendresse* for Lady Hester Stanhope, but his allegiance to duty and service to the country was far too strong to allow himself the luxury of a private indulgence. By 1801 he had been Prime Minister for seventeen years, and by this time also, after eight years of war with revolutionary France, 'the tide had turned', as Bryant put it, 'in England's favour'. It was true that France under Bonaparte seemed to be unchallengeable in western and southern Europe, yet at sea Britain, with nearly 500 warships (more than 200 ships of the line and more than 275 frigates), was absolute master, while the British Army was shortly to be more than 300,000 strong. Both services were to win some famous victories in 1801, but Pitt was by then no longer at the head of affairs. Early that year his attempt to introduce a measure of Catholic Emancipation met with such violent opposition from the King that in March 1801 he laid down his office, and Addington formed an administration. We all know the jingle that 'Pitt is to Addington as London is to Paddington', yet at the beginning of his premiership, Addington was to enjoy some remarkable successes. Pitt himself had pointed out on handing over power that England's resources were entire, her honour and integrity complete. No territory had been lost – and 'we have given the rest of the world many chances of salvation'.

The British Army was now to set about turning the French out of territory which, strictly speaking, was part of the Turkish Empire. The gallant Abercromby, whom we last met floundering about in Flanders, departed with 15,000 men to Egypt. With him also was Major-General John Moore and Colonel Edward Paget – both future heroic stars of the army. In a letter to his father on the day before the British landed at Aboukir, Edward Paget was eloquent in depicting the bold confidence of his soldiers, a feeling of superiority which seemed to inspire the whole army and to enable John Bull to hold his enemy almost in contempt. Certainly they displayed just such superlative qualities when John Moore and his division landed to the west of Aboukir Castle, charging up a hill to their first objective and so overwhelming the French brigade defending it that they fled in disorder, leaving their guns to be captured by the British. By 12 March 1801 Abercromby had landed his entire force and was advancing on Alexandria. He then took up positions a few miles to the east of the port, with his flanks secured by the sea on his right and Aboukir lake on his left. The French commander, General Menou, came marching up from Cairo with 10,000 men (no doubt glad to be leaving his plain elderly Mohammedan bride behind in the harem) to reinforce the Alexandria garrison, and with characteristic *élan*, together with the advantages of more guns and a substantial force of cavalry (the British had none), attacked Abercromby on 21 March. It was then that John Moore's division won more glory, notably by the actions of those renowned regiments the Black Watch (42nd Highlanders) and the Gloucester Regiment (28th Foot). It was in fact then that the Gloucesters earned the right to wear their badge on both the front and the back of their head-dress. Under Edward Paget's cool command they simultaneously engaged a French infantry attack from the front and a cavalry charge from the rear. So successful was the British defence that the French were obliged to retire behind Alexandria's walls.

John Moore had shown once more what an inspiring, courageous commander he was. We will before long be meeting him again in his finest hour at Corunna. Abercromby too had commanded with great intrepidity and skill, but alas, a wound in the thigh, neglected until the battle was over, caused his death a week later. He had lived, as the Duke of York recorded, 'a life of honour' and ended it with a 'death of glory'. No soldier could ask for more. It was under Abercromby's hand that the British Army had triumphed in the gorgeous east, just as the Royal Navy had three years earlier. In less than a month, Alexandria had fallen and the reconquest of Egypt quickly followed. It all showed how futile had been Napoleon's oriental adventure. Egypt was safe. Napoleon had wanted it as a stepping-stone to India. That dream, however imaginative and strategically desirable, was over. In India itself Wellesley would shortly be consolidating British power even more firmly, as we shall see. But at this time the thwarting of French policy was not confined to the deserts of Egypt. It was also manifested in the waters of Scandinavia. It was clear to all that if England were to strike a blow at Bonaparte by sea, there was but one man to do it – the very man who had made possible the British Army's freedom of manoeuvre in the Mediterranean enabling them to reconquer Egypt, Vice-Admiral Lord Nelson.

Bonaparte's manipulation of the Baltic powers, Russia, Sweden and Denmark, together with the formation of the Northern League to exclude British trade from the Baltic, called for stern measures, and on 12 March 1801, the same day that Abercromby landed his troops in Egypt, Nelson sailed from Yarmouth with a powerful fleet, containing fifteen battleships, frigates, brigs and 1,000 redcoats. He was nominally second-in-command to the wealthy, cautious and uxoriously just-married Admiral Sir Hyde Parker, but no one was in any doubt about who would be in charge when it came to fighting. Nelson, aware that to Parker keeping a good table was as important as gratifying a young wife, succeeded in reaching Parker's heart by sending him a fine turbot. They were then able to discuss operational plans, and Parker was characteristically alarmed when he realized that Nelson was in favour of instant and offensive action. However, Nelson's assurance that the boldest measures were also the safest gave Parker some comfort, and he accepted his Vice-Admiral's plan of sailing through the narrow waters between the Danish Kronborg Castle and the Swedish coast, keeping as close as possible to the latter, and so beyond the range of Danish batteries. All this was accomplished by 30 March and with Copenhagen now in sight, Nelson set about the Danes – both their fleet and their shore batteries – on the following day. It was 'warm work' as Nelson himself put it, and at one point his renowned gesture of putting a telescope to his blind eye when Parker signalled a discontinuation of the action – 'I really do not see the signal' – was necessary in order for the gallantry and expert gunnery of the British sailors to prevail. His victory plus his subsequent diplomacy, together with the assassination of the mad Russian Czar Paul, brought the Northern League to an end. Everywhere, it seemed, Napoleon was being thwarted by the British.

It is therefore not surprising that he was prepared to listen to peace overtures. While hostilities on land and at sea continued, Addington's government proposed in 1801 what Arthur Bryant calls 'a business deal'. In the simplest terms it was that France should be allowed to hang on to her European conquests, while Britain retained the colonial ones – in particular, the Cape, Malta, Ceylon, Trinidad and Martinique. As Bonaparte was more or less invincible on European battlefields and the Royal Navy absolute masters of the sea, it seemed a rational enough arrangement. But as Bryant has emphasized, Addington was not dealing with a man who really wanted peace. Bonaparte's aim in accepting peace with England was simply to gain time in order to be able to return to the charge when powerful enough to destroy England. The only way to world domination as he saw it was to re-establish France's naval power, and this could not be done while the war persisted and the Royal Navy effectively blocked all the ports and construction bases under France's control. Besides, British sea-power also strangled Continental commercial enterprise, and thus robbed France of the wealth and means necessary to recreate a navy. Therefore, from Bonaparte's point of view, peace was a desirable expedient – for the present. Further British naval victories at sea against the Spanish and the French, together with the collapse of France's position in Egypt, persuaded the First Consul that serious negotiations for peace must get under way. But like the great bluffer and bully that he was, he threatened Britain with invasion – by a largely phantom flotilla of barges and proclamations of army artillerymen manning mythical gunboats. Nelson, back from his Baltic success, was appointed to guard the Channel, and although he failed to capture the French invasion barges at Boulogne, he was in no doubt that such an enterprise by the French was an impossibility. Negotiations continued and, as was to be expected, the wily First Consul had little difficulty in getting the better of Addington and Hawkesbury, his Foreign Secretary. These two lacked Pitt's vision of the commercial and strategic value of overseas colonies, and were content to return to France and her allies innumerable pre-war possessions in the West Indies, India and Africa in exchange for empty promises that France would withdraw garrisons from certain Italian ports, restore Egypt to Turkey (Britain's reconquest of Egypt was not yet known to Addington) and honour the independence of Portugal. Britain even agreed to restore Malta to the knights of St John and Minorca to Spain. A preliminary treaty was signed on 1 October 1801, and the Peace of Amiens was formally concluded in March 1802. A few weeks afterwards Bonaparte received an overwhelming vote of confidence from the French people, confirming him as Consul for his life. Henceforth he would be known as Napoleon. The peace was to last for little more than a year. When war came again, Napoleon, Wellington and Nelson would enjoy their most renowned victories. By the time peace finally returned, Nelson would be dead, Wellington the first man of Europe and Napoleon at St Helena.

CHAPTER 5

The Emperor Napoleon
and the Sepoy General

Look here upon this picture and on this.

Hamlet

I T would hardly be possible to conjure up a greater disparity of position between our two men than was the case in the year 1804. Napoleon was crowned Emperor of the French. Wellesley was awarded the Order of the Bath. We will now examine the events which immediately preceded and followed these two acknowledgements of distinction. Lord Castlereagh, who in 1802 was President of the Indian Board of Control, and later War and Colonial Secretary,[1] declared that what he desired was that France should feel England could not be trifled with. Yet, despite Napoleon's noting that 'England never sleeps, she is always on the watch,' during the Peace of Amiens, the First Consul began a calculated programme of trifling with England. It might in fact have been thought that England *was* going to sleep, for Addington's administration pursued a policy of retrenchment, most particularly in the armed forces. Within weeks of the peace treaty's being signed, his reduction of the army and the Royal Navy had begun. Indeed these steps were made inevitable by his abolition of Pitt's income tax – whose whole purpose had been to raise revenue to pay for the war. The British Army was to be more or less halved. Its regular strength was to be a mere 95,000, excluding 18,000 in Ireland. The volunteers were to be disbanded. The militia would be 50,000 and half of these were to be

---

[1] His greatest achievements were, of course, as Foreign Secretary from 1812 to 1822.

in reserve. Even worse than these measures reducing the army were Addington's proposals for the navy. Instead of a hundred ships of the line, there would be a mere forty. 50,000 seamen were to be discharged. And yet throughout this programme of British military economy, Napoleon was steadily preparing for a renewal of war. Most menacingly he was determined to create a navy which would, like the army, be invincible. It was just as well that war came sooner than Napoleon either wanted or expected, for not only did he not have time to complete his rebuilding of the navy – the plan was for seventy ships of the line – but he also squandered what time he had by setting the ship builders the task of making invasion barges, failing to grasp that without mastery of the Channel these barges would be useless.

History is full of ironies and one of them is that it was Addington – amiable, peace-loving, economizing, conciliatory Addington – who declared war on France in May 1803. Why did he do it? In the simplest terms, because the First Consul pushed him too far. By the Peace of Amiens Britain had agreed to return her overseas conquests to France – those in India were included – and to both Holland and Spain. There were some exceptions, notably Trinidad and Ceylon. Malta was to be returned to the Knights of St John of Jerusalem, and British troops were to leave the island. But this had not occurred, when it became clear to Addington and his administration that Napoleon had not the slightest intention of fulfilling his side of the bargain in relinquishing some of France's conquests in Europe. Moreover, it was not just that the First Consul intended to hang on to what he had and to regain what France had lost in war. He was after even bigger game by adding still further to his overseas territories. Thus he acquired from Spain – which was wholly subordinate to his influence – Elba, Parma and Louisiana. Still more serious from Britain's point of view, the strategically vital island of Malta was the subject of a threat to its independence by Spain's assumption of authority over the Malta Knights. Nor was this all. Napoleon reasserted his grip on northern Italy. All these things together were too much even for Addington. It was clear that some riposte was necessary. Britain therefore did not withdraw her troops from Malta, nor did she restore to France the Indian territories.

It was the dispute over Malta which caused the final break between Britain and France. During the early months of 1803 the British

Ambassador in Paris, Lord Whitworth, was required to undergo some disagreeable exchanges with the First Consul. Like most men who had risen from relatively humble origins to positions of almost supreme power, Napoleon, when confronted with reasoned argument which contradicted his own morally insupportable ambitions and predetermined courses of action, resorted to the methods and manners of a bully. He began to shout. Because he wanted Malta in order to swing the scale of Mediterranean mastery in his favour, he was willing to indulge in any sort of political manoeuvring or military threat to obtain his ends. But the British were well aware of Malta's indispensable role in their naval strategy. Whitworth therefore refused to budge. He was able to remind Napoleon that Parliament had voted funds to augment the Royal Navy by 10,000 more men and went on to infuriate the First Consul by saying that unless absolute guarantees as to Malta's independence were given, the British would continue to garrison the island. Napoleon lost his temper and bellowed that if Britain armed, so would he. 'If you fight, I will fight also.'

On and on the argument went, until it became plain to the British government that there was no dealing with Napoleon. In the first place he was unreasonable. In the second place no reliance could be placed on his honouring any agreement, reasonable or not. On 18 May 1803, therefore, Great Britain declared war. It had come too soon for Napoleon. Although he wanted war, he wanted it at a time of his own choosing – that is, when his fleet would be large enough and skilled enough to take on the Royal Navy. It was the very strength and omnipresence of the Royal Navy which determined Addington's war policy. He had none of the worldwide strategic vision or boldness of Pitt. He was not for despatching expeditions here, there and everywhere. It was probably just as well, for many of Pitt's attempts to regain a foothold in Europe by supporting a real or supposed royalist or anti-republican group had ended in failure and evacuation. No, Addington's strategy was essentially a defensive one, albeit reliant on the offensive power of the Royal Navy. While Napoleon might have his way in Continental Europe – indeed, how was he to be prevented? – the Royal Navy would continue to exercise mastery of the seas, protecting and enlarging British trade, stimulating the country's economy and financial strength, while denying these advantages to the enemy by blockading their ports and destroying their shipping. In order to counter this strategy, France would be obliged to attempt the invasion and subjugation of England. The Royal Navy would then inflict an overwhelming defeat on the French venture and the war would have been won. So ran Addington's theory of waging war.

To some extent it was a sound theory, for Napoleon, although thwarted of his intention to strengthen the French navy until it could challenge the British, was certainly setting his mind and his resources to the idea of invading England. With this very purpose in mind, he set about the task of creating the Grande Armée, and as A. G. Macdonnell reminds us, 'It was to be a real, full-dress, organized, trained fighting machine. Its training ground was to be the north-east coast of France, and its objective was England.' This was the army which was to be Napoleon's tool for dominating the affairs of Europe for the next decade, and against which a British army under Wellington – albeit in comparatively small numbers and in a theatre of war which the by then Emperor of the French regarded as a side-show – was to try its hand in a series of battles, which by their persistence and duration gradually acted like a cancer in draining the Grande Armée's strength away. We had therefore better take a look at this army of Napoleon's. Originally called the Army of the Coasts of the Ocean, it was a highly efficient fighting force, both as regards numbers and quality. Organized into seven corps, positioned at Hanover, Utrecht, Flushing-Dunkirk, Boulogne, Montreuil and Brest, it contained in all some 200,000 men. The corps commanders – all of whom were destined to become Marshals of the Empire and against some of whom Wellington would play a hand or two – represented about the most glittering array of military talent that could be gathered together. They were Bernadotte, who, despite his fence-sitting during the 1799 coup and his lack of affection for the First Consul, did at least promise co-operation; Marmont, Napoleon's friend and artillery expert, who was very earnest, painstaking, concerned with his men's well-being and loved building things; Davout, who was later said to be the only one of the marshals who really understood what Napoleon's theory and practice of war was all about; Soult, who was another great builder and an excellent trainer, if somewhat severe, of young officers; Lannes, the courageous leader of so many attacks, who had been so furious in Egypt to hear of his wife's giving birth to a bouncing boy when he had been parted from her for more than a year – he had since divorced her and married again – and who recently had been the First

Consul's envoy in Portugal to bully England's oldest ally into neutrality; Ney, the fiery red-headed cavalryman, who worshipped war and battle for their own sake, and who studied hard to master infantry tactics (his Chief of Staff was Jomini, whom we met earlier, and Ney's conduct of warlike operations could be summed up by the admirable concept of 'fast marching and straight shooting' – a battle-winner if ever there was one); and lastly Augereau, swaggering, rough-mouthed and full of intrigue as always, but a bold man in a tight corner. There remained the cavalry, under, of course, Napoleon's brother-in-law, Murat (he had married Caroline Bonaparte), who was not only the most dashing of cavalry commanders himself, but whose subordinates, Lasalle, Colbert, Sainte-Croix and Montbrun, were, as A. G. Macdonnell writes, 'symbols in themselves of the whole Napoleonic saga with its mixture of fantasy, high adventure and tragedy. None of these four were yet thirty years of age, and all were handsome, brilliant and reckless, and all were generals.' Finally, from 1804 onward, there was the Imperial Guard under Bessières.

About 100,000 of this Army of the Coasts of the Ocean were concentrated in the area of Dunkirk and Boulogne, training, drilling, shooting, preparing and waiting for the day when the barges and other transports would be assembled and ready, the escorting battle fleet concentrated and powerful enough for the world's greatest soldier to sail across the Channel in command of an invasion force which would subdue a nation of shopkeepers once and for all. In the event Nelson put paid to any such grand strategic ideas and the world's greatest soldier turned elsewhere. But before he did, Wellington was adding to his already growing prestige by winning some remarkable campaigns against the Mahratta powers in central India.

Even during the Peace of Amiens, Napoleon had once again been in league with the Mahrattas, offering military assistance in order that the British could be turned out of India. But the Governor-General (by now Mornington had become Lord Wellesley) had anticipated the breakdown of the Amiens agreement, delayed returning the French possessions and persuaded the Peshwah, titular ruler, to accept British protection, a subsidy, and an alliance with the East India Company in exchange for allowing British troops and advisers into Mahratta territory. An agreement of this sort was quite unacceptable to the Mahratta princes, who wished to continue their policies of plunder for personal gain, so that conflict between the British and the Mahratta chieftains was bound to break out. At hand to conduct the military side of Wellesley's policy was his own brother, Arthur, Governor of Mysore, and now a major-general – on the India list – commanding the Company's army there. Once again Arthur Wellesley was presented with a huge administrative problem: how to move his army of some 10,000 men over 600 miles of wild, lawless country and at the same time have sufficient provisions of every sort – forage, food, ammunition, stores – so that the movement of his troops would be entirely at his own discretion and decision. Wellesley explained it like this. The Mahrattas would always attempt to cut the communications of a British and Sepoy force, and if this force were dependent on its communications, it would be surrounded and annihilated. They, the Mahrattas, would 'follow him with their cavalry in his marches and surround and attack him with their infantry and cannon when he halts and he can scarcely escape from them. That, therefore, which I consider absolutely necessary in an operation against a Mahratta power is such a quantity of provisions in your camp as will enable you to command your own movements and to be independent of your magazines.' It all hung on having enough rice and enough bullocks. If he had these, he had men, and 'if I had men I knew I could defeat the enemy'. So thoroughly did Wellesley make his preparations that his march from Seringapatam to Poona, a matter of 600 miles, took less than two months, without the loss of any draught animals. The secret of rapid and secure movement was, of course, having 'good cattle' well cared for. In this way the Peshwah was restored to his nominal throne by May 1803 – when France and Britain were once more at war. The next task for Wellesley would be to deal with two powerful Mahratta chieftains of the north – Scindia of Gwalior and Bonslah of Nagpore. Their joint armies numbered some 50,000 men, greatly outnumbering the forces under Wellesley's command. He offered them peace in August 1803 – peace, as he put it, 'on terms of equality honourable to all parties; you have chosen war and are responsible for all consequences'. His first great objective with his army of 15,000 British and sepoy soldiers would be to lay siege to and take the great hill fortress of Ahmednuggur on the north-west frontier of the Nizam of Hyderabad's territory, an ally in name if not in performance. The capture of this key fortress turned out to be quicker and easier than he had expected.

The reduction of the fort at Ahmednuggur was a remarkable feat of arms, and illustrated once more how frequently and devastatingly during the British subjugation and exploitation of India, from the time of Clive at Arcot and Plassey to the ups and downs of the mutiny a hundred years on, a handful of British redcoats, well-trained and well-commanded, displayed a kind of insolent disregard for daunting odds and routed with careless ease native armies many times their number. Perhaps the most telling comment on the affair came from one of its eye-witnesses, Gooklah, the Mahratta chief, who observed that the English were a strange people, their general a wonderful man, for they had come to Ahmednuggur in the morning, looked at the fortress's wall, walked over it, killed all the garrison and returned to breakfast. 'What', he asked 'can withstand them?'

Can such things be and overcome us like a summer's cloud, without our special wonder? enquired Macbeth. Certainly we may understand Gooklah's wonder when we appreciate too the sheer strength of the fortress, how solid and high were its walls, how formidable its armaments. Ahmednuggur was constructed of solid stone and chunam. Encircling it was a deep, dry ditch, mounting bastions all the way round with short spaces between them. Each of these bastions contained up to four guns in casemated embrasures. Above them were terraces, from whose loopholes musket fire could be poured on any assaulting troops. Altogether the bastions mounted sixty guns – and thirty feet of the walls were covered by a steep glacis. But none of these dreadful obstacles and weapons of destruction could deter Wellesley. He took Ahmednuggur and meant to hang on to it, declaring that he would fill it with provisions, and when that was done not all the Mahrattas in India would be able to budge him. He had in short secured a more or less impregnable base from which to pursue further offensive operations. Although obliged to take his supplies with him – his army could not live off the country like Bonaparte's – yet his rapid, bold movement rivalled that of Bonaparte himself. Wellesley was determined to break the Mahratta confidence. Once he had the upper hand, he was certain that he would keep it. Wellesley made no secret of the extent to which he relied on his British regiments, to whose morale and fighting spirit he paid such tribute (he was to do so again in the Peninsula despite his periodic outbursts about British soldiers being the scum of the earth, enlisted solely for drink). This is what his Memorandum on

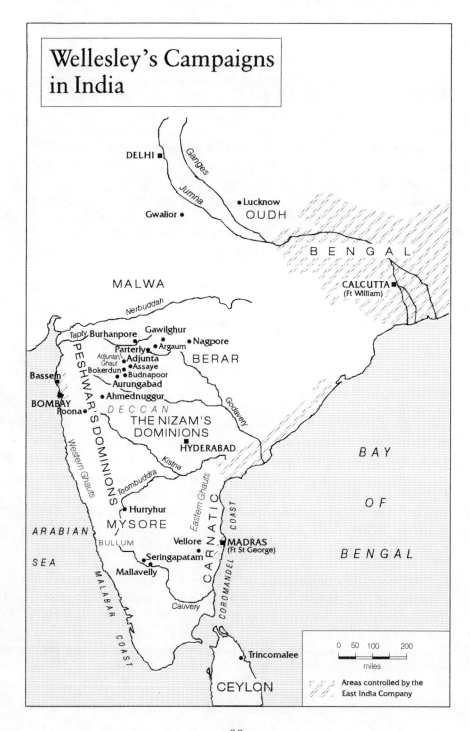

Wellesley's Campaigns in India

DELHI ■

Ganges

Jumna

Gwalior •

• Lucknow

OUDH

B E N G A L

MALWA

CALCUTTA ■
(Ft William)

Nerbuddah

Tapty Burhanpore • Gawilghur

PESHWAR'S

Parterly • • Argaum • Nagpore

Adjunta\ • Adjunta

Ghaut

Bokerdun • Assaye

BERAR

Bassein

• Budnapoor

Aurungabad

BOMBAY ■

DOMINIONS

• Ahmednuggur

Poona •

DECCAN

Godavery

THE NIZAM'S
DOMINIONS

Western Ghauts

HYDERABAD ■

BAY

Kistna

Toombuddra

Eastern Ghauts

OF

ARABIAN

• Hurryhur

MYSORE

BULLUM

Vellore • MADRAS
(Ft St George)

BENGAL

SEA

• Seringapatam

Mallavelly

COROMANDEL COAST

CARNATIC

MALABAR COAST

Cauvery

• Trincomalee

0   50 100   200

miles

CEYLON

Areas controlled by the
East India Company

88

British Troops in India, composed when the campaign was over, had to say:

> They are the main foundation of British power in Asia. Bravery is the characteristic of the British Army in all quarters of the world, but no other quarter has afforded such striking examples of the existence of this quality in the soldier as the East Indies. An instance of their misbehaviour in the field has never been known; and particularly those who have been for some time in that country cannot be ordered upon any service, however dangerous or arduous, that they will not effect, not only with bravery but a degree of skill not often witnessed by persons of their description in other parts of the world.
>
> I attribute these qualities, which are peculiar to them in the East Indies, to the distinctness of their class in that country from all others existing in it . . . Add to these qualities that their bodies are inured to climate, hardship and fatigue by long residence, habit and exercise . . . I have made them march 60 miles in 30 hours and afterwards engage the enemy, and it will not be surprising that they should be respected as they are, throughout India . . . They show in what manner nations, consisting of millions, are governed by 30,000 strangers.

Wellesley might have added that his own meticulous planning and preparations, which ensured his soldiers abundant supplies of food, forage, ammunition, clothing, shoes and so on, had much to do with the successful record of the men he commanded and led. Moreover this careful, dedicated leadership was reflected at all levels of command. It would have been impossible to imagine Napoleon composing a memorandum like this one. The Emperor would have been more likely to recall history, gratify his own pride and ambition, and make eloquent appeals to glory, conquest and plunder. Herein lay one of their essential differences of character and conduct. Wellesley was now to go on to win one of his greatest, perhaps – in purely military terms as opposed to its instant political result – *the* greatest of his victories.

The battle of Assaye, fought in September 1803, was, like Waterloo, a near-run thing. Wellesley's method of bringing the joint armies of Scindia and Rajah Bonslah to battle was to harry them to the north and east until the opportunity came to strike at them effectively. He had linked forces with the Hyderabad division under Colonel Stevenson, but their two contingents had divided on 22 September in order to cross a range of hills more quickly by using two defiles rather than one. On the following day, when Stevenson had still not arrived at the agreed rendezvous, Wellesley with his 7,000 men and some twenty guns – of whom only three regiments were British, the 74th and 78th Foot and 19th Light Dragoons – found himself confronting the entire Mahratta armies of some 50,000 infantry, countless cavalry, and a hundred guns. Wellesley, like Nelson believing the boldest measures are usually the safest, realized that only by attacking so formidable an army from the flank could he hope to prevail, and he staked everything on being able to cross the River Kaitna. Despite his native guides' assurance that there was no crossing, Wellesley caught sight of two villages divided only by the river, and, in his own words: 'I immediately said to myself that men could not have built two villages so close to one another on opposite sides of a stream without some habitual means of communication either by boat or a ford – most probably by the latter. On that conjecture, or rather reasoning, in defiance of all my guides and information, I took the desperate resolution, as it seemed, of marching for the river, and I was right; I found a passage, crossed my army over, had no more to fear from the enemy's cloud of cavalry, and my army, small as it was, was just enough to fill the space between the two streams, so that both my flanks were secure.'

Yet his position was still one of great and immediate danger. Even though his flanks were secure, his army was facing one vastly superior in infantry and artillery. Furthermore, behind him were rivers which were without bridges – and on the far banks of what fords there were, swarmed Mahratta cavalry. If the taking of calculated risks, backed by extreme boldness and determined leadership, is the key to winning battles, Wellesley certainly showed at Assaye that he was the equal of Napoleon.

The battle itself was a very bloody affair, amounting as it did to a frontal assault on vastly superior infantry and guns. Although Wellesley warned Colonel Orrock, whose pickets were leading the 74th Highlanders, to be wary of the strongly defended village of Assaye where there was a massed battery of Mahratta guns, Orrock, who was on the right flank of the British advance, lost direction and went straight at them – suffering terrible casualties from combined attacks by infantry and cavalry together with devastating artillery fire. The British battalion was reduced to company size, and was only rescued by Wellesley's sending the 19th Light Dragoons and the 4th Native Cavalry in a splendid charge which routed both enemy cavalry and infantry. That Wellesley had been able to do this at all was explained by his own personal command of the left flank with the 78th Highlanders who swept over and cut down the Mahratta gunners, leaving their infantry with little appetite for the fight. Wellesley himself was at the very centre of things and his great qualities of courage and leadership were recalled by Colin Campbell of the 78th (who was later to achieve great fame in the Crimea and the Indian Mutiny): 'The General was in the thick of the action the whole time ... I never saw a man so cool and collected as he was ... though I can assure you, till our troops got the orders to advance the fate of the day seemed doubtful.' At the end of the day Assaye itself was taken by the Highlanders who captured ninety-eight of the enemy guns. The two enemy chieftains, Scindia and the Rajah Bonslah, had fled. The victory was complete – but at what a cost! Wellesley had lost half his British troops, some 650 in all, and more than 900 sepoys. But the enemy suffered far greater losses – more than 6,000 soldiers killed or wounded, and virtually all their guns.

This victory at Assaye was the prelude to further battles and pursuits which enabled Wellesley to complete the campaign by the end of 1803. He had won such a reputation for invincibility – Wellesley Bahadur was his Indian name – that he had attained a kind of moral dominance over his enemies which almost won battles before they were joined. He was in no doubt about his own contribution to victory. In November 1803, he again fought the forces of the Scindia and the Rajah in the plains of Argaum. At one point two sepoy battalions broke under enemy artillery cannonade, but Wellesley calmly rallied them, and led them round by another route to the position they were to have occupied. Afterwards he was to note – as he did in slightly different words about another affair of even greater moment, Waterloo – that if he had not been there to restore the situation, the day would have been lost. This action of his, cool, confident and just what was needed to reassure shaken troops, was described by a witness as a masterpiece of generalship, displaying in particular a knowledge of human nature 'only to be found in great minds'.

After the Mahratta power was finally broken, Wellesley displayed another great trait of character – magnanimity. 'When war is concluded,' he recorded, 'I am decidedly of opinion that all animosity should be forgotten. The war will be eternal if nobody is ever to be forgiven. When the empire of the Company is so great, little dirty passions must not be suffered to guide its measures.' It was a sentiment he preserved in his dealings with a defeated France more than a decade later. Nor was this the only non-military lesson he learned in India. Apart from mastering the business of command in the field, he had absorbed the techniques and subtleties of administration and diplomacy. He had created order out of chaos, stability out of dissolution and peace out of freebooting. But perhaps most important of all – in view of the duties and service which lay before him when he returned to Europe – was the experience he had gained of how to handle armies in the field and the robustness, both mental and physical, that went with this experience. Moreover, he appreciated that the essence of command was in itself an understanding of the raw material with which the military commander plies his trade – the private soldier. Bryant puts his finger on the point when he writes that Wellesley's 'imaginative enterprise, celerity and daring had been matched by the meticulous forethought and industry with which he attended to every detail that could ensure success and safeguard the health, comfort and lives of his men'. Nothing, in his view, was so valuable as 'the life and health of the British soldier' – and here we see once more how fitting was Bagehot's reference to the Duke in his definition of a great general. Wellesley praised alike the soldiers' courage, perseverance and patience, and – unlike many in senior positions of command – gave to them the credit for his army's success in travelling great distances under constant threat, time after time coming through it all without loss of supplies or property. Wellesley was equally generous in recognizing the sterling qualities of the sepoy, and in recommending to the Company that provision should be made for those Indian soldiers who risked their lives in the Company's service – for themselves in the case of disablement and for their families should they fall in battle.

'Be clear,' observed Napoleon, 'and all the rest will follow.' It was clarity of mind that was one of Wellesley's greatest attributes. It enabled him not only to see the absolute essentials of whatever problem confronted him, but also to make these things plain to those about him in unequivocal terms. However, there was more to it than this – and here we see once more a great gap between Wellesley and Napoleon.

Wellesley stood for perfection of behaviour. 'An officer to command must be worthy of command; be both a gentleman – honourable, faithful to his trust, truthful, self-controlled and considerate to others – and a soldier dedicated by study and experience to the mastery of his profession.' Wellesley himself passes both requirements with flying colours. Napoleon sails through the second test; falls down badly on the first. He cared nothing for honour in the sense Wellesley meant it; was utterly unfaithful to the trust imposed in him by fellow sovereigns; was untruthful, completely lacking in self-control when thwarted; was frequently and maliciously inconsiderate of the feelings of others. But then, as we have already noted, he was not a gentleman.

For his services in India Wellesley was honoured with the Order of the Bath and in March 1805 he sailed for home. He gave as his reasons for success that he saw everything and did everything for himself. It was for this reason, he believed, and for being very young in command – he was not quite thirty-six when he left India – that he was able to cope with so many aspects of command and administration. Yet for Major-General Sir Arthur Wellesley it was not all work and no play. There was time for dalliance with the ladies too. A brace of Calcutta's belles, Mrs Coggan and Mrs Gordon, were lovesick for him or pretended to be, and Wellesley himself, as Elizabeth Longford reports, 'lost his heart to Mrs Freese' and their relationship caused a certain scandal, although Mrs Freese's husband, a captain in the Madras Artillery, appeared to be complacent. Wellesley and Mrs Freese remained friends after he left India. And at home he would find Kitty Pakenham still unmarried. He reached England on 10 September 1805 and shortly afterwards, while waiting to see the Secretary of War and the Colonies, Lord Castlereagh, he had his only meeting with Nelson.

But before we join them in Castlereagh's ante-room, we must see what enormous strides the First Consul has been making on his way to becoming Emperor of the French. His almost feverish activity during the Peace of Amiens and after the renewed outbreak of war was principally aimed at two objectives: first, the organization of France so that order would replace disorder, proper administration take the place of corrupt practices, and a system of beneficial government would be subject to the will of one man, however dictatorial that man might be; second was Napoleon's passionate concern to heal old wounds, to bind together all the conflicting interests and causes of those loyal to the

Bourbons or the Jacobins, those who had embraced or recoiled from revolutionary excesses, those to whom the Catholic Church was still all in all or to whom it was anathema – in short a programme of reconciliation and stabilization, which by gradually merging interests and grappling loyalties together would fuse the nation into one single France. One of the measures, which ironically was greeted with both enraged dismay and fervent enthusiasm, was the Concordat. This dismay was not, A. G. Macdonnell writes, 'diminished in intensity when it was seen that the First Consul's prestige, immense already, was actually increased among the common people to whom a thousand years of rooted Catholicism meant more than a dozen years of compulsory atheism.' Having got so far from the ideas of the Revolution, the next step was hardly to be wondered at. In May 1804 Napoleon became Emperor of the French (he crowned himself in December of that year) and in May also he appointed eighteen Marshals of the Empire. Among them were Berthier, Murat, Masséna, Augereau, Bernadotte, Soult, Lannes, Ney and Davout. Before long there would be some stern work for them to do. For in that same month, May 1804, Pitt had formed his second administration, and in the King's Speech two months later, Pitt's intended policies were outlined to Parliament. The Prime Minister had concluded that although England could if necessary continue to fight alone against France, only by convincing other European powers to fight too could he put a stop to Napoleon's territorial ambitions. Pitt was seeking 'the re-establishment of such a system in Europe as would rescue it from the precarious state to which it is reduced'. There was only one way to counter the Emperor's schemes of aggrandizement – an effective barrier had to be raised against him.

The barrier at sea was already in place. It was not only essential that the Royal Navy should ensure that Napoleon could not successfully invade these islands – preparations for which he had already set in train. British sea-power had also to establish mastery over the oceans elsewhere to guarantee Britain's empire and trade, and deny such freedom of the sea to the French. But there remained the question of keeping the French army busy and away from England's shores, and for this allies were indispensable. Pitt's diplomatic activities led to what became known as the Third Coalition against France. To start with only Russia responded to Pitt's overtures. Their new Czar, Alexander I, was self-opinionated and over-sensitive. His ambition was equalled only by his pride, and any setback to his territorial aspirations or rebuff to his self-esteem would be bound to provoke instant hostility. Small wonder, therefore, that when Napoleon took possession of Naples and Hanover without hearing what he, the Czar, might have to say about it, and furthermore pursued an expansionist policy in the eastern Mediterranean – a policy which particularly exasperated Alexander, with his eyes firmly fixed on Constantinople – these moves should have had a powerful effect. It was clear to Alexander that only if Napoleon could be restrained, could he himself gratify his own imperial aspirations and become what he longed to be – a kind of major-domo of Europe. Alexander's aggrieved feelings towards Napoleon were further aggravated when the French Emperor reacted violently to the supposed royalist intrigues of the Duc d'Enghien and had him both kidnapped and executed. All this resulted in a diplomatic coup for Pitt and in May 1805 an Anglo-Russian alliance was signed.

Pitt was not satisfied with one ally, however. In that same month, May 1805, Austria had been so infuriated by Napoleon's having himself crowned King of Italy that she joined the alliance with Great Britain and Russia. Prussia, on the other hand, stayed neutral for the time being, for Prussia still had an eye on Hanover. Broad allied strategy was that they would force France to remove her troops from northern Germany and Italy by advancing from the east. They would also free Naples, Switzerland and the Netherlands. With France engaged on both her eastern and southern flanks, so reasoned Pitt, the threat of Napoleon's invasion of Britain would be removed. There was, however, an unanticipated obstacle to this strategic plan. It was easy enough for Pitt to promise subsidies which would support half a million Russian soldiers on their march westwards, but to get at France it would be necessary to march through Prussia and this Prussia would not allow. An alternative strategy therefore had to be put together. More limited in scope, it envisaged an attack on the French positions in northern Italy by sending Russian troops through Austria and by despatching a British force from Malta and Sicily. In the event neither of these ventures came off, for in the summer of 1805 Napoleon took a hand in the game himself. Unlike the slow-moving nations of the Third Coalition, when Napoleon took it upon himself to do something, he acted with the swiftness and decision of an eagle.

Yet even as late as July 1805 he had been hoping for the chance to rush his army at Boulogne across the Channel to subdue England. Nelson had been kept busy pursuing the French fleet across the Atlantic and back. As early as March 1804, two months before Pitt became Prime Minister again, Nelson had written to a friend: 'Day by day, I am expecting the French to put to sea – every day, hour and moment; and you may rely that, if it is within the power of man to get at them, it shall be done; and I am sure that all my brethren look forward to that day as the finish of our laborious cruize.' Napoleon knew full well that he could only hope to cross the Channel with his Boulogne army if he could lure the battle fleets of the Royal Navy away from there, and so be in a position to deploy a superior force of French ships of the line. His long-suffering admirals were mercilessly bullied. First they were required to sail to the West Indies to threaten British possessions there and so draw the British warships away from home waters. Next they were ordered to concentrate in the English Channel and win temporary superiority so that the French transports could effect a crossing with veterans of the Grande Armée and show the British regular troops, militia and volunteers alike, what soldiering was really all about. It was just as well that Napoleon's army did not land in Kent or Sussex because the defensive preparations made by Addington in his last year as Prime Minister had been ludicrously inadequate. His idea of waging defensive war was to do it on the cheap and to get as large a number of men into uniform as possible. However large the number of English yeomen and burghers he might have mustered, with no knowledge of war, no training or discipline, and probably armed with nothing more deadly than a pike, they would have been unlikely to achieve much in competition with Napoleon's veterans except perhaps rapidly to have been turned into mincemeat.

Fortunately for them it was never put to the test, for in August 1805, on hearing that Austria had entered the war against him, the French Emperor changed his plans. 'The great camps along the coast of the Pas-de-Calais were struck', writes A. G. Macdonnell, 'and the most superb army in equipment, training, experience, morale, men, officers, and Commander-in-Chief, that the world had ever seen, turned its back on the white sails of England's fleet and the white silhouette of England's cliffs, and went swinging across France and Holland and Germany, sixteen miles a day, to its first concentration line.' We will follow the fortunes of this splendid army shortly, but before that we must join

Nelson and Wellesley in Lord Castlereagh's ante-room. It is 12 September 1805.

Nelson had returned to Portsmouth in HMS *Victory* on 18 August, having chased, pursued and searched for Admiral Villeneuve and the French fleet for 14,000 miles without getting at him. Nelson had been concerned that his failure to bring Villeneuve to battle might have affected the feelings of the people for him. He need not have worried. His reception was wildly enthusiastic. The separation from his wife, his obsession with Emma Hamilton, his long absence from England's shores in the Mediterranean and the West Indies, could not distract from his legendary fame and the hero-worship which the people felt for him. Such adulation warmed him. He had always thought of himself as the child of opinion. Recognition was everything to him. And there was more than just affection and admiration for the frail admiral who had made the Royal Navy so glorious in its victories and so feared by the French. Somehow England felt safer with Nelson and his Mediterranean fleet at home. Moreover, it would now be possible not only to guarantee the integrity of England's shores, but to take the war to England's enemy – in other words to play one of Nelson's greatest aces of leadership: to reassume the offensive. It had become crucially necessary to do so, for to allow an enemy naval concentration freedom of action would endanger England's very lifeline. Villeneuve with the combined French and Spanish fleet might be at the naval base, Ferrol, in northwest Spain or might be at sea in the Bay of Biscay, and from such deployment could threaten Britain's sea communications both with the Mediterranean and with the East Indies. This threat had to be removed. On 12 September 1805, when Nelson saw Castlereagh in Downing Street, plans were laid which would lead to Nelson's last great venture to carry out that vital duty which England expected of him.

The one meeting between Nelson and Wellesley in Castlereagh's ante-room brought into sharp contrast their different natures. Nelson, for all his great qualities, was consumed by vanity. It was a quality quite foreign to Wellesley. Yet Nelson had another ace of leadership which endeared him to his subordinates and inspired them to emulate his example – it was what Elizabeth Longford defined as 'the delightful impression of consultation, of welcoming advice, of taking the younger colleague into his confidence and spontaneously disclosing what he hoped to achieve'. We shall shortly see a supreme example of this graceful way of command when Nelson explained his proposed tactics for what became the battle of Trafalgar. Wellesley could not match this particular touch of confidentiality. Indeed, before Waterloo, when Uxbridge, in command of the cavalry and the Duke's nominal second-in-command, asked Wellington what his plan was – in case he, Wellington, should fall – Uxbridge was duly snubbed. Wellington made it plain that since Napoleon would attack first, and all depended on the form of this attack and the Allied response to it, there was no way of revealing what the Allied plan might be. This difference in attitude also emphasizes, of course, the contrasting strategic circumstances in which Nelson and Wellington commanded – the former always on the offensive, the latter required to play a more Fabian part.

It was perhaps characteristic of Nelson on meeting an unknown gentleman in Castlereagh's ante-room that he should begin to speak of himself in trivial and self-indulgent language, much to Wellesley's disgust, for he recorded a conversation, if it could be called that, 'almost all on his side, and all about himself, and really, in a style so vain and silly as to surprise me . . .' It is not difficult for us to imagine that Wellesley's response to this was of a nature – cold, aloof yet authoritative – that prompted Nelson to leave the room, to find out who it was and, on discovering he had been talking to no less a person than Major-General Sir Arthur Wellesley, victor of Assaye, to create upon his return a very different impression, as Wellington later recorded:

> All that I thought a charlatan style had vanished, and he talked . . . with good sense, and a knowledge of subjects both at home and abroad, that surprised me equally and more agreeably than the first part of our interview had done; in fact, he talked like an officer and a statesman . . . I don't know that I ever had a conversation that interested me more.

What did they talk about? asks Elizabeth Longford. In answering her own question, Lady Longford suggests not only that both the general state of the country and the affairs of the Continent were covered, but also that each man touched on strategic matters of particular concern to the other. While Wellesley deplored the failure of Admiral Calder to bring Villeneuve to the kind of decisive naval action which Nelson's glorious victories had 'taught the public to expect', Nelson in his turn hoped that Wellesley would be put in command of an expedition to attack Sardinia. Lady Longford adds one extremely significant comment on the outcome of this hour-long conversation: 'Nelson undoubtedly helped to form the future Duke of Wellington's ideal of the great captain who could see far beyond his own flagship or headquarters.' In his subsequent actions as a soldier both in the Peninsula and in Belgium, as a diplomat in Paris and Vienna, and as a statesman at home, the Great Duke, despite occasional blind spots, lived up to this reputation for foresight.

Meanwhile the petticoats were not idle. On leaving London Nelson went to his beloved Merton, there to take leave of Lady Hamilton. That same evening, 12 September, Nelson's friend, Lord Minto, dined at Merton and noted in a letter to his wife: 'Lady Hamilton was in tears all yesterday, could not eat and hardly drink [this was something of a feat, for Emma was an advanced alcoholic] and near swooning all at table.' Minto was puzzled by the mutual devotion of Nelson and Emma – who told him that nothing could be more pure and ardent than the flame of love they felt for each other. Before he left Merton next day, Nelson went through a form of religious ceremony, saying to her in the priest's presence: 'Emma, I have taken the Sacrament with you this day to prove to the world that our friendship is most pure and innocent and of this I call God to witness.' After painful farewells and after praying at the bedside of his and Emma's daughter, Horatia, he set off for Portsmouth, noting in his diary that he was leaving 'all which I hold dear in this world to go to serve my King and Country'. He asked God to enable him to fulfil the expectations of his country. If he should return, his thanks would never cease – if not, God would protect those dear to him. He wrote one last note to Emma before embarking on his barge to *Victory*: 'My dearest and most beloved of women, Nelson's Emma ... I shall be at sea this day. God protect you and my dear Horatia prays ever your most faithful Nelson and Bronte.' As the barge left Southsea, hundreds of people were there to give him three cheers. 'I had their huzzas before,' he told his flag-captain, Thomas Hardy, 'I have their hearts now.'

Wellesley's petticoat dealings were less passionate and less dramatic. In October 1805 he formally proposed marriage to Kitty Pakenham by letter. Her reply was one of great gratitude, but while clearly favourable, offered him release should he not be positive when they again met that she was indeed the chosen companion and friend for life. Military duty in command of a brigade took him to the Elbe in December 1805. He returned in February and married Kitty in Dublin on 10 April 1806. By that time the battles of Trafalgar and Austerlitz had been fought, Pitt was dead and Napoleon had decreed that the Continental System would impose a blockade on Britain's trade with Europe. We will look first at Trafalgar.

In October 1805, while Napoleon was driving the Grande Armée forward to the first of several spectacular triumphs over the Austrian and Russian armies, Nelson was about to be rewarded for all his patience and vigilance with the most famous of all naval victories in the Royal Navy's history. It was a victory which a few years later would facilitate the deployment of a British army on the south-western extremes of Napoleon's empire, and keep it there properly supplied and reinforced until the Emperor's own armies had been driven back to France by Wellesley. For the British fleet there was a good deal of searching, planning, doubting and manoeuvring before Nelson at last sighted the combined French and Spanish fleet off Cape Trafalgar on 21 October 1805. He and his captains, his band of brothers, knew exactly what they were about. Nelson had repeatedly outlined to his subordinates how they would 'surprise and confound the enemy', bring about what he always sought – 'a pell-mell battle' – and so bring about too the annihilation of the enemy's fleet. When Nelson first expounded his tactical plan – to sail direct for the enemy centre, split and divide them, so that each half could be destroyed in detail, the plan which he lightly defined as 'the Nelson touch' – his audience of subordinate commanders was electrified by the sheer beauty of the idea. 'It was new, it was singular, it was simple . . . it must succeed.' Indeed some of his captains were so moved by what Nelson had to say that they wept.

Never were Nelson's four aces of leadership played with greater effect. His first ace, imagination – an ace he shared with Napoleon – was at the height of its brilliance. He was somehow able to picture the circumstances of a forthcoming battle with such clarity, such boldness and such an unrivalled determination to bend the enemy to his will that his spirit permeated the whole fleet: so much, indeed, were they all with him that just before the battle was joined and the renowned 'England expects . . .' signal flew from *Victory*'s masthead, his second-in-command, Collingwood, complained that he wished Nelson would stop signalling, for they all knew what to do. The second ace, his ability to inspire, was so strong that it animated not only the whole fleet, but the whole nation. His confidence, his enthusiasm, his dedication to duty, and the sheer professional heights of seamanship and gunnery that the fleet's training and preparation had achieved meant that every captain under his command aspired to be another Nelson. And this is to say nothing of his genius in gaining the absolute trust and affection of the lower deck. We have touched already on his third ace, while describing his one meeting with Wellesley – that grace of command which consulted subordinates, took them into his confidence, listened to their views, and gave them credit for their performance. Never before surely did such mutual confidence, trust and reliance exist between a commander and his lieutenants (despite Napoleon's astonishing triumphs at Austerlitz, his marshals were constantly at loggerheads). Dominating all Nelson's greatness as a fleet commander was the offensive spirit, the absolutely overriding resolution to engage the enemy at the closest possible quarters and utterly destroy him. It was the very apotheosis of all that Nelson stood for.

It could hardly have been possible for Nelson to have succeeded more brilliantly and devastatingly than he did. As the admiral lay dying in the cockpit of *Victory*, and Hardy congratulated him on his success, saying that he was sure that fourteen or fifteen enemy ships had surrendered, Nelson replied that it was well, but he had bargained for twenty. Nelson's last words were characteristic of him. He begged Hardy to take care of 'poor Lady Hamilton' and Horatia, and he thanked God that he had done his duty. Indeed he had. Trafalgar *was* a battle of annihilation. Of the thirty-three enemy ships engaged in the action, eighteen were captured on the day of the battle, four were taken two weeks later, and the other eleven returned to Cadiz, never to take to the open sea again. The victory removed once and for all the practicability of a French army invading Britain. It also gave Britain and its army the opportunity to land on the Continent whenever it chose and take on the French army.

The price of this victory which struck hardest was the loss of Nelson, 'the darling of the British navy, whose death has plunged a whole nation into the deepest grief'. One of Napoleon's greatest adversaries was down. His memory would be immortal. It was significant that Collingwood's despatch to the Admiralty began not with details of the victory, but 'the ever to be lamented death of Vice-Admiral Lord Nelson, who, in the late conflict with the enemy, fell in the hour of victory . . .' Nelson's chaplain in *Victory* wrote of 'the greatest and simplest of men' and 'I could for ever tell you of the qualities of this beloved man'. As St Vincent himself had put it years earlier: 'There is but one Nelson.'

There was also only one Napoleon and on the day before Trafalgar he had confounded the Austrian army under General Mack at Ulm. A. G. Macdonnell describes the Emperor's move to trap Mack's 30,000 men as more than a great stroke of strategy. 'It was,' he writes, 'an exquisite work of art, and the beauty of it is the beauty of anything that is symmetrical.' It is here that we see Bagehot's point about a general's being surrounded by maps and charts, exact in calculations and a master tactician immersed in detail. Napoleon's plan of movement was at once an astonishing example of deception and a classic masterpiece of concentration, for within just over six weeks of striking camp at Boulogne he had succeeded in positioning some 150,000 soldiers – coming from as far apart as Hanover, Utrecht, the Rhineland and the Pas-de-Calais – to the north of Mack's 30,000 men, and clouding all this movement by deploying an enormous screen of the reserve cavalry under Murat to conceal his intentions. Before Mack knew what was happening he was surrounded, and his entire army of 30,000 was captured. There had been one brief encounter at Elchingen in which Ney and his 6th Corps distinguished themselves at the expense of Murat, whose faulty dispositions had aroused the ire of his Emperor brother-in-law. Ney as usual led the attack and as usual took the objective. During this encounter also, Napoleon had again displayed his indifference to danger, and was quite unmoved when he and his staff came under fire from an Austrian artillery battery. It required the equally intrepid Lannes to remove the Emperor from this dangerous position by the simple expedient of grasping his charger's bridle and bustling him away.

For Napoleon then, so far so good. Better was to come. The first Austrian army in his sights had been satisfactorily disposed of. There remained two more rather larger armies – a mixed force of Austrians and Russians thought to be near Vienna; fortunately for Napoleon they had with them their respective sovereigns, whose knowledge of Napoleonic warfare was limited, if it existed at all. Further east, no doubt, there were more Austrian and Russian reserves. Pitt, whose health was failing, had been heartened by the victory of Trafalgar, but it could not be said that the Third Coalition's endeavours on land had begun auspiciously. For this ill-fated coalition a far more deadly blow was about to be delivered. Despite the appalling weather, despite the Grande Armée's exhaustion and lack of food, forage and other supplies, Napoleon pushed on, entered Vienna without having to fight for it, then crossed the Danube at Spitz. The rapid capture of the great wooden bridge there – which was vital if Napoleon were to take on the Austro-Russian army before it could be reinforced – showed the marshals at their flamboyant peak of sheer daring and effrontery. Murat and Lannes, dressed in their dazzling uniforms, simply rode across the bridge, which was mined and defended by the Austrians, declaring to the elderly enemy commander that an armistice had handed the bridge over to them, and while the point was being disputed, Oudinot with some grenadiers defused the mines and rushed the bridge.

Napoleon finally confronted the combined Austro-Russian army at the Moravian village of Austerlitz on 2 December 1805. Nominally in command were the two Emperors, Alexander I of Russia and Frances II of Austria. Doing the actual thinking for them, however, was Kutusov, the professional expert. As A. G. Macdonnell so eloquently put it, all they had to do was 'to wait for Bennigsen and young Charles [both of whom were bringing up reinforcements] and the game was in their hands. But prestige is a terrible malady, and the prestige of the two dynasties, Romanov and Habsburg, had to be maintained against the dirty little Corsican usurper, and the Allied Emperors decided that they should stand and fight.' They had cause to regret it. With the sun of Austerlitz looking down on them, Napoleon ordered Marshal Soult's corps forward, together with those of Bernadotte and Oudinot, with Bessières' Imperial Guard in reserve. The vital piece of ground in the centre of the Allied position was taken: when the Emperor had asked Soult how long it would take him to get there, Soult had replied: 'Twenty minutes, Sire' – and twenty minutes after Napoleon had given the order to advance, it was in Soult's hands. The Austro-Russian centre was destroyed, their left wing rolled up, and it was all over. Austria made peace, the Russian armies faded away, the Third Coalition was finished and, as Sir Charles Petrie puts it, 'Napoleon's domination of the Continent was more firmly established than ever.'

Little more than a month after Austerlitz, on 23 January 1806, the Prime Minister, William Pitt, died. The second great adversary to Napoleon was down. Pitt had, according to J. H. Rose, killed himself by

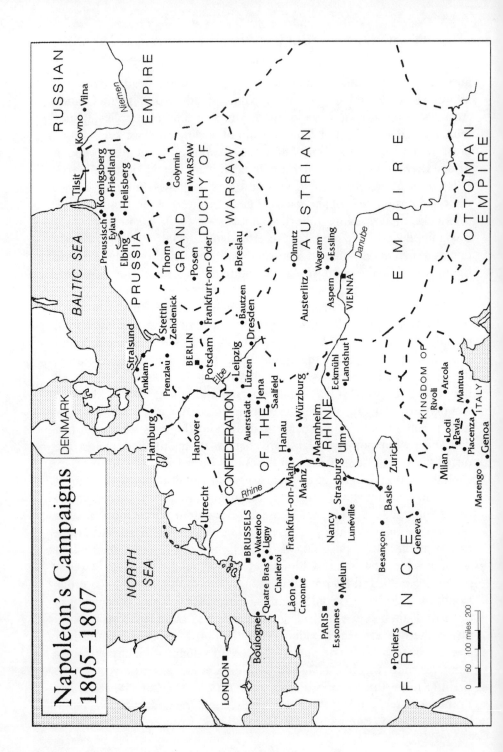

Napoleon's Campaigns
1805–1807

RUSSIAN EMPIRE

EMPIRE

Niemen

Vilna

Kovno

Tilsit

Koenigsberg
Friedland
Eylau
Heilsberg
Preussisch
Eylau

Golymin
WARSAW
GRAND
DUCHY OF
WARSAW

Thorn
Posen
Frankfurt-on-Oder
Breslau

BALTIC SEA

PRUSSIA

Stettin
Zehdenick
Elbing

AUSTRIAN

Olmutz
Wagram
Essling
Aspern
Austerlitz
VIENNA

EMPIRE

Danube

OTTOMAN
EMPIRE

Stralsund
Ankam
Prenzlau
BERLIN
Potsdam
Elbe
Leipzig
Lützen
Bautzen
Dresden

Eckmühl
Landshut

KINGDOM OF

Rivoli
Arcola
Mantua
Milan
Lodi
Pavia
Placenza
Genoa
Marengo

ITALY

DENMARK

Hamburg

Hanover

Utrecht

CONFEDERATION

OF THE

RHINE

Auerstädt
Jena
Saalfeld
Würzburg
Hanau
Mannheim
Mainz
Ulm
Strasburg
Zurich
Basle

NORTH
SEA

Rhine

Frankfurt-on-Main

Nancy
Lunéville
Besançon
Geneva

BRUSSELS
Waterloo
Ligny
Quatre Bras
Charleroi
Lâon
Craonne

PARIS
Essonnes
Melun

Poitiers

FRANCE

LONDON

Boulogne

0 50 100 miles 200

104

endlessly overworking for the well-being of a country which failed to understand him and for a King who was unwilling to allow him the additional ministerial support he needed. Before he died, Pitt had rolled up the map of Europe – 'it will not be wanted these ten years'. He had lamented the state in which he left his country. And he had said of Arthur Wellesley: 'He states every difficulty before he undertakes any service, but none after he has undertaken it.' He also paid Wellesley the great compliment that he knew no other soldier with whom it was so satisfactory to converse. Clarity, soundness, rationality – all were his. 'He is a very remarkable man.' So too was Pitt, and Petrie judges him to be the greatest of Prime Ministers in that he saw that Britain passed from 'the old order to the new without any violent upheaval . . . unless a genius had been in office from 1784 to 1792 Great Britain must have gone the way of France'. His obituary in *The Times* spoke of 'the splendour of his talents, the powers of his eloquence and his indefatigable attention to the objects of his administration' – and went on to praise the way in which these talents and powers were made use of with incomparable energy for the benefit of his country. Of all Napoleon's enemies, Pitt had been the most steadfast and Wellesley by his own perseverance was to prove worthy of Pitt's high opinion.

So, as the year 1806 gets under way, we see our two men of destiny at very different levels. Bonaparte is Emperor of the French, conqueror of the Austrian and Russian armies, Commander-in-Chief of the Grande Armée, whose marshals have been swaggering about in the Imperial Palace of Schönbrunn; Napoleon was now to start ennobling them in order to keep them in order and bind them even closer to his Imperial dynasty. 'What duke in his senses would contemplate a return to Bourbonism if it entailed the instant loss of his dukedom?' Thus Murat was made Grand Duke of Berg and Cleves, Berthier was given the Princedom of Neufchâtel, Talleyrand became Prince of Benevento, and Bernadotte was promoted to be His Highness and Marshal, Prince and Duke of Ponte-Corvo. The Emperor was welding them all to the Bonapartist legend. Soon, however, there would be sterner affairs for them all to think about. Prussia had been temporarily bribed by the prospect of Hanover, while Napoleon dealt with Austria and Russia. But now Prussia was stirring and would therefore have to be dealt with. Up to this time – even now it was Prussia who started the war – it could be said that Napoleon's campaigns in Europe had been defensive, to preserve the integrity of France, whether Jacobin, Consular or Imperial. But before long, having no regard to the ultimate demands of time and space and rejecting totally the principles of singleness of aim and concentration of force, Napoleon was to overreach himself and embark on an aggressive war in Iberia. And this was where the other man of destiny came in.

In 1806 Wellesley was still very small beer by comparison – appointed Colonel of the 33rd Foot and a mere brigade commander. His own answer to the question put to him by a friend – how could Sir Arthur Wellesley KB submit to such paltry employment? – was characteristic of him: 'I am *nimmukwallah*, as we say in the East; that is, I have eaten of the King's salt, and therefore I conceive it to be my duty to serve with unhesitating zeal and cheerfulness, when and wherever the King or his Government may think proper to employ me.' He might have been writing his own epitaph.

CHAPTER 6

Peak of Power and a Fatal Blunder

War in Spain has, from the days of the Romans, had a character of its own; it is a fire which cannot be raked out; it burns
fiercely under the embers; and long after it has, to all seeming,
been extinguished, bursts forth more violently than ever.

Macaulay

D URING the years from 1806 to 1808 Napoleon reached the
zenith of his career. During these same years Wellesley began
for the second time to show what a fine field commander and
diplomatist he was. It was because the French Emperor took one step
too far that the British general came once more into prominence. After
the death of Pitt, Grenville formed what was called the 'Ministry of all
the Talents' – a curious and ironic title, for the only man in it really
possessing talent was Fox, who became Foreign Secretary. Alas, he did
not have long to live. During his short time in office, however, he came
to understand that it was impossible to negotiate sensibly and securely
with Napoleon. The Emperor's success at Austerlitz had simply fed his
appetite for more conquest and before long he was waging war once
more with Prussia, with Russia, and in Spain.

The forthcoming conflict in Spain would at last give the British Army
– and Wellesley – something to do other than land in Flanders, be
defeated and be re-embarked. Moreover by this time two men had more
or less transformed the British Army. Although he had not distinguished
himself as a commander of armies in the field, when the Duke of York
became the army's Commander-in-Chief at home, it seemed that he
had found his true vocation. An excellent administrator, extremely hard-
working, a master of detail and blessed with a disciplined mind, he set
about correcting the army's deficiencies – which he had witnessed at

first hand while campaigning – with a devotion and a perseverance which were wholly admirable. It was already abundantly clear that there was little wrong with the army's regiments. It was the system that was at fault. In particular, command of these regiments was frequently given, not to those most competent or experienced, but to those with money and influence. There was also the question of organization and support, for the army lacked a proper structure of artillery, engineers, transport and supply. All these things had to be put right, together with a proper system of training and the provision of good weapons and equipment. The Duke of York accordingly not only corrected the selection and training of officers. He instituted a regular programme of training exercises, at both regimental and brigade level. Slowly but surely the army was being turned into an orderly and first-class fighting force.

The other man who did so much in this respect was Major-General Sir John Moore. As far back as 1802 Moore had been charged by the Duke of York to supervise the training of British regiments in light infantry tactics. He was not only a fine trainer of soldiers. He possessed, like Nelson, that indispensable quality of the true commander – humanity. He was at once practical and idealistic. His orders were a model of clarity and his methods a model of precision. His integrity and sense of justice were absolute, his sense of duty inviolate. He would never avoid an unpleasant task and would insist that hardship be shared by general officer and private soldier alike. Above all, although insisting on firm discipline, he encouraged the individual soldier to use his initiative and his common sense. The traditions of regimental spirit and pride were there already. The *foundations* of a fine army had long been in existence. What Moore did was to build on them. His great aim was to have 'thinking, fighting men', whom their officers knew and between whom there would be mutual trust. What is more, conditions of training were, under Moore, as close as possible to war itself. By these means the famous Light Brigade (later the Light Division) was raised and made ready for operations. Arthur Byrant, recording his great admiration for the Rifle Corps in his majestic *Jackets of Green*, had this to say:

At the back of every rifleman's mind Moore instilled the principle that the enemy was always at hand ready to strike. Whether on reconnaissance or protective duty, he was taught to be wary and on guard ... It was the pride of a light infantryman never to be caught napping; of a light infantry regiment or company never to have an outpost or picket surprised.

Of course the light infantry was only a small part of the British Army, but by the time Wellesley was to lead his first expedition to Portugal, Castlereagh, Secretary of War, had seen to it that the total size of the regular army was nearly a quarter of a million, and this meant that, when the time was ripe, some overseas adventures could be indulged in. This was not to be until 1808. In the two previous years Napoleon had defeated both the Prussian and the Russian armies.

In September 1806, the month in which Fox died, Prussia, no doubt harbouring memories of Frederick the Great's exploits, was unwise enough to declare war on France. The Prussian war machine was pretty rusty by this time, and it took a good deal of overhauling before what had been Frederick's army, with its invincible infantry, got itself into position – 150,000 of them in all – to the north of the Thuringian Forest near Weimar. By the beginning of October 1806 they were there. Napoleon did not permit them to stay very long. It was during this campaign, A. G. Macdonnell reminds us, that Napoleon first made use of what became known as the *battaillon carré*, a kind of flexible deployment and marching order for the army which enabled it to respond instantly to intelligence gained by the screen of cavalry which preceded the main body. It was as if the army advanced in a huge diamond formation and each point of the diamond could if necessary turn right or left, and so alter the army's direction and order of march. The point division or corps could become the left or right flank, and the left or right angles of the diamond could become the leading or reserve formation at will.

Yet in spite of this innovation of movement, at the outset of the campaign, Napoleon did not exert his customary grip on affairs. He delegated command of the army first to Berthier – a brilliant Chief of Staff, but no commander – then, without informing Berthier, to Murat, a superb cavalry leader, but no strategist; it was therefore hardly surprising that when the Emperor arrived at Mainz to take command of the army himself, he found, to say the least of it, a confused situation, made worse by the fact that Berthier was not there. And so, despite having had virtually no sleep since leaving Paris a day and a half earlier, he then began dictating orders to his various corps commanders for the next three days, snatching an occasional pause for rest and refreshment when he could. 'But even the Napoleonic brain began to flag,' A. G. Macdonnell says, 'and many of the later letters of this outburst of energy were almost incoherent.' What must amaze us and command our admiration, however, is that Napoleon was able to do it at all.

This somewhat inauspicious start to the campaign was to some extent corrected when the Grande Armée finally got under way on 8 October 1806. Less than a week later the Emperor had succeeded, by his customary furious marching, in positioning his army of nearly 200,000 men on the Prussian left flank – and was poised, as he had been at Ulm against the Austrians, to win the battle with a minimum of shooting and fighting. But it did not turn out like that. There was to be a good deal of blundering – by Lannes, Ney, Bernadotte and even the Emperor himself. The underlying problem was that there had been no proper reconnaissance so that Napoleon knew neither exactly where the Prussians were nor how strong they were. Nevertheless he had decided to attack them and on 14 October, he did. The trouble now was that although Lannes's corps got into its proper position on the Landgrafenberg plateau near Jena, Ney's corps, which should have been on Lannes's right, lost its way in the morning mist and fog and emerged on Lannes's left. By early afternoon the muddle had been straightened out and the French line went forward to take the plateau. Meanwhile Napoleon had ordered Davout and Bernadotte to bring their corps round the flank to the Prussian rear, so that the Prussian army would not merely be pushed back, but annihilated. The strategy was sound enough except that it was based on a complete misapprehension as to the whereabouts of the main body of the Prussian army. It was not at Jena at all. This meant that the action so far had dealt merely with a relatively small Prussian force. The Prussian main body under the King and his field commander, Brunswick, had moved north-east, and when Davout advanced with his corps to complete the encirclement of the enemy at Jena, he ran headlong instead into 60,000 Prussians at Auerstädt – more than twice his own number. Since Bernadotte was unaccountably slow at reinforcing him, it meant that Davout had to stand and fight greatly superior numbers. In successfully doing so he won the admiration of the entire Grande Armée, having proved himself on the field of battle to be as brilliant a tactician as Ney, as dogged as Masséna, and as brave as Murat or Lannes. Yet it had been Napoleon's error, and he, Emperor and Commander-in-Chief, had been saved from his own mistakes by the action of one of his own corps commanders, Marshal Davout. It has been said that Davout, cold, hard, unpopular, ambitious and devoted to the Emperor, was the only one of the marshals who really understood the Napoleonic concept of war. This concept was that, whereas the battle itself should be regarded as the breaking of the crest of a wave, it was the flood which swept irresistibly after it that constituted the actual victory. The classic example of this – made possible by Davout's stubborn action at Auerstädt and by his Commander-in-Chief's then taking a real grip of the situation and showing Europe what it was he was up to – was now to be revealed. Again A. G. Macdonnell sums it up admirably:

> Napoleon hurled his army northwards in the greatest sustained pursuit in history. The pursuit is sometimes called the Pursuit of the Three Marshals, because Murat, Bernadotte and Soult were in at the death.
>
> On November 6th Blücher surrendered in Lübeck, and the mighty machine of Frederick the Great vanished. There was not a single man, horse or gun left. Twenty-three days of fighting had done the entire trick, and Murat wrote to the Emperor that the fighting was over for lack of opponents.
>
> So fell the Prussian Army, and Napoleon symbolically removed the sword of Frederick from the tomb in Potsdam.

'Hats off, gentlemen,' Napoleon told his generals. 'If he were alive we should not be here.' Frederick the Great's successor, King Frederick William, had fled to East Prussia. So we see that Napoleon's activity during 1806 had been continuous and devastating. Prussia had been eliminated. Next it would be Russia's turn. Meanwhile, what of Arthur Wellesley?

His year had been somewhat milder. He had married Kitty Pakenham, was a Member of Parliament and was still a soldier. In the summer of 1806, shortly before the Prussians declared war on France, we find him writing from Hastings to an old friend, Malcolm, in the following vein:

> I am here now in command of a force stationed in this part of the coast, the old landing-place of William the Conqueror. You will have seen that I am in Parliament, and a most difficult and unpleasant

game I have had to play in the present extraordinary state of the parties.

The fact that he was a Member of Parliament did not endear him to those in power at the Horse Guards. Even his triumphs in India were regarded by some of the senior army people as no triumphs at all. Indeed many of them were simply envious that Wellesley was a member of the nobility, who had entered the army not to be of any use, but simply to adorn it. It was not long before they were again proved totally wrong. When he finds that several of his regiments are being prepared for overseas service – in the autumn of 1806 the government nurtured a forlorn hope about intervening in Europe, a hope instantly dashed by Prussia's collapse – he wishes to go too, in a subordinate capacity if necessary, noting that the Prime Minister, Grenville, might not realize that he, Wellesley, was eager to serve abroad if others were going. It did not have to be the chief command for him. Any command would do. Nothing came of these ideas. Early in 1807 Wellesley had become a father – a son was born to Kitty – but he was far from happy in his marriage. Appointed to the Irish Secretaryship in the spring of 1807 when a new Tory administration under Portland replaced Grenville's Ministry of all the Talents, he found that Kitty was quite incapable of managing his household. Extravagant, disorderly, emotional and depressed, she simply irritated him, as he later explained to Mrs Arbuthnot. It was, he said, distressing to be married to someone with whom there could be no understanding or confidence. Whereas his mind was occupied with matters of importance, hers was filled with trivialities. Try as he might to live with her on affectionate terms, she could take no interest in his pursuits and responsibilities. Worse, she not only had no common sense or grasp of significant matters, she had a high opinion of her own cleverness and infallibility. He longed for a happy domestic atmosphere. But it was not to be found with Kitty.

Napoleon, on the other hand, was having better fortune with the petticoats, for in January 1807, advancing for his campaign against Russia, he had met the enchanting Marie Walewska in Warsaw. She, a girl of twenty, married to a rich provincial governor who was almost seventy, may have sacrificed her youth and romantic dreams in order to save the family fortunes. But in front of her lay the greatest possible romantic adventure. Regarding Napoleon as a heroic saviour of her country – for he had defeated Poland's enemies, Prussia and Russia – she welcomed the Emperor, who at thirty-seven was still vulnerable to feminine charms, with flowers and a few words: 'Sire, Poland is overwhelmed to feel your step upon her soil.' Napoleon thought the child exquisite. She became his mistress and was, as Vincent Cronin puts it, 'the least pretty, but the most sensitive, loyal and passionate'. She bore him a son in 1810, and 'was to remain faithful to Napoleon even in adversity.'

Just how faithful is told by A. P. Herbert in his enchanting *Why Waterloo?* His book begins with the touching tale of how the Countess Walewska vainly waits outside his room to see Napoleon at Fontainebleau, where in March 1814 the Emperor, unable to halt the Allies' inexorable advance on Paris, deserted by his closest adherents, including his wife, Marie-Louise, an Empire gone, his capital abandoned to the enemy, is moodily contemplating his far from certain future. She has been let in at a side door of the palace by Constant, Napoleon's valet. The Emperor himself is in a small room, silent, unwilling to see anyone, telling Constant to send the Countess away. She replies that she will wait. Constant believes that Napoleon has attempted suicide, but does not tell Marie this, for he believes the Countess would then force her way in to see the Emperor. Constant too is about to desert his master, having been given money enough by Napoleon. He slips away, leaving Marie still there. While waiting, Marie recalls their first meeting on 1 January 1807 in Warsaw when the Emperor showers her with questions. 'What is your name? How old are you? Do you speak French? Do you know that you are charming?' In recounting this passage A. P. Herbert draws a curious parallel with Wellington. 'Napoleon', he writes, 'had the habit found in other great men, of asking a number of questions and not waiting for the answers. Sometimes it was intended to fluster: sometimes it was only the impatience of a swift mind. Wellington had it too. Harriette Wilson, a fond friend of his, writes: "As I was one day taking a solitary drive up the Champs Élysées, the Duke of Wellington galloped past ... he returned and was at the side of my carriage: 'I thought it was you,' said Wellington, 'and am glad to see you are looking so beautiful. I'll come to see you. How long have you been in Paris? When may I come? Where do you live? How far are you going?'"' Once more we may remark, so much for Bagehot's assertion that the great soldier had no time for fancies as to a lady-love.

In the early days of 1807, however, there was not much time for dalliance in Warsaw. The Grande Armée had to push on north to find and engage the Russian army. The weather was appalling, the country flat and bare, mud everywhere, the villages mean, the billets disgusting, the language incomprehensible, the people dirty, the rations nothing but potatoes, and all in all it was turning out to be a campaign utterly distasteful to the Grande Armée. It might have been redeemed had the army's first encounter with the Russians at Eylau on 8 February been an unqualified success. It was anything but this. There had already been evidence during clashes at Heilsberg and Pultusk that the Russians were hard, brave, determined opponents, and at Eylau itself Napoleon, with only 50,000 men, including the corps of Augereau and Soult, the Guard, and Murat with the cavalry, came up against 75,000 Russians. Davout and Bernadotte – as at Jena – were still to come up on the flanks, and when the Emperor sent Augereau forward to engage the Russian bulk, it all went awry. He exposed his flank to the Russian guns by advancing in the wrong direction and suffered severe casualties. It was a situation that called for a desperate measure, if the Grande Armée were not to be totally destroyed. Fortunately, A. G. Macdonnell tells us, the very man to deliver such a measure was on parade:

> 100,000 men of the two armies watched one of the most famous spectacles in the whole history of warfare, when ninety squadrons of the Reserve Cavalry galloped across the snow to attack unbroken infantry and artillery, with Murat himself at their head, wearing his gold-embroidered uniform, his ostrich feathers in his hat, with his saddle over a great leopard skin, and carrying a gold-headed cane in his hand.

The Grande Armée remained in possession of the battlefield, but they had failed to win the battle and lost 15,000 men. Augereau's corps had virtually ceased to exist and before long was disbanded; what remained of it was parcelled out to other formations. Eylau had been the first serious setback to Napoleon's astonishing series of victories. Henceforth, despite a few blazing comets here and there, his star would begin to shine less brightly, the sun begin to set and the shadows begin to make their appearance. Even Napoleon himself commented that the Russians had done them great harm, while the ordinary soldier was heard to cry 'Vive la Paix' instead of 'Vive l'Empereur'.

One of the brightest comets appeared only four months after Eylau at a battle nearby – Friedland, when in June 1807 Napoleon smashed the Russian army, making use, as became an artilleryman, of massed artillery batteries, and brilliantly supported by those two intrepid marshals, Lannes and Ney. The result was the treaty of Tilsit. The two Emperors, Alexander I and Napoleon, first conferred on a raft in the middle of the Niemen on 25 June and the treaty was formally signed on 7 July. The most important articles in the treaty were meant to be secret, although in fact they were soon known to George Canning, Foreign Secretary, and to the British government. This was just as well for they essentially concerned the subjugation of Great Britain. The two Emperors required that the British should lift their ban on trade with France and her allies, and, a fantastic demand, that all territories conquered by the British since 1805 should be restored. If these conditions were not met, Portugal, Denmark and Sweden would all be constrained to close their ports to British shipping. Such arrangements would, of course, gravely threaten Britain in two ways – both commercially and strategically. When Napoleon had abandoned his plans to invade Britain in 1805, it was in order to remove any dangers to his position from the European powers. Since then he had dealt with Austria, Prussia and Russia – the latter twice, at Austerlitz and Friedland. With Europe at his feet, he could now if he wished – and with the aid of warships from Portugal, Sweden and Denmark, plus what little Nelson had left of the Spanish and French fleets – turn his attention once more to invading the British Isles. Napoleon recorded his intentions thus:

> After Russia had joined my alliance, Prussia, as a matter of course, followed her example; Portugal, Sweden and the Pope alone remained to be gained over, for we were well aware that Denmark would hasten to throw herself into our arms. If England refused the mediation of Russia, the whole maritime forces of the Continent were to be employed against her, and they could muster 180 sail of the line. In a few years this force could be raised to 250. With the aid of such a fleet, and my immense flotilla, it was by no means impossible to lead a European army to London. One hundred ships of the line employed against her colonies in the two hemispheres would have sufficed to draw off a large portion of the British navy; while eighty more,

assembled in the Channel, would have sufficed to assure the passage of my flotilla and avenge the outraged rights of nations. Such was at bottom my plan.

There is one key word in all this rhetoric, and we must give Napoleon credit for his strategic thinking in continents: 'Portugal'. For it was here that the British were able to turn affairs to their advantage. Before doing so Britain had seized the Danish fleet – Wellesley played his part here by defeating a Danish force at Roskilde – and attempted to bolster Sweden by sending Sir John Moore there with 12,000 troops. Sweden's mad King Gustavus, however, rejected the offer of help and tried unsuccessfully to arrest Moore. Portugal was a different matter. To start with she was England's oldest ally, and when Napoleon reached an agreement with Spain for permission to march French troops through Spanish territory in order to subdue Portugal, and acted on it, Britain was able to persuade the Portuguese Regent (later John VI) to quit Lisbon and sail to Brazil, thus robbing France of the all-important Portuguese fleet. 'It was not until the French were in the very suburbs of the Portuguese capital,' writes Petrie, 'that the Prince Regent handed his ships over to the British, and set sail for Rio de Janeiro. Canning had won the race with Napoleon by a very short head indeed, but he had won; and the Portuguese fleet, like the Danish, was under the White Ensign, not the tricolour.'

Napoleon had despatched Junot with 24,000 men – the so-called Corps of Observation of the Gironde – across the Spanish frontier on 18 October 1807. It took him about six weeks to reach Lisbon by which time his corps had been reduced to 1,500 men, who by this time were without food, horses, guns or ammunition. But such was the fame of the Grande Armée and the Emperor Napoleon that even this ineffectual force was quite sufficient to ensure that there would be no resistance from the Portuguese. Junot appointed himself Governor of the country. There seemed little doubt that on land the French Emperor could do more or less what he liked. At sea, however, it was a different story. Napoleon's determination to teach not only Portugal, but Spain too, a lesson gave Britain the very opportunity to exploit her sea-power by making use of innumerable points of entry to the Iberian peninsula with relatively small numbers of redcoats. Moreover, such was the nature of the country there that it was ideal for the operation of native guerrilla forces, whose numbers, mobility, fanaticism and sheer hatred of foreign invaders were able to multiply infinitely the effect of a small British army. Once Napoleon turned on the Spanish people he acquired an enemy of such unquenchable hostility that it accounted for untold thousands of French soldiers, and became a kind of cancer in the side of Napoleon's empire. It forced him to abandon any kind of concentration of force. Instead, together with his other insatiable designs for conquest, it obliged him to string the Grande Armée out between Cadiz and Moscow. And once singleness of aim and concentration of force were gone, so too was the Napoleonic recipe for success in battle.

Macaulay has vividly described in his essay on the War of the Spanish Succession that, although it was easy for an army to overrun Spain, it was immeasurably difficult to conquer the actual people. No matter how unprofessional, ill-organized and badly disciplined Spain's regular troops might be, when these professionals had been defeated and put aside, another kind of resistance, hard, unforgiving, steadfast and fanatical, took the place of regular soldiers. The very word, guerrilla, was born in this way. Small, independent, secretive, merciless bands of guerrillas were to become far more deadly to Napoleon's veterans than the ill-disciplined rabbles of the regular army. These were the enemy which the Grande Armée were shortly to encounter when Napoleon decided to make war on Spain.

He did not do so at first. At first, as we have seen, he sent General Junot and his Corps of Observation of the Gironde *through* Spain to Portugal. But Spain had already aroused his anger by its attitude during his campaign against Prussia in 1806. Heading the Spanish government at this time was about as repulsive a group of human beings as could be imagined. The nominal king, Charles IV, dithering, not wholly sane, had a passion for only one thing – hunting; when we regard his queen, Maria-Luisa, strong in character, deficient in looks, loose in morals, insatiable between the sheets, we may comprehend Charles's preference for *la chasse*. It was hardly to be wondered at that the offspring of such a couple, Ferdinand, should be hideous, vulgar, bloated, a bigoted tyrant and a venal coward. The real ruler of Spain, the Queen's favourite, was the oddly named Prince of Peace, Manuel Godoy, described by Lady Holland as 'a large, coarse, ruddy-complexioned man, with a heavy, sleepy, voluptuous eye'. At the time of Napoleon's Prussian campaign, Godoy had made the crass error of trying to assert Spain's independence from France by calling on the Spanish people to come forward *en masse* to fight the enemy. It was quite clear to everyone, including Napoleon, that by 'the enemy' he meant the French, particularly as he called for a substantial reinforcement of the army – horses were a special need. So that when, after the French Emperor's destruction of the Prussian army, he tried to reassure Napoleon that by 'the enemy' he had referred to the British, even though there had been no demand for more ships, it did not ring very true. For the time being, Napoleon let it go. There would be plenty of time to deal with Spain later. A start could be made by arranging the passage of French troops through Spain to close Portuguese ports to British shipping and trade.

So Junot made his way to Lisbon and, having successfully sent one corps into Spain, Napoleon followed this success by sending more. Army after army crossed the Pyrenees and slowly but surely occupied northern Spain, Barcelona, Madrid and the frontier fortresses. Having induced King Charles IV and his heir, Ferdinand, to come to Bayonne in April 1808, Napoleon had them seized, then bullied Charles into abdication; after Murat – who needed no lesson in how to subdue insurrections with a whiff of grapeshot – had ruthlessly suppressed a rising by the mobs of Madrid, Napoleon convinced Ferdinand too that abdication might be preferable to the firing squad. Spain was to be ruled by Joseph Bonaparte, Napoleon's elder brother, while Murat, who had hoped for the Spanish crown, went off to be King of Naples instead. He got the better bargain. It might have been supposed that the Spanish people would have been glad to see the backs of Charles, Maria-Luisa and Ferdinand, but such was their perversity and pride that they clamoured for the return of their legitimate rulers, and in May 1808 took up arms against the French.

It must again be remembered that with this move the whole nature of the Napoleonic wars underwent a change. In the opening passages of his masterly *History of the War in the Peninsula*, William Napier makes this point: 'Up to the treaty of Tilsit, the wars of France were wholly defensive – for the bloody contest that wasted the continent for so many years was not a struggle for pre-eminence between the ambitious powers, not a dispute for some accession of territory, nor for the political ascendancy of one or more nations, but a deadly conflict, to determine whether aristocracy or democracy should pre-dominate, whether equality or privilege should henceforth be the principle of European governments.' But Napoleon's attempt to turn Portugal and Spain into mere provinces of Imperial France changed all that. His invasion of Portugal and Spain was naked aggression, and it met with a fittingly aggressive response. The rising against the French was country-wide. Everywhere the Spanish army and the peasants declared war on the invading French armies, which now numbered over 100,000. From Andalusia in the south, Estramadura in the west, Murcia, Aragon and Valencia in the east and Old Castile, Galicia and Asturias in the north, resistance to the French began. At first the Spanish had some successes. Worst of all from the French point of view, and to Napoleon's fury, at Baylen in July 1808 General Dupont with 17,000 men had capitulated to the Spanish army. In the same month Lieutenant-General Sir Arthur Wellesley with an army of about 9,000 had landed in Portugal.

Pitt had foreseen the whole thing when shortly before his death he told Arthur Wellesley that sooner or later Napoleon would interfere in Spain and then he would find himself for the first time conducting a war against partisans. For although the Spanish government might be made of poor stuff and the nobility was corrupt and debauched, the people themselves still possessed fine feelings of patriotism and honour. They would resist any attempt to stamp out such feelings, and if Napoleon sought to do so, such a war would be started as would not end except by his own destruction. How accurately Pitt prophesied the cancer of Spain![1] The British government had decided to take a hand in the Iberian game, and the Spanish uprising gave them just the opportunity they needed. Although Canning had wished at first to despatch a British expedition to Venezuela to assist the rebels there *against* Spain (regarded before Spain took up arms against her as France's ally), what was happening from May 1808 altered the destination of the army. Indeed, as Wellesley himself noted, it would be far more effective to strike a blow nearer home to Napoleon's European empire than on the other side of the Atlantic. Accordingly it was decided to send Wellesley and his 9,000 men to the Peninsula. Such a move was strongly supported by both Spanish and Portuguese emissaries. Before setting out, Wellesley had confided to his friend, Croker, his thoughts about once more finding himself in command of troops against the French. It had

---

[1] It was Napoleon himself who after his downfall observed: 'The Spanish ulcer destroyed me.'

been more than a dozen years since he had been in action against the then revolutionary armies. They had been excellent soldiers then, and no doubt all the Napoleonic victories in between would have made them even better. Moreover, he noted, Napoleon's system of making war was a new one and had outfought by manoeuvre and sheer weight and speed all the European armies. It was enough to make him thoughtful. However, he, Wellesley, was not frightened of them, and from what he had heard he believed the French system of manoeuvre would not prevail against steady troops. He would certainly not be outmanoeuvred. Whether he might be overwhelmed was another matter. But whereas the Continental armies, he suspected, were all half beaten before the battles even started, his would not be. His prophesies were as sound as Pitt's and it was not to be long before he was putting his tactical ideas into devastating practice.

Wellesley called first at Corunna on 20 July and talked to the Spanish Junta there. It was clear from the discussion that at this time the Spaniards would not welcome *any* foreign troops in their country, not even allies. Wellesley therefore agreed to their recommendation that the most promising course of action would be to proceed to northern Portugal to reinforce the uprising there, and then mount an offensive against Junot, now calling himself Duc d'Abrantés, and his corps. Further consultation at Oporto with both the Junta there and with Admiral Cotton, who commanded the blockading British fleet, led to a decision to land his army at Mondego Bay, some 80 miles north of Lisbon. Here Wellesley would be able to disembark his men, horses, stores and guns without interference, and concentrate in order to take on Junot. His army of 9,000 was strengthened by a further 4,000 under Major-General Brent Spencer, which had been in transports off southern Spain. An additional 2,000 Portuguese troops brought Wellesley's total up to some 15,000.

Even before operations got under way, Wellesley had received some unwelcome news from Castlereagh, Secretary of State for War. This was to the effect that he was not to remain in sole command for long. The tortuous reasoning behind it all was that since the government intended that a further 12,000 troops under Sir John Moore should also join the expedition, and since they did not wish Moore to be in overall command because of his criticism of government strategy, they were also sending General Sir Harry Burrard (whose nickname

Betty summed up his dithering incompetence) *and* General Sir Hew Dalrymple, the ancient Governor of Gibraltar. We are reminded of Napoleon's point that one bad general does better than two good ones. In this case – for Moore did not in the event participate in the campaign – we have one good general, Wellesley, on the ground, with two bad ones, Burrard and Dalrymple, following on. Wellesley sensibly determined to get on with the business while his two seniors were still on passage and defeat Junot before they could interfere.

On landing his army, Wellesley made it plain to those under his command that Portugal was an ally, a country friendly to His Majesty George III, and that the normal soldierly practices of plundering everything in sight and making light of the local women's virtue were not to be indulged in or tolerated. He also proclaimed to the Portuguese themselves that his army was there to liberate their country from the French invaders and to restore their rightful sovereign to the throne. By 8 August he had completed the disembarkation of his army and its accoutrements, and on the 10th he began to advance southwards towards Lisbon. In the mean time, Junot had not been idle.

Junot had sent General Laborde with about 4,000 troops to encounter Wellesley's advancing army in order to impose some delay on the British, while he, Junot, gathered a second French force under General Loison to reinforce Laborde. In was therefore important for Wellesley to engage Laborde's force as quickly as possible in order to enjoy to the full his present advantage in numbers. During their first encounter with the French, the two rifle regiments trained by Sir John Moore, the 60th and 95th (which were to achieve such lasting fame in war after war and still do so as the Royal Green Jackets) proved their worth in bold skirmishing, making skilful use of their fire and movement drills, and actually charging the enemy's rearguard positions. Then the two armies engaged in the first battle of the Peninsular War – at Rolica on 17 August 1808. Many of Wellesley's subsequent battles in the Peninsula were essentially defensive battles. His first one, however, was an attack on the positions taken up by Laborde behind the village of Rolica. His tactics were traditional – a central advance by the main body under his personal direction, while Ferguson with 5,000 men attempted to outflank the French to their right and the Portuguese troops did the same to the enemy's left. Things did not go quite according to plan. They rarely do in war. Indeed the great von Moltke, years later, pronounced that no plan survives first contact with the enemy. In this case the over-eager 29th Foot, under the brave but precipitate Colonel Lake, got too far ahead without proper support and suffered heavy casualties. Wellesley, however, realizing that the outflanking manoeuvre was now unlikely to succeed, pushed on with his main force, the 60th and 95th Rifles skirmishing ahead, and ejected Laborde from his defensive position. As he had insufficient cavalry to mount a pursuit, he had to be content with an indecisive outcome to his first Peninsular encounter. Yet he described the battle as a desperate action – he had never seen such fighting.

On the following day Wellesley, like Macduff, found it hard to reconcile welcome and unwelcome things. On the one hand, 4,000 extra troops, a complete brigade, had arrived off the coast to reinforce him – welcome indeed. Less so was the arrival of General Sir Harry Burrard. Having arranged for the disembarkation of the reinforcing troops and having repositioned his army at Vimeiro, Wellesley went to confer with Burrard in the frigate *Brazen*. It became instantly clear to Wellesley that any ideas of his own about rapid, bold movements to outflank Junot's army at Torres Vedras would have little appeal to 'Betty' Burrard, who counselled caution. Burrard was in favour of waiting until Sir John Moore and his 12,000 soldiers arrived. But, as things turned out, it was neither Wellesley nor Burrard who made the next move. Junot, with some 20,000 men altogether, decided to march against the British with about two-thirds of his force, leaving the other third to secure his communications with Lisbon and the capital itself. Regarding the British army as a bunch of amateur soldiers, he was confident that with 13,000 men and twenty-four guns, and by employing the traditional French tactic of first disrupting the British with his *tirailleurs* and artillery, and then delivering a *coup de grâce* with his grenadier columns and the cavalry, he would soon drive the enemy back into the sea.

The result was somewhat different. Junot's advance and attack – although coming from the east, not the south as Wellesley had expected, and necessitating some last-minute readjustment of his defensive arrangements – gave Wellesley the opportunity to show how right he had been in telling Croker that he believed the French system of manoeuvring was unsound and would not work against steady troops. Wellesley disposed his men in characteristically reverse slope positions – the main body on a ridge to the north and east of Vimeiro, another

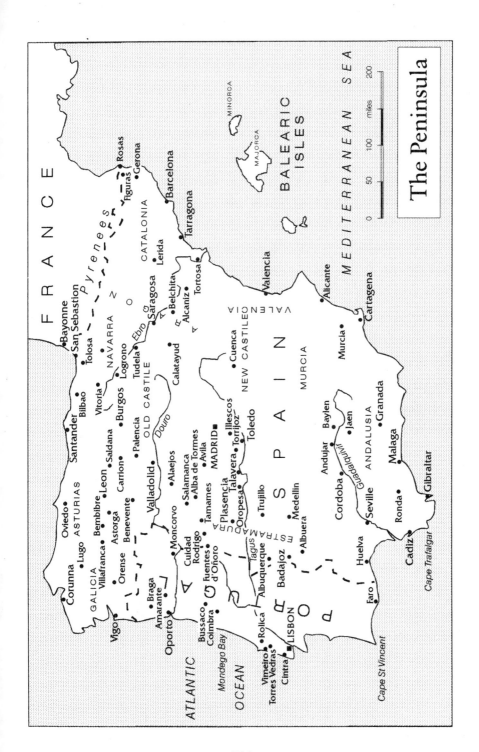

The Peninsula

123

group on a hill to the south, with a British brigade, the Portuguese and a squadron of cavalry in reserve further west. His orders to the infantry were to remain in position behind the crests on the reverse slopes – and thus relatively immune to enemy artillery fire – and to wait until the last moment before *they* opened fire. His battery of twelve guns were further forward to give them good fields of fire, and the light infantry were posted at the foot of the hills for their skirmishing, reconnoitring and disruptive tactics. It was a recipe for a defensive battle which Wellesley employed time and again, with almost invariable success.

At Vimeiro it took only a few hours. The French columns did not lack courage. They advanced with their customary *élan*, and were then treated to a variety of more or less continuous shot and shell, first from the sharp-shooting, skirmishing light infantry, then from the artillery, and most devastating of all from the musketry of the British infantry who, because they deployed in line, were able to pour a deadly hail of bullets into both the front and the flanks of the advancing French columns. As these columns came to a halt and began to disperse, they were treated to further discouragement by the sight of British bayonets charging at them. It was more than enough. The French grenadiers broke and ran. Such was the form of the fighting which took place at Vimeiro, Wellesley's first Peninsular victory. It was a pattern oft to be repeated.

One of the best descriptions given by a French general as to what it was like to be a member of an attacking column against Wellington's troops was that of Marshal Bugeaud, who explained the unnerving nature of the steadiness of the British line. His men would hoist their shakos on their muskets, break into a run, ranks getting mixed up, agitation growing, the advancing soldiers beginning to fire ineffectually, and all the time, only 300 yards away, the line of redcoats remained still and silent, seeming quite indifferent to the advancing column. Then at length the redcoats would do a quarter-turn, their muskets up to the shoulder – this was enough to give the French column further cause to pause – and at last a precise, co-ordinated and deadly fire would crash into the column, which reeled under its effect. Finally the redcoats with three cheers would break their silence and be down on the French with the bayonet, forcing them into an ill-disciplined retreat. Even as late on as Waterloo Wellington observed that the French came on in the old style and were then beaten back in the old style. At Vimeiro, Wellesley had succeeded in capturing three-quarters of the enemy's guns, inflicting 2,000 casualties and forcing them to retire. It was still only midday. A pursuit now might have turned the French retreat into a rout. But the old-womanish 'Betty' Burrard, who had arrived on the battlefield without making any contribution to the affair, would have none of it. He insisted on waiting for Sir John Moore. Such was Wellesley's disgust that he commented to his fellow officers that they might as well go off and shoot partridges. Worse was to follow, for instead of Sir John Moore and his 12,000 men, there arrived next day General Sir Hew (known as 'Dowager') Dalrymple, another old woman.

This particular old woman was so delighted to hear from Junot's emissary, General Kellermann, that the French now wanted an armistice that he gave up all idea of continuing the fight, and concluded the Convention of Cintra on 30 August 1808. Under this extraordinary agreement it was arranged that the French army should be evacuated from Portugal and that together with their armies and accoutrements they should be shipped to a French port in *British* transports. The dismay with which the news of this agreement was received in London may be imagined, for the initial despatches announcing Wellesley's successful action at Vimeiro had heralded much rejoicing, great satisfaction that the formally dismal days of defeat were things of the past, and the anticipation that shortly Junot's entire army would have capitulated and that Wellesley and his men would ride in triumph through the streets of Lisbon. When such high expectations were disappointed, it was not long before attribution of blame began. The politicians held the soldiers to be at fault – they always do when things go wrong – and maintained that victory had been thrown away. Wellesley himself – for his signature was also on the Cintra agreement – bore some of the responsibility, although it soon became clear that the principal culprit was Dowager Dalrymple. It was even said that henceforth, the word humiliation would be spelt with a 'hew'.

For Wellesley himself it was a bitter disappointment. He had brought his army to Portugal to destroy the French there, and then take the war into Spain. Two battles had been fought and in each he had been successful. But Junot's army would now be at liberty to re-enter the contest, and he himself was under the command of two old gentlemen who had neither the capacity nor the inclination to wage war. Also now under this inept direction was Sir John Moore and his 12,000 men who had at last arrived from their abortive expedition to Sweden. It was no wonder that Wellesley, in writing to his brother William, had cause to complain. He had had enough and wished to be gone. Things could not flourish as now conducted. Burrard and Dalrymple had no ideas and no plans. They could not even arrange for the extra supplies necessary to feed and accommodate the additional men of Moore's army. 'The people are really more stupid and incapable than any I have yet met with, and, if things go on in this disgraceful manner, I must quit them.'

And quit them he did, but not until after he had shown in another letter to his brother how every sensible principle of command had been breached by the two old women, who proceeded to break up the existing grouping of regiments (soldiers always value the 'family' associations of the officers they know and the fellow regiments they have fought with and admire) and switch them to unfamiliar commanders. What is more – and here we are again reminded of Bagehot – 'they have annoyed the soldiers ... having no shoes to their feet and feeling a very natural desire to see the place for which they had fought'. Wellesley also made the point – one he was often to reiterate – that orders and regulations issued by him were ignored, contracts for supply of food broken, and as a result utter confusion was caused by 'these Gentlemen'. He realized that hard things might be said of him for leaving Portugal, but he had never cared much for the unjustified poor opinion of others, and he was willing either to return to Ireland, to serve on the army staff in England, or to amuse himself by hunting and shooting.

Before he left Portugal, however, and with characteristic honesty and generosity, he wrote to Sir John Moore, who was to remain in Portugal commanding the British Army there and whose fortunes against Napoleon himself we must shortly follow. In his letter to Moore, Wellesley made it clear that, whereas the existing command arrangements of Burrard and Dalrymple were impossible, Moore must not allow his former disappointment with and criticism of government strategy to preclude him from the service for which he was most fitted, that is in high command. He, Wellesley, would use what influence he had to ease matters at home so that Moore could have the command-in-chief. Moreover, he, Wellesley, would, as he told Moore when they met at Queluz palace outside Lisbon, be willing to serve under his command. Next day Wellesley left for home and at the same time Burrard and Dalrymple were recalled to London. Wellesley had also told Moore that one of the two of them must liberate Spain. It was to be Moore who made the first brief, gallant but unsuccessful attempt. It was left to Wellesley to make the second, equally gallant, but prolonged, perseverant and ultimately triumphant one. In October 1808 Wellesley was back in England, Sir John Moore in Portugal was receiving his orders to support the Spanish armies, and the Emperor Napoleon was setting out for Spain himself with the bulk of the Grande Armée in order finally to settle the Spanish business.

In parenthesis here we may perhaps observe that, whereas Wellesley had descended on Portugal in July 1808 with a mere 9,000 men, subsequently made up to about 15,000, the French Emperor's total command was somewhat grander. Leaving about 40,000 men to keep an eye on Austria, the Emperor resolved to advance into Spain with no fewer than eight corps, commanded respectively by Victor, Soult, Moncey (later Lannes), Lefèbvre, Mortier, Ney, St Cyr and Junot. Together with the reserve cavalry under Bessières, Napoleon had the best part of 200,000 men, and a plan which was the very acme of simplicity. He would smash straight through the Spanish centre, then split into three groups, two of which would outflank and destroy the Spanish left and right, while the third group took Madrid. Then he could drive on to engage the hated and despised English leopards and turn them out of Portugal.

As Sir John Moore's activities interfered with this master plan of Napoleon's, we may perhaps consider these activities first. His orders were clear enough. King George III, he had been told, was determined to employ some 30,000 infantry and 5,000 cavalry in northern Spain to co-operate with the Spanish armies and expel the French from that kingdom. He, Moore, was to be entrusted with the command-in-chief. A simple enough requirement – the only problem was how to do it. His position was not an easy one. At this time, October 1808, he had only 30,000 men in Portugal, and he would have to leave 10,000 to secure his base there before setting off for Spain. He was to be reinforced with a further 17,000 under General Baird, but they had not yet arrived in the country. Nor had the 5,000 cavalry commanded by Lord Henry Paget. Convinced as he was that Napoleon would shortly be attacking the Spanish armies, he had to move quickly if he were to be able to support them at all.

Moore's problems were not only those of awaiting reinforcements. The mere matter of moving what troops he had into Spain over the most difficult and unmapped mountain roads, where there were no pre-positioned depots of stores, food, forage and ammunition, would have daunted most commanders. Moore was made of sterner stuff. He set off on 16 October from Queluz to march his army over the Portuguese mountains to the frontier fortress of Ciudad Rodrigo and then on to Salamanca with the idea of joining Baird and his 17,000 men in Old Castile. Then with his concentrated force he would be able to support the Spanish army. His heavy artillery had been sent by another route because he had received inaccurate intelligence about the state of the roads.

In war, situations change rapidly and when Moore reached Salamanca a month later, he found himself and his army in a strategically most uncomfortable position. The French were already at Valladolid, and Moore – still without Baird, who was at Lugo, or Paget's cavalry, at Corunna, or even his artillery under Hope, a hundred miles away – was in danger of being overwhelmed. We must see what it was that Napoleon had done to bring about these totally different circumstances. His grand design of smashing the Spanish centre, curling round its left and right flanks and so annihilating the entire enemy army, had not quite come off. The centre had been smashed as planned, but neither of the flanking operations had fully succeeded. One of the reasons for Napoleon's failure in Spain was one wholly uncharacteristic of him. He did not appreciate that whereas some of the main routes, such as the one he himself took from Bayonne to Madrid, were properly metalled and therefore conducive to fast movement by horse, foot and guns, most of the minor routes were dreadfully inadequate mountain tracks. Long after Napoleon had quitted Spain at the beginning of 1809 – for he never entered that country again – he would continue to send totally unrealistic orders to his marshals in command there, based on an absolutely false understanding of what communications were like, what a dreadful threat the Spanish guerrillas posed, and what impossible conditions the army operated under, without regular supplies, reliable intelligence or any sort of master plan to which they could conform.

Yet for what was achieved during his one and only campaign there, Napoleon had some reason for satisfaction. It was true that the Spanish left-wing army had largely escaped the net because dear old Marshal

Arthur Wesley as Lieutenant-Colonel of the 33rd Foot, aged about 26, by John Hoppner

Catherine Dorothea Sarah
('Kitty') Packenham,
Viscountess Wellington,
by Slater, 1811

William Pitt the Younger,
by John Hoppner

Arthur Wesley as Lieutenant-Colonel of the 33rd Foot, aged about 26, by John Hoppner

Napoleon crossing the St. Bernard Pass, by David

The Battle of Rivoli, 14 January 1797, by Felix Philippoteaux

Catherine Dorothea Sarah
('Kitty') Packenham,
Viscountess Wellington,
by Slater, 1811

William Pitt the Younger,
by John Hoppner

Talleyrand, from a portrait
by Gérard

Napoleon at the Battle of Jena, 14 October 1806, by Horace Vernet

Major-General the Hon Sir
Arthur Wellesley, KB,
by John Hoppner, 1806

Admiral Nelson,
by Lemuel Abbott

Marie Walewska,
by Robert Lefevre

Czar Alexander I

The Passage of the Bidassoa,
1813, from a painting
by James Prinsep Beadle

Pause in the Attack,
Hougoumont Farm,
Waterloo, by J. Crofts, 1861

The charge of Ney at Waterloo, by Flameng

Wellington at Waterloo, 18 June 1815, by Sir William Allan

Napoleon at Waterloo, 18 June 1815, by Sir William Allan

Joachim Murat, later King of
Naples (1771–1815),
by Gérard

Wellington's funeral procession

Lefèbvre, unable to comprehend the Emperor's overall strategy which depended on precise timing, could not resist the temptation of attacking prematurely. It was true that the appalling state of the mountain trails over which Ney's 6th Corps was trying to entrap the Spanish right wing prevented his doing so. It was also true that the Grande Armée was beginning to discover that soldiering in Spain was not a very comfortable business, for isolated groups of French soldiers, stragglers, messengers, indeed any French soldiers at all, were subject to ruthless shootings, stabbings and stranglings, which merely grew worse when the French dealt out terrible reprisals by burning villages, shooting hostages or sacking nunneries. Such measures simply inflamed the spirit of the Spanish people still more. Nonetheless Napoleon had smashed the central part of the Spanish army, entered Madrid on 4 December 1808, restored his brother Joseph to the throne, and was now ready to push on to Portugal, destroy the British army and retake Lisbon. It was then he heard the news that Sir John Moore with an army of English leopards was chasing Soult in Old Castile and even threatening his communications with France. Once more Napoleon pulled on his long boots and acted with speed and decision.

What Moore had succeeded in doing was to concentrate his army near Salamanca, and now with some 30,000 troops, sixty guns and the cavalry, he was advancing on Soult – who at Carrion de los Condes was guarding the western sector of Napoleon's communications with France. On 22 December Napoleon got the news, and as Sir Charles Oman described it in his classic *History of the Peninsular War*, the Emperor acted with unsurpassed energy. Abandoning all ideas of advancing on Portugal, Napoleon gathered 80,000 men and hurled them furiously northwards to entrap Moore's army. It was during the march that Napoleon was to discover (a discovery he conveniently discarded in later years when dictating orders for future strategic moves in Spain) that the roads were not all metalled, for in crossing the mountain passes over the Sierra Guadarrama, so strong were the winds and so deep was the snow that the cavalry and light horse artillery could not get on. The Emperor himself dismounted and marched on foot with the Guard, but sixteen horses were lost, and by this time – Christmas Eve 1808 – Moore had heard about the torrent that was about to engulf him, and halted his advance across the Carrion against Soult, for to continue would have been to invite encirclement and destruction, and had given orders initially for retreat to Astorga, then for a further retirement over the Cantabrian mountains to Lugo and Corunna.

It was a retreat in which the British redcoats, angered and dismayed by the need to do so at all, descended to previously unseen depths of drunkenness and ill discipline. It lasted three weeks and covered a distance of some 230 miles through ice and slush; food and firewood were scarce, progress was impeded by the disintegrating remnants of a so-called Spanish army, and they were harassed by the pursuing French. Fortunately Moore could rely on magnificent support from some of his subordinates, notably Robert Craufurd commanding the Light Brigade, Edward Paget with the Reserve Division and the incomparable Lord Henry Paget with the cavalry. Moore reached Astorga on 30 December, and there split his force into two. Craufurd and the Light Brigade would protect his southern flank and make for Vigo. He himself with the main body would continue to Corunna. Further disgraceful scenes of plunder, disorder and drunkenness occurred, and any stragglers were mercilessly dealt with by the French cavalry in pursuit.

Napoleon himself reached Astorga on 1 January 1809, and there received news that in Paris, Talleyrand, Fouché and Murat were intriguing against him. Furthermore, Austria was rearming. Handing over the command to Soult, he departed at once for Paris, and never set foot in Spain again. Meanwhile, the nightmare retreat of the British army to Corunna continued. On 6 January Moore halted the main body at Lugo and hoped to give battle to the French. They did not oblige, and on the retreat went, the army by now a disorganized rabble, although their spirits were raised five days later when, as they neared Corunna, the sea was visible and supplies were more plentiful. Moore's army pulled itself together and marched into Corunna in some sort of order. The defence of Corunna was made especially difficult by a shortage of infantry, so that Moore could not base it on the outer higher hills, but on those closer in and therefore overlooked by the enemy. The British transports escorted by a squadron of men-of-war had arrived at Corunna; stores and ammunition were now plentiful. On 16 January the battle took place, and Moore handled his troops so skilfully that he beat off Soult's main infantry attack and successfully engaged the principal French artillery position; at the very moment of victory he was struck by a cannon-ball. Hope took over the command, as Baird too was wounded, and successfully embarked 24,000 of Moore's original

30,000. In his despatch to Castlereagh two days earlier Moore, while condemning the troops' infamous behaviour during the retreat, yet expressed his confidence in their readiness to fight and their devotion to duty while doing so. At Corunna they had lived up to his high expectations and standards. Soult raised a monument in his memory, well after the British army which Moore had trained and commanded had 'left him alone with his glory'.

The strategic consequences of Moore's campaign, even though it had led to one more retreat and evacuation, were all-important, for he had prevented Napoleon from resolving the Spanish problem. His timely intervention and boldness in laying his small army across Napoleon's lines of communication had stopped the French from advancing on Lisbon to crush Portuguese resistance. Moreover the remnants of the Spanish army had been awarded a breathing space, and the Spanish guerrillas were shortly to be active again. The legacy of it all would be for Wellesley to enjoy, for the British Army was soon to return, this time under Wellesley's command, and this time to remain, until – together with the activities of Spain's regular troops and guerrillas – it would form such a cancer in the side of Napoleon's Europe that, as Pitt had prophesied, it would in large measure contribute to his downfall.

Less than two months after Corunna, Wellesley is advising Castlereagh about both the practical problems and the potential strategic advantages of raising an army in Portugal and reinforcing it with a British one. His summing-up of the matter in a famous memorandum is masterly. 'I have always been of the opinion,' he wrote, 'that Portugal might be defended whatever might be the result of the contest in Spain.' Moreover, given a Portuguese army trained by British officers and NCOs, together with a British army of 20,000 to 30,000, of which 4,000 would be cavalry, he believed that Lisbon could be held even against a French army of 100,000. Of course, absolute command of the sea was an essential feature of such a strategy, for, as he enumerated, if this plan were to be adopted, everything to support the army would have to be sent from England – arms, ammunition, clothing and accoutrements, ordnance, flour, oats and so on. So convinced were Castlereagh and the British government by Wellesley's reasoning that they determined to adopt his plan and send him out in command of the expeditionary force. His instructions were clear. His primary task was the defence of Portugal. Should he consider it advantageous in addition to co-operate with the Spanish armies, he was to make his views known. But actually doing it would require the British government's authority.

On 22 April Wellesley landed in Lisbon. He was to remain in Portugal and Spain for five years, win battle after battle, execute retreat after retreat, advance after advance, storm frontier fortresses and manoeuvre with infinite boldness. And when, as was frequently to happen, he received harsh criticism from England, he would quietly observe that, although affairs in the Peninsula always seemed to have the appearance of being lost, the contest itself continued. It is Wellesley's conduct of the first three years of the contest, together with the gradual lengthening of the shadows over the Napoleonic legend elsewhere in Europe, which we will now take a look at.

CHAPTER 7

The Shadows Lengthen

No one understands this man's character [Napoleon's] . . .
no one realizes how good he is.

Alexander I to Talleyrand

I N the same month that Wellesley landed in Portugal, April 1809, Napoleon had arrived at Donauwörth to take command of the army. For Austria had completed mobilization by February and the Austrian army under Archduke Charles, by far the ablest of their commanders, was pushing along the Danube and into Bavaria to take on the dispersed corps of the Grande Armeé before they could be concentrated under the Emperor's hand. It was just as well that Napoleon arrived when he did for he found, as he had before Jena, that leaving command of the army in the hands of his Chief of Staff, Berthier, was about the best method of encouraging mismanagement. It required all the Emperor's brilliance to save the situation and, characteristically, he chose a bold counter-stroke rather than a retirement to regroup. First Davout was to engage Archduke Charles's force while retiring westwards from Regensburg to Ingolstadt, then Napoleon, with Oudinot, Lannes and Masséna – whom he had summoned with the famous message, '*Activité, activité, vitesse, je me recommande à vous*' – intended to strike east to get round Archduke Charles's left flank, and so cut his lines of communication with Vienna. In the event Davout was obliged to stand and fight at Eckmühl, and in order to prevent Davout's being destroyed by sheer weight of numbers, Napoleon, together with Masséna and Lannes, attacked the Austrian left flank. It resulted in what the Emperor's bulletin referred to as one of the most beautiful sights in war – the retreating back of the enemy. Napoleon himself was slightly wounded in the battle. This was followed by another example of

Lannes's spectacular courage under fire when, inspired by his example, the grenadiers of his corps rushed a demolished part of the Ratisbon fortress and took the place by storm. Once more Napoleon entered Vienna – this time on 13 May 1809 – and once more he was faced with the same problem that he had had to deal with after Ulm and before Austerlitz in 1805. He had taken Vienna but the Austrian army was still on the northern bank of the Danube, and to get at them would once more mean crossing the river. While Napoleon could always be relied upon to act boldly, the plan he now conceived bordered on rashness. In crossing the river at Aspern-Essling, he fell into the trap prepared for him by Archduke Charles who was able to bring superior numbers to bear on the 20,000 Frenchmen who had so far crossed to the northern bridgehead. The French were driven out of the two villages and back to the bridge which was itself destroyed by the Austrians. The supposed invincibility of Napoleon and the Grande Armée – which had been called into question by the Russians at Eylau – was now challenged by the Austrians, for Napoleon withdrew to Lobau, and all Europe was soon to know that the Archduke Charles had actually inflicted a defeat on the Emperor. The French had lost about 20,000 men, and one of the bravest and most brilliant of the marshals – Lannes. For some six weeks, Napoleon prepared for the next move, sending for reinforcements, including Marmont's corps. After rebuilding bridges across the river, he issued his orders at the beginning of July for what became known as the battle of Wagram – a bloody, slogging match on the Marchfeld with maximum use of artillery and an advance by 36,000 Frenchmen under General Macdonald against the enemy centre. This finally left Napoleon in possession of the battlefield on which lay over 30,000 French dead and wounded and a similar number of Austrians. Macdonald was made a Marshal of France on the field of battle. It was a technical victory for Napoleon, but at what a cost! Apart from the huge general losses at Wagram, Bessières was wounded – at first thought killed, to the dismay of the Imperial Guard. Lasalle, of the Light Cavalry, was struck down mortally by a chance bullet when the battle was virtually over. An armistice was signed on 12 July 1809 to be followed in October of that year with the treaty of Schönbrunn, by which the Emperor Francis II ceded territory in Poland and the Adriatic. If there had been some similarity between the situations *before* Jena and Auerstädt and *before* Aspern-Essling and Wagram, there was little *after* these two brace of battles. In 1806 the French pursuit of the Prussian army had led to its total annihilation. In 1809 there was no pursuit of the Austrian army at all. Napoleon's star was beginning to set, the shadows over the legend lengthening still further. What is more, the news from the Peninsula was from the Emperor's point of view far from reassuring.

For Wellesley had already demonstrated both his coolness and his determination to get to grips with the enemy. He was quite undismayed by the arithmetical odds against him. While it was clear that to conduct his campaign he would at first have fewer than 40,000 soldiers – 20,000 British, 3,000 of the King's German Legion and 16,000 Portuguese under Beresford – he knew that the French armies in Spain totalled 200,000. Fortunately they were widely dispersed and not under one central command, if, that is, we may exclude the wholly unrealistic orders despatched to his marshals in Spain by the Emperor. This great disparity in numbers puts us in mind of a revealing comment made by Marmont on the business of directing armies. 'With 12,000 men', he said, 'one fights; with 30,000 one commands; but in great armies the commander is only a sort of Providence which can only intervene to ward off great accidents.' Wellesley, who according to Marmont's definition falls into the second category, was soon to show that he commanded brilliantly. With regard to Spain and indeed other theatres Napoleon becomes 'a sort of Providence', but whatever he was from now on, he was less and less able to ward off great accidents.

The French forces most nearly threatening Wellesley's position were Soult at Oporto with some 20,000 men, Victor with 25,000 stationed about 50 miles east of Badajoz at Medellin, and, at the frontier fortress of Ciudad Rodrigo, General Lapisse with 6,000. Thus even those enemy forces relatively near to Wellesley's army outnumbered him and this was to say nothing of the remaining 150,000 elsewhere. It was difficult, therefore, to see how Wellesley could achieve any great strategic victories against such odds. Yet to view the matter in this light is to misunderstand the nature of the Peninsular War. Even A. G. Macdonnell is guilty of this sort of misunderstanding when he declares that Wellesley's task in the Peninsula was the easiest one that had ever faced a general. He argues that, although Wellesley enjoyed the advantages of a mercenary army, speedy and reliable intelligence, an indigenous population which was utterly hostile to the French invaders, interior lines of operation, absolute mastery of the seas, and thus abundant supplies of everything needed to wage war – all of which Macdonnell suggests put the game into his hands – it nevertheless took him six years to get his army from Portugal to France. In making this accusation, Macdonnell completely misses the point, which Liddell Hart so eloquently stressed. It was not the *battles* fought by Wellesley which were most damaging to the French. 'The overwhelming majority of the losses which drained the French strength, and their morale still more, was due to the operation of the guerrillas, and of Wellesley himself, in harrying the French and in making the countryside a desert where the French stayed only to starve.' The old saying that in Spain a small army is defeated, while a large army starves, reiterates the point. In Wellesley's case, of course, his small army was neither defeated nor did it starve, but then not only did he enjoy the support of the Spanish and Portuguese people, he never hesitated to retreat along secure lines of communication to a firm base with plentiful supplies, knowing, as he did so, that the French, should they pursue him, would be denied these very strategic necessities.

In accordance with this broad plan of campaign, Wellesley decided to deal first with Soult at Oporto. He instantly displayed a boldness quite at odds with the fashionable notion of him as an essentially cautious general. First he concentrated his main body of 18,000 British soldiers at Coimbra, midway between Lisbon and Oporto, while sending Beresford and his Portuguese corps as a right flank guard and leaving a sufficient force to watch the Tagus – for Victor and his army were not far away at Medellin – and then on 7 May advanced north to the Douro river south of Oporto. Soult laboured under the comfortable conviction that the Douro would be sufficient protection against an attack. But he had reckoned without the victor of Assaye. Finding a concealed crossing place and mustering boats and barges, Wellesley rapidly ferried a brigade of infantry and two squadrons of the 14th Light Dragoons to the northern bank. The expected French counter-attack was met and checked by heavy fire from a well-positioned British artillery battery, and Wellesley quickly reinforced success by sending across the river four more battalions, including regiments of the Brigade of Guards, to assault Oporto itself. This was enough for Soult, who withdrew his force, only to find that his main routes east into Spain had been cut by Beresford's outflanking movement. Soult was therefore left with no choice but to withdraw northwards to Galicia over difficult mountainous tracks, leaving all his guns and baggage wagons behind. It was on occasions like this that the Portuguese guerrillas took terrible revenge on straggling or ambushed French soldiers. Castration and crucifixion were not uncommon. Yet three-quarters of Soult's men escaped. Proper pursuit was not possible for Wellesley. He had insufficient cavalry and, as he pointed out to Castlereagh, an army like Soult's without guns or transport could move a good deal faster than one still possessing these indispensable sinews of war. In any event other developments demanded Wellesley's attention. Intelligence had reached him that Marshal Victor was advancing into eastern Portugal. Wellesley therefore ordered a concentration of his army at Abrantes. Thus far he had turned Soult out of Portugal. Now he must turn on Victor. This would mean that the second phase of his strategic design must be embarked upon. The fight would have to be taken to Spain, and this would demand co-operation with the Spanish army.

By the end of June, and with news of the most welcome reinforcements on their way to him – the Light Brigade and the Chestnut Troop of the Royal Horse Artillery – Wellesley was ready to move his 20,000 men into Spain to join General Cuesta's army of 30,000 (if such a mob of badly armed and ill-disciplined men could be called an army). The broad plan was that between them they would engage and eliminate Victor's 23,000 men now *en route* to Talavera. Wellesley was by no means satisfied with either his allied or his own troops, who had fallen into their customary bad habits of plunder. This ever-ready tendency had been aggravated by a shortage of supplies, which was caused by a delay in the arrival of money from England. Soldiers short of food and money were inclined to help themselves, much to the fury of their Commander-in-Chief, who condemned his army as a rabble, which would rapidly disintegrate into disorder and outrageous behaviour even though they had just taken part in a victorious action. But the fact is that action was what the British redcoats were best at. Idleness bred ill discipline. Fortunately some sharp action was shortly in store for them.

By mid-July Wellesley's army, having concentrated at Plasencia, moved on eastwards to join General Cuesta and his motley collection of ill-armed, ill-trained peasants whose principal occupations were chewing garlic, smoking cigarillos and enjoying siestas. Never do today what may be put off until tomorrow, was a fair way to sum up the Spanish attitude to making war, and Wellesley was soon to get a taste of it. For when their joint armies were at Talavera on 21 July and made contact with Victor's outposts, it was plain to Wellesley that an immediate attack – for the Allies had twice as many men as Victor – could overwhelm the enemy. But Cuesta, who was picturesquely labelled by a rifleman as a deformed lump of pride, ignorance and treachery, refused to budge, greatly to Wellesley's annoyance. When Victor moved eastwards towards Madrid, however, Cuesta was unwise enough to set his disorderly gang of troops in pursuit. Pursuers soon became the pursued when Victor, reinforced by the garrison from Madrid and by Sebastiani's corps and now totalling 46,000 men, turned on them and gave battle. Cuesta's men fled back to Talavera and took refuge on the right flank of the defences established there by Wellesley, who now faced some 40,000 French veterans with 20,000 men of his own and some shaky Spanish allies. Happily, however, Wellesley was about to conduct one of his classic defensive battles.

On 28 July 1809 the battle of Talavera took place. It was a pattern to be re-enacted time after time. Victor's army advanced at dawn in the old style, skirmishers ahead, column after column of infantry, cavalry behind ready to exploit success, all being observed by the thin red lines of British foot. Then when the French cannonade began, the redcoats lay down under cover of the crest in front of them and, as the enemy columns appeared, stood up and poured volley after volley into the packed ranks in front of them. The moment the enemy faltered, forward went the redcoats in a bayonet charge. The French were driven back and the first part of the battle was over. In the afternoon their attack was renewed against the British right and centre, and was preceded by another huge bombardment from a battery of eighty guns. There were two dangerous developments for Wellesley – one when his centre was threatened by enemy reserve columns and again when it appeared that his left might be outflanked. The first danger was averted by the British Reserve Brigade, the second by Wellesley releasing two cavalry brigades supported by Spanish horse artillery. The French attack had been decisively checked. Talavera was an unusual battle in that Napoleon's brother, King Joseph, was present and unlike the Emperor was not prepared to risk all on one throw of pitch and toss. He overruled Victor who wished to continue the battle and the French army withdrew. Next day it was clear that although Wellesley had lost 5,000 men, the French losses were half as much again, together with seventeen guns. Moreover Wellesley was now reinforced by the promised Light Brigade under

General (Black Bob) Craufurd. Those famous regiments, the 43rd, 52nd and 95th plus the Chestnut Troop, were a sight for sore eyes. For his victory at Talavera, Wellesley was elevated to the peerage as Viscount Wellington.

Although Wellington had reason to be pleased with the performance of his British soldiers at Talavera, he had even more reason for dissatisfaction with his Spanish allies. His own comments on the battle, which he described as murderous, revealed the measure of his achievement: 'We had about two to one against us; fearful odds; but we maintained our positions and gave the enemy a terrible beating.' He had once again shown that against steady troops and sound generalship, the French reputation for invincibility was a myth.

While the news of Talavera was welcomed at home, there was little cause for general rejoicing there. Austria, as we have seen, had made peace, and the British government, set it seemed on repeating past failures, had sent yet one more expedition to the Low Countries, this time to Walcheren, so that a British army could dither about achieving nothing and then re-embark to return to England. If there was one thing in the field of military affairs which the British Crown and its ministers were good at, it was choosing incompetent, slow-witted and thick-skinned commanders to lead enterprises which required the touch of a Nelson or a Wellington. But in this case George III and his Prime Minister, Portland, excelled themselves. They chose the late William Pitt's elder brother, the Earl of Chatham, who was principally renowned for doing nothing and being unpunctual even about that. The naval commander was Sir Richard Strachan, and between them these two men had 40,000 soldiers and thirty-five ships of the line. The entire force was completely misused. The broad plan had been to capture Antwerp while Napoleon was busy in Austria, but the customary British dithering ensured that the expedition did not even set sail until after Wagram; when it did finally leave, it was not to capture Antwerp – regarded as too risky – but to take Flushing after two weeks besieging it, and then send half the troops home, leaving the other half, because of the poor climate and total lack of medical support, to rot at Walcheren. The well-known ditty about Chatham waiting with sabre drawn for Sir Richard Strachan and Strachan eager to be at 'em, waiting for the Earl of Chatham, is the best thing that came out of it all.

When we consider what use Wellington might have made of these wasted troops, which would have doubled the size of his army, the blunder is greatly multiplied. There was a good deal of gloom in England when, in addition to their failure at Walcheren, it became clear that the aftermath of Talavera was by no means auspicious. Wellington was obliged to retire once more to Portugal, for Napoleon's peace with Austria released more French troops for Spain. But Wellington had also made plain his opinion of the Spanish army with whom he was obliged to co-operate. In writing to his brother, William, he complained that Spanish troops would not fight. They were ill-disciplined, without officers, provisions, ammunition, resources of any sort which meant that if he, Wellington, acted with them, the whole burden of war would fall upon the British and almost inevitably the blame for failure. He was not exaggerating. Although he too had hardly believed all the bad things he had heard about them, he was now sure that no troops were so inefficient. At the same time the Spaniards so hated the French that he thought it impossible for Napoleon ever to establish a government of his in Spain.

By no means discouraged, however, Wellington was determined not to give up the game in the Peninsula, so long as it could be played. The British game, both at sea and in the Peninsula, was in the latter part of 1809 and for more than two years thereafter the only one that was being played against Napoleon. The Continent otherwise was at peace. It was not, however, a very comfortable peace because of the blockade imposed on Europe by the Royal Navy. Never had there been such an illustration of the omnipresence and omnipotence of the British navy. Between 800 and 900 vessels were deployed, including 150 ships of the line. They kept watch on the entire coastline of Europe, and imposed an almost absolute paralysis of trade. Napoleon's determination to continue the fight against England simply caused ever-increasing hardship on the people of France and her satellites. One form of subjugation and misery, exemplified by the *ancien régime*, had been replaced by another, which sprang from Napoleon's own insatiable ambition and will to dominate. Far from uniting Europe in the spirit of a natural desire for freedom, he was alienating the very liberal forces which had presented him with his opportunity in the first place. Arthur Bryant puts his finger on the point when he writes of Napoleon that 'his ultimate legacy to the Continent he dominated was not unity but a romantic and intensely dangerous nationalism'.

It was, of course, in Spain that the British were able to take maximum advantage of this nationalism. Wellington's great merit was that he was able to see the strategic importance of this unquenchable Spanish nationalism. In December 1809 he was writing that the Spanish people were like gunpowder – 'the least spark inflames them; and when inflamed, there is no violence or outrage they do not commit, and nothing can stop their violence'. The Spanish might be undisciplined savages, obeying no law, defying all authority and instantly ready to commit murder, but these very defects when added to the appalling state of their country were such that they lent hope to the result of the contest against the French which he and they were engaged in. Therefore there could be no question of honourably withdrawing from this contest. For Wellington persevered in maintaining that, provided he and his army could continue to be secure in Portugal and the guerrillas could continue to operate in Spain, the game would be kept in play. These two distractions for the French complemented each other. Dispersion of French forces in order to contain guerrilla activity would give him, Wellington, the opportunity to engage and damage some part of their army, yet a total concentration of the French army against his own would permit the guerrillas to operate unchallenged. Yet to make assurance doubly sure, on the withdrawal of his army to Portugal after Talavera, Wellington took the strategically vital step of giving orders that three great defensive lines should be constructed north of Lisbon, the renowned Lines of Torres Vedras. He would leave nothing to chance. Either these defences would be effective in stopping the French, or if they were not, sufficient delay would be imposed on them to give him time to re-embark his army. This measure showed Wellington at his patient and perseverant best. Nothing was too much trouble. He thought, not impulsively only about the present, but with foresight about what might happen next. The rewards for such anticipation and preparation were to be very great. Above all he was resolved to keep the army in being. Therefore transports were to be positioned in the Tagus, ready if the need arose – which he did not for one moment expect – to sail his army away. Moreover, if this latter course were forced upon him, they would go 'like gentlemen out of the hall door'. Wellington's confidence in pursuing his strategy was fortunately shared by members of the government at home. When Perceval succeeded Portland as Prime Minister in 1809, Liverpool became Secretary of State for War and the Colonies and, having complete faith in the strategic value of the Peninsular campaign and Wellington's ability to conduct affairs there, agreed to a request for further reinforcements, in order to bring Wellington's strength of British soldiers up to 30,000. Further powerful support in the Cabinet was to be found in Wellington's brother, the Marquess of Wellesley, who was Foreign Secretary.

In 1810 there was a marked difference between those directing the activities of the French and British armies in the Peninsula. The Emperor Napoleon, having failed to persuade Alexander I to allow him to marry his sister Anna (Napoleon had his marriage to Josephine annulled in December 1809), turned instead to Marie-Louise, Francis II of Austria's eighteen-year-old daughter, whom he married in 1810.[1] This distraction, however, did not interfere with Napoleon's continuing to issue orders – quite unrelated to the military realities – as to what was to be done in Spain. Soult was to conquer Andalusia, a task he set about with his customary thoroughness, while Masséna, greatly against his inclination, was appointed by Napoleon to command the Army of Portugal, and with 70,000 men was ordered by the Emperor to drive Wellington and the English leopards out of Portugal altogether. Masséna, still, as Wellington himself put it, one of the first soldiers in Europe, completely failed in the task given him. This failure was primarily due to the very special conditions prevailing in Spain and Portugal – never understood or appreciated by Napoleon – and to the immensely thorough defensive preparations which Wellington had made against just the situation which then came about.

The special conditions were, as we have seen, exactly those which would most effectively aid the British and hinder the French. The Spanish armies might be crushed and dispersed, their towns might be sacked and burned, their guerrilla commanders tortured and hanged, time and again, yet the fanatical and merciless resistance of the Spanish people went on. Amongst other things this meant that Wellington was kept constantly supplied with intelligence about French troop movements, whereas not only were the French denied comparable infor-

---

[1] When Wellington heard of Napoleon's marriage to Marie-Louise, he called it a terrible event, which would prevent any great changes on the Continent. But characteristically he did not despair of a check sooner or later to the Bonapartist system, which was so 'inconsistent with the wishes, interests and even existence of civilized society'.

mation about the British, but their marshals could not even communicate with one another unless a messenger was escorted by hundreds of cavalry. Thus they had little notion of what the others were up to. No central co-ordination was possible, so that any grand strategic directions from the Emperor, even if they got through, were of no use in producing master plans for a concentrated drive against the British. It was not only intelligence which the French were starved of. There was also the question of supplies – abundant and assured for Wellington's army, precisely the opposite for the French. Before long starvation in a literal sense would be their lot.

Nevertheless Masséna duly arrived at Salamanca in May 1810, with Marshal Ney as his impetuous and brilliant second-in-command. In order to get at Wellington's army in Portugal they had first to capture the two frontier fortresses of Ciudad Rodrigo and Almeida. As they set about doing so, Wellington bent every sinew to delay the enemy as long as possible, both to complete his defensive arrangements further south and to get in the harvest. He succeeded in holding Ciudad Rodrigo until July and Almeida until August, but then it was time to fall back – not at this point all the way to Torres Vedras, but to Bussaco, north of the Coimbra. Here late in September 1810 another display of Wellington's defensive tactics was enacted, the French gallantly pushing forward to take the positions held by the long line of British infantry, then the defending artillery and steady rifle fire taking such toll of the advancing enemy columns that they paused, and were then subjected to a furious bayonet charge by apparently unstoppable men. Especially distinguished and courageous in their actions were the 88th Foot, the famous Connaught Rangers, and Craufurd's Light Infantry, the 43rd and 52nd. Avenging the death of Sir John Moore, 1,800 of these two regiments moved forward just as the French were about to capture the crest of a vital ridge, and poured so deadly a fire into the massed ranks of 6,000 French grenadiers that they were dashed down to the bottom of the ridge again.

Although Wellington had once more fought a successful defensive battle, he knew that he must retire further in order to ensure the integrity of Britain's only army, and so back he went to the Lines of Torres Vedras, with his cavalry and the Rifle Brigade as rearguard, and confident that his knowledge of the country would enable him to take up firm positions in the by now impregnable Torres Vedras defences well before Masséna caught up with him. So closely guarded had the secret of these defences been that Wellington's own army knew nothing of them, let alone the French. When Masséna reached the Lines of Torres Vedras in October, he and his men were flabbergasted. It was not just that he had been told nothing of the elaborate defensive works. His Portuguese guides had informed him that there would be no obstacles south of the Coimbra. The country would be open, rolling and easy to traverse. Now, not merely was he up against complex lines of trenches, earthworks, gun emplacements in great depth, and so sited and mutually supporting that any attack – if it could get past the innumerable defiles, marshes, palisades and parapets – would be exposed to the most appalling and devastating cross-fire, but the whole position was based on a range of mountains. When his Portuguese friends excused themselves by saying they had not known what Wellington had been up to, Masséna could contain his annoyance no longer. '*Que diable, il n'a pas construit ces montagnes!*' he declared bitterly. The highest compliment paid to these defences was from the intrepid Marshal Ney, who took one look and declined to attack them.

It soon became plain that Wellington's Fabian strategy would pay a huge dividend, for Masséna's army, sitting down in front of the Lines of Torres Vedras,[2] was, as one French cavalry officer put it, faced with a terrible dilemma – there was a wall of brass in front of them and a region of famine behind them. Masséna's men suffered enough throughout the winter, but they suffered still more when, after grimly hanging on for more than four months – and only getting enough food by ill-treating the local peasants to such an extent that their hidden supplies were handed over – he ordered the retreat to Spain in March 1811. Although Wellington too had been obliged to retreat – he said once that the mark of a great general was to know when such a move was necessary and to have the courage to do it – on more than one occasion, he had always been careful to arrange for secure lines of communication, defences prepared for occupation, and a proper reserve of supplies. Moreover he was able to enjoy the support of the local people. No such comforts awaited Masséna and his army as they retreated. The whole affair was terrible from start to finish. In his *History of the War in the*

---

[2] 'Masséna is growing old,' said the Emperor, unwilling to admit that the Empire itself was running out of steam.

Peninsula, Sir William Napier uses some extravagant language to describe it. Every conceivable horror accompanied it. It was a tale of death, destruction, starvation, pitiless revenge and cruelty, the wounded untended, the dying left to be set on by dogs driven to such brutishness by their Portuguese masters, baggage mules and asses hamstrung and left helpless to starve, fearful atrocities committed by French soldiers on the natives, including burning women and children in their houses, pointless vandalism, wanton smashing of homes and goods. 'All passions', writes Napier, 'are akin to madness.' But Masséna's army itself paid a terrible price. Although in this instance he was able to fall back on the frontier forts of Almeida and Ciudad Rodrigo, which together with Badajoz the French still held, the passage of his army over the mountains of central Portugal cost him more than a third of his army. When he reached Spain in April 1811, he had lost over 25,000 men and 6,000 horses together with transport, baggage and munitions. Far from obeying Napoleon's order to turn the British out of Portugal, Masséna had himself been out-fought by the British and forced to abandon Portugal and return to Spain, where he was to engage in one more battle – his last – against Wellington.

The task now facing Wellington was that, if he were to take the fight into Spain effectively, he had to capture the three frontier fortresses of Almeida, Badajoz and Ciudad Rodrigo. It was fortunate that at this time the Duke of York, who had been obliged to resign as the army's Commander-in-Chief in 1809 because of his mistress's sale of promotions and other privileges, was reinstated. His continued improvement and simplification of administrative matters removed a great burden from Wellington. Formerly when the inflexible and bureaucratic Dundas had been at the Horse Guards, Wellington was constantly irritated by the ceaseless flow of drivelling letters written to him from there. If he were to deal with them all, he complained to Liverpool, there would be little time left for campaigning. And it was as a field commander that Wellington excelled. He always maintained that the first duty of any commander in the field, no matter at what level, was so to train and care for the men that when they came up against the enemy, they would without question win. He had nothing but contempt for 'croakers' and those who avoided their duty. When one of his brigadiers complained of rheumatism, Wellington instantly snapped at him that no doubt he wished to go to England for a cure and therefore should go immediately.

He was equally scathing when a court martial 'honourably acquitted an officer' of brawling in a brothel, commenting that the mere presence of such a man in a brothel could under no circumstances be regarded as honourable. Although himself a man who enjoyed society and was by no means impartial to the ladies, he could not stand dereliction of duty or shirking of responsibility.

Wellington's own duty now turned towards the investment of Almeida – where he sent the 1st Division under Spencer – and to the problem of capturing Badajoz. While conferring with Beresford, still in command of the Portuguese army, Wellington heard that Masséna had recovered from his appalling defeat, and with a refitted army of 47,000 men, including 5,000 cavalry (of which the British Army was still short) and forty guns, was heading for Almeida to attack the British force investing the fortress there. The outcome was the battle of Fuentes de Oñoro which took place on 11 May 1811. Wellington was never closer to defeat – indeed he commented later that 'if Boney had been there we should have been beaten'. As it was, with their right flank unprotected, the British line was in danger of being outflanked by cavalry, but the magnificent work of Craufurd's Light Division, with what British cavalry and horse artillery there was in support, succeeded in stemming the French advance, while in the centre of Wellington's position there was a desperate fight for the village itself against Masséna's main attack. The British line held and Masséna withdrew, having lost over 2,000 men. Contenting himself with some further manoeuvring and martial displays, he moved his army back to Salamanca. Shortly afterwards he was replaced by Marmont. Masséna, whose two passions were money and women, had much to console himself with when he returned to France. Throughout the campaign he had been accompanied by a charming young mistress, who sported the uniform of a captain of light dragoons. Moreover, before leaving the so-called Army of Portugal, he was able to award himself all the back pay owing to him from cash that had just arrived at Salamanca. The arrival of Marmont, still only thirty-seven, to take command greatly cheered the French army, for Marmont possessed boundless enthusiasm and great organizing ability, gave command of divisions to younger men and generally so raised morale that he was soon ready to take the field once more against Wellington.

Wellington had succeeded in preventing the French relief of Almeida but not, to his great annoyance, the escape of the French garrison there, giving rise to his oft-repeated complaint that unless he were present himself everywhere, things would go wrong. Meanwhile another danger was to be encountered. For Soult was now marching to counter Beresford's efforts to reduce Badajoz, and their two armies clashed in a bloody slogging match at Albuera on 16 May 1811. Wellington was not able to reach the battle in time to take command, but could hardly complain of Beresford's conduct nor of his soldiers. In a seven-hour battle, the British infantry again distinguished itself for sheer refusal to countenance defeat. The casualties were frightful. Soult lost 7,000 men. Of the 6,500 British infantry engaged, two-thirds had fallen, and Soult went so far as to complain that even when the British were defeated, their right turned, their centre pierced, they still did not know how to run. Beresford and his men remained in possession of the battlefield, but his despatch had to be rewritten by Wellington so that it proclaimed a victory rather than a defeat. The scale of casualties, however, was such that losses like this could not be sustained if Wellington were to renew the offensive and pursue his strategy of capturing the frontier fortresses, before hounding the French army out of Spain. Therefore he was forced to retire once more into Portugal, with Almeida still in his possession. He crossed the Agueda to cantonments at Sabugal, but this time Marmont and Soult did not follow. French efforts to conquer Portugal were at an end.

Thus Wellington's campaign of 1811 ended with his army in winter quarters, but with his eye firmly on the need to take Ciudad Rodrigo and Badajoz in the New Year. Until then he could rest his army, build up supplies, demand the indispensable siege-trains for reducing fortresses and plan his next offensive. By the end of the year 1811 he had most of what was needed. From the government at home, he had strong support. The Prince Regent may have been darling of the Whigs, who had hoped for so much when the Regency began, but they were duly disappointed when Prinny stuck to the existing administration. Moreover, the energetic and able Castlereagh was back as Foreign Secretary, replacing Wellesley who had resigned. Castlereagh, like Liverpool, was a staunch friend and supporter of Wellington.

On the other side of the hill, things were a little different. Napoleon might rejoice in the birth of his son and heir in March 1811, and declare himself to be at the summit of his happiness, but although his alliance with Austria had been strengthened by this event, the attitude of Russia was changing. Alexander might have told Talleyrand that no one realized how good Napoleon's character was. But this was hardly a view shared by Talleyrand himself. It had been Talleyrand's influence which had largely persuaded Alexander not to ally himself with Napoleon during the Austrian war of 1809. Nor was this view of the French Emperor held by the Russian hierarchy. The coming year, 1812, would see the differences between the French and Russian Emperors come to a head. However, these circumstances did not discourage Napoleon from interfering in the one theatre of war, Spain, where the Grande Armée was in action in 1811 and the early part of 1812. The marshals in Spain were still privileged to receive unrealistic orders from the Emperor, who persisted in telling Marmont that the British Army could not possibly take the field for months to come – at the very time Wellington was about to do just that and resume his offensive. Marmont himself recorded later that, in the early part of 1812, Napoleon was 'living in a non-existent world, created by his own imagination'. He was making pictures which conformed not to actuality, but to what he, Napoleon, desired should be actuality. And this from a man who in the past had insisted that what mattered in war was clarity and accuracy. General Thiébault, one of Marmont's subordinates, observed that it was impossible to direct a war from a distance of 1,000 miles. Yet this is what Napoleon did! Soon, however, he would be less concerned with sending ridiculous orders to Spain, and he himself once more at the head of the Grande Armée, indulging in the ultimate folly – the march on Moscow. In 1812 the shadows would lengthen inexorably and bring about those conditions which would enable even Napoleon to see that his game was finally going wrong.

CHAPTER 8

1812

Though Napoleon at that time, in 1812, was more convinced than ever that to shed or not to shed the blood of his peoples – *verser ou ne pas verser le sang de ses peuples*, as Alexander expressed it in his last letter to him – depended entirely on his will, he had never been more in the grip of those inevitable laws which compelled him . . . to perform for the world in general – for history – what was destined to be accomplished.

Tolstoy

IF we wanted to repudiate the determinist view of history, we would need to look no further than at the career of Napoleon Bonaparte. For time after time he demonstrated that when his will to dominate was in the ascendant, as it very often was, he could and did bring about events. Perhaps the supreme example was his decision to invade Russia. Although Tolstoy maintained that Napoleon only fancied that he had brought about the war of 1812, other observers, some of them contemporary, take a different view. We may nod at Tolstoy's suggestion that the will of an historical hero is subject to events, while questioning his assertion that this same hero cannot rule the actions of a multitude. We may endorse Tolstoy's observation that there is a difference between the man who says the Grande Armeé marched east because Napoleon ordered it and the man who maintains that this great event occurred because it had to occur. Of course there is a difference. This is not in question. What is in question is which standpoint is more firmly supported by those actually concerned in the event.

Few men were better qualified to contribute a relevant opinion on this matter than Caulaincourt,[1] who was Napoleon's Ambassador at St Petersburg from 1807 to 1811. On his return to France he conversed with the Emperor for five hours about the Czar's attitude to war and peace. He told Napoleon that Alexander I did not want war, but was understandably concerned about hostile troop concentrations in Danzig and Prussia. He further said – although in this he was mistaken – that Russia had not breached the Continental System, which had been agreed at Tilsit and was designed to cripple Great Britain by preventing trade with her. Caulaincourt went so far as to remind his master that he himself had authorized French merchant vessels to trade with England. He concluded by urging Napoleon to maintain the Russian alliance, reiterating that Alexander did not wish to make war on France, yet adding the Czar's prescient warning that if it came to war, it would not be a short one. He, Alexander, while not being the first to draw his sword, would certainly be the last to sheath it. Space, the infinite space at his command, was a barrier. The Russian climate, the Russian winter, would fight on his side. It was, therefore, for Napoleon himself to decide between peace or war, and Caulaincourt beseeched the Emperor in choosing his course to bear in mind not only his own welfare, but that of France. For all the good it did, he might just as well have remained silent.

That this was so became clear two months later in August 1811, when Napoleon held a reception at the Tuileries to celebrate his forty-second birthday. Of all inopportune occasions, Napoleon chose this one to vent his grievances about the Czar's behaviour to the Russian Ambassador. What is more, as is often the way with powerful men who convince themselves that their wishes are being thwarted, he did so with raised voice and violent words. He complained that Russia was conducting two-way trade with England, that they had laid heavy duties on French imports, that Russian troops were menacing peace, that the Czar was putting an end to their alliance. He, Napoleon, did not want war, but if obliged to make war, he would win. He had 800,000 troops at his command. Besides, he always had won. Where was Alexander to get allies? Not Austria, 'from whom you have seized 300,000 souls in

---

[1] General Armand Augustin Louis Marquis de Caulaincourt, Duke of Vicenza (1772–1827) accompanied Napoleon on the Russian campaign. One of the Emperor's most devoted followers, he was later Minister for Foreign Affairs.

Galicia' – in fact Napoleon had given Alexander part of this Austrian province in recognition of Russia's supposed, but insubstantial, assistance in France's 1809 campaign against Austria. Certainly not Prussia, soundly defeated by Napoleon in 1806 and whose King, Frederick William III, was in total awe of Napoleon. Nor Sweden, argued Napoleon, with the former humiliation of having Finland stolen from her by Russia to avenge. Here, of course, Napoleon miscalculated for one of his own marshals, Bernadotte,[2] had been adopted by the Swedish King, Charles XIII, as his heir, and had his own ideas about restraining Napoleon's power. Nevertheless, Napoleon concluded his outburst by assuring the Russian Ambassador, Prince Kurakin, that 'the entire Continent will be against you'.

While we may deprecate Napoleon's bullying methods, it must be acknowledged that he had cause for anger at Alexander's shilly-shallying. The Czar was torn between his inclination to remain on friendly terms with Napoleon and his realization that such friendship, involving as it did the acceptance of certain liberal principles, would be incompatible with his continuing to be the Czar. The Russian nobles were understandably concerned that Napoleon's establishment of the Civil Code in the Grand Duchy of Warsaw introduced such dangerous ideas as political rights for all races and freedom for serfs. What effect the proximity of these liberal ideas might have on Russia's own countless serfs was hardly to be thought of, and the nobles made it plain that unless Alexander changed his ways, he would end up like his father – strangled to death. Alexander did change his ways. After toying with the idea of seizing Poland, he demanded from Napoleon a large part of the Grand Duchy of Warsaw. It was now becoming clear to Napoleon that the Czar, far from being content to remain a kind of secondary planet subordinate to his own all-powerful sun, was intent on expanding his empire at the expense of France and her allies. Towards the end of 1811, therefore, Napoleon began to put in train preparations for a great expedition. He confided in the Minister for War, de Cessac, that the army would be covering long distances and operating in several directions. The whole thing would start by crossing the River Niemen, the

[2] Jean-Baptiste Jules Bernadotte (1764–1844) became Crown Prince of Sweden in 1810 and Charles XIV in 1818.

frontier with Russia. Thus Napoleon chose war before even investigating the chances of peace.

In the months that followed both Napoleon and Alexander sought to conclude alliances. Prussia agreed to supply the Grande Armée with supplies and a corps of 20,000 men. Metternich, the Austrian Chancellor, as was his custom, made assurance doubly sure by promising Napoleon the support of 30,000 men on the right wing, while confiding to Alexander that this Austrian army would not advance very far or fast. While Napoleon had therefore gained some security for his centre, Alexander, by concluding treaties with both Sweden to the north and Turkey to the south, had thrown some doubt about what might happen on the flanks. By the spring of 1812 it became clear that nothing would induce the French Emperor to drop his plan. Caulaincourt returned to the charge, pointing out the dangerous situation in Spain; questioning why it was that such huge concentrations of troops were assembling in Prussia and Poland – if, as he maintained, Napoleon did not seek war with Russia; arguing that France's frontiers were far too widely spread already, that to extend them still further to gratify his obsession with conquest could only end in disaster; maintaining that the one thing which would satisfy England would be a return to a Europe of states within reasonable boundaries. Napoleon brushed all this sound advice aside, even claiming that as Russia was set on war, he must strike first. Even a last-minute proposal by the Czar to conform to the Tilsit agreement about the Continental System – provided Napoleon honoured his undertaking in that agreement to withdraw from Prussia – was also brushed aside. On 9 May 1812 Napoleon set out for Dresden.

About a month later, while having dinner in Danzig with three of his comrades in arms – Berthier, Chief of Staff, Murat, Commander of the Reserve Cavalry, and Colonel Rapp, aide-de-camp – the Emperor asked how many leagues they were now from Cadiz. It was a pertinent question, for while the Grande Armée was about to launch itself into a perilous adventure, the game was going badly wrong for another French army in the Peninsula. Rapp's reply was also pertinent: 'Too many, Sire.'

While Napoleon is preparing to invade Russia, Wellington has been setting the scene for his last but one entry into Spain. On the first day of 1812, despite the bitter cold, he set his army on the road to Ciudad Rodrigo, and within a week had invested the fortress. During the night of 8 January several hundred soldiers of the élite Light Division under the command of Colonel Colborne mounted so silent and swift an attack on the San Francisco redoubt that it fell into their hands before the French defenders had fully understood that something was up. The next step, which Wellington instantly took, for he had intelligence that Marmont was intending to send a relieving force, was to dig entrenchments for the main assault and to bombard the fortress defences with such effect that two breaches were made. The very next night, 9 January, two of his most renowned divisions led the assault itself – Thomas Picton's 3rd Division and the Light Division under Robert Craufurd. The men of both divisions behaved magnificently during the fighting, and some of both were guilty of gross ill discipline and drunkenness after the town was taken.

It was no small matter to be a member of the leading assault parties, who would have to face enemy shells, grapeshot, canister and bullets, and the expression on the faces of the Light Division soldiers told its tale to one who observed them marching by on their way to attack. There was 'an indescribable *something* about them', he noted. It was as if they knew how desperate and serious an undertaking they were to be entrusted with, and the quiet resolution of their demeanour, or the friendly greeting called out to comrades as they passed, seemed to confirm this. No less determined were the men of Picton's division, who with grim enthusiasm endorsed his declared intention not to waste powder, but to do their part of the business with cold steel. These manifestations of courage and devotion to duty were more than confirmed when the assault itself took place, despite the suffering endured by the storming parties as they met a hail of shot and shell. Their commanding generals, who in those days led from the front, set a fine example. Craufurd, the incomparable Black Bob, was killed when the Light Division advanced, and General Mackinnon, who was directing the 3rd Division's assault, was also killed by the explosion of a French magazine. Yet within half an hour of the attack going in, the thing was done, and the Governor of Ciudad Rodrigo surrendered the town to an officer of the Light Division. It was then that the inhabitants of the town were subjected to the uncontrollable fury of British redcoats on the rampage for loot, drink and women. It is perhaps no surprise that after the frenzied excitement of battle, seeing their comrades blown to pieces, suffering still from the shock of 'seeking the bubble reputation even in the cannon's mouth', bloodstained, scorched, half-mad with thirst, and exulting in their hard-won victory, they should have turned to sacking the town completely. For the whole of that night they ran wildly from house to house, pillaging, burning, destroying, terrifying the inhabitants, slaking their thirst and lust in such fury that neither their own officers nor the provost marshals were able to restore order until the next day. It was utterly deplorable, and worse was soon to come, but from Wellington's point of view, the important thing was that the second of the three key frontier fortresses was in his hands. Now he could set his sights on what would be the hardest nut of all to crack – Badajoz!

Badajoz was, like another of his battles, a close-run thing. So desperate was the fighting and so grievous the losses that on the morning after the attack, so moved was Wellington by the sight of the innumerable dead that he actually wept. Sir Thomas Picton, whose 3rd Division had once more distinguished itself by successfully breaching the defences at a time when Wellington was about to call off the assault, was amazed by the sight of his Commander-in-Chief absolutely biting back the tears when he came to congratulate him on the capture of Badajoz. Wellington was obliged to hide his emotion by falling to swearing and cursing the government for not providing the sappers and miners who were so badly needed to breach the defences more effectively and so ease the task of his brave soldiers. For although from time to time he would utter cutting comments on both officer and private soldier alike, in reality he was now commanding an army of rare quality, whose contradictory elements somehow enabled its men to rise to extraordinary heights of heroic gallantry and sheer doggedness, and then, after bringing off well-nigh impossible feats, descend uncontrollably into the very depth of depraved bestiality. These men, whom Wellington once described as the mere scum of the earth, enlisted for drink, had become hardened by four years' campaigning, were skilled fighters and, like all British soldiers throughout the centuries, individually eccentric. Eager for a fight, full of strange oaths, scroungers *par excellence*, unstoppable in their craving for liquor, bronzed and tough, yet touchingly soft-hearted when it came to a wounded comrade or 'an enemy soldier', even to ill-treated peasants or animals. United in their cheerful contempt for the French, Johnny Crapaud, and confident in their absolute superiority over him, they were also fiercely proud of their own regiment and, despite the treatment they received from England, their own country. In the desperate excitement of battle, their cool musketry and headlong rush upon the enemy with the bayonet would be accompanied by patriotic hurrahs, and cheers for Old England. In all their almost insolent independence of spirit, they were wonderfully well supported by the calibre of their regimental officers who were brave, honourable, dedicated soldiers, Hotspur-like in their scorn for the malingerer, putting duty, loyalty and service first, with a care for their men and a joke on their lips, and whose principal concern was to follow Polonius's advice to Laertes – to be true to themselves, never to disgrace the regiment or let down their comrades. They were a band of brothers in the pattern of Prince Hal or Nelson's Captains. No wonder that this team of rough, jesting, pillaging, hard and quietly confident soldiers, officered, as Wellington himself put it, by gentlemen 'who have something more at stake than a reputation for military smartness', was so formidable in action.

At the head of this remarkable army, its Commander-in-Chief was shortly to bring off one of the most successful offensive coups of his career. But first he had to take Badajoz. And it was there that his confidence in the army, despite its shortcomings, was wholly vindicated. Wellington never fell into the error of underestimating his problems. Although well served by subordinate generals, he was determined to keep the reins of command in his own hands. Despite this resolution, his instructions were not always carried out, and when he comments on this deficiency to the Military Secretary, Colonel Torrens, we may note an agreeable irony in some of his despatches. In the same way that he referred to a village as not having been greatly improved by having a battle fought over it, so he says that no one in the British Army would ever read one of his orders or regulations except as an entertaining novel. When some complicated arrangement or manoeuvre was to be executed, therefore, and everyone involved in it simply pleased himself, it was hardly surprising that things went wrong. Then they all came to him to set it right again, and so his work was greatly augmented. Wellington also made the point – one which all of us who have been in command of troops would wholly endorse – that it was not enough to give good clear orders; you had also to ensure by your own personal activity and presence that they were obeyed to the letter. That this did not always occur roused Wellington to another of his playfully ironic observations when he tells the British Minister at Lisbon that the foundation of all military ventures is composed of what one's own troops and those of both allies and the enemy are up to, and if it were impossible to be sure of even what his own troops were doing it would be unlikely for him to be able to formulate, still less carry out, any military plan. Yet the actual regiments with which he did both make plans and execute them were such that time after time – whether under his command or someone else's – they indelibly marked out Britain's glorious record on innumerable battlefields. These regiments included the green-jacketed 95th Rifles, their red-coated comrades of Light Infantry, the 43rd and 52nd, together with the majestic and incomparable Foot Guards, the Fusilier regiments, the kilted Highlanders, the Diehards, the Buffs, the roistering Irish regiments – indeed all the infantry of the line, backbone of Wellington's army, of which he was later to say that with them he could have gone anywhere and done anything.

Now on 6 April 1812 the Light Division and the 4th Division were required to storm the south-eastern breaches of Badajoz, while the 5th Division under Leith was to make a demonstration to the north-west of the fortress and attempt to capture the San Vincente bastion. At the same time Picton's 3rd Division would make an attempt on the castle to the city's north. It was a terrible business, and one soldier who was there wrote later of hundreds falling as the defenders discharged their deadly shot, losses which both maddened those behind and somehow inspired them to deeds of great fury and vengeance as, making bridges of the dead bodies in front of them, they stormed forward in their determination to take the town. 'Slaughter, tumult and disorder' prevailed. It was impossible to hear the words of command, as the officers somehow led and urged their men forward, and the French guns fired again and again tearing bloody lanes through the assaulting British infantry. For three hours the main assaults continued – and failed. At midnight Wellington, shaken by the losses, called off the assault. But even as he was giving orders to this effect, unknown to him, the other attempts by Picton and Leith were succeeding. In the north, men of the 3rd Division had scaled the cliffs and captured the castle, but at a terrible price for one-third of the 3rd Division's attacking infantry was lost, among them the noble and gallant Colonel Ridge, Commanding 5th Fusiliers. William Napier wrote of him that, during a night when many men died with much glory, no man died with more glory than he. It was not only Picton's division which triumphed. Leith's 5th Division had also entered the city by taking the San Vincente bastion and followed up with such numbers that the French garrison surrendered. Badajoz was then subjected to the same fiendish sack as Ciudad Rodrigo, an unspeakable ordeal of murder, rape, plunder and drunkenness, which went on for two days and nights before Wellington sent in fresh troops and, with gallows erected, set about the task of restoring order.

His losses had been grievous: 5,000 men, of whom about two-thirds were from his precious Light and 4th Division, some of the best troops he had. In his despatch to Lord Liverpool (shortly to become Prime Minister, after Perceval's assassination), Wellington made known his feelings and his urgent need of special siege troops: 'The capture of Badajoz affords as strong an instance of the gallantry of our troops as has ever been displayed, but I anxiously hope that I shall never again be the instrument of putting them to such a test as they were in last night . . . When I ordered the assault I was certain I should lose our best officers and men. It is a cruel situation for any person to be placed in, and I earnestly recommend to Your Lordship to have a corps of sappers and miners formed without loss of time.' Strategically, the position was now greatly altered in Wellington's favour. With the key fortresses of western Spain in his hands, he at last held the initiative and could advance against Marmont or Soult as he chose. Moreover he had cut direct communications between the two French marshals by sending Hill to seize Almarez. Yet the total number of French troops in the Peninsula – some 250,000 – was still more than three times that at Wellington's disposal, with about 45,000 British and 25,000 Portuguese. Wellington would soon be across the frontier and into Spain, yet Napoleon, refusing to acknowledge the danger developing in the south, was still intent on eliminating Russia.

On 18 May 1812, while Wellington is planning to destroy Marmont's army and Napoleon is at Dresden, Alexander I is granting an audience to one of Napoleon's aides-de-camp, Count Narbonne. He gave that emissary a stern warning. First he asked what it was Napoleon wanted. If Napoleon wanted to get Alexander on to his side in order to impose ruinous conditions on the Russian people, and if when Alexander refused to comply Napoleon made war on him, believing that after he had won a few victories and occupied several provinces then Alexander would sue for peace and agree to Napoleon's own terms, then he would be disappointed. Alexander thereupon predicted with uncanny accuracy the course of things to come: 'I am convinced that Napoleon is the greatest general in Europe, his armies are the best trained, his lieutenants the most courageous and experienced. But' – and here the Czar indicated a huge map which he had unrolled – 'space is a barrier, and if, after several defeats, I withdraw, sweeping the inhabitants along with me, if I let time, deserts and climate defend Russia for me, then perhaps I shall have the last word.' In short, Alexander was saying again what he had said to Caulaincourt before, and again – for all the effect it had on Napoleon when Count Narbonne reported back to the Emperor at Dresden – he might as well have not said it at all. Napoleon simply observed that there was no more time to be lost in fruitless negotiations. From then on the pace accelerated. At Danzig early in June, Napoleon was joined by Murat and Davout; further administrative preparations were made and he inspected the assembled troops. It was during the time before the invasion actually began that Napoleon made the sort of mistake that Wellington would never have made. He allowed his armies to ravage the very country where lived the people of his allies, Prussia and Poland, and so built up such hostility that when later he needed reinforcements from them, they were not forthcoming. Another great contrast between the respective 1812 campaigns of Napoleon and Wellington was, of course, the sheer scale of each – both in numbers and distance. When Napoleon arrived at the Russian frontier on 23 June, he was 1,200 miles from Paris. At Badajoz Wellington was little more than 100 miles from Lisbon. Under Napoleon's command was an army of 675,000 men, of whom 500,000 accompanied him into Russia. Wellington's army of British and Portuguese together was a mere 70,000, only just more than a tenth of the Grande Armée. But whereas Wellington husbanded his army, Napoleon squandered his. The squandering had begun long before any fighting took place. When Mortier, who together with Bessières commanded the Imperial Guard, reached Vilna he wrote in a letter home that between the Niemen and Vilna, he had seen nothing but ruined villages and abandoned wagons and equipment. 10,000 horses had perished because of the cold, wet weather and unripened corn. The stench of these dead horses was appalling. It was not only forage that was in short supply, however. There were not enough rations for the soldiers and some of Mortier's Young Guard were already dead from starvation.

Having crossed the frontier on 24 June 1812, Napoleon had taken only four days to reach Vilna, some seventy miles from the Niemen, and he then dallied there for eighteen days, far too long, for up to this time he had achieved nothing. Alexander's First Army, commanded by Barclay de Tolly, had simply retreated in his path, and already, as Mortier made plain, the heavy cost of advancing into such inhospitable country was becoming clear. Conditions for horses and men could hardly have been worse. A combination of poor roads, thunderstorms, mud, mingled with oppressive heat, choking dust, insect bites, lack of forage, bread and fresh water – all these took their toll. Loss of horses further aggravated the problem of bringing up supply wagons and guns. Nevertheless, having arrived at Vilna, Napoleon planned his strategic moves in a way which he thought would enable him to destroy in detail the enemy armies facing him. First with the main body he would defeat Barclay's army at Drissa to the north-east, and at the same time he would send Davout's corps, supported by Jerome's corps with Poniatowski's Poles, to the south-east to cut off and eliminate Bagration's Second Army. The whole of Napoleon's strategy was based on the notion that the two Russian armies would not be able to link up. Yet this is exactly what they did – at Smolensk. The French Emperor was again 'making pictures', living in a world created solely by his own imagination and wishes. Yet there was no shortage of evidence that the Russians would *not* conform to his ideas of what was going to happen.

He had been at Vilna only two days when on 30 June he received an emissary from the Czar – Balashov, Minister of Police. Balashov had brought with him a letter from the Czar:

Monsieur mon frère. I heard yesterday that in spite of the loyalty with which I have kept faith with your majesty, your troops have invaded Russia. If Your Majesty is not determined to spill the blood of our people in an unnecessary war and will withdraw, I will regard this event as something that has not happened, and we can come to terms. If not, I shall be obliged to resist an attack which I have done nothing to provoke. It rests with Your Majesty to prevent the calamity of another war.

Even at this stage therefore Napoleon *could* have come to terms with Alexander. But it was not in his nature to withdraw voluntarily. It would not be long before he had no choice between withdrawal or total disaster.

In *War and Peace*, Tolstoy gives us a memorable picture of how the French Emperor appeared to Balashov. Having just finished getting dressed for his ride, he was wearing a blue uniform coat, which opened in front to reveal a long white waistcoat, covering his round stomach. His doeskin breeches tightly enclosed fat thighs and short legs; his feet were encased in Hessian boots. Short hair was neatly brushed with the familiar lock in the centre of a broad forehead. The black collar of his coat emphasized the whiteness and plumpness of his neck. Napoleon was not quite forty-three, his full face still looked youthful, with its conspicuous chin, and at the outset of the audience he wore an expression of welcoming benevolence.

The benevolence, however, did not last long once Napoleon heard that Balashov had nothing to add to what was in the Czar's letter. When it became clear that Alexander demanded the withdrawal of the French army beyond the Niemen, before he, Alexander, would enter into negotiation, Napoleon, like other men of great ability and will-power who suddenly discover that these qualities are insufficient to gain their objectives, began to shout. Alexander must be joking. Did the Czar imagine that he, Napoleon, had advanced all the way to Vilna to trade treaties? No, he had come to finish the thing off. The Russians would be pushed back so far that for the next twenty-five years, they would be unable to have any influence on what was happening in civilized Europe. Even if offered St Petersburg and Moscow, he would not accept the Czar's conditions. Indeed he would himself dictate peace terms in Moscow. What hope had Russia of resisting him? His army was three times the size of Alexander's. When Balashov told Napoleon that the Russians would fight a terrible war and, despite the apparent odds against them, would do what they could, the French Emperor's tirade continued. He, Napoleon, was accused of starting the war, yet it was Alexander who had first joined his army. Why had Russia formed an alliance with England? What good could it bring Russia? The British were practically on their knees already. Besides, the Czar's generals were incompetent. Barclay had done nothing, Bagration was stupid, even though he had some experience. As for Alexander himself, no sovereign should be with an army unless he were also a general. And so it went on. Balashov was hardly able to get a word in. But Napoleon did at least ask Balashov to dine with him, pinched his ear – a special mark of favour – and even sent the envoy off with some of his own horses to take a letter to the

Czar. Before long the war began in earnest. Fortunately for the Russian army, before it did, Alexander was persuaded by his senior commanders – Balashov was in fact their spokesman – to give up his supposed role as supreme commander (he knew nothing of strategy or command in the field), and return to Moscow, where – and in St Petersburg – he could assume his proper duties of leading the nation itself. On 14 July he handed over command of his army to Barclay at Drissa, making it plain to the general that he entrusted the army to him and charging him not to forget, indeed always to bear in mind, that it was the only army he had. To Barclay this meant that if continuous retreat were necessary to keep the army in being, then continuous retreat it would be.

It was a strategy of which Wellington would have approved, although at this time, July 1812, Wellington himself was not thinking in terms of retreat. On the contrary, he was very much on the offensive. Eleven days before Napoleon invaded Russia, on 13 June 1812, he had crossed the Agueda with just over 50,000 men, of whom about 30,000 were British, the rest Portuguese and Spanish. Marmont, whose army was dispersed, had no alternative but to retire, and four days later the British army entered Salamanca to an ecstatic welcome by the people there. Wellington himself was mobbed by a group of admiring females – the sort of treatment no discerning soldier objects to. There then followed a good deal of manoeuvring by both armies either side of the Douro. Marmont attempted to threaten the British lines of communication with their bases in Portugal, while Wellington contemplated yet one more withdrawal unless he could be sure of winning a decisive victory. Yet it was then, on 22 July 1812, that Wellington – whose battles up to this time had been largely defensive, infantry ones – showed that, given the opportunity, he could be quick and bold in an offensive operation and make devastating use of cavalry. Although not always complimentary about the behaviour of British cavalry, and with some justification for their courageous impetuosity often landed them in trouble through sheer lack of discipline and control, Wellington was fortunate at the time in having a Heavy Cavalry Brigade commanded by someone who knew what he was doing – Major-General Le Marchant. Although Wellington had always maintained that he would never risk Britain's only army in a major engagement which might put him at a disadvantage, he was constantly on the look-out for an opportunity which would enable him to exploit the disadvantage of an adversary. Herein lay the principal contrast of his own generalship and that of Napoleon – comprehensible, of course, when we appreciate the difference in numbers which each had at his disposal. Napoleon could afford to be a spendthrift, Wellington could not. Napoleon would very often engage the enemy without any very clear idea of how many of them there were, or what they were up to – and then rely on his own versatility and speed, together with the courage and experience of his soldiers, to pull him through. Wellington preferred to be more circumspect – to prepare for every eventuality and then when the balance of odds appeared to be in his favour either to stand in order to defeat attack, or to attack in order to exploit an enemy's faulty dispositions. At Salamanca he did the second of these two.

During the afternoon of 22 July 1812 Marmont, while he and Wellington were manoeuvring their armies south-east of Salamanca, attempted to envelop the British right, and in doing so greatly extended the gap between his left wing and his centre. This was enough for Wellington, who on seeing it flung away the piece of chicken he was eating, despatched ADCs with orders, and himself galloped 3 miles to where his brother-in-law, Edward Pakenham, was in reserve with the 3rd Division. Wellington instantly ordered Pakenham to move forward, take the heights in front of him and drive the enemy away. The battle of Salamanca, which Wellington himself regarded as one of his greatest victories, was a classic model of what an army which is balanced, concentrated, manoeuvrable and wholly under the hand of its commander can achieve against one which is none of these things, but on the contrary off balance, dispersed and unresponsive to orders for rapid redeployment. Marmont's army was moving in a huge semicircular column spread out over a front of some 5 miles in the vain hope of encircling Wellington's force, which because of its concealment allowed Marmont no inkling of either how powerful or compact the British force was. Thus in presenting his right unprotected flank to Wellington, Marmont gave him a perfect opportunity to bring superior numbers to bear on the French not just in one place, but in several.

Pakenham's 3rd Division supported by Portuguese cavalry was the first to engage the enemy, when, emerging from their undetected advance through woods, they fell on the strung-out advance guard of Thomière's division like a thunderbolt. Thomière lost half his division, his own life and all his guns. Further east, where Wellington was in personal command of the main body, his 4th and 5th Divisions were moving against the French centre, and at this moment Marmont, who had realized far too late that Wellington was not after all the cautious, defensive general he had supposed, desperately trying to retrieve an irretrievable situation, was wounded by a shell, and removed from the field. Clausel took over command. The next blow to the French was a double one. First the fire-power of Wellington's 4th and 5th Divisions shattered Maucune's infantry, and this was instantly followed by a brilliant charge from Le Marchant's heavy cavalry including the 4th[3] and 5th Dragoons, which not only cut to pieces Maucune's flying remnants, but also drove into Brennier's division following up behind Maucune. Wellington, usually chary of praising the cavalry, told Cotton, the senior cavalry commander, that he had never seen anything so beautiful in his life. By this time almost a third of Marmont's army had been eliminated. Although Clausel tried with his own division and Bonnet's to rescue something from the battle by attacking the ridge from which Wellington had launched his assault, the French were countered by three further British divisions, the 1st, 6th and 7th, which Wellington had positioned in reserve. The best part played by the French in the whole affair was the action of its rearguard which successfully covered the escape of the withdrawing French army. Had one of Wellington's Spanish officers obeyed his orders to guard the crossing of the Tormes Alba, it may be doubted whether the French would have got away at all. But not only did he abandon his position at Alba Castle, he even neglected to inform the Commander-in-Chief that he had done so. Thus was the chance of absolutely annihilating the French thrown away. But it was nevertheless a famous victory.

Wellington's own part in it had been crucial. His coolness, his precise orders, his presence wherever it was needed, his total *grip* of the battle ensured its triumph. Pakenham, his brother-in-law, concerned about the way in which his chief was utterly regardless of his own safety – and indeed Wellington was hit by a spent bullet during the action – added that never were his energy or clarity more marked. Napier, at the time commanding that splendid regiment of Light Infantry, the 43rd, noted that at the realization of victory, Wellington still spoke calmly and quietly, but his eyes were full of alertness and anticipation.

---

[3] The author's Regiment.

It was no mean achievement to have inflicted 15,000 casualties on Marmont's army, to have captured two eagles, twenty guns and 7,000 prisoners. One of the French divisional commanders there, Foy, commented that, although they knew all about Wellington's prudent defensive tactics, at Salamanca he had shown himself to be a master of manoeuvre, winning a battle 'in the style of Frederick the Great'. Wellington's own despatch to Bathurst, Secretary of State for War, hoped that at home they would be pleased for 'there was no mistake; everything went on as it ought, and there was never an army so beaten in so short a time. If we had had another hour or two of daylight, not a man would have passed the Tormes. And, as it was, they would all have been taken if Don Carlos de España had left the garrison in Alba de Tormes as I wished and desired, or having taken it away (as I believe before he was aware of my wishes), he had informed me that it was not there.' More than thirty years later, on 8 November 1843 in conversation with Stanhope, the Great Duke recalled the affair, and according to Stanhope recollected in particular the irresponsible behaviour of Don Carlos d'Espagne. During the battle, the Duke told him, Don Carlos came to ask whether the fort in Alba de Tormes ought not to be evacuated. In spite of a decided negative from the Duke, Don Carlos without informing Wellington, in other words in direct contradiction of the Duke's wishes, sent orders to the officer commanding the garrison at the fort to quit it. 'Had he only told me,' the Duke added to Stanhope 'it would not have signified.' Wellington also mentioned that Lord Combermere (at the time of Salamanca, General Cotton) was wounded by a British sentry on returning from a reconnoitring patrol – the sort of accident which has repeated itself all too often in innumerable wars. After his Salamanca victory, Wellington advanced on Madrid, entering the city – Napoleon's brother, King Joseph, had left for Valencia – on 12 August 1812 to a tumultuously joyous welcome.

While Wellington is being fêted in the Spanish capital, Napoleon is driving his doomed army ever deeper into Russia. No fewer than ten of those who were already or were to become marshals accompanied the Emperor for this campaign, and none of them thought much of it. They would not have revised this view if they had heard Napoleon while still dallying at Vilna in conversation with Jomini and others making some pretence of planning a prolonged stay in Russia. Mortier and Bessières were there, as already noted, Berthier, who hated the whole thing, Davout and Oudinot, Victor, St Cyr, Murat, Macdonald, and, of course, Ney who won immortal fame commanding the rearguard during the retreat, who was made Prince of the Moskowa and of whom Napoleon said that he would rather have given 300 million from his treasury than have lost him. It was Ney who commanded the leading troops when the Grande Armée smashed its way into Smolensk on 18 August 1812, for, before leaving Vilna on 16 July, Napoleon had half-jestingly told his staff that if Barclay thought that he, Napoleon, was going to chase Barclay's army all the way to the Volga, he would find himself mistaken. On the contrary, he intended to go as far as Smolensk, fight a good battle there, and then go into winter quarters. The Emperor himself would then return to Vilna, spend the winter there with opera companies and actors from Paris, and, short of making peace during the winter, finish the job the following May. Of course, it was all talk, intended for Barclay's ears to deceive him. In fact Napoleon hoped for and expected a battle between Vilna and Smolensk. He very nearly got one. The conditions during his advance from Vilna to Vitebsk continued to take heavy toll of his army, particularly the cavalry. The advance from Vilna to Vitebsk was made under conditions which demanded the sort of thorough planning and meticulous administrative arrangement which Wellington had been accustomed to ensure in India and in the Peninsula. In the midsummer heat and storms of Russia, men and horses suffered alike. The discipline of the soldiers, choked by dust or soaked by marching through swamps, was severely strained and often broke. For the horses it was even worse for by day they were covered in sweat, their furniture then causing terrible sores, which in the cold wet nights became so painful that they would break free from the horse lines and gallop frantically away. Murat's Chief of Staff made it clear to the Emperor that he was destroying the cavalry. There was never enough forage. The forced marches were too long and too exhausting. You could not ask cavalry to go into action – even for reconnoitring purposes, let alone the charge – with dangerously weakened and starving mounts. The supply situation, on which everything else depended, was hopelessly inadequate. Wellington would have ensured that there were enough bullocks, cattle, wagons, drivers, forage and food for all. Napoleon not only did not provide these indispensable sinews of war. He refused to admit even when reminiscing about the campaign years later that he had been at fault. A further 8,000 horses died on the march from Vilna to Vitebsk together with untold numbers of cattle. Caulaincourt, who had tried to dissuade the Emperor from embarking on the campaign in the first place, ascribed all the French army's initial disasters to this utter failure of the commissariat.

The Russian army's withdrawal was not the first example of a so-called scorched-earth policy. It had occurred throughout the history of war. But it was clear enough that the Russians would leave nothing to their enemies. Indeed very often there was nothing to leave, for although Barclay's troops were able to fall back on depots, stocked with food, forage, water and ammunition, on the march itself their supply system was just as useless as the French one. This was not the only sense in which there was a similarity between the two armies. The Russians were as good at looting villages and terrorizing peasants into revealing hidden food stocks as their enemies. Napoleon hailed Barclay's abandonment of the fortifications at Drissa as an illustration of Russian degeneracy, and he urged his Chief of Staff, Berthier, and his marshals to make a renewed effort to engage and defeat Barclay's army. There was a short, sharp engagement west of Vitebsk on the River Dvina on 25 July. But Barclay then withdrew further and with his 80,000-strong force occupied a plateau near Vitebsk. It seemed for a time as if he would stand and make a fight of it there. On 27 July Napoleon made the appropriate reconnaissances and rested his troops for a battle on the morrow, yet that night Barclay again silently crept away, no doubt concerned that with the numbers he had at his disposal – and with no prospect of linking up with Bagration, who could not join him as Davout and his corps were preventing a movement north – a pitched battle could end only in his destruction. So Napoleon entered Vitebsk with the main body of his army, still without having brought the Russian army to battle, and there he spent a further two weeks, fruitlessly debating what strategy to adopt, while in the north Macdonald had advanced to Riga, an operation which had as little effect on the main strategic issue in the centre, as had that of Schwarzenberg and Reynier who with their Austrian and Saxon corps were arguing the toss with Tormassov's Third Army hundreds of miles to the south beyond the Pripet Marsh. Davout meanwhile was pushing Bagration and his Second Army further east where he was to join Barclay at Smolensk. There was little love lost between these latter two; Bagration detested Barclay for the simple reason that, although Barclay was junior to Bagration in the service, yet he, Barclay, a foreigner at that, would be in overall command once their two armies did unite.

But Napoleon at Vitebsk, while assuring his subordinates that they would not repeat Charles XII's folly,[4] was wavering between either pushing on to Smolensk, winning a battle, entering Moscow and dictating peace there, or wintering his army where it was, resting and replenishing it, then renewing his offensive in the following year. But this latter course was entirely foreign to his nature, his longing for action. His advisers were divided. Berthier and Caulaincourt were all for staying put; the fiery Murat advocated a further advance. When Napoleon's quarter-master-general even questioned the whole purpose of the campaign, pointing out that the entire army did not understand either its purpose or its need, and warning that further advance would simply exacerbate an already critical supply problem, Napoleon made up his mind. They would push on to Smolensk and fight a decisive battle there which would finish the whole thing off. On 11 August the Grande Armée left Vitebsk. Two weeks before this Barclay and Bagration together with their armies, now mustering some 125,000, had joined together. The two generals then accused one another of the very faults each himself was guilty of – abandoning strategically important cities without engaging the enemy at all. It was therefore unlikely that two such dubious candidates for hitting upon a sound and achievable strategic plan should do so. The question was: should they sally forth and challenge Napoleon's advance upon Smolensk, fortify and defend Smolensk, or dither about, do neither and continue to retreat? It was hardly to be wondered at that they chose the last. This in turn meant that there would be no decisive battle at Smolensk.

There was, however, a battle of sorts. Four days after leaving Vitebsk, 15 August, was Napoleon's forty-third birthday. At first irritated by the action of Ney and Murat in firing off a one-hundred-gun salute, because of the sheer waste of powder involved, he was instantly mollified by the two marshals' assurance that the powder had been captured from the Russians on the previous day. On 17 August powder was used more earnestly, when Ney, Davout and Poniatowski with their customary *élan* stormed their way into Smolensk, thus presenting the French Emperor

---

[4] Charles XII of Sweden was defeated at Poltava in 1709 and obliged to take refuge in Turkey.

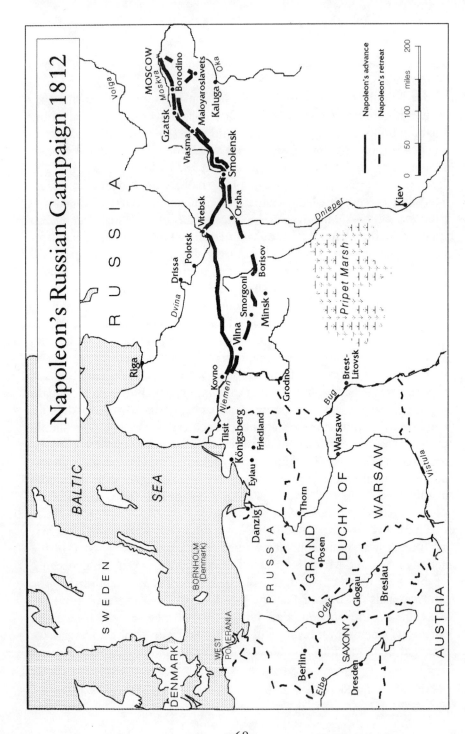

Napoleon's Russian Campaign 1812

with yet another opportunity of halting the great gamble, finding winter quarters, refurbishing the army and sending for opera dancers from Paris. But he refused to take it. Having already horrified his staff when he saw Smolensk burning with the comment that the corpse of an enemy always smelled good – we see now what Talleyrand meant about ill-breeding – he went on to horrify them still further by going back on his promise to Caulaincourt to remain at Smolensk and announcing his intention of going on to Moscow. Not even the appeal of his brother-in-law, Murat, who never wanted for dash or daring, and actually went down on his knees to beg Napoleon not to advance to Moscow, which would destroy them, had the least effect. The decision was to go on, and on they went with Murat in command of the advance guard, which consisted principally of Davout's corps. Murat and Davout had never been on good terms, and this arrangement merely led to a serious worsening of their relationship. Having left Smolensk on 25 August, Napoleon finally came up with the armies of Barclay and Bagration nearly two weeks later – on 7 September at Borodino.

By the time Napoleon finally engaged the main body of the Russian army at Borodino the army under his own hand had dwindled to a total of 130,000 men – less than one-fifth of the 675,000 he had reached the frontier with two and a half months previously. Casualties, garrison troops, flank guards, reserves, stragglers had eaten up the rest. Even with 130,000, had the greatest general of his time been at his best, he would no doubt have given the Russians a severe thrashing. But he was not. Davout pleaded with him to employ his corps on the left of the Russian position, which was strongly based on redoubts and the village of Semenovski. The French Emperor, however, was not only in a totally unimaginative, sluggish frame of mind, he had caught a bad chill from the previous night's rain, and had lost his voice. All this made for late and bad orders. He could think of nothing better than a straightforward, frontal slogging match led by Ney on the left and Davout on the right, with Murat commanding the cavalry. At six that morning the sun was shining and Napoleon called it the sun of Austerlitz, but all it was doing was helping the Russian gunners and dazzling the French. After furious fighting by Ney and Davout, with Murat leading one of his great cavalry charges, the Russian positions were at last taken during the afternoon, and the moment had arrived for the Napoleonic pursuit which would turn initial success into a victory of annihilation. The three marshals implored Napoleon in message after message to send up the Imperial Guard, who had not yet been in action, to finish the job. But when Bessières reminded the Emperor that they were 1,800 miles from Paris, Napoleon, unlike himself a mile in rear of the action and unable to judge the real situation, hesitated and declined to risk the Old Guard. Ney was furious and condemned Napoleon for being too far back, suggesting that if he were no longer to behave like a general, he might as well stay in Paris and leave the commanding to them. In all at Borodino 50,000 men and 30,000 horses were killed. The Russian army left the field unmolested further. 'The Napoleonic fantasy', observed Macdonnell, 'was fast descending into the deep shadows.' But the road to Moscow was open and Napoleon entered the city on 14 September.

In Spain, the shadows were being somewhat capricious. Wellington, having left Madrid for the north, arrived in front of Burgos on 16 September with four divisions. But he was not to get much further on this occasion, for his attack on Burgos went badly. The siege went on for more than a month, and surprisingly Wellington underestimated its strength. Having had such terrible losses at Badajoz he was reluctant to commit too many of his precious soldiers in storming the well-sited and well-manned defences. Nor had he yet received a full complement of the sappers and miners which he had so urgently requested after Badajoz. The weather was contrary – cold and wet. When it became clear not merely that Burgos was holding out, but that the French had rallied and were threatening Madrid, Wellington had little choice if he were to keep his army in being, but to retire from Burgos, reconcentrate his forces and retreat once more – for the last time in fact – via Salamanca and Ciudad Rodrigo to Portugal. This further retreat was greatly to the disgust of his soldiers, who could not understand the need for it after their former successes. Their tempers were not greatly improved by the appalling autumn weather, and on this occasion, rare for Wellington's normally excellent commissariat arrangements, a severe shortage of food. As a result discipline was by no means good and Wellington lost some 4,000 stragglers and as many again from disease and fever. Almost one-third of his army suffered some form of sickness.

The whole unhappy business was further aggravated by Wellington's thereupon blaming the regimental officers for failing to maintain proper discipline and generally neglecting their duty. This harshness was uncharacteristic of the Commander-in-Chief, who knew well enough that the failure of the system to supply clothing, shoes, rations and forage could not be laid at the door of regimental officers. There was, therefore, among these latter profound resentment at their Commander-in-Chief's strictures. In what way, they very reasonably asked, could they be held responsible for bad planning and staff work which resulted in supply convoys being in the wrong place at the wrong time? Of course, the whole army, and most of all Wellington himself, was profoundly disappointed that the campaign of 1812 had not finished the French off. It was humiliating to be obliged to retire for one more winter in Portugal. Yet strategically, it was undoubtedly the proper course of action. Indeed the fruits of Wellington's entire handling of his Peninsular campaign were about to be harvested. Victory was near. The French had still not mastered the problem of co-ordinating their various armies' actions in Spain, nor had they found an answer to the ceaseless toll taken of their numbers by the Spanish guerrillas. They had suffered huge losses of men, material and morale. And they were soon to suffer more such losses, not only in the Peninsula, but in the depths of Russia too. For as Wellington withdrew to Portugal, Napoleon had been obliged to wait in vain for Alexander to make peace, and was soon to embark on one of the most disastrous of all his extraordinary enterprises – the retreat from Moscow.

In *War and Peace* Tolstoy reminds us that at the beginning of October – when Napoleon had been in Moscow for more than two weeks and had already written to the Czar proposing a compromise peace, to which he received no answer – he wrote another letter, this one to Kutuzov, Commander-in-Chief of the Russian army, which at this time was positioned at Tarutino, some 50 miles south-south-west of Moscow. Napoleon's letter, taken by his adjutant-general, Lauriston, was a supreme example of the French Emperor's ability to 'make pictures', to believe that the situation was as he desired it to be, not as it actually was. In any event it was plain to Kutuzov that the French were making overtures for peace. Napoleon wrote that Lauriston had been sent to discuss matters of interest and begged Kutuzov to credit what was said, adding with what great sentiments of esteem and admiration he, Napoleon, had always regarded the Russian general. Kutuzov curtly rejected Napoleon's overtures, saying that posterity would curse him if he made any move towards a settlement. The spirit of his nation would never allow it. Tolstoy's comment is that while the French army is pillaging Moscow and the Russian army is encamped at Tarutino, their respective positions, both in morale and in numbers, are changing – greatly to the advantage of the Russians.

That this was so was further reinforced by the Czar's comment on Napoleon's letter, to the effect that there was no question of making peace. On the contrary he had not yet begun to make war. His campaign was only just beginning. Nevertheless Napoleon tried a third time, on 14 October. Again Lauriston went to Kutuzov bearing a letter from Berthier to the Russian Commander-in-Chief. This time the proposal was that arrangements should be made whereby the war should conform to established rules – in other words that inhuman excesses by Russian peasants should somehow be restrained. Kutuzov replied that the Russian people knew nothing of what did or did not constitute civilized warfare, and they were ready to sacrifice themselves for their country – which had not experienced war within its frontiers for several hundred years. After this third rebuff Napoleon made no more overtures for peace, but concerned himself more with the acute problems of his lines of communication and of supply. As he had decided on 17 October to retire from Moscow, these matters would of course be crucial, if he and his army were to conduct an orderly withdrawal from Russia. On the following day, 18 October, Napoleon gave orders for the Great Retreat to begin, and rather more than 100,000 soldiers with some 570 guns set out – initially south-west to Maloyaroslavets, then north-west to Borodino, via Gzatsk and Viasma to Smolensk, Orcha, Borisov and Smorgoni, back to Vilna, and so to Kovno, where the ghastly adventure had all started. Throughout the retreat what was left of the Grande Armée was harassed by three Russian armies – from the east by Kutuzov, from the north by Wittgenstein and from the south by Chichagov. The Cossacks were never far off and ever ready to seize their opportunity to pounce and kill. The Russian soldiers were not the only enemy which Napoleon's army had to contend with. There was also the Russian winter, about which Caulaincourt had frequently warned the Emperor. But in these days the Emperor believed only what he wanted to believe.

In fact at the beginning of the retreat, the weather was not particularly unkind. Indeed for the first ten days it was uncharacteristically mild, and the interminable column marched on with reasonably high morale. Davout, who was commanding the rearguard, had little understanding of how to combat the Cossacks' irregular tactics and footled about with conventional defensive formations which were quite ineffective and simply resulted in the rearguard's falling further and further behind the main body. Far grimmer things were awaiting the retreating army. First they had to file past the battlefield of Borodino with its 50,000 corpses – or what was left of them after the ravaging of wild animals. It was enough to strike a chill into the stoutest heart of the most battleworn veteran of an army which had already been fighting more or less continuously for twenty years. On top of these terrible sights, the weather began to wage its own campaign, as Alexander I had always claimed it would. By the end of October the snow had started falling and there were 9 degrees of frost. During the first days of November there was more snow, and heavy rain which froze; the lakes themselves were frozen, the horses slipped and stumbled – broken legs meant they had to be destroyed – and then, as A. G. Macdonnell so dramatically depicted it: 'The 5th November was the last day of autumn, for later that night there came a terrible change. Out of the lowering, grey, foggy, over-clouded sky came down the Cold of Russia, and that grim morning of the 6th was the beginning of the tragedy.' One good thing occurred during these early days of November. Ney and his corps relieved Davout of the rearguard, and Ney, Bravest of the Brave, began to conduct his epic display of an unconquerable will and courage never to submit or yield. Ney, like the Emperor himself, was not one given to despair, and even the 30 degrees of frost which descended on and struck down the Grande Armée on 6 November 1812 did not succeed in disheartening Michel Ney. All the time the rearguard and the main body itself were being watched, pursued and harried by the Cossacks. Three days later the weather was milder again, and some 50,000 men staggered into Smolensk by the middle of November. Then, with the prospect of food and vodka, the discipline of Napoleon's army melted away as surely as had that of Wellington's army after taking Badajoz. At this point it seemed to the Emperor that Ney and the rearguard were lost, cut off by many times their number, and Napoleon was obliged to push on westwards without the news that Ney, by unbelievable feats of resolution, deception and courage, had succeeded in crossing the Dnieper with what remained of his rearguard, less than 1,000 men, to rejoin the main body at Orcha. It was then that Napoleon declared that he would have preferred to lose 300 million francs than lose Ney.

In his admirable *Napoleon 1812*, Nigel Nicolson reminds us that there were many conflicting views of the Emperor's conduct of the retreat. He himself tried to avoid seeing the horrible results of the campaign. It was as if he were continuing to deny recognition of the appalling mistake he had made. To observe untold numbers of dead, dying, naked and starving men, to look upon thousands of dead and mutilated horses, broken guns, abandoned stores, all the flotsam and jetsam of war, hear the curses, screams and prayers of wounded and dying soldiers – such things would do nothing for the Napoleonic legend of invincibility. He therefore held himself aloof, riding with his Guard at the head of the retreating columns, or travelling in his comfortable carriage, and sometimes marching. The Marquis de Chambray recorded that many soldiers – from general to grenadier – reproached the Emperor for the pride and ambition which had driven him to undertake so hazardous an enterprise and then, having led the Grande Armée into a disastrous situation, to compound the disaster still further by refusing to recognize the facts and the true circumstances. Some went so far as to accuse him of being responsible for every single death, and for deliberately not witnessing the horror and tragedy of the retreat so that he would not be brought face to face with his own blundering. Even Caulaincourt, devoted and loyal follower of Napoleon though he was, utterly condemned the handling of the retreat. Nothing had ever been worse planned or executed with such ill discipline. Lack of foresight had caused the disaster. Decisions were taken far too late. Self-delusion as to the possibility of making a stand resulted in the retention of too much materiel – which in itself slowed progress, and resulted later in even greater loss. 'Fortune had so often smiled upon him,' concluded Caulaincourt, 'that he could never bring himself to believe that it might prove fickle.' Here Caulaincourt strays from the truth – nearly twenty years earlier Napoleon had asserted that 'fortune is a woman', and no one knew better than Napoleon how fickle women could be. It was not the fickleness of fortune that misled Napoleon, but the steady onset of megalomania, so powerful that he could not reconcile himself to failure or compromise.

It was not only military affairs in Russia that were of concern to Napoleon during the early part of November. There were also political affairs in Paris. Even while still in Moscow Napoleon had reflected that had he simply been Commander-in-Chief of the army, he could have taken his time, stayed there all winter if necessary and resumed the campaign in the spring – always assuming, of course, that the army could have been properly supplied. But as Emperor too, he had always to be thinking of the dangers inherent in being out of touch with the Empire's mainspring – Paris. So when in November he heard of an attempted coup there by General Malet – a coup which in the event proved abortive – he again had his mind concentrated on political affairs. But even if he decided to return to Paris ahead of the army – a decision which he later did take – there was still the little matter of crossing the Beresina to consider, and although normally in the latter part of November the Beresina would have been frozen, allowing easy passage for horse, foot and guns, the abnormally mild weather that November, which followed the earlier deadly freeze, meant that the river was *not* frozen over. Moreover Napoleon's 40,000 men were being pressed on three sides by Russian armies totalling 120,000. It was in desperate situations like this that the general, who never despaired, was at his best, and Napoleon then set about manoeuvring and bridge-building with such skill and energy, boldly and ably supported by the remnants of Ney's, Oudinot's and Victor's commands, that he succeeded in crossing his now relatively small army on 27 November. Next day, the Russians furiously attacked on both sides of the Beresina, and another 20,000 soldiers of the former 600,000 were lost. The crossing may have enhanced the Emperor's reputation as a military genius. It did not enhance the size of his army. What was left of it was then subjected to the intense cold of late November and early December – when there were 54 degrees of frost. This finished off the rest of the Grande Armée except only for Ney's tiny rearguard and about 1,000 of the Old Guard. On 5 December Napoleon left Smorgoni in a sledge, handing over command to Murat. Ney continued to muster a rearguard of sorts and, despite the refusal of Victor to help, Ney's spirit and courage never broke. He was the last to cross the Niemen, and had won unquenchable fame for his utter refusal to be beaten. Napoleon's celebrated observation when he reached Paris on the night of 18/19 December that the Grande Armée was destroyed, while the Emperor had never been in better health, can only be explained as an ultimate manifestation of megalomania.[5]

In his study of Bonaparte Correlli Barnett argues that in losing this

[5] Napoleon's maxim: '*A la guerre, les hommes ne sont rien; c'est un seul homme qui est tout.*'

campaign and in throwing away the largest army he had ever commanded, Napoleon lost something else, something of supreme importance to a gambler – his credit. Not altogether, we might say, for as we shall see, he did succeed on two more occasions in raising yet another army to challenge his adversaries. Yet the initiative, except for one brief and tragic episode, had passed from Napoleon for ever. Wellington, on the other hand, still had it. Before we examine how Wellington began once more to advance and this time went on advancing, while Napoleon began to withdraw and went on withdrawing, we may perhaps note one other incident. Talleyrand, who had described the Russian campaign as the beginning of the end, the end itself being not far off, was invited by Napoleon after his return to Paris to resume office as Minister of Foreign Affairs. In refusing this offer Talleyrand gave as his reason that Napoleon's views were contrary to what he, Talleyrand, believed to be 'for the glory and happiness of my country'. In subsequent years Talleyrand's views and actions more than vindicated these words he used to Napoleon.

CHAPTER 9

Wellington Advances, Napoleon Withdraws

All the world, except one man, knew that the game was up.

A. G. Macdonnell

I N April 1813 both Wellington and Napoleon were commanding armies in the field. 1813 had begun rather better for the former than the latter. In January of that year, while he was travelling in a landau through Cadiz, the people had acclaimed Wellington with cries of 'The Eagle! The Eagle!' – a rather curious greeting given the symbolism of this particular bird of prey in the Napoleonic legend, although it is true that Wellington's nose was more eagle-like than the French Emperor's. Honours had been showered on Wellington since his Salamanca victory. He had been made a Marquess in August 1812, Generalissimo of the Spanish armies in September and in January 1813 he became Colonel of The Blues. Two months later, in March, he was given the Garter. With characteristic modesty and common sense, he commented on his rapturous reception in Cadiz and Lisbon by suggesting that he needed someone behind him to remind him that he was 'but a man'. He regarded himself as most fortunate and most favoured, while confident that in what still remained to be done 'I may yet do well'. Indeed he would, and had already, by February 1813, made his plans for expelling the French from Spain with one more daring campaign.

For Napoleon at this time things were more comfortable in the petticoat line than the political line. He knew now that Talleyrand was in touch with the Allies, but such were the memories of all they had done together in the past and of the sound advice that Talleyrand had invariably given him – advice he had as often spurned as accepted – that the Emperor decided against cutting Talleyrand down. Such violent action would seem to be, Duff Cooper suggested, like 'striking down the pillars of his own house when storm was threatening'. Instead Napoleon, with a repeated show of ill breeding, denounced Talleyrand in the court's presence as a traitor and threatened him with execution. As on that previous similar occasion, Talleyrand passed off this ugly scene by murmuring to those assembled that the Emperor was in a charming mood. On the family front, Napoleon was most fortunate – he loved Marie-Louise and his son, now eighteen months old. He even went to see Josephine at her beautiful home, Malmaison. But he needed more powerful allies than petticoats, and in order to please Francis II of Austria, he hit upon the notion of making Marie-Louise Regent of France when he himself went off campaigning once more. It was not long before this was necessary, for in the middle of March, the Prussian King, Frederick William, having mobilized his army in Silesia and having concluded an alliance with Czar Alexander, declared a war of liberation against Napoleon. The Emperor meanwhile had been raising yet one more army and by April 1813 he was in personal command of nearly quarter of a million men on the Elbe and Weser, preparing to take on a joint Prusso-Russian army. But Napoleon's army, large though it was, suffered from two serious deficiencies. In the first place the French were desperately short of cavalry, which would make it virtually impossible to cap a successful breach of an enemy's position by artillery bombardment and infantry assault with the annihilating crescendo of cavalry pursuit. There were only 15,000 cavalry in the entire army of Saxony, whose open, rolling country was ideal for the *arme blanche*. Secondly there was the physical and mental state of Napoleon's marshals and the Emperor himself. After all, they had by now been campaigning almost continuously for twenty years, and apart from the appalling gaps in their ranks, they were no longer the men of Austerlitz, Jena and Friedland. And the Russian campaign had ended only four months previously. Nevertheless Napoleon was able to count on six of his most reliable and experienced corps commanders – Macdonald, Marmont, Ney, Oudinot, St Cyr and Victor, while Murat commanded the albeit diminished cavalry, Bessières as usual had the Guard and Berthier was still Chief of Staff. Between them they were to win two famous victories. Yet, as Napoleon himself had observed, whereas he could beat legitimate kings and emperors time after time without their being obliged to forfeit their thrones, he had to be defeated but once for his own right to the throne to be put in instant jeopardy. The battle of Lützen was fought on 2 May 1813, Napoleon personally leading a charge by the Young Guard, and the joint army of Prussians and Russians was driven beyond the Elbe. But Bessières had been killed. Not just the Guard but the whole army mourned him – Ney's comment was '*C'est une belle mort.*' Duroc was mortally wounded and lack of cavalry robbed the Emperor of a decisive victory. He confided in Marmont as he rode back from the battlefield that although his Eagles had been victorious, his Star was setting. Indeed it was. The game was going badly wrong, and in spite of another victory at Bautzen, when Napoleon pushed the enemy back across the Oder, the last hand but one in the game was about to be played at Leipzig – and when it was, there would be very few winning cards in the Emperor's hand. Bautzen was fought on 20/21 May and on 4 June the Allies requested an armistice to which Napoleon – he would never have done so in his prime – agreed. It was a fatal move, for his enemies simply made use of the breathing space thus provided not only to re-equip their forces and reinforce their numbers, but also to augment the alliance against France – *with Austria and Sweden.* Only one thing might have come to Napoleon's rescue at this time: the abandonment of the Spanish campaign and the withdrawal of the best part of 200,000 French troops, many of them seasoned campaigners. But Wellington had already seen to it that the time for such an option was fast fading. Indeed it was his success in Spain that had been influential in persuading Austria to change sides once more.

It was Napoleon's underestimate of Wellington, both the man and his resources – a crucial mistake he was to make again at Waterloo – that had caused him already to withdraw from Spain both regiments of the Guard and a number of veterans from other regiments. Napoleon had assumed, in the way he always distorted the facts to suit his own desired perception of the truth, that Wellington had no more than 30,000 troops under his command. The actual position was very different. At the end of April 1813, when Napoleon was preparing to fight the Prusso-Russian army in Saxony, Wellington was in command of an army comprising more than 80,000 soldiers, of whom more than 50,000 were British and the rest Portuguese. As he was also now Generalissimo of the Spanish armies, there were a further 21,000 Spanish regulars

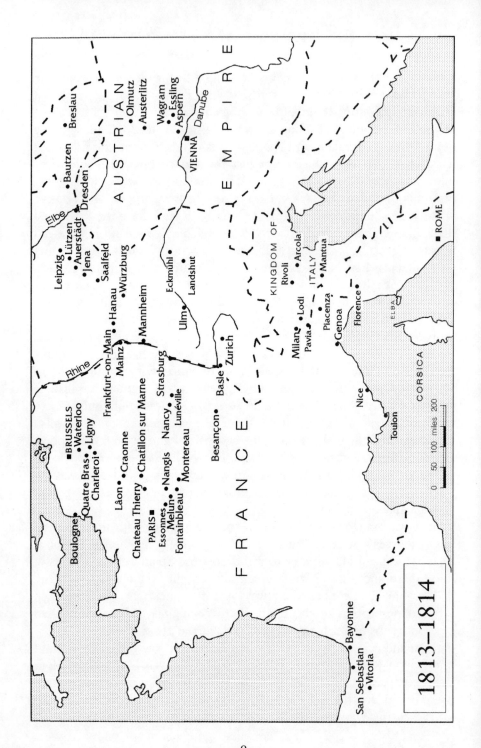

1813–1814

AUSTRIAN EMPIRE

FRANCE

KINGDOM OF ITALY

CORSICA

•Breslau
•Bautzen
•Olmutz
•Austerlitz
•Wagram
•Essling
•Aspern
■VIENNA
Danube
•Dresden
•Auerstädt
Elbe
Leipzig•
•Lützen
•Jena
Saalfeld•
•Würzburg
•Hanau
•Eckmühl
•Landshut
Ulm•
•Zurich
Frankfurt-on-Main
Mainz•
•Mannheim
Rhine
Strasburg•
Basle•
Rivoli•
•Arcola
ITALY
•Mantua
Milan•
•Lodi
Pavia•
Piacenza•
Genoa•
•Florence
ELBA
■ROME
BRUSSELS■
•Waterloo
Quatre Bras•
•Ligny
Charleroi•
Nancy•
•Lunéville
Strasburg•
Chatillon sur Marne
Besançon•
Laon•
•Craonne
Chateau Thiery•
PARIS■
Nangis•
Essonnes•
Melun•
Montereau•
Fontainbleau•
•Nice
•Toulon
•Boulogne

0   50 100 miles 200

•Bayonne
San Sebastian•
•Vitoria

180

and 50,000 irregulars – a formidable array. He was to make excellent use of them. Moreover his prudent decision to winter in Portugal had given him the time and opportunity to improve the condition and composition of his army. Every soldier had three pairs of shoes and a spare set of soles and heels in his knapsack – not as grand, perhaps, as having in it the baton of a marshal of France, but at least they all had them. The soldiers were also provided with tents and 'light tin' kettles – Wellington's insistence on the latter had provoked one of his ironic asides to the Horse Guards that the men could not cook their food properly without camp kettles. A siege-train had at last arrived plus more sappers and miners. With his own army in excellent fettle and his enemy's depleted and harassed by guerrillas, Wellington proposed to take the field as soon as possible and place himself 'in Fortune's way'. As always, he made thorough preparations amidst strictest secrecy. He still enjoyed the overwhelming advantage of assured supplies by virtue of Britain's sea-power. Indeed Arthur Bryant calls him 'Neptune's General'.

It was a fitting title for it was on the manipulation and adaptability of sea-power that Wellington was to base his entire strategy for his last Peninsular campaign. In 1812 he had devised a more or less frontal attack on Marmont's position by crossing the Douro. This time he intended to outflank the French defences based on that river by moving the bulk of his army in Portugal to the northern side of the Douro and then, by crossing the Esla, which joined the Douro some 20 miles west of Zamora, position his forces in the rear of King Joseph's army, about 55,000 men dispersed over several hundred miles from the Douro to the Tagus. It was a bold idea for it would mean not only negotiating the very mountainous territory of northern Portugal which bordered Spain but also ensuring that all the guns and supplies would be available to support him. Yet strategically it contained the very key to success, for Wellington with the thoroughness and foresight of genius had it also in mind to transfer his main source of supply from the Portuguese ports of Lisbon and Oporto to the Spanish ones of Santander (which the Royal Navy had seized) and Bilbao. Thus his grand design conformed to Jomini's great principles of disrupting the enemy's lines of communications while preserving one's own. By setting his army in a position to appear *behind* the French lines and so threaten their northern communications to France itself – the Bayonne route – he would achieve Jomini's first objective. And by advancing towards and securing his own communications with Santander, which would now become his principal supply point, he would achieve Jomini's second requirement. It was a masterly plan, and the absolute antithesis of how Napoleon set about designing his Russian campaign.

What is more important, Wellington's plan worked. The main body of his army began its outflanking through the Tras-os-Montes during the second week of May 1813, while Wellington himself, as part of his deception plan, crossed the Portuguese frontier with 'Daddy' Hill and 30,000 men *en route* to Salamanca. As he crossed the frontier, the Commander-in-Chief bade farewell to Portugal, declaring that he would never see that country again. Three days later Hill drove in the enemy's outward defences of Salamanca and the French, believing – as Wellington had intended they should – that his main thrust would be in the same direction as it had been against Marmont in the previous year, withdrew from Salamanca. Joseph deployed his army on the line of the Douro between Toro and Tordesillas. Having succeeded with his plan thus far, Wellington called a halt to this diversionary push in order to give time for Graham with the main outflanking body to complete his difficult march through the mountains. On 31 May Graham's advance guard was at Zamora and by then Wellington had rejoined the main body. He had already made sure that the French positions on the Douro would be useless to them, and sure enough, realizing that Wellington's army had now crossed the Esla, the enemy abandoned Toro. This further withdrawal by the French enabled Graham's 30,000 men to cross the Douro, so that by 4 June Wellington had concentrated his entire army of 81,000 men and so begun his march to the north-east across the plains of Old Castile preceded by a cavalry screen. The difference in the state of the two armies may be judged by the recollections of those serving with them. For the British the blue skies, the overjoyed greetings of the Spanish people, the plentiful food and supplies meant that it was the sort of campaigning that every soldier dreams about. In Palencia the soldiers were even showered with rose petals thrown by nuns from a convent's windows. Wellington's Peninsular army was in excellent spirits and eagerly anticipating further victories and advances. They would not have long to wait. The French army on the other hand, now some 60,000, was retreating – three of their former strongholds, Vallodolid (where Joseph had had his headquarters), Palencia, even Burgos were all abandoned between 2 and 12 June. Moreover, there was none of the efficient commissariat staff work, which the British enjoyed, to keep the French army well supplied. Having left behind the agriculturally abundant Douro country, they were now retiring across a desert-like waste land, with no assured supplies, and therefore for men and horses alike hunger was as great a threat and fear as the steady musketry or impetuous sabring of the British redcoats. And then, the French army was encumbered by a huge collection of what Nelson would have described as fiddlers, whores and scoundrels – in other words a kind of court accompanying the army, with all the paraphernalia of wagons, loot, silver and useless accoutrements. A travelling brothel was how one French officer summed it all up. But then, of course, Masséna had not set the best of examples when, while commanding the Army of Portugal some years previously, he had rendered campaigning more agreeable by sharing it with the delectable young female dressed – when she was wearing clothes – in the uniform of a light dragoon.

The task now facing the French army was anything but light, for Wellington now intended to outflank and encircle the French in the Ebro valley. A real victory in Spain was even more urgent now that the news from Germany was of Napoleon's two successes at Lützen and Bautzen and there were murmurings of armistice and peace. If he could drive the French right out of Spain, so reasoned Wellington, he would then have the Pyrenees as a defensive barrier, should the French return in strength. So his advance went on – and this time Wellington aimed his army at Vitoria, 20 miles behind the French defences. The march itself was remembered by Major Harry Smith as a wonderful one, the men in splendid fighting condition, better, as he put it, than that of a trained pugilist. The end product of this march was the battle of Vitoria on 13 June 1813 during which Wellington's 80,000 men utterly trounced Joseph's 65,000. Joseph's principal military adviser, Marshal Jourdan, had advised against making a stand there and, on hearing that his advice had been rejected, went to bed. By the time he got up again, the battle had been irretrievably lost.

A. G. Macdonnell is persistently unkind to Wellington, and in his account of Vitoria he refers to his being 'master of the interminable stalk followed by the modified pounce'. We understand Macdonnell's partiality and forgive him because his is an incomparably readable book, but Vitoria could not accurately be described as a modified pounce.

When the combination of circumstances – Joseph's choosing to fight in such a place with totally unsound tactical dispositions, the numerical superiority of the British and their unquenchably confident spirit (as exemplified by Picton, wearing a blue frock coat and a generously brimmed top hat and shouting to his men as they attacked a vital bridge, 'Come on, ye rascals . . . you fighting villains') and the ever-present French fear of being cut off from the route of retreat to France itself – resulted in Joseph's realizing that Wellington's left wing was about to effect this very cutting off, his entire army made a run for it along the Pamplona road, leaving behind them more than 150 guns, a million pounds in cash, untold treasure[1] looted over the years of French occupation of Spain, and even Marshal Jourdan's baton – which when sent to the Prince Regent caused him to return a Field Marshal's baton to the triumphant Commander-in-Chief. 'You have sent me,' wrote Prinny to Wellington, '. . . the staff of a French Marshal, and I send you in return that of England.' Vitoria was more than a modified pounce. It was the *coup de grâce* for France's Army of Spain. Jourdan was sacked and Soult took over command.

The sheer success of Vitoria and the resultant temptation of drink and booty which presented itself to the victorious British soldiers proved too much for them. It was the old story all over again. They might be lions in the field – they might even be gentlemen in quarters – but with the prospect of unlimited wine and the abandoned riches of a king after a five-week march and a furious contest, discipline evaporated. Wellington made known his displeasure in letters to Earl Bathurst, Secretary for War and the Colonies: 'We started with the army in the highest order and on the day of the battle nothing could get on better. But that event has, as usual, totally annihilated all order and discipline. The soldiers of the army have got among them about a million sterling in money . . . The night of the battle, instead of being passed in getting rest and food to prepare for the pursuit the following day, was spent by the soldiers in looking for plunder. The consequence was that they were

---

[1] Wellington himself did not do badly out of it, acquiring some masterpieces by Correggio, Rubens and Velásquez, including the last-named's *The Waterseller of Seville* – all stolen from Spain's royal collection by Joseph Bonaparte. Characteristically, Wellington offered to return them. Uncharacteristically King Ferdinand declined. They had come into Wellington's possession, he declared, by means as just as they were honourable.

incapable of marching in pursuit of the enemy and were totally knocked up.' Again he goes on: 'It is quite impossible for me or any other man to command a British army under the existing system. We have in the service the scum of the earth as common soldiers . . . The officers of the lower ranks will not perform the duty required from them for the purpose of keeping their soldiers in order . . . As for the non-commissioned officers, as I have repeatedly stated, they are as bad as the men . . .' In spite of all these complaints, Wellington was later to say of his Peninsular army that in his later campaigns, and especially when they crossed the Pyrenees, there never was an army in better spirits, better order or better discipline. 'We were pretty near perfect.' It was to be in the Pyrenees that the final battles of this long campaign were to be fought. By the end of June his army had reached the Bidassoa.

Napoleon was understandably furious at the news of Vitoria and sent Soult to put some backbone into the demoralized Army of Spain. But however unwelcome the information might have been to the French Emperor, to the Austrians it was exactly what they wanted to hear in order to end their neutrality and enter the field once more in alliance with Prussia and Russia against France. On 26 June 1813 Napoleon received Metternich, the Austrian Foreign Minister, at the Marcolini Palace in Dresden. When we read of what passed between these two men, it is difficult for us to *like* Metternich. He may have had infinite charm – he was after all one of Caroline Bonaparte's lovers; he was no doubt a diplomat of the premier class; he had the interests of his country always at heart – and his own family's interest even closer; and he did try to preserve the orderliness and stability of the existing autocratic order. But compared with Napoleon Bonaparte – a king on any chess-board of history – Metternich was a pawn. Whereas Napoleon had turned the world upside down, risked his life in a hundred encounters on the battlefield, and given new ideas and rules to his adopted country, Metternich had risked nothing more than his own reputation in the bedchamber or the counsel room. Yet he got the better of Napoleon in this interview. In this particular game the pawn check-mated the King. It was as plain to Metternich as to everyone else – except Napoleon himself – that France was running out of the resources to go on waging war, and the subsequent discussion, with Metternich holding most of the cards, went something like this.

The great strength of Metternich's position was that it had been agreed by Alexander of Russia, Frederick William of Prussia and Francis II of Austria that he, Metternich, would mediate between Napoleon and the two monarchs with whom France was at war. Thus, with Austria's neutrality in the balance – a key consideration for Napoleon – Metternich was not required to concede anything. Nor indeed was it his intention to mediate in the sense of bringing about a reasonable settlement. He was angling for Napoleon's humiliation and downfall – by peaceful means if possible, but if not possible, by war. Up to the time of their meeting negotiations between the two men had been inconclusive. Although Napoleon had accepted Metternich's proposal for an armistice between France and Prussia, his attempts to deal directly with either Prussia or Russia were thwarted by the proviso made by these countries' sovereigns that all communications be made through Metternich as mediator. The armistice enabled both sides to improve their positions – the French by augmenting their cavalry – but most menacingly Austria, still at present neutral, set about rearming to the tune of 200,000 men. Austrian neutrality thus became vital to Napoleon – he had already offered Austria Illyria to secure it – while Austria's potential strength became a winning card in Metternich's hand.

When the two men met on 26 June, Napoleon wanted at once to get down to the details of peace arrangements, while Metternich talked in general terms of the balance of power so that peace could be preserved by a number of independent states. Napoleon demanded a more precise statement of Austria's own position. He had offered Illyria to secure their neutrality. Would that do? His own armies could take care of the Russians and Prussians, provided Austria stood aside. Metternich, however, continued to prevaricate, even making the unlikely suggestion that Austria could not remain neutral, but must fight on one side or the other, and that it was in Napoleon's power to double the fighting men at his disposal by gaining the Austrian army for himself. Such an alluring prospect was rapidly dashed when the two men consulted a map of Europe. It was then that Metternich revealed his hand. The sheer scale, immoderation and audacity of his proposals were such that Napoleon could scarcely believe them. Metternich was suggesting nothing more or less than the dismantling of the French Empire. Austria would receive not just Illyria, but northern Italy as well; Prussia was to be awarded the west bank of the Elbe; Poland would go to Russia and the Rhine Confederation – one of Napoleon's principal weapons against England

– would come to an end. Napoleon's outburst of angry rejection of such terms was only to be expected. He pointed out that his armies were still on the Oder and the Vistula, and yet without a single blow being struck he was quietly to withdraw from his conquest of Europe. If Francis II imagined that his son-in-law would accept such conditions, he was profoundly mistaken. When in further discussion, Napoleon attempted to persuade Metternich genuinely to mediate between the combatants, it became clear that the Austrian Foreign Minister was not willing to enter into any form of bargaining. Either Napoleon gave up the great bulk of his conquests, or Austria would join Russia and Prussia in their war against him. This would swing the odds most unfavourably against Napoleon. To fight two powers was one thing. To engage three – to say nothing of what England was doing at sea and in Spain – was another. Besides – and in this respect there are considerations other than military ones – there was the whole question of all that Napoleon's France stood for and had achieved. Napoleon's entire career – and if ever confirmation were needed of his contention that almost any goal was open to talent, it was in his own – owed its origins and glittering successes to all that the Revolution had done in tearing down the former barriers of privilege and opening opportunity to all. The fundamental difference between Metternich's ideas and Napoleon's was that whereas the former strove always for holding back the advance of new ideas, new liberties, and the gradual redistribution of political power and social position, the latter was concerned, genuinely so, with the rights of man and saw the French Empire as the embodiment of the new order. In his masterly biography of Napoleon, Vincent Cronin makes this point very strongly, and also points out that it was the *honour* of France which most mattered to the French Emperor, that Napoleon's ambition was not personal, but national. 'It was not his will', Cronin writes, 'that drove the supposedly peace-loving French people forward, for no man in recorded history has ever led a people unless he marches dead in step with them. Napoleon's inflexibility could never have stemmed from so feeble a thing as personal ambition; it was rooted in the principles of the Revolution. The conclusion is that Napoleon was not, more than most men, ambitious for himself; but he was very ambitious for France and he embodied the ambitions of thirty million Frenchmen.' This point is supremely important for our understanding of Napoleon's character and our judgement of his career. It also goes a long way to explain why after military defeat – which now could not long elude him – he threw away the chance to rule a France robbed of its former Empire.

Negotiations between Metternich and Napoleon were designed by the former to ensure that there would be no agreement. Although, when Napoleon made some attempt to bargain, repeating his offer of Illyria to Austria, even conceding that Russia could have part of Poland, and suggesting that the four powers should meet to discuss the whole problem, Metternich accepted this last idea, he never had any intention of allowing such a thing to happen. Indeed he instantly concluded the treaty of Reichenbad with Napoleon's enemies, by which the three powers, Austria, Russia and Prussia, simply reiterated the original conditions put to Napoleon by Metternich on 26 June. Unless France agreed, they said, and moreover agreed by 10 July, Austria would join the other two powers and declare war. Napoleon made one more effort to make an honourable peace by despatching Caulaincourt to negotiate with Russia and Prussia. But Metternich prevented any such meetings and on 12 August (the deadline of 10 July had been extended by one month) Austria declared war. All Napoleon's hopes for peace with honour were for the time being at an end and he now faced three enemies, whose joint armies totalled 430,000 men. The Austrians under Schwarzenberg in Bohemia had 230,000 men, Blücher in Silesia commanded 100,000 Prusso-Russians, and Bernadotte, formerly one of Napoleon's marshals and now Crown Prince of Sweden, had 100,000 Swedish and Russian soldiers near Berlin. Napoleon, never one to despair, made brave attempts to overcome these various opponents separately, but although he himself was in excellent form and defeated Blücher in Silesia and Schwarzenberg at Dresden, his marshals were not. Indeed Bernadotte had offered advice to his allies that whenever possible they should attack the French where opposed to one of the marshals, but *not* where Napoleon commanded in person. Bernadotte could hardly have paid a greater compliment to his former master's military prowess. And by following Bernadotte's advice, the Allies slowly but surely beat back the French. Macdonald was defeated by Blücher on the Katzbach, Oudinot was driven back by Bernadotte, Vandamme was worsted at Kulm, St Cyr, renowned for his skill in a defensive battle, held on at Leipzig. It was here at Leipzig that Napoleon, having abandoned his bold idea of capturing Berlin in order to advance into Poland and cut off the Russians – abandoned only, it should be said, because Marshals Berthier, Macdonald, Murat and Ney advised so strongly against it – decided to make his stand. For a general who had previously made such tactically decisive use of ground where hills and valleys, rivers and ravines had offered infinite variety for manoeuvre, deception and sudden descent on a flank, the broad, flat plains of Leipzig were a surprising choice. Not all the great man's military genius would enable him to surprise the enemy on such a battlefield. Napoleon was moreover still at a numerical disadvantage – some 170,000 Frenchmen against the Allies' 260,000. The battle of Leipzig raged for four days, from 16 to 19 October. It was a desperate slogging match, which not even all the efforts of Napoleon himself and ten of the marshals – one of them, Poniatowski, was awarded his baton during the battle – could turn to their country's advantage. The odds were too heavily against them. Apart from Schwarzenberg's and Blücher's armies, the Allies were reinforced by Bernadotte with 60,000 men and Bennigsen with 50,000 Russians. The other marshals present were Berthier, Ney, Mortier, Marmont, Oudinot, Victor, Macdonald, Augereau and Murat, the last-named indulging in one last charge, riding as usual at the head of the Reserve Cavalry in his glittering uniform and ostrich-plumed headgear. It availed them nothing and 20,000 of Napoleon's last but one army were stranded on the east bank of the Elster when the last bridge over it was prematurely blown; among others, Poniatowski was drowned in trying to swim the river on a horse as exhausted as himself.

The game had gone badly wrong in Saxony. Leipzig had cost Napoleon more than 70,000 men killed and wounded, and the remnants of his army made their way sullenly back into France. France itself would now be threatened, not only from the west, but from the south too, for ten days before the battle of Leipzig, Wellington's soldiers had crossed the Bidassoa and were on French soil. They had not had an altogether easy time of it since their victory at Vitoria, for the big, bustling, bullying Marshal Soult had arrived in Bayonne on 12 July 'to re-establish the imperial business in Spain', and his rapid and brilliant reorganization had soon put heart back into the French army. Indeed, before long he was actually to launch a counter-offensive against Wellington's necessarily dispersed forces – necessarily, because of the nature of the Pyrenean country, and his need to capture the two Spanish fortresses remaining in French hands, St Sebastian and Pamplona. Wellington was advancing with three columns: on the left Graham was to take

St Sebastian, on the right Picton and Cole were advancing from Roncesvalles to St Jean Pied-de-Port, while in the centre Hill was operating in the mountainous area of Bastan. Wellington himself with his headquarters was at Lesaca, very much on the left flank of his front, for it was here that he expected the French to be most active. For once his intelligence failed him. Soult's intention was quite different – no less than to assault the Roncesvalles sector, while also advancing across the Maya pass through the Bastan. In this way he hoped to drive a wedge between Wellington's forces, relieve Pamplona, capture supplies from its besiegers and then push on to Vitoria, so outflanking the British in a manoeuvre similar to that in which Wellington had swept round Joseph and Jourdan before and during the battle of Vitoria. That Soult had considerable success with this bold plan owed much to a circumstance to which Wellington was often to draw attention: that unless he were there himself things invariably went awry.

Early on 25 July, while Graham was hammering away at St Sebastian, d'Erlon attacked the British outpost positions in the Maya pass, at the same time as Soult's columns further south-east were attempting to force their way through the Roncesvalles passes. Although the British succeeded in holding the French attack at Roncesvalles for the whole of that day, at night, fearing an outflanking movement, Cole, in command of the 4th Division, decided to fall back towards Pamplona to join Picton's 3rd Division at Zuburi. Thus despite the staunch defence of the Maya pass – and here the 92nd Highlanders (now the Gordon Highlanders) greatly distinguished themselves – there was already a rearward movement by the British extreme right, which was made even worse when Picton withdrew still further – like Cole, concerned about his flanks – to the tactically less favourable hills north of Pamplona. On hearing of Cole's withdrawal, Hill had already ordered a retreat from the Maya pass to conform and level out the line, so that on the morning of 26 July Soult found both the vital passes abandoned by the British and open to his columns. It was not until that evening that Wellington was able to take a proper grip on the situation and order a concentration on the area north of Pamplona. Yet at this point Soult had the advantage and despite having sent a triumphant despatch to Napoleon at Dresden (which the Emperor, as was his custom, instantly exaggerated to the effect that the British had suffered a major reverse), Soult wavered and, instead of attacking on 27 July when only two hours' march from

Pamplona and with a numerical superiority of two to one, he delayed his move until the following morning, by which time Wellington had mustered sufficient strength to take on Soult's men at the battle of Sorauren. It was the same old story of the French massed columns coming up against the British infantry drawn up in line behind crests, who then with their steady musketry subjected the French to devastatingly accurate fire-power. But it was a bloody affair. 'Bludgeon work' was how Wellington described it and as usual he was in the thick of things, always appearing at the vital spot of enemy pressure, and ensuring that his dispositions were such that the French were beaten back again and again. Not for the first time Wellington, although many of those riding with him were struck, seemed to bear a charmed life. 'I begin to believe that the finger of God is upon me.'[2]

Having lost his chance of a successful counter-offensive at Pamplona, Soult now made the classic error of marching his men across Wellington's positions in an attempt to relieve St Sebastian. Nothing could have suited the British Commander-in-Chief better. Falling on Soult's rearguard, he destroyed most of it. The rest of Soult's men, having failed to obtain adequate supplies, by capturing those of the Allies, had little choice but either to starve or to make their demoralized way back into France. Wellington did not pursue. He still had 80,000 men, but a quarter of them were Spanish troops, and he was determined to avoid the repercussions of letting loose in France Spanish soldiers whose vengeful behaviour would inevitably provoke fanatical national resistance. Instead, during August and September, he waited in the Pyrenees while the St Sebastian and Pamplona fortresses were reduced.

The Peninsular War had not long to run now, but there were a few more battles to be fought and we will look at them briefly before turning back to the man who had brought it all about. As soon as Wellington heard the news that Napoleon's armistice with Prussia and Russia was over, and Austria too had declared war, he determined to invade France. It is agreeable to record that by this time Wellington's fame was widespread and that he enjoyed the dinner parties which celebrated his various victories. His Judge-Advocate-General, Francis Larpent, who had joined Wellington's staff in the previous autumn, noted in his journal that there were so many of these victory days that over-indulgence in

---

[2] He used the same phrase after the battle of Waterloo.

food and wine would be the ruining of them all. He also recorded how lively and universal was the curiosity about his chief – 'as one of the great men of the age'.

The great man meanwhile was making his plans to cross the Bidassoa in strength, and having again deceived the enemy as to his strategy, launched an assault across the river estuary at dawn on 7 October. By the end of the next day the French right was retiring to the Nivelle river. Again Wellington paused. He still awaited news of the fall of Pamplona and of what was happening in Germany. Pamplona finally surrendered at the end of October and early in November Wellington heard of Napoleon's defeat at Leipzig. Thereupon Wellington renewed his attack, and despite the good defensive country which Soult's men were manning, with all the strength given them by redoubts, entrenchments and guns, they were required to hold far too extensive a line, so that the British, able to concentrate wherever they chose, broke through the French defences on 10 November. It was a sure illustration of the pitch of efficiency, spirit and sheer unstoppability of the British infantry, to which Wellington's diligence and tactical dexterity had brought them. Soult's line was duly penetrated and his army's morale melted away. To escape encirclement at Bayonne, the French abandoned St Jean de Luz, a valuable port, leaving fifty guns and over 1,000 prisoners in enemy hands.

Six days before the battle of the Nivelle, the Allied armies had entered Frankfurt; a few days later they were on the Rhine. Now Napoleon would be fighting on French soil. Yet, almost incredibly, on 9 November the Allies were prepared to make peace. Napoleon was offered France's natural frontiers – the Rhine, the Alps and the Pyrenees. Equally incredibly Napoleon turned the offer down. He interpreted the offer as evidence of his own powerful position – although how a soldier of his ability and experience could have so misjudged it, when the Allied armies were poised to march on Paris from the east with irresistible strength and Wellington was pushing all before him from the south, must be beyond our comprehension. And then the pity of it! Had he accepted the offer, what might he not have done with his extraordinary inventiveness, energy, talent, administrative genius and sheer enthusiasm to have helped rebuild France and mould Europe to better ways than those to which subsequent revolutions in 1830 and 1848 led? But as Duff Cooper put it, 'Whatever may be thought of his generalship during these months' – for in February and March 1814 Napoleon was once more wearing his long boots and astonishing the world with whirlwind tactics and breathtaking manoeuvres – 'it cannot be denied that the faults in his statesmanship and diplomacy were never more gross or glaring'. In any event the time for diplomacy or statesmanship or even brilliant military operations was all but over. France was bankrupt – not just in money, but in all the commodities for making war – and was being invaded by seven powers: Austria, Bavaria, England, Prussia, Russia, Saxony and Sweden. Still the general who never despaired fought on, and between February and March 1814 he who had shown himself to be such a consummate master of the lightning offensive, the irresistible attack, the shattering flank manoeuvre and the wholly annihilating pursuit, now demonstrated to the world what he could do in a campaign of mobile defence with 50,000 men against invading armies totalling almost ten times that number. Despite a repulse at La Rothière on 1 February 1814, Napoleon hurled his 50,000 men here and there defeating in turn Blücher, Schwarzenberg and the Russians. It all took place near Brienne, where Napoleon had been pursuing his military studies thirty years earlier. Victory after victory was won – Châtillon-sur-Marne, Montmirail, Château-Thierry, Vauchamp, Champaubert, Nangis, Montereau – but all to no avail, for at length Blücher saw what he should have seen much earlier, that the key to it all was Paris, and to Paris he marched. It was then that Napoleon's marshals finally made the Emperor understand that the game was up. On 4 April at Fontainebleau, Ney together with Lefèbvre and Moncey were received by Napoleon – Berthier at his side – and demanded that both the fighting and the Emperor's reign should be brought to an end. They were joined by Oudinot and Macdonald, and Napoleon's appeal to continue the fight was listened to in deadly silence. Ney pronounced the terrible verdict that the army would not march, and capped the Emperor's assertion that the army would obey him with the words: 'The army will obey its generals.' It was enough, and that very night Napoleon signed an Act of Abdication.

When Wellington heard of it on 12 April he had just ridden into Toulouse – scene of his last Peninsular victory – and Colonel Ponsonby arrived with extraordinary news. 'Napoleon has abdicated.' 'How abdicated? Ay, 'tis time indeed.' And then realizing what it meant, 'You don't say so, upon my honour! Hurrah!' and the great man absolutely spun on his heels snapping his fingers. On 3 May he was created Duke of Wellington. Byron's reaction to Napoleon's downfall was somewhat different:

> 'Tis done – but yesterday a King!
> And arm'd with Kings to strive –
> And now thou art a nameless thing:
> So abject – yet alive!

In fact when Napoleon, 'Emperor and Sovereign of the Isle of Elba', stood on the deck of the Royal Navy's frigate *Undaunted* in the bay of Portoferraio on 4 May 1814, he was not notably abject.

Indeed Sir Neil Campbell, British commissioner on Elba, recorded that he had never seen anyone so active or perseverant, taking great pleasure in being constantly on the move and evidently unwilling or unable to pursue a life of retirement as he himself had stated to be his intention. There was a miniature court at Elba, there was the local gentry such as it was to attend levées, there were farms to be inspected, industries to be developed, loyal adherents to be welcomed, among them his sister, Pauline, his mother, Letizia, and the ever-faithful Marie Walewska. And of course there was the Guard to review. On 20 April 1814, before setting out from Fontainebleau, Napoleon had bid adieu to the Guard with all the ceremonial stage management of which he was a master. It was all to be part of the legend, a memorable set-piece which would go down in history, a tale to be told countless times, to touch many a sentimental and simple heart:

Soldiers of my Old Guard, I bid you goodbye. For twenty years I have found you uninterruptedly on the path of honour and glory. Later no less than when things went well you have continually been models of courage and loyalty. With men like you our cause was not lost; but the war could not be ended: it would have been civil war, and that would only have brought France more misfortune. So I have sacrificed our interests to those of the *patrie*; I am leaving you; you, my friends, are going to go on serving France. France's happiness was my one thought; and it will always be what I wish for most. Don't be sorry for me; if I have chosen to go on living, I have done so in order to go on serving your glory. I want to write about the great things we have done together! . . . Goodbye, my children! I should like to press you all to my heart; at least I shall kiss your flag!

What a flag it was! Surmounted by the eagle, emblazoned with battle honours of unimaginable fame and glory, embracing twelve years of victory and triumph, fields of combat never to be forgotten and twenty years later to be indelibly recorded on the Arc de Triomphe – the battlefields on which we have in these pages seen Napoleon exercise his unique mastery of command: Marengo, Austerlitz, Jena, Friedland, Wagram, Vienna, Berlin, Madrid, Moscow – this was the colour that the Emperor embraced, before the final words to the Guard: 'Adieu! Keep me in your memory!' This dramatic and moving scene was played in front of the palace at Fontainebleau. The words were addressed to members of the Old Guard who would not accompany Napoleon to Elba. 1,000, however, did, more than twice as many as originally agreed by the Allies, for so many had volunteered to do so. At Elba, therefore, the Emperor still had the Guard to review, and before a year was out to accompany him on yet one more enterprise, one last throw in his legendary game. Although he might have the consolation of the Guard, however, he was not to enjoy the company of his wife and son. Despite all Napoleon's longing and hoping for them to share his exile, Metternich and Francis II were too much for him. Marie-Louise was instructed to proceed to Rambouillet, thence to Vienna and finally to Parma – of which she was created Duchess – there to succumb to the attentions and ardour of the wicked and dashing Hussar general, Count Neipperg. The Duchess of Parma never went to Elba. But the Countess Marie Walewska did.

Before we join her there, we must return to the conquering hero of the Peninsular War. Wellington had achieved all that he had set himself to do in the long campaign. He had successfully defended Portugal; he had co-operated with the Spanish army and assisted the guerrillas to hold down and account for huge numbers of French soldiers; he had defeated marshal after marshal in both defensive and offensive battles; and although required to retreat all too often, for his army was always greatly inferior to the total French forces, he had in the end turned them out of Spain altogether and invaded France itself. During his command of the army he had won the total confidence of his subordinate generals together with that of the regimental officers and men. He had always been commissariat-minded. He had to be, and having learned how to conduct campaigns in the deserts and jungles of India he applied these lessons to the plains and mountains of Portugal and Spain. The Lines of Torres Vedras had been a masterpiece of defensive foresight and preparation. The brilliant coup of Salamanca had been an illustration of sound deployment and the seizure of fleeting opportunity. From time to time, caution and the preservation of Britain's only army prevailed over bolder measures, for he could not afford one single serious reverse. He immersed himself in detail and saw to everything possible himself, for unless he did, things usually went wrong. The courage of his soldiers, the steadiness and marksmanship of his infantry, the excellence of his regimental officers – these were priceless assets that he came to rely on, even though he would sometimes condemn his army for ill discipline. He may have called them infamous and scum of the earth, but he took infinite pride in their fighting qualities and in the confidence they bestowed upon him. He could hardly have awarded them higher praise than when he said of his Peninsular army that with it he could have gone anywhere and done anything.

At home, of course, Wellington was the idol of all, including, not greatly to his taste, his wife, Kitty. It was perhaps unfortunate that whereas Napoleon on Elba was yearning for the presence of Marie-Louise, Wellington in London – he had after all been a huge favourite of the ladies during his five years of separation from Kitty in Portugal and Spain – could probably have borne it if he had been deprived of her presence. But he did not in fact spend all that amount of time with her. Indeed he did not spend long in England. He returned there in June 1814 and by August he was in Brussels on his way to Paris to take up his new appointment of British Ambassador to the Court of the Tuileries. One of the first things he did was to acquire a residency, formerly that of Napoleon's sister, Pauline. How subsequent ambassadors must have blessed him for buying the Hôtel de Charost in the rue de Faubourg St Honoré! As Brussels was to figure prominently in a forthcoming scene in the great Napoleonic and Wellingtonian drama, we may perhaps pause there for a moment and join the family of Lady Caroline Capel, sister of that great and gallant 7th Light Dragoon, Henry Paget (whom we have already met in the Peninsular War with Sir John Moore), later Lord Uxbridge, 1st Marquess of Anglesey, and known after Waterloo as One-Leg. Here is his niece, Maria, known as

Muzzy, one of Lady Caroline's thirteen children, recording the celebrations in Brussels on the occasion of the Prince Regent's fifty-second birthday (his birthday was on 12 August, Muzzy's letter written a week later):

> On the Prince Regent's birthday we had a Magnificent Parade & Feu de Joi which extended all round the Park. Lord Wellington, who attended it was recd. with enthusiasm. In the Evening Lord Clancarty gave a very Good Ball to 500 People. On the Duke of York's Birthday *The Guards* gave a Ball & Supper in the handsomest way possible . . . The Walls were hung with Banners, Standards, & other Military Trophies which had a very good effect . . . Lord Wellington went to the Play one night and was received with great applause – he came here with the Prince of Orange the same Evening to our Great Delight . . .

Muzzy would have done well as Jennifer in the *Tatler*, and we will join her family again when Wellington was once more in Brussels for a more momentous purpose. Meanwhile we will accompany Wellington to Paris. Although the Duke may have been surprised at his appointment as Ambassador in Paris, commenting as he did that it was a situation for which he would not have thought himself qualified, in fact his character, accomplishments, ability and experience fitted him remarkably well for the post. He was immensely distinguished, an English nobleman who spoke French with effortless elegance, he had had endless dealings with difficult and susceptible allies, he knew the customs and niceties of the *ancien régime*, he was acquainted with almost everyone who mattered, he was firm in strategic purpose, adaptable in tactical method, above all his character was such that it inspired confidence in others. Just as Napoleon had told Talleyrand that cleverness was not needed in war – what *was* needed was accuracy, simplicity and character – so Wellington believed that these three attributes, especially the last, made for confidence in diplomacy. What better equipment could a man have had for dealing with the restored Bourbon government of Louis XVIII?

His diplomatic skills, however, were insufficient for him to make much progress in his principal mission of trying to persuade the French government to abolish the slave trade. The Abolitionists in London, led by Wilberforce and his friends, were fanatically opposed to the idea of returning to France her colonies unless there were assurances that the slave trade would come to an end. There was wholly comprehensible opposition to this notion in French commercial circles to whom it seemed that the British simply wished to stifle the economy of French colonies. These difficulties together with a growing concern for the Duke's safety from assassination threats (Wellington's military success against French armies did not endear him to French opinion in all quarters) led to suggestions that he should take command of the British army in America – for Britain and the United States had been at war again since 1812. Fortunately it was a somewhat inconclusive affair comprising clashes on either side of the Canadian frontier and some sharp naval actions. A peace was agreed at the end of 1814, and the main effect on Wellington was that, when shortly afterwards his veterans of the Peninsular War were badly needed in Europe, many of them were not to be had. In any event affairs in Vienna demanded Wellington's attendance there. After Napoleon's abdication, Britain's Foreign Secretary, Castlereagh, whose great aim was to set up in France a government which would at once be stable and lasting, had welcomed the idea of a Bourbon restoration. As was the way with the British, in victory they were magnanimous, and Castlereagh's concern was not to punish France, but to carve out a settlement which France itself would regard as just and which would thus be workable.[3] Talleyrand, who came into his own again at this time – he was a great survivor – had already laid it down that the only alternative to Napoleon was Louis XVIII. When the Czar Alexander made the suggestion that Bernadotte – the former French marshal, now Crown Prince of Sweden, who had led armies *against* his native country – might succeed to the throne, Talleyrand had dismissed the idea with the splendid remark that if the French wanted a soldier for the job, they still had the finest one in the world. Yet Alexander did agree with Castlereagh that Prussia's vindictive desire for vengeance had to be curbed.

In April 1814 a provisional treaty of Paris to settle Napoleon's future had been signed by France (Caulaincourt, Ney, Macdonald), Great Britain (Castlereagh), Austria (Metternich), Prussia (Hardenberg) and Russia (Nesselrode). In the following month a further treaty, signed by Louis XVIII himself, gave France her 1792 boundaries and restored

---

[3] If only Clemenceau had been blessed with such wisdom!

the bulk of her colonies. Thus France was treated with generosity and there was to be no indemnity. It had been further agreed by the Powers that they 'would send plenipotentiaries to Vienna for the purpose of regulating in General Congress the arrangements which are to complete the provision of the present treaty'. In September 1814 therefore a glittering throng of peace-makers gathered at Vienna to settle Europe's future and, as the Prince de Ligne observed, to enjoy themselves with an endless procession of fêtes and balls, for as he put it: '*Le Congrès ne marche pas; il danse.*' There were so many sovereigns in Vienna that de Ligne complained he had worn out his hat doffing it to them all as he encountered them at street corners. He notes the graceful, martial figure of Czar Alexander and the dignified appearance of King Frederick William of Prussia; Francis II of Austria is all affability even though attired in a stiff Venetian suit; the Kings of Bavaria, Württemberg and Denmark are there. Princes, archdukes, reigning monarchs are two a penny. The English are distinguished not so much by their lavish titles, as by the extravagance of their clothes.

The real work, of course, was done by the statesmen – Metternich, manager in chief of the Congress; Hardenberg of Prussia; Nesselrode, the Czar's spokesman; Talleyrand, whose patience and diplomacy were so crucial; and Castlereagh. It was a curious irony that France and Great Britain, so long bitter enemies, were now at one in striving for moderation and a peace that would last; Metternich too was all for balance. Between them these three succeeded in obtaining the admission of France on an equal footing with the other Great Powers and in restraining the territorial greed of Russia and Prussia, who respectively coveted Poland and Saxony. Neither France nor Great Britain had territorial ambitions in Europe, for France's frontiers had already been settled by the Peace Treaty, and Great Britain was satisfied that the Low Countries, Spain and Portugal were free from aggressive French influence and that her own supremacy at sea and commercial welfare had been enhanced by the acquisition of the Cape of Good Hope and Guadeloupe. It was the struggle between Austria, Prussia and Russia over the future of Poland and Saxony that constituted the Congress's main business, and it was a somewhat unlikely secret agreement between France, Britain and Austria that resolved this tricky question. Their agreement, made in January 1815, was to counter the demands of the Czar who wanted an enlarged Poland under Russian control and of the

Prussian King Frederick who would settle for all of Saxony. When it became known to Alexander and Frederick that France, Britain and Austria would if necessary resort to force to prevent these acquisitions, they both climbed down and agreed to accept far less. Russia was to get Napoleon's former Duchy of Warsaw, Prussia to have only a small part of Saxony. By the time this arrangement had been concluded on 11 February, Wellington had been in Vienna for just over a week. Castlereagh had decided that he must go home to explain these agreements to Parliament and it had therefore been determined by the British government that Wellington would replace Castlereagh in Vienna for the closing activities of the Congress. It was just as well he was there at that time for in the following month there came startling and ominous news from Elba. Napoleon had escaped.

One of the most readable, and yet perhaps nowadays least read, of books about Napoleon is A. P. Herbert's *Why Waterloo?* In it he gives us a sympathetic portrait of the King of Elba and we get tantalizing glimpses of him, pining for his wife and son, briefly enjoying the company of Marie Walewska, his sister Pauline and his mother, going about the island, visiting, inspecting, improving, planning, worrying the British Commissioner, Colonel Neil Campbell, as to his intentions, and behaving more like an ordinary mortal than an Emperor. On 4 May 1814 he had written to Marie-Louise:

Ma bonne Louise,
I have been four days at sea in fine weather, and was quite well. Here I am at the Isle of Elba, which is very pretty. The accommodation is mediocre. I shall arrange something in a week or two. I have no news of you. That is the sorrow of all my days. My health is very good. *Adieu, mon amie,* you are far from me, but my thoughts are with my Louise. A tender kiss for my son. *Tout à toi.*

NAP

Ten days later Colonel Campbell notes that the people of Elba are favourably inclined towards their new sovereign, partially no doubt because they believe that his presence will bring them previously unknown advantages, but mostly, as A. P. Herbert points out, because 'it was the sight of a great little man, not too great to go about among the people on a mule and talk to them about mulberries and radishes, to find out what was wanted and try to provide it'. In his talks with Campbell, Napoleon ranged widely and paid England and the English extravagant compliments, saying they could do what they liked now as the other Powers were nothing. They even discussed Napoleon's plans for invading England. It had been his firm intention to carry it out, but only if superiority at sea could first be gained. He had needed only three or four days. His flotillas of assaulting infantry escorted by the fleet could have sailed instantly, followed rapidly by artillery and cavalry. 'We should have been in London in three days.' When Campbell enquires what he would have done on getting to London, Napoleon is again generous in his praise of a spirited people. 'I should have separated Ireland from England, and made it a Republic. But the English I should have left to themselves' – except, he adds wryly, for sowing some Republican seed there.

On 29 May 1814 Josephine died at Malmaison. 'She is happy now,' murmured Napoleon when he heard the news. Later in July and August, there is some little petticoat comfort for him. Marie Walewska writes to say that she is in Florence with their son Alexandre. Napoleon sends a guarded answer, but receives her brother in Elba on 8 August. By then, Madame Mère, the redoubtable Letizia Bonaparte, mother and mother-in-law of innumerable European sovereigns, is with her most famous son and a consolation to him. Little consolation was to be had from Marie-Louise. Méneval, Napoleon's former secretary, had delivered her to Aix and from there she wrote various letters to Méneval, which made it clear that she was not intending to join her husband at Elba. As to what she would do, there was nothing but vacillation. She asks whether she will be allowed to establish herself at Parma; she will never consent to return to Vienna; she has heard from Napoleon who begs her to go to Tuscany; how can she do what her husband wants if it does not accord with her father's wishes? The fact is, of course, that she was already under the influence of Count Neipperg – who was himself totally subservient to the political intrigues of Metternich, and Metternich would never allow Marie-Louise to rejoin Napoleon. Nonetheless on 18 August the Emperor writes to her again, unhappy that he has had no news of her or of their son. '*Cette conduite est bien bête et atroce.*' No one had the right to keep them apart. He waited impatiently for her. She knew his feelings for her. Madame Mère was with him and Pauline would join them soon. It availed him nothing.

In spite of more appeals by Napoleon – his letters were often unanswered or stopped – on 8 September Marie-Louise writes to the Duchess of Montebello, the beautiful and charming widow of Marshal Lannes, lightly dismissing the idea that she should make an 'escapade' to Elba: 'I have answered him [Napoleon] frankly that I could not come at present . . . I shall give the Ministers my most sacred word of honour that I shall not go to the Isle of Elba for the moment, that I shall *never* go . . . *mais l'Empereur est vraiment d'une inconséquence, d'une légèreté.*' Napoleon may justly have been accused of many shortcomings, but among them would hardly have figured inconsistency or slightness. These were qualities better ascribed to herself. There was, however, the other Marie – Walewska, the Polish wife, who proved more true 'than those that have more cunning to be strange'. On 1 September 1814 she and Alexandre came to the shores of Elba – not to Porto Ferraio itself – and were reunited with the Emperor. But not for long. They talked, and Napoleon confided in her that he wished to be remembered not only for his victories, but for his docks, his roads and canals, bridges and buildings, his sewers ('Do you know, Marie, before me there was not a single sewer in Paris?'), his prefects and his laws. He had built something and left behind him something that was good and lasting. Another twenty years and he could have changed the face of France and of Europe. He would have shown France the difference between a constitutional emperor and a selfish king. He was more particular about the great harbour at Cherbourg. 'The docks excavated in the granite rock are works worthy of the greatest periods of Rome, and the Romans never executed anything grander . . . I wanted to concentrate at Cherbourg an immense naval force, in order to have it in my power to threaten England . . . It would have been a struggle, hand to hand, of forty millions of Frenchmen against from fifteen to twenty millions Englishmen: and who could doubt the result? What should I have done with England then? Destroyed her? Certainly not. I should only have put an end to her naval domination, her intolerable assumption of the rights of all. I should have insisted on the freedom of the seas, the independence and honour of the flags of all nations . . . Do I weary you, my sweet Marie?' She would not have been wearied by a hundred such confidences, but her stay in Elba was but a short one. There could be no secrets in the eagle's little cage at Elba, and the *on dit* was that the Empress Marie-Louise and the King of Rome had arrived – a comprehensible mistake for Marie Walewska and Alexandre. Napoleon still hoped that his wife and heir might come, and he could not afford that 'wicked gossip' might prevent her coming. He was, of course, deluding himself, but Marie Walewska was despatched back to Italy. She was brave and noble until the end, telling Napoleon that she would have stayed with him for ever – and 'if you ever call me, I will come'. She even hoped as she bid him *au revoir* that the other Marie would come.

She did not, but his sister Pauline did. Napoleon's sister, Princess Pauline Borghese – whose house Wellington had acquired as the British Embassy in Paris and whose sculpted figure, naked except for a sheet just covering her lower stomach and thighs, had raised eyebrows (her explanation was that it was quite all right as the studio was well heated) – had, as Pons[4] reported: '. . . all the qualities of a consorting angel. Only the King of Rome could have been a more welcome visitor . . . She was sweet, affectionate and kind, and her gaiety gave life to everything about her. She could be considered the most precious treasure in the Imperial Palace.' Pauline arrived at Elba on 30 October 1814. She brought a little extra joy into life at Porto Ferraio. She also had a most disturbing effect on Colonel Neil Campbell. Yet Campbell's principal concern was still with Napoleon himself. On 6 December he records in his diary that he has written to Castlereagh, giving it as his opinion that if Napoleon continued to receive the means of subsistence he had been promised 'he will remain here in perfect tranquillity, unless some great opening should present itself in Italy or France'. But, of course, the promised means of subsistence did not continue, a great opening did present itself in France and Colonel Campbell made the almost inconceivable error of relaxing his vigilance. Napoleon was given cause enough not to remain in perfect tranquillity. First there were whispers that he would be deprived of his minute kingdom and sent to St Helena or the Azores. Then Louis XVIII approved a report proposing to remove all the Bonapartes' property in France. On 1 January 1815 Napoleon heard that French frigates were patrolling the island and was displeased,

---

[4] André Pons de l'Hérault, administrator of iron mines in Elba, said that at Elba – and only there – Napoleon could be properly understood. There he was himself – neither too remotely exalted as a reigning Emperor, nor playing a part and promoting his own legend as he was at St Helena.

but nevertheless January and February were Carnival months. Then on 13 February a felucca from the Gulf of Spezia arrived in Elba, its principal passenger, Fleury de Chaboulon, one of Napoleon's most devoted adherents. He had brought with him a message from Maret, Duc de Bassano, formerly Napoleon's Foreign Minister, a man noted for caution. His message contained the very information for which Napoleon had been waiting and longing. 'Come back,' said the message, 'the Bourbons cannot last. There will be a rising. If you do not come, it will be the Duc d'Orléans. The people want you. The Army loves you still, and is unhappy. Come and rescue France from misfortune.'

It was hardly surprising that such a message should have been sent. The Bourbons had done just about everything possible to alienate the French people and more particularly the army. Although at times Napoleon's former Imperial Guard had been employed on parades for purely ceremonial purposes, they had – like our own Foot Guards – earned the right to enjoy such undemanding duties by virtue of the matchless valour they had displayed on a score of battlefields. The Bourbons, however, chose to replace them with several thousand youths of the Household Corps – which had last been seen in the days of Louis XIV, when they did at least undertake some fighting. But the sight of these silken-clad sprigs of nobility, whose only engagements were those of exchanging *bons mots* in the elegant salons of Paris and whose only conquests were those of the bedchamber, had the same effect on Napoleon's veterans as that 'Certain lord, neat, and trimly dress'd,/Fresh as a bridegroom, and his chin new reap'd . . ./He was perfumed like a milliner' had had on Hotspur when the fight was done and, leaning upon his sword, he was 'dry with rage and extreme toil'. Quite apart from the appointment of this bunch of popinjays in place of the Guard, it had to be remembered that nearly all Frenchmen had served with Napoleon during his innumerable campaigns and, although they might deprecate the Emperor's seemingly insatiable ambition, although they might welcome peace after nearly a quarter of a century of war, nevertheless they were ever mindful of France's glorious military achievements and Napoleon's own indispensably leading part in them. That Louis XVIII should appoint as Minister of War Dupont – the very man who had put a question mark against French invincibility by surrendering an army to the Spaniards at Baylen in 1808 – showed an insensitivity to national pride which bordered on idiocy. Equally insensitive was

Louis's lavish distribution of the Legion of Honour – Napoleon's own exemplification of honourable service to the state whether on the battle-field or not – to fat, comfortable, civilian nobodies, to whom the word honour meant no more than to be born well. Even worse perhaps was the creation of a new military decoration, the Order of St Louis, and its award to some of the shallow, pink-cheeked, uniformed fops who had never seen and never would see a shot fired in anger. Such goings-on were hardly calculated to excite the approval of those many thousand veterans of Napoleon's Grande Armée who had returned from captivity or were dismissed on half-pay. Indeed, when serving soldiers of the day were being numbered on parade, they would call out: '*Quinze, seize, dix-sept, gros cochon, dix-neuf!*' Such was the respect and admiration which the restored Bourbon King was able to inspire in the ranks of his not inconsiderable army. In the more exalted circles of royal drawing-rooms, the reinstated *émigré* noblemen and their ladies of the court, who had passed the years of danger and glory in exile, were now able to snub and turn their backs on the Marshals of the Empire and their wives, yet France's real feelings were made plain in January 1815, when General Excelmans, one of Napoleon's many dashing cavalry com-manders, was acquitted by a military court on a charge of insubordi-nation. It was the very same French people who now acclaimed their overjoyed approval of his acquittal who had been glad to see the back of Napoleon only nine months earlier. France ceased to count, says the Contessa Pietranera in Stendhal's great novel, after Napoleon left it.

It was not only this general dissatisfaction with the Bourbons which made Maret's message to the Emperor at Elba so timely. There was also the consideration that Colonel Campbell chose this very time to leave Elba. On 16 February he sailed for Italy in HMS *Partridge*. Ten days later, having made all the necessary preparations, the Emperor sailed for France in the *Inconstant* together with six other vessels. With him went nearly 700 of the Old Guard, a hundred Polish lancers, some Corsican and Elban volunteers and members of the Imperial staff. On 1 March, having evaded the Royal Navy brig *Partridge* with Campbell on board, and having deceived the French brig *Zéphyr* as to their desti-nation, the tiny flotilla appeared off Cap d'Antibes. 'At one in the after-noon,' writes Vincent Cronin, 'the landing began; a thousand men against the whole of France.'

It was not until early in the morning of 7 March that the news of

Napoleon's escape from Elba reached Metternich at Vienna. Later that morning the five great Powers' plenipotentiaries met to decide what was to be done. Talleyrand thought that Napoleon would make for Italy or Switzerland. Metternich knew better and asserted that he would head straight for Paris. Wellington expressed the – for him somewhat vain – hope that Louis XVIII's armies would arrest Napoleon. There soon followed a declaration by all the Powers in Vienna that Napoleon was now beyond the pale, an outlaw, who deserved and would be dealt the joint opposition and punishment of Europe. Wellington's own position was instantly changed for Castlereagh wrote to say that both he and the Prince Regent left it to the Duke's judgement as to where his services would best serve the public interest, strongly implying that it was at the head of the army in Flanders that he should be. On 25 March the Great Powers had declared that they would not lay down arms until after the final defeat of Napoleon. Wellington had already decided to go to the Low Countries to take command of the army there. He got to Brussels late on 4 April 1815. By this time Napoleon had been in Paris for two weeks, and we will now join them both as they make their respective preparations for war.

CHAPTER 10

Face to Face

By God! I don't think it would have done if I had not been
there.

Wellington

THE spring of 1815 reveals the Duke and the Emperor in strikingly and characteristically different lights. The Duke is
matter of fact, the Emperor grandiloquent. We will look at the
heroics first. Even before landing in France, Napoleon had prepared
no fewer than three proclamations: one was addressed to the French
people, calling upon them to dismiss the Bourbon King and his government who had betrayed their promises and France's glory; one was for
those officers and men of the Guard who were with him to appeal to
their comrades-in-arms to trample on that badge of shame, the white
cockade, which represented a King who owed his throne to Britain's
Prince Regent, and to return to their duty; the third was addressed
to the Grande Armée itself and was couched in fittingly extravagant
language:

The eagle with the tricolour will fly from steeple to steeple until it
reaches the pinnacles of Notre Dame itself. Then you may show your
scars, your medals. And in your fading years your countrymen will
gather round and give you all the glory you deserve. You will tell
them the tales of your great deeds, you will proudly say: 'Yes, I was
there. I was one of the Grande Armée that marched into Vienna,
twice – into Rome, Berlin, Madrid, and Moscow, and at last redeemed
our beloved Paris from the shame of foreign conquerors, when we
brought back peace and honour to France.'

There was never much doubt about the honour. If only he could have brought back peace too! Napoleon had pledged himself in the first of his proclamations to abandon all ideas of conquest and to devote his efforts to the welfare of France.

While making his way from the Golfe Juan to Paris the Emperor was able to add another page to the Napoleonic legend. As he was leading members of the Guard through the wild, mountainous country of Haute Provence, he encountered on 7 March a regiment of royal troops, deployed to stop his march astride a snowy defile: just such a scene as to bring out the most theatrically impressive side of his character. Stepping forward in front of the Guard to face the aimed muskets and throwing open his coat, he declared: 'Soldiers, if there is one among you who wishes to kill his Emperor he can do so. Here I am!' But back came the cry, '*Vive l'Empereur!*' Not for the first time the sheer magic of the man in his grey overcoat and bicorne hat had demolished any doubts the soldiers might have had. It was a magic that was to work again and again. It did not, however, work with all of Napoleon's marshals. That old fox, Masséna, commanding the Marseilles Military District, tried to have it both ways. On 9 March his proclamation to the people of Marseilles assured them of his zeal and devotion, of his allegiance to the legitimate king. He would never leave the path of honour and was ready to shed his blood in support of Louis XVIII's throne. A month later, having received definite orders from the now-restored Napoleon, he was singing a different tune, and in another proclamation hailed the return of The Great Napoleon, 'our chosen sovereign', who had returned to the bosom of a family which held him dear. It was a day of rejoicing and for prayers to ensure that his days and his dynasty would be preserved. Yet despite this show of loyalty, Masséna made sure that his state of health did not permit his accepting an active command in the field.

Of all the marshals, perhaps the most disconcerted by the Emperor's return was Ney, whose loyalties were fatally divided. When Napoleon landed, he was in command of the 6th Military District at Besançon. Despatched by the King, to whom he expressed absolute allegiance, he dashed off with a brigade of troops to the Rhone valley to intercept and capture the usurper, then bring him to Paris in an iron cage. But on 12 March, while at Lons-le-Saulmier, he received a scribbled message from his former master who had reached Lyons (where another marshal,

Macdonald, had completely failed to rally the troops to fight for Louis). The message read:

> I am sure that as soon as you learn of my arrival at Lyons you will have ordered your troops to hoist again the tricolour flag. Follow the orders you receive from Bertrand and come and join me at Châlons. I shall receive you as I did on the day after the battle of the Moskowa.
>
> N.

It was enough. After agonizing all that night over where his loyalties lay and drafting a proclamation (there was a great fashion for proclamations in these heady days), Ney assembled his brigade next morning and got no further than declaring that the Bourbons' cause was lost, when his troops burst out with *'Vive l'Empereur!'*, and the thing was done. He joined the Emperor on 14 March. After this, there was little more that Louis could do. Although two days later he made a futile attempt to put some backbone into the two Assemblies of Peers and Deputies by suggesting that there could be no better way of ending his life than in the defence of his country, and although this suggestion was enthusiastically endorsed, the Assemblies echoing the King's determination to die in their country's defence, yet on the night of 19 March they all fled the capital, pursued by a jubilant General Excelmans, and the following evening the Emperor of the French entered the Tuileries and climbed the stairs. 'His eyes were shut, his hands stretched forward like a blind man's, his happiness showing only in a smile.' He observed that it was the will of the people that had done it, and it was this will that he had divined and acted upon.

As we have noted, the reaction of Allied leaders at Vienna was instant and uncompromising. Napoleon's efforts to make known his peaceful intentions – he even went so far as to send a special emissary to Metternich and to pen a letter in his own hand to the Prince Regent – were rejected out of hand. The Allies' joint declaration, inspired principally by Talleyrand, branded Napoleon as an outlaw and an enemy of the world's peace. Talleyrand understood well that whereas Napoleon would find support in France from the army he would not find it from those democrats for whom the Revolution had meant above all a share of political power. Whereas Napoleon's aim was to make the forthcoming war – for war was now inevitable – appear to be one of national survival, the Allies were equally determined to make it clear that their fight was against Napoleon himself, not against France. Thus the Emperor, while preparing to counter the Allied declaration that England, Austria and Prussia would each put into the field an army of 150,000 men, was also obliged to make concessions at home by proclaiming an *Acte Additionel* which would modify his former Imperial dictatorship by introducing a strain of parliamentary participation. Thus the triumphant entry into the Tuileries on 20 March 1815 was already being overshadowed by the Great Powers' implacable hostility and the less-than-universal enthusiasm of the French people themselves. Moreover there was little to console him on the domestic front – Marie-Louise and the King of Rome were as remote as ever. Already the 'enterprise of great pitch and moment' which had inspired his escape from Elba and his adventurous march across France had begun to 'turn awry and lose the name of action'. Yet action was the only thing that could save him.

For such action he would have no shortage of troops. In addition to the army of 200,000 which he had inherited from the Bourbon King, he had raised half as many again. There was also the National Guard, some 200,000 strong, to guarantee the security of French cities. Nearly all the soldiers were, of course, veterans of Napoleon's former campaigns. 'Their morale', writes Vincent Cronin, 'was higher than that of any army since at least 1809. The troops were determined to wipe out the shame of their defection the previous year, and Allied spies reported their almost frenzied enthusiasm for the Emperor.' It was, however, not so much the fighting spirit of the army nor its numbers that Napoleon was to feel the lack of when it came to the actual battle. It was more in experienced and balanced commanders. It is true that Ney had come back to him, but ever since the battle of Borodino, when the fiery red-headed marshal had launched his tirade against his Commander-in-Chief for not being up at the front and for refusing to release the Imperial Guard, Ney, despite his heroic rearguard action in the Russian campaign and unfailing courage at Leipzig, had been unbalanced, at times hysterical. Although temporarily in disgrace because of his promise to Louis XVIII to bring the usurper back to Paris in an iron cage, Ney was to be entrusted by Napoleon with absolutely crucial responsibility in the forthcoming battle, not once but twice – a responsibility which Ney was temperamentally and psychologically incapable of fulfilling. Apart from Ney there were few of the old hands who supported the Emperor or accompanied him for the last of all his campaigns. Marmont, St Cyr, Victor and Macdonald stuck to their new Bourbon loyalties. Augereau and Berthier had gone to ground. Soult, however, despite his former allegiance to Louis, had rejoined the Emperor. So had Mortier and Suchet. Masséna was unwell. Murat, King of Naples, impetuous as ever, on hearing of his brother-in-law's resumption of the throne, committed the egregious folly of turning on his Austrian friends and attacking them with Neapolitan soldiers, who of course ran away, leaving Murat no choice but to make an ignominious flight to Toulon. There was one new marshal created in April – Grouchy, who might have turned the scales at Waterloo had he acted as a marshal of France should. But after Ligny he and his corps did nothing but march aimlessly about far from the action itself. One other supporter of proved worth Napoleon did have – the iron, uncompromising Davout, who accepted the Ministry of War and did what he could to put the army in order. But all in all the Emperor would not be fielding the first eleven for the battle to come.

Nor would Wellington. Although the Czar Alexander had told him before he left Vienna: 'It is for you to save the world again,' the Duke was far from satisfied with what he found waiting for him when he reached Brussels on 4 April 1815. Yet his mere presence was a great consolation to the British community in Brussels as Lord Uxbridge's sister, Caroline, recorded in a letter to her mother: 'We are in as perfect Security here as you are in London – Lord Wellington is arrived in the highest Spirits & it seems generally believed that Napoleon never was in such a Scrape before – *Certainly* there is a strong party against him in France & there is *already* a Cordon of 100,000 men between Us & him, without the Russians & Austrians who are yet to join . . .' All four powers had pledged themselves to take the field against France, but by the time of the battle only two armies had assembled in Belgium: the Prussians under Blücher had by June 1815 113,000 men holding the frontier from the Ardennes to Charleroi, while Wellington had a mixed force of British, Dutch, Hanoverian and Brunswicker troops totalling about 70,000 positioned between Mons and the coast. Very few of Wellington's veteran Peninsular men were with him, as the bulk of them were in America, in overseas garrisons or on their way home in transports. 'I have got an infamous army,' he wrote on 8 May, 'very weak and ill-equipped, and a very inexperienced staff.' He condemned those at home for doing nothing, not raising more men, not even calling out the militia.

Yet even though many of his soldiers had not previously seen action, about half of his 24,000 British troops had been with him in Portugal or Spain, including the Guards, the Highlanders, the incomparable 52nd and 95th Rifles, and some splendid horse and field artillery; he was also strong in cavalry, including the Household Regiments and the Union Brigade all under the finest cavalry leader in the British Army, Lord Uxbridge. The latter's appointment had caused that famous comment by Wellington when it was pointed out to him that Uxbridge (who had formerly eloped with the Duke's sister-in-law, Lady Charlotte Wellesley) had the reputation of running away with anybody he could: 'I'll take care he don't run away with me!' Also not to be forgotten is the exchange between Creevey[1] and the Duke when they were conversing in the park at Brussels some weeks before Waterloo. It was then that Wellington expressed the opinion that he thought he and Blücher could do the thing; that he expected no desertions in Bonaparte's army from colonel to private, but that they might pick up a marshal or two – 'not worth a damn'; and most significant of all, pointing to a small scarlet British infantryman, that it all depended on him whether they did the business or not. Given enough of 'that article' and he was sure.

Correlli Barnett has emphasized that the strategic odds were heavily against Napoleon. By midsummer the Allies would have mustered armies of more than 600,000 to threaten France from its frontiers with the Low Countries, Germany and Italy. Yet in the past, despite numerous Grand Coalitions against him, he had defeated his enemies' armies either one by one, or even two of them at a time. If therefore he could now successfully engage the Prussians under Blücher and the mixed force commanded by Wellington, he might then be able to turn on the Austrians and defeat them before the Russians even entered the field. Correlli Barnett, however, maintains that although Napoleon's strategy of defeating former Coalitions' armies in detail had worked in the early days from 1800 to 1808, from 1812 until his first abdication it had been thwarted by the Allies' policy of simply pushing on towards Paris with

---

[1] Thomas Creevey (1768–1838), politician and diarist, MP and follower of Fox, Treasurer of the Ordnance 1830. He quarrelled with Wellington in 1806, but Wellington did not resent it.

one army or another until, at length, Napoleon ran out of resources. So, Barnett concludes, as this was to be the Allied intention again, even if Napoleon had won the battle of Waterloo 'it would only have proved another Lützen or Bautzen or Champaubert; a delusory prelude to inexorable defeat'. This, of course, is what Jac Weller calls one of the 'ifs' of Waterloo, making him wince, but perhaps making us not so sure. The defeat of Wellington and Blücher by Napoleon would certainly have changed the attitude of the Belgians and Dutch, Louis XVIII would have shambled off to retirement at some English watering place, and such an event might have made even Alexander think twice. But of two things we *can* be sure. The British would have fought on, and Talleyrand somehow or other would have survived.

The events of June 1815 put paid to such speculation and determined the fate of Europe. On the first day of that month one of the most highly valued, and in the past devoted, of the Emperor's marshals perished. Berthier was at Bamberg and there he heard the tramp of Alexander's infantry soldiers and the jingle of harnesses as the Czar's horse artillery made its way westwards intent on the invasion of France and the overthrow once more of the Emperor whom he, Berthier, had so faithfully served with his maps and compasses and brilliant staff work. This time he would not be there, and his remorse was such that he hurled himself from the window of his house on to the cobblestones below to his death. In Brussels at this time there was a very much lighter mood. As in Vienna, balls were the order of the day. The Duke of Wellington gave several, but according to Lord Uxbridge's sister, Lady Caroline Capel, the Duke 'has not impressed the *Morality* of our Society, as he has given several things and makes a point of asking all the Ladies of Loose Character – Every one was surprised at seeing Lady John Campbell at his House & one of his Staff told me that it had been represented to him her not being received for that her Character was more than Suspicious, "Is it by—," said he, "then I will go & ask her Myself". On which he immediately took his Hat & went out for the purpose.'

Yet if the Duke was continuing to be lax in his regard for the petticoat company and for the moral rectitude of Brussels society, he had been his customarily sensible, energetic and thorough self as far as his military preparations were concerned. He had organized his somewhat multinational army into three corps, and made each part of it more solid by including in each formation some British or King's German Legion troops. 'He could not transform into reliable soldiers the Belgian or Dutch peasants or raw German mercenaries from the petty Teuton principalities who were sent to swell his numbers,' wrote Arthur Bryant. 'Yet by dint of common drill, organisation and, above all, the immense morale-raising prestige of his name and the personal attention he gave to every unit of his command, irrespective of nationality, he did everything possible to blend his force into a single international whole accustomed to working together.' This was the very stuff of which proper generalship is made.

On 12 June Napoleon left Paris to take command of the Armée du Nord. There were five corps commanded by d'Erlon, Reille, Vandamme, Gérard and the Count of Lobau. Grouchy had the Reserve Cavalry and Soult had been appointed Chief of Staff. In an almost last-minute, haphazard appointment, the Emperor put Ney – who had accompanied the army on its northward move along the Charleroi road and met the Emperor outside an inn – in overall charge of some 50,000 men, comprising two corps, ten cavalry regiments and over seventy guns. Given Ney's extraordinary state of mind and formerly desperate doubts, it was a curious and, as it turned out, fateful choice. In all the Emperor had about 128,000 men, of whom over 20,000 were cavalry, and nearly 350 guns, so that under Ney's direction would be nearly half his strength. Opposing him would be Allied armies totalling some 200,000 men, rather more cavalry than the French and half as many guns again. On 14 June, the day before he began his attack, Napoleon resorted once more to one of his dramatic orders of the day:

> Soldiers, today is the anniversary of Marengo and Friedland, which twice decided the destinies of Europe. Then, just as after Austerlitz and Wagram, we were too generous; we believed in the oaths and protestations of the princes we left on their thrones! Today, then, in a coalition against us . . . they have begun the most unjust of aggressions. Let us then march to meet them; are not we and they still the same men?
>
> For every Frenchman with a heart, the moment has come to conquer or perish.

On 28 April George Canning had written to Castlereagh with reference to Wellington, saying what a happy consummation of the Duke's story it would make if the final destruction of Bonaparte's power would be determined by a direct conflict between the two of them. This conflict and this consummation were now about to occur. Wellington's first received intelligence as to Napoleon's advance was neither timely nor accurate. Indeed the reports sent to him were conflicting. Although Napoleon began his advance into Belgium at dawn on 15 June, it was not until that afternoon, about 3 o'clock, that Wellington received his first news of it – to the effect that General Ziethen's 1st Prussian Corps had been attacked at Thuin. From the very beginning the great question facing Wellington was whether the French would make their main effort through Charleroi and advance north to Brussels, or whether their principal thrust would be further west via Mons. He was inclined to think the latter more likely. On the answer to this vital question would depend the deployment of Wellington's army. The information that he had so far, for Thuin was south-west of Charleroi and south-east of Mons, somewhat nearer to Mons, gave him no clear indication of Napoleon's intentions. Moreover, nor did what immediately followed. The Prince of Orange, one of Wellington's subordinate commanders (and a thoroughly inexperienced yet over-confident one at that), arrived to say that the Prussians had been ejected from Binche and fighting seemed to be in progress at Charleroi. As Binche is roughly equidistant between Charleroi and Mons, Wellington still did not know whether Napoleon was feinting at Charleroi – with a view to making the main assault further west – or whether it really was the principal effort. Nevertheless it was clearly time to get his own army ready for action. Accordingly he gave orders for his troops to assemble and to be at short notice to move. These warning orders were despatched between 5. p.m. and 7 p.m. on 15 June, and if executed would deploy the bulk of the army, under the Prince of Orange and Lord Hill, between Grammont and Nivelles, that is to say, in accordance with Wellington's notion that the main attack would be further west than the direct route to Brussels from Charleroi via Quatre Bras. No positive order to march was, however, yet issued – for Wellington, as he made clear in assuring Fitzroy Somerset, one of his aides-de-camp, that they 'would be able to manage those Fellows', all would depend on there being no false movement. Fortunately the Duke was shortly to receive more, and this time definite, reports as to what Napoleon was actually about. At ten o'clock, while he was dressing for the Duchess of Richmond's ball, Wellington received General

Müffling with a message from Gneisenau stating that Blücher was concentrating his army at Sombreffe; Müffling wished to know what were the Duke's intentions as to supporting the Prussians. Wellington, still awaiting a report from General Dörnberg at Mons, sent Müffling back to his quarters with a promise that as soon as this Mons report was in his hands Müffling would hear from him. Sure enough the report from Dörnberg arrived; it was now clear that the main French attack *was* at Charleroi. Wellington therefore ordered his troops to concentrate at Nivelles and Quatre Bras; then he and his staff went to the Duchess's ball in order to reassure the assembled company there.

It was while he was still at this ball that Wellington made a remark which Napoleon would have been incapable of. Having received yet more intelligence that the Prussians had been forced back from Fleurus – only 8 miles from Quatre Bras – and then, from the Prince of Orange himself, that the French had actually reached Quatre Bras, Wellington casually took his leave, asking the Duke of Richmond as he began to leave if there was a good map in the house. Having studied it in an ante-room, he made the characteristically Wellingtonian comment: 'Napoleon has *humbugged* me, by God! He has gained twenty-four hours' march on me.' When asked by Richmond what he intended to do, he replied that he had instructed the army to concentrate at Quatre Bras, adding, 'But we shall not stop him there, and if so, I must fight him *here*,' passing his thumbnail over the Waterloo position.

It must be a source of satisfaction to many historians to be reminded of Frederic Maitland's contention that 'the essential matter of history is not what happened but what people thought or said about it'. Adherence to this idea enables us to concentrate on the latter. Nevertheless for our purposes here it is also important to understand in outline at least what happened in order to put into context what people did think and say about the battle of Waterloo, not least the impressions and observations of those who actually took part in it. There have been so many detailed accounts of the battle – those of Elizabeth Longford, Arthur Bryant, Jac Weller, David Chandler and John Keegan must still rank among the most laudable[2] – that perhaps here a summary of events

---

[2] Although, of course, we must not overlook novelists like Thackeray, Georgette Heyer and Bernard Cornwell for sheer entertainment combined with authenticity.

will be sufficient to preface both contemporary comment and the hindsight of those who followed.

On 15 June, having humbugged Wellington by the speed of his concentration and the secrecy of his advance, Napoleon crossed the Sambre and drove a wedge between Wellington's and Blücher's armies, and on 16 June proceeded to maul, but not destroy the Prussians at Ligny. 'We have scotch'd the snake, not kill'd it,' declared Macbeth, and then proceeded with the murder of Banquo. Napoleon, however, failed to finish off Blücher. His failure to do so was brought about firstly, by Ney's tardiness in seizing Quatre Bras quickly enough to conform to Napoleon's intention that he, Ney, should envelop the Prussian right flank, and secondly, by Wellington's hastening to come to Blücher's aid by occupying the vital Quatre Bras crossroads, and fighting a fierce battle there. Yet as soon as he knew that Blücher had withdrawn towards Wavre, Wellington was obliged to conform and during the night of 17 June, with the British cavalry under Uxbridge expertly conducting the rearguard, Wellington established his army astride the road to Brussels on the ridge south of the village of Waterloo and the forest of Soignes. Two substantial farms, which were to be crucially important in the forthcoming battle – La Haye Sainte on the Brussels road and the Château de Hougoumont, about a mile to the west and slightly south – reinforced his line, which measured about 3½ miles. As was his custom, Wellington had deployed his troops on a crest, behind which they would be able to shelter from the enemy's artillery.

The course of the battle has been admirably summarized by John Keegan in his uniquely distinguished account of it.[3] First, beginning at eleven o'clock in the morning, came the French attempt to capture Hougoumont, an attack which persisted all day and never succeeded. It was intended to draw Wellington's reserves away from his centre, but instead ate up French reserves. Second was d'Erlon's attack on the British centre which started about one o'clock and was checked by Picton's counter-attack, then dispersed by British cavalry. Thirdly, at four o'clock in the afternoon, Ney sent the French cavalry forward to break the British line to the west of d'Erlon's attempt; they were stopped by British artillery and infantry. Next, at about six o'clock, Ney with infantry, having at last taken La Haye Sainte, almost penetrated the

---

[3] *The Face of Battle*, Cape, 1976.

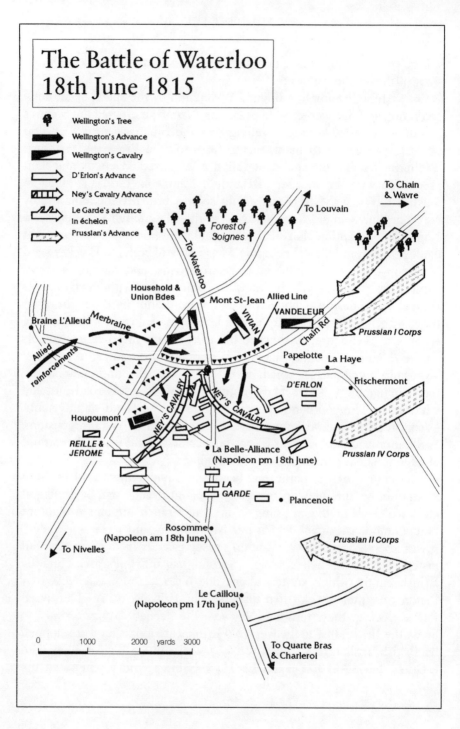

The Battle of Waterloo 18th June 1815

Wellington's Tree
Wellington's Advance
Wellington's Cavalry
D'Erlon's Advance
Ney's Cavalry Advance
Le Garde's advance In échelon
Prussian's Advance

To Chain & Wavre

To Louvain

Forest of Soignes

To Waterloo

Household & Union Bdes

Mont St-Jean

Allied Line

VANDELEUR

VIVIAN

Chain Rd

Prussian I Corps

Braine L'Alleud

Merbraine

Allied reinforcements

Papelotte

La Haye

D'ERLON

Frischermont

NEY'S CAVALRY

NEY'S CAVALRY

Hougoumont

REILLE & JEROME

La Belle-Alliance (Napoleon pm 18th June)

Prussian IV Corps

LA GARDE

Plancenoit

Rosomme (Napoleon am 18th June)

Prussian II Corps

To Nivelles

Le Caillou (Napoleon pm 17th June)

| 0 | 1000 | 2000 | yards | 3000 |

To Quarte Bras & Charleroi

Allied line, but was halted by Wellington's rapid deployment of reinforcements to the threatened position. In the last phase of all, with
the Prussians pressing ever closer to the right flank, Napoleon launched
the Imperial Guard just east of Hougoumont. This last thrust was so
effectively countered by the British infantry both from the front and the
flank that the unthinkable occurred – 'La Guarde recule!' Wellington
then gave orders for a general advance, and except for the Prussian
cavalry's pursuit, the battle was over. Napoleon retired from the battlefield, protected by the Guards as far as Genappe, then, transferring
from his campaign carriage to his mare, Désirée, rode for Charleroi
with an escort of lancers. The Duke had seen off the Emperor.

One or two aspects of the battle deserve further emphasis before we
see what others, particularly Wellington and Napoleon themselves, had
to say about it. The first point of interest is that there was virtually no
manoeuvring by Napoleon, none of the tactical dexterity which in the
past had enabled him to produce decisive concentration at a crucial
time and place. He had not believed it to be necessary. When warned
by Soult, his Chief of Staff, that the steadiness of British troops and
the skilful command of Wellington were things to be taken seriously
(after all, Soult had good reason to know), Napoleon simply dismissed
such advice, saying that the whole thing would be a picnic. Having laid
it down that Wellington was a bad general and the English bad soldiers
(he would never have said such things about the Royal Navy), he resorted
to his original trade, that of an artilleryman, and arranged for his massed
batteries of guns to bombard the Allied positions as a prelude to frontal
attack after frontal attack. Against Wellington's infantry and his knack
of always being in the crucial place at the right moment, and instantly
redeploying his troops to counter threat upon threat, such tactics would
not do. In any event it was not until later on in the battle that Napoleon
took a personal grip on it. During the hours when his army was fighting
only Wellington's mixed force – for once the Prussians appeared on the
battlefield at a time, when the British and Allied line at Waterloo still
held firm, there was no further chance for the French to prevail –
Napoleon left most of the business to Ney, and Ney, despite all his
bravery and skill in conducting the rearguard action after Moscow, was
not renowned for imagination or improvisation. Indeed for this last
campaign Ney was never to show the coolness and steadiness of which
he had formerly been capable. It was all fire and fury and frustrated

rage. Such things had little effect on the calm confidence of Wellington and his redcoats. As we have already noted at the beginning of this story, when Wellington observed what the Emperor was up to, he dismissed it with the laconic comment that 'the fellow was a mere pounder after all'.

Another feature of the battle which will always arouse admiration and invite controversy is the role played by the Château of Hougoumont. Victor Hugo went so far as to say that its conquest was one of Napoleon's dreams and that, had he seized it, it would have given him the world. Hougoumont had two doors to its court, one to the château itself on the southern side, one belonging to the farm to the north. It was the door to the north that was smashed open by a huge French officer who, followed by a number of his jubilant men, rushed into the courtyard. They were instantly set upon by the defending Coldstream Guardsmen, five of whom succeeded in pushing to the doors and barring them with a huge wooden beam. Wellington was later to observe that the success of the battle of Waterloo depended on the closing of these doors. Yet apart from some Nassau and Hanoverian troops, there were at first only four light companies of Coldstream and Scots Guards plus a battery of horse artillery to defend Hougoumont until Wellington, appreciating the scale of the French attack on this vital feature of his defences, sent four more companies of the Coldstream Guards to reinforce the garrison – with the simple order: 'There my lads, in with you and let me see no more of you.' The remarkable achievement of these Foot Guards may be gauged when we consider that, as Victor Hugo put it, they held out for seven hours against the attacks of an entire army. After the initial failure of Napoleon's brother, Prince Jerome, to take Hougoumont, neither he nor Napoleon himself took the decision to mask and bypass this stubborn centre of resistance, so that the main attack could proceed. Jerome allowed what was a diversionary, albeit important, objective to take his eye off the main requirement which was to attack and pierce Wellington's centre; instead of getting this principal attack under way, Jerome poured more and more troops into the desperate struggle for Hougoumont. Victor Hugo's account tells us that the divisions of Foy, Guilleminot, and Bachelu hurled themselves against it; nearly the entire corps of Reille was employed against it, and miscarried; Kellermann's balls were exhausted on this heroic section of wall. Bauduin's brigade was not strong enough to force Hougoumont on the north, and the brigade of Soye could not do more than effect the beginning of a breach on the south, but without taking it. In other words Jerome was making one of the classic errors of war – *reinforcing failure*, and on such a scale that he was dissipating the very strength needed by the French army to sweep Wellington aside before the Prussians came up. Wellington on the other hand had reinforced success. Thus the contribution which Hougoumont's defenders made to the victory at Waterloo was incalculable, and Wellington's praise – 'no troops could have held Hougoumont but British, and only the best of them' – was wholly just. If, as some historians have claimed, the battle of Waterloo was a series of French blunders, Jerome's failure to deal properly with Hougoumont was certainly one of them – as was his brother's failure to overrule him. Yet other even more serious blunders had been made earlier. Perhaps the most significant were Grouchy's incomprehensible refusal to march to the sound of the guns on the afternoon of 18 June 1815 and Ney's inexplicable dithering in not rapidly seizing Quatre Bras two days earlier.

One of the most agreeable and undemanding books about Napoleon's campaigns is Vyvyan Ferrers' *The Brigadier*. In it he gives us a lively account of the career of Marcellin Marbot, a cavalry officer and eventually *général de brigade* in the Grande Armée, who served at Austerlitz, Jena, Eylau, in Spain, at Aspern-Essling, Wagram, in Russia and at Leipzig. The principal source for this biographical piece is Marbot's own book of memoirs, and Ferrers suggests that these memoirs gave Conan Doyle his inspiration for writing his stories about Brigadier Gérard. He reminds us that in naming his hero Brigadier, Doyle is, of course, using it in the English sense, for in French the word *brigadier* means corporal of cavalry. Ferrers also notes that the choice of the name Gérard was surprising: as we have seen, one of the corps commanders at Waterloo was General Etienne Gérard, and on the fateful afternoon of 18 June he was with the newly appointed Marshal Grouchy, who was vainly attempting to obey Napoleon's order to follow up Blücher's army to Wavre and engage it. It was while Grouchy was pondering what to do, that the thunder of guns at Waterloo was heard. If ever the initiative inherent to any great military commander needed to be employed, it was now. To march to the sound of the guns – at a time when your own force was contributing nothing to the battle's resolution – was so fundamental that Grouchy should have given instant orders to do so. Yet at this very moment General Gérard intervened and publicly told Grouchy that it was his duty to march upon the guns. In spite of his own indecision the one thing Grouchy was not prepared to tolerate was a lesson in command from one of his own subordinates and, after an ill-tempered dispute, the marshal made it plain that his duty was to carry out the Emperor's orders and proceed to Wavre.[4] And so he turned his back on the struggle which was to determine Europe's future. Had he marched to the guns with his 33,000 or so men, he would have intercepted the Prussian movement towards Waterloo and reinforced Napoleon at a moment when such reinforcement could have been decisive. Another 'if' constantly recurs, when we consider the behaviour of Ney. When Napoleon was engaging the Prussians at Ligny – by which time Ney should already have seized Quatre Bras – and sent to Ney for d'Erlon's Reserve Corps to complete the business at Ligny, Ney, finding the fight for Quatre Bras becoming ever more severe because his own delay had allowed Wellington to bring up reinforcements, countermanded the order and brought d'Erlon back towards Quatre Bras. In the event d'Erlon took no part in either battle, so that the great 'if' here is this: had Ney allowed d'Erlon to help finish off the Prussians at Ligny, there would have been no need to detach Grouchy with his 33,000 men, who would then have been available for Napoleon in his fight at Waterloo against Wellington – who in turn would not have been reinforced by Blücher. In the event, when at about midday on 17 June Napoleon joined Ney for the decisive attack on Quatre Bras, the information soon afterwards that the village was clear of Wellington's army – which had by this time withdrawn to conform to the Prussian retreat – gave rise to the Emperor's comment to d'Erlon, referring of course to Ney's mistakes: '*On a perdu la France.*' Once more the contrast in temperament and expression of our two great men is emphasized when we compare this hyperbole with Wellington's response that evening to Uxbridge's enquiry as to the Duke's intended strategy. Wellington asks who will attack first – Bonaparte or himself. Uxbridge names the former. The Duke then somewhat ungraciously remarks that, as Bonaparte has not yet revealed his plans, he himself can hardly say what his are. But the sheer generous nature of the man breaks through when, conscious of

---

[4] Napoleon's actual written orders were: 'His Majesty desires you will head for Wavre *in order to draw near to us* . . .' (my italics). Yet this in itself was contradictory for whereas Wavre was to the north of Grouchy, Napoleon was to the west. This lack of clarity puts us in mind of Lord Raglan's imprecise order before the Charge of the Light Brigade.

his brusqueness, he puts his hand on Uxbridge's shoulder, assuring him that whatever happens, it is certain that the two of them will do their duty. The Napoleonic equivalent would have been to pinch someone's ear.

These differences were echoed by the various actions and pronouncements of the opposing Commanders-in-Chief during their single, historic encounter. 'Ask me for anything but time,' Napoleon had once declared. Yet on the morning of 18 June 1815 he treated time as if it were a commodity of which he had a limitless store. Whereas Wellington was up and about at six o'clock that morning, riding his chestnut, Copenhagen, inspecting his line, encouraging his soldiers, selecting a command post (the famous 'Wellington Tree' at the crossroads just north of La Haye Sainte) and telling Müffling that Bonaparte would now see how a sepoy general could defend a position, Napoleon did not breakfast until eight o'clock and, leaving Hougoumont aside, did not start his main attack on the British centre until one o'clock in the afternoon. Elizabeth Longford makes a particular point of contrasting Wellington's 'intense activity' together with 'his habitual calm and unusual geniality' with Napoleon's dilatory behaviour and contemptuous comments. When Soult advised the recall of Grouchy's 33,000 soldiers, the Emperor insulted him; when Reille suggested that the British infantry, posted by Wellington, would be well nigh undefeatable but that manoeuvre might do the trick, Napoleon turned away dismissively; even his brother Jerome, speaking of a junction between Wellington and Blücher, got short shrift. Napoleon said there could be no link-up for two days. In fact within four hours the vanguard of Bülow's corps would be visible to the French. Such a misappreciation of the situation by the greatest captain of the age is hard to explain. For the general who formerly had been a master of concentration to have indulged already in two actions – Ligny and Quatre Bras – in which real concentration would have destroyed the Prussians, and not just humbugged, but overwhelmed Wellington, and now to have split his army so that he had some 72,000 men with 250 guns to attack Wellington's roughly 68,000 men and 150 guns – when with Grouchy his strength could have been 105,000 – was no recipe for success. And the Prussians still had 100,000 men and were marching towards the battlefield. Yet at this stage the battle was still to be lost or won. At half-past one in the afternoon Napoleon had positioned himself and his staff at La Belle-Alliance. The orders to attack were passed to Ney and on to d'Erlon. It says much for the courage and discipline of d'Erlon's corps that, following the renewed cannonade by eighty guns of Napoleon's artillery, they advanced in their columns against the Allied cannon fire, and having swept past La Haye Sainte arrived on the crest of Wellington's line to be met by Picton's division, whose brigades were commanded by those Peninsular veterans, Pack and Kempt. While Pack's men advanced to meet the French with bayonets, Kempt's battalions fired their deadly and disciplined volleys into the densely massed enemy columns. Picton himself was at the head of Kempt's men when he was killed by a bullet which penetrated his famous beaver hat and struck his forehead. The situation was a desperate one for Pack's brigade which, weakened by its losses at Quatre Bras, was in danger of being pushed back by weight of numbers alone, and it was then that Uxbridge with his two brigades of heavy cavalry took a hand in the game. To Napoleon at La Belle-Alliance it seemed as if d'Erlon was about to break through the Allied line, and Wellington too from his tree had seen that Picton's men needed instant support. Once more desperate appliance was to relieve diseases desperate grown. The very man to take desperate measures was fortunately at hand. With the Household Brigade and the Union Brigade under his command, Uxbridge did not hesitate. He galloped to the commander of the Household Brigade, Lord Edward Somerset, told him to form line and went on to Sir William Ponsonby, commanding the Union Brigade, with similar orders, and then, with more encouragement from Wellington himself – 'Now, gentlemen, for the honour of the Household troops' – the two brigades charged with Uxbridge at their head. The charge was both a triumphant success and a tragic disaster, for having sent d'Erlon's divisions into disintegrating flight, the British cavalrymen – renowned for dash, but not for disciplined control – pursued their enemies too far then, blown and scattered, they were themselves subjected to furious counter-attacks by fresh, numerous French cavalry, who inflicted terrible casualties on them – 2,500 in all. Napoleon had observed this event and commented in particular on the spectacular performance of the Scots Greys – 'Those terrible grey horses, how they fight.' Apart from his cavalry losses, d'Erlon's attack, though repulsed, had cost Wellington 4,500 infantry. But the line was restored – with both La Haye Sainte and Hougoumont still in Allied hands.

The British cavalry had certainly resolved a difficult crisis, but had been mishandled. An even more spectacular misuse of cavalry was now about to take place – this time by the French. While the struggle for Hougoumont continued and d'Erlon was attempting to reform his shattered divisions, another intense artillery bombardment caused Wellington to withdraw his infantry under cover of the ridge's reverse slope. Thereupon Ney, interpreting this movement as a general retirement of the British line, sent forward 4,500 of his cavalry to sweep the ridge clear and so bring about the victory which had hitherto evaded him. To attack unbroken infantry with cavalry alone was to break all the rules of war, and it was soon to be shown, as Ney's regiments of cuirassiers came up against the battalion squares of redcoats, with Horse Artillery batteries deployed between them and the British cavalry behind, what a heavy price the French were to pay for so tactically unsound a manoeuvre. Not only did the Horse Artillery's nine-pounders, loaded with round-shot and case-shot, take terrible toll of the French cavalry's leading ranks, but the British and Hanoverian squares, unintimidated by the glittering array of lancers and cuirassiers who could inflict little damage when confronted with disciplined ranks of bayonets, stood their ground and, when ordered to fire, brought down great numbers of horses and men. Wellington's reply to a question put to him much later as to whether the cuirassiers had not come up very well, was that they had 'gone down very well too'. In spite of all this, Ney was reinforced by a further 5,000 heavy cavalry and the whole process was repeated. All in all Ney's attacks persisted for the best part of two hours in spite of appalling losses. During this phase of the battle, which lasted until about five o'clock, Wellington was everywhere, riding up and down the line, encouraging and directing, and now and again making one of his pithy, matter-of-fact comments: 'The battle is mine; and if the Prussians arrive soon, there will be an end to the war.' And it was during Ney's second attempt with the heavy cavalry, observing that Napoleon's tactics seemed to be confined to pulverizing artillery bombardments followed by frontal assaults, that the Duke damned the fellow for being a mere pounder after all. What a difference there was between Wellington astride Copenhagen looking perfectly composed and the glimpsed sight of Ney – whose fourth horse had been killed – 'his uniform blackened, his epaulettes shot away, his helmet lost, madly beating an English cannon with the flat of his sword. A telescope, a writing-pad and a pencil', notes A. G. Macdonnell, 'would have been more effective weapons.'

Yet Ney was still to engineer one last chance for the Emperor. At six o'clock, abandoning at last the fruitless charges by cavalry alone and ordered by Napoleon to take La Haye Sainte, he launched an attack on it with combined infantry, cavalry and guns in a renewed attempt to break the British centre. He succeeded in taking La Haye Sainte and, with a very real prospect at last of penetrating the British line, sent urgently to the Emperor for more troops. Napoleon's dilemma was acute: pressing in on his right flank were the Prussians and Lobau was clamouring for reinforcements to check them; in front Ney was similarly demanding reinforcements, to execute the *coup de grâce*. It was then that the great gambler misplayed his hand. Unwilling at this time to risk the Imperial Guard, he refused Ney's urgent appeal with the peevish question: 'Troops? Where do you expect me to find them? Do you expect me to make them?' The last chance had been chucked away. During this crisis we again see the contrast in character between the petulant Emperor and the cool perseverant Duke, whom when asked by an artilleryman if he might fire at Napoleon, dismissed any such idea – 'Generals commanding armies have something else to do than to shoot at one another'[5] – and, as the enemy artillery bombardment resumed, commented: 'Hard pounding this, gentlemen; try who can pound the longest.' During the short lull after Napoleon's refusal to send the Guard up to reinforce Ney, Wellington, calm as ever, took personal control of the threatened sector in his position and steadily reinforced it. The thinning red line still held on, the Prussians were temporarily checked by Lobau, and now at about seven o'clock, in a final throw of the dice and himself leading them to La Haye Sainte, the Emperor launched the Grenadiers and Chasseurs of the Imperial Guard. At no time could the two Commanders-in-Chief have been more closely face to face, but whereas Napoleon handed over his cherished 'Immortals' to Marshal Ney, and spread the lie that the approaching Prussian army heralded the long-awaited arrival of Grouchy, Wellington first restored the threatened positions of Halkett's brigade and the Brunswicker battalion, then galloped up to Maitland's 1st Guards, who were concealed from the advancing Imperial Guard, and told them to stand up and fire.

---

[5] His comment becomes even more illustrative of his character when we recall that Napoleon's will included a legacy to Cantillon, the man who attempted to assassinate Wellington in 1818.

This check to Napoleon's élite troops was then turned into absolute defeat by the initiative of Colborne and his 52nd Regiment, who with tactical boldness of the first order advanced to the flank of the Imperial Guard and subjected them to shatteringly accurate and deadly volleys. It was characteristic of Wellington to be on the spot shortly afterwards. Having ordered the 95th Rifles forward as well, he congratulated Colborne and urged him to follow up his success: 'Go on . . . They won't stand.' Indeed they did not stand. *'La Guarde recule'* was the terrible cry heard throughout the French ranks.

It was almost over. The Prussians were on the battlefield at Papelotte and La Haye, and at about half-past seven that evening Wellington gave another expression to the English language when he determined on a general advance by his army: 'Oh damn it! In for a penny, in for a pound' – and, with the signal of waving his hat three times towards the French, his cavalry and infantry swept down on to the plain in front of them. It was the end. While Ney, in a further frenzy, yelled at d'Erlon that, if caught, they would be hanged;[6] while Napoleon vainly tried to stay the general retreat of his army with what reserves of the Guard he could muster; while Wellington with Uxbridge at his side rode forward on Copenhagen, a shell passing over his charger's neck to hit Uxbridge's right knee; while the Duke and Blücher met on the Brussels road near La Belle Alliance – by which name Blücher wanted to call the whole affair, to be overruled by Wellington; while 40,000–50,000 men and untold numbers of horses lay dead or wounded on the field of Waterloo; while the Prussians began their pursuit and Napoleon slipped away – the Emperor's last army disintegrated and Wellington turned Copenhagen back to Waterloo. After supper, waiting in vain for some of his personal staff to appear, he pronounced that the hand of Almighty God had been upon him that day. After a few hours' sleep he arose to be confronted by a list of casualties that caused the tears to furrow through the sweat and dirt on his face, saying to Dr Hume that although he did not know what it was to lose a battle, nothing could be more painful than to gain one with the loss of so many friends. He sat down to compose his Waterloo despatch. Meanwhile Napoleon, not far away at Charleroi, who *did* know what it was to lose a battle and had few friends,

---

[6] A prophetic comment, for Ney was tried and condemned by his peers, and executed by firing squad in December 1815.

was contemplating rallying his army to continue the fight, until he was advised that the deputies in Paris might surrender and make peace behind his back. Thereupon he made for his capital.

The point has been made many times that Wellington's despatch after the battle was characteristically restrained and brief. We may imagine with what extravagant triumph Napoleon would have hailed a victory. Wellington simply assured Bathurst, Secretary of State for War, that the Guards division set an example to all, that everyone behaved well, that the assistance he received from the Prussians was decisive, that the army's losses had been grievous, but, as in all his writings, he said nothing of glory. It was a tale of duty well done. Wellington's own subsequent comments on the battle were comparably laconic – it had been a damned serious business, a damned nice thing, the nearest run thing you ever saw in your life, a pounding match, in which Napoleon did not manoeuvre at all. The French had moved forward in the old style, in columns, and were driven off in the old style. Yet others were lavish in their praise of his own conduct in command. He had been everywhere, galloping here to engage the enemy, darting there to issue orders, always in the thick of it, his attention concentrated on each crisis, his calm perseverance and mere presence an inspiration. Even he admitted as much when he told Creevey: 'By God! I don't think it would have done if I had not been there.' His indispensable contribution to victory was fittingly and uniquely acknowledged when the Waterloo medal was later issued to all British soldiers who had been there, for on its reverse side, together with the name and date of the battle, is the word 'Wellington'.

'No two men', wrote Charles Petrie, 'could be more unlike than the great commanders who decided the fate of Europe that Sunday in June at Waterloo.' He went on to say that Napoleon had no very high opinion of Wellington. Perhaps one reason for this was that whereas Napoleon had conducted war on a grand scale for campaign after campaign, Wellington had been obliged to husband a relatively small army in a defensive campaign, where he could not afford to suffer a single serious reverse. Napoleon was prodigal with his armies, Wellington never. Yet Wellington had a genius for improvisation. He himself echoed this point by likening the French marshals' plans of campaign to a splendid piece of harness which was good enough until it was broken, then you were done for, compared with his own method of making a campaign of ropes, so that if anything went wrong, he tied a knot and went on. Moreover, as Sir William Napier, who served under Wellington in the Peninsula and wrote an incomparable history of the war there, summed it up: 'Wellington possessed in high degree that daring promptness of action, that faculty of inspiration for suddenly deciding the fate of whole campaigns with which Napoleon was endowed beyond all mankind.' At Waterloo, however, the promptness of action and inspired decisiveness belonged not to Napoleon, but to Wellington.

A. G. Macdonnell, on the other hand, finds fault not so much with Napoleon as with Marshals Ney, Soult and Grouchy. Grouchy, as we have seen, marched his 33,000 men about without engaging the enemy at all and ignored the classic requirement of marching to the sound of guns; Soult, as Chief of Staff, did nothing to stem the tide of mistakes; and Ney, in Macdonnell's view, lost the battle by his ill-tempered countermanding of the Emperor's order on 16 June to send up d'Erlon's corps so that he, Napoleon, could have destroyed Blücher's army rather than simply mauling it and pushing it back. Had this been done, says Macdonnell – and others have said it too – Grouchy would never have been despatched to follow up the Prussians and so Napoleon would have had an extra 33,000 men to dispose of Wellington – who in turn would have received no last-minute support from the Prussians. To which we may reply that when Soult urged Napoleon to send for Grouchy before attacking at Waterloo, the Emperor pooh-poohed the idea; and he did nothing to correct Ney's initial mistakes either in allowing Jerome to get too involved at Hougoumont, or in attacking the enemy crest with cavalry alone. Moreover, at that one fleeting moment of opportunity which occurred late in the day when Ney had almost penetrated the Allied centre and urgently sent to the Emperor for more troops, Napoleon declined. We may be sure that he would have taken full credit for victory, and so must bear responsibility for defeat. Victor Hugo summed up Waterloo as the strangest encounter in history for Napoleon and Wellington are such opposites:

On one side, precision, foresight, geometry, prudence, all assured retreat, reserves spaced with an obstinate coolness, an impenetrable method, strategy which takes advantage of the ground, tactics which preserve the equilibrium of battalions, carnage executed according to rule, war regulated, watch in hand, nothing voluntarily left to chance, the ancient classic courage, absolute regularity; on the other, intuition, divination, military strangeness, superhuman instinct, a flaming glance, an indescribable something which gazes like an eagle and strikes like lightning, a prodigious act in disdainful impetuosity, all the mysteries of a profound soul, association with destiny.

Bagehot would have approved of the first list of qualities, Byron of the second. It was indeed a strange encounter – in the end determined, as Hugo himself emphasizes, by the circumstance that Napoleon waited for Grouchy in vain, while Wellington's wait for Blücher was at length rewarded. Vincent Cronin finds less fault with Napoleon's actual supervision of the battle itself, but more with the preface to it – in particular his failure to ensure that Ney crushed Wellington at Quatre Bras on 17 June. Thus the Emperor's '*On a perdu la France*' really applies most damningly to himself. Cronin also blames Napoleon for his total misjudgement both of the British soldier and of his Commander-in-Chief, which sprang from over-confidence, the very over-confidence which also persuaded him to attack the Allies without Grouchy, indeed without even giving Grouchy clear, sensible orders. Yet the Emperor had himself laid it down that clarity was uniquely important: 'Be clear,' he declared, 'and all the rest will follow.'

Whereas it must be conceded that Napoleon and his subordinates made mistakes, if we look at the other side of the coin, it must also be conceded that Wellington, the same age as the Emperor, did not. On the contrary, he was at the peak of his form; as he himself asserted later, he never took so much trouble about any battle, yet it was 'the most desperate business' he was ever in and never had he been 'so near to being beat'. John Keegan's excellent portrait of Wellington in *The Mask of Command* contains one passage which puts into a nutshell the reasons for his success:

If he was not beaten, much indeed had to do with the trouble he had taken. Wellington's energy was legendary; so too was his attention to detail, unwillingness to delegate, ability to do without sleep or food, disregard for personal comfort, contempt for danger. But in the few days of the Waterloo campaign he surpassed even his own stringent standards of courage and asceticism.

How different was Napoleon's conduct! He showed little of his former superhuman energy, he ignored significant detail, he delegated recklessly, required both sleep and food, was made as comfortable as field conditions would allow, and despite his legendary courage, largely kept out of the firing line, while as to this last point Wellington was constantly at the place of danger, risking his life more frequently and for longer periods than anyone in his army. If ever a general deserved victory, it was Wellington at Waterloo. If ever a general forfeited victory, it was Napoleon at Waterloo. There for the moment we will leave it, although a further look will be needed when we finally contrast the Duke and the Emperor. One later remark about Waterloo from each of them will again highlight the difference in their perspective. At St Helena the Emperor is nursing his regrets: 'It was a fatality, for in spite of all I should have won that battle ... Poor France, to be beaten by those scoundrels. But 'tis true there had already been Cressy and Agincourt.' Wellington at Deal is questioning the very idea of accurately recording anything: 'Thus there is one event noted in the world – the battle of Waterloo – and you will not find any two people to agree as to the exact hour when it commenced.'

However much historians may deprecate the uselessness of speculating as to the 'ifs' of history, we may all applaud Stendhal's diverting suggestion that had Napoleon won at Waterloo, not only would there have been no Liberals to be afraid of in the 1820s, but all the ancient sovereigns of Europe would only have kept their thrones by marrying the daughters of Napoleon's marshals. Judging by the mettle of these marshals, the sovereigns in question could have done a great deal worse.

CHAPTER 11

Prisoner and Politician

Now thanks to my misfortune, one can see me nakedly as I
am.

Napoleon at St Helena

The ball is at my foot, and I hope I shall have the strength
to give it a good kick.

Wellington

T HE contest was over. The Emperor had played his last hand.
The Duke was to go on playing his own game. Napoleon was
condemned to six years as a virtual prisoner on an island in the
Atlantic. Wellington would reach the highest offices of state during
more than thirty-six years of diplomatic, political, military and social
activity and become one of the most renowned and revered Britons of
his age or any age. Since the actions of these two men during the years
1815 to 1821 were so greatly separated, we had better consider them
separately. Any impartial account of Napoleon's journey to and long
exile at St Helena must enhance our sympathy and admiration for the
fallen Emperor. The sheer magic of the man cast its spell not only over
the soldiers of France, but also the sailors of the Royal Navy. Just as
the ship's company of HMS *Undaunted*, which took the Emperor to
Elba, had wished him 'long life and prosperity' and 'better luck another
time', so the crew of the *Bellerophon*, the man-of-war commanded by
Captain Maitland under whose protection Napoleon sailed from
Rochefort to England in July 1815, recorded their feeling that 'if the
people of England knew him as well as we do, they would not touch a
hair of his head'. These sentiments were echoed again by the men of
the *Northumberland* who, during the voyage to St Helena, had every

opportunity to study their celebrated passenger: 'He is a fine fellow, who does not deserve his fate.'

Napoleon was not greatly impressed by what he saw on sighting this remote, mountainous island, 5,000 miles from France. It was not in his view an attractive place and he would have done better to have remained in Egypt. On landing he pronounced it a disgraceful island and a prison. He would need great courage and strength to endure life there. Fortunately he had both and during his five and a half years at Longwood – a wooden farmhouse, high up on a plateau, where his suite of rooms included a study, drawing- and dining-rooms, ante-room and bathroom – he spent most of his time dictating his memoirs, reading or talking to those who had chosen to accompany him and indulging in formal evening gatherings. There were four friends with him. Three were generals – Bertrand, de Montholon and Gourgaud. The fourth was Count Las Cases. Inevitably they recorded their impressions and noted down the great man's sayings. In choosing from those willing to come with him to St Helena, Napoleon was able to please himself. In the selection of a gaoler, he was not. The first of these, Admiral Sir George Cockburn, was not precisely congenial, for initially he was unwilling to treat Napoleon with the courtesy that might be thought of as proper for someone of such consequence. But later, on observing the Emperor's patience and reluctance to make difficulties, he was more considerate. Cockburn remained responsible for Napoleon at St Helena until the arrival of Colonel Sir Hudson Lowe, whom Wellington, while assembling his staff in Brussels before the battle of Waterloo, had thought so stupid that he would not accept him as quartermaster-general. It was in April 1816 that Lowe arrived – 'a narrow, ignorant, irritable man without a vestige of tact or sympathy,' according to Lord Rosebery, and one whose 'eye', observed Napoleon on first catching sight of him, 'is that of a hyena caught in a trap'. It was perhaps not surprising that the British government had appointed such an unprepossessing Governor of St Helena for they had never wanted the responsibility of guaranteeing Napoleon's security in the first place. Liverpool, the Prime Minister, had expressed to Castlereagh the wish that Louis XVIII would 'hang or shoot Buonaparte as the best termination of the business'. But as Napoleon had placed himself under British protection and as the Allied powers wished Britain to accept the charge, they did. Liverpool, on realizing that the Bourbon King of France was not in a position of sufficient strength to treat Napoleon as a rebel, agreed that the British government would take it upon themselves to be responsible for his custody. Yet Liverpool was in no doubt as to the dangers of harbouring so renowned a hero of the French Revolution in Britain itself – where unrest was widespread and insurrection just below the surface, as was to be shown a few years later by the Peterloo massacre and the introduction of the Six Acts.[1] Indeed Liverpool told Castlereagh that in Britain Napoleon would become an object of both curiosity and compassion – a view reinforced by Admiral Lord Keith, who suggested that if Napoleon had been received by the Prince Regent, the two of them would have become the best of friends within half an hour.

On the tiny island of St Helena, friendships were more difficult. Reverence, pettiness, jealousies, pretences, recollections, fabrications, regrets were commonplace. In his majestic *Napoleon: The Last Phase*, Lord Rosebery comments shrewdly on those members of the Emperor's entourage who recorded in their journals both for posterity and for personal gain the doings and sayings of the most illustrious prisoner in the world. Las Cases, who was genuinely devoted to the Emperor, fabricates too much. His motive – vindication of his beloved master – may be praiseworthy, his consequent effort to distort the truth of the matter is less so. An outstanding instance is the controversy surrounding those circumstances which led to the Duc d'Enghien's execution in 1804, centring on whether or not Talleyrand received – and suppressed – a letter from the Duc, declaring his abandonment of claims to the throne and his willingness to serve the First Consul. Although Las Cases's attempt to clear Napoleon of what Duff Cooper calls 'the blackest deed in [his] career' was supported by another of Napoleon's St Helena companions, de Montholon, the whole idea that Talleyrand was principally to blame was exploded by Napoleon himself, who before his death inserted in his will a statement that for the 'safety, interest and honour of the French people' he had had the Duc arrested and tried. That Talleyrand was implicated has never been in doubt. But to Talleyrand – whom at St Helena Napoleon branded a *scelerato* (villain)

---

[1] In August 1819 an assembly of some 50,000 people with revolutionary banners was to be addressed by Henry 'Orator' Hunt. When the authorities tried to arrest him, scuffles with the troops caused the yeomanry to charge. Eleven people were killed, 400 wounded. The Six Acts were designed to prevent revolutionary outbreaks.

and a *briccone* (rascal) – the Duc's execution was not so much a crime, as a blunder – for the Duc was not just innocent of conspiracy; he was a romantic hero and his death deeply shocked French public opinion.

Such goings-on by the recorders of St Helena's events show to what lengths Napoleon's adherents would go in order to magnify the Emperor's reputation and legend. From time to time Las Cases, like Napoleon himself, descends from the sublime to the ridiculous, as when, on observing Napoleon rubbing his stomach after enjoying coffee and saying that it felt good, Las Cases writes how difficult it would be to express his own feelings at these simple words. Of course at St Helena Napoleon's life was simple, but the petty restrictions imposed by Hudson Lowe made it less tolerable than would have been the case if Wellington's advice had been taken. In the first place the Duke would never have chosen Lowe – 'a very bad choice' as 'he was a man wanting education and judgement'. Moreover he, Wellington, would have adopted a different plan for supervising the prisoner at St Helena. As there were very few landing places, these would have been strictly guarded, and Napoleon would have been required to show himself to an English officer every night and morning. 'For the rest of the time I would have let him do or go wherever he pleased. This would have avoided most matters of dispute, and then he might have received or sent as many letters as he chose.' But Lowe posted 125 sentries to watch Longwood by day and 72 at night. For a man to whom the whole idea of *Liberté* was something he had been championing all his life, such a reminder of his captivity was unnecessarily mean and pettifogging. To Las Cases Napoleon called Lowe not just a gaoler, but a hangman.

Apart from dictating his memoirs, reading, playing chess, Napoleon talked endlessly and his conversation was duly noted down by those who heard it. The subjects he ranged over were very varied. It was clear from what he said of the English people that he held their character in great respect. Having at one time dismissed them as a nation of shopkeepers (not Napoleon's own phrase, but Paoli's), he later declared that the English character was superior to that of the French. They were decisive and brave. With an English army he would have conquered the world. There were only two nations – France and England. The rest were nothing. Yet it was also clear that he was totally ignorant of England and its people, when for example he states that had he gone to London in 1815 he would have been carried about in triumph. Everyone in

England would have been on his side. How much the Emperor really believed what he was saying and how much was for posterity is never quite plain. But he certainly puts his finger on what Englishmen of the time were like when he says there is something of the bulldog in them, they are ferocious and live from day to day. British magnanimity in victory is a puzzle to him. 'For a thousand years such another opportunity of aggrandizing England will not occur.' England should have insisted on a commercial monopoly on the seas of India and China. No other nations should have been allowed to put their noses beyond the Cape. 'The English can dictate to the world, more especially if they withdraw their troops from the Continent, relegate Wellington to his estates and remain a purely maritime power. She can then do what she likes.' Napoleon recommends the return of 'old Lord Chatham' as Prime Minister. Here we might echo Polonius, 'How pregnant some of his replies are.' It is almost as if Napoleon foresaw the resumption of a great blue-water policy, with Wellington – by no means relegated to his estates, however – preserving the British army once withdrawn from Europe by hiding it in the Colonies, and then Great Britain, under the influence of such men as Palmerston, Disraeli and Salisbury and by means of an all-powerful navy and relatively small numbers of British redcoats, supplemented by splendid sepoys, both building and maintaining the greatest empire yet seen and establishing a *pax Britannica* to go with it.

Napoleon talks too of his family and his amours. His father had been a man of pleasure, wanting to play the part of a great nobleman; his mother, most faithful to him of all, wished to join him at St Helena, old and blind though she was. As for his wives, he had loved Josephine. She, like Madame Mère, would have accompanied him to Elba. Marie-Louise was true, honest and innocent, until seduced by the wiles of the Duchess of Montebello and the wicked ways of Count Neipperg. Of his brothers he has little good to say, nor of his sisters. He should never have made Joseph King of Spain, nor given to Murat and Caroline the Kingdom of Naples. He talks of his mistresses – among them Marie Walewska was the only one for whom he felt a real attachment. Apart from the petticoat encounters – and in order to make time pass he even discusses whether fat or thin, dark or fair women are to be preferred – there is always another favourite subject: the battlefield. He calls war a strange art. Having fought sixty battles, he had learned nothing from them that he did not know at first. Reduced to absolute first principles, the statement is supportable. For these principles do not change. Correctly to select your primary object and then so to concentrate and deploy your forces to achieve this object were, are and will remain the two master rules of strategy. And tactically you cannot go far wrong if you conform to the requirements of good intelligence, rapid movement, concentrated force, surprise and sound administration – all combined with overwhelming fire-power and adaptable manoeuvre. The trouble with Napoleon's later campaigns was that although he knew what ought to be done, he did not do it. Yet at St Helena he admits his mistakes. The blame for the Russian campaign rests entirely with himself. He should never have remained in Moscow so long. Indeed, he had been wrong even in embarking on the advance into Russia at all without first making certain of support from Austria (his marriage to Marie-Louise had – he thought mistakenly – given him this assurance) and dealing with Prussia before crossing the Niemen.

Napoleon also concedes that his policy in Spain had been a fatal blunder. He should have pulled his army out of Spain after the Russian débâcle, restored Ferdinand to the throne and had the benefit of nearly 200,000 more soldiers. What a difference there might then have been in the defensive campaign of 1813! He does not, of course, say how the southern borders of France would have been protected against an advancing Wellington with British redcoats and a vengeful Spanish army, but it may be supposed that the defence of the Pyrenees would have presented no great military problem to a substantial French army fighting on French soil with abundant supplies and no guerrillas to harass them. Not surprisingly Napoleon refers to Austerlitz as a brilliant victory, and also Eckmühl and the splendid manoeuvre there when with 50,000 men he defeated more than double that number. Then, curiously, he picks on Borodino as a fine achievement. It is true that Borodino was fought at the end of unbelievably long lines of communication – 1,800 miles from Paris – but it was a brutal slogging match, with no proper manoeuvring, and the Russian redoubt and position were taken by sheer perseverance. Moreover, the Emperor himself was sitting inactive a mile back from the action and so aroused Ney's fury for not sending up the Old Guard to clinch the whole affair by pursuing the retreating, defeated Russians that Ney broke out with his condemnation of his Commander-in-Chief for being so far behind, adding that if no longer a general, he should clear off back to Paris and leave it to the marshals to do the commanding. During and immediately after the Russian campaign Napoleon could not have spoken more highly of Ney, yet when at St Helena he hears of his execution, he swings from one extreme to another. First, de Montholon records, the Emperor is saying that Ney's death is a crime, his blood is sacred, his conduct in the Russian campaign unequalled. But Gourgaud reports otherwise. Ney got what he deserved. Traitors were to be despised. He should never have made Ney a marshal in the first place, but should have left him as a divisional general, for on the field of battle he was invaluable. When Napoleon referred to traitors, he could not have failed to have in mind – quite apart from Ney's abandonment of the Bourbon cause before Waterloo – that it was Ney who had told the Emperor in 1814 that the army would no longer obey him, but its generals. Reports by his entourage of Napoleon's reaction to the news of Murat's death are equally capricious: at one moment it is horrible; at the next Murat has got his desserts; he too had been overpromoted – a marshal, yes, for he was a brave man; a King, no.

Napoleon may not have had too many regrets as to the death of his former comrades in arms. His own great regrets concern himself: first that he should not have died in a truly heroic way – at Moscow, in Dresden before the Russian campaign when all Europe was at his feet, or at Waterloo; secondly he regrets the lost dream of the East; he himself had said that to destroy England, France had to possess Egypt, and had they done so, England could have bid farewell to India. For France to be master of Egypt would have been to be master of India too (almost every British statesman from Pitt to Churchill would have agreed with him); 'If I had been able to get to India from Egypt I should have driven them [the British] from India.' His foresight was remarkable. He would have constructed canals from the Red Sea to the Mediterranean and to the Nile at Cairo. And now, Napoleon went on, the danger to the British position in India would come from the Russians. As we know, British campaigning on the north-west frontier and the Great Game which was played there lasted for a hundred years. The third great regret is Waterloo. How had he lost the battle? He could not understand it. 'Had he had Suchet at the head of Grouchy's army, had he had Andréossi in Soult's place, could Bessières or Lannes have commanded the Guard, had he given the command of the Guard to Lobau, had Murat headed the cavalry, had Clausel or Lamarque been at the War Office, all might have been different.'[2] Yes, we may say, but Lannes had been killed at Essling, Bessières at Leipzig, Murat had been in hiding during the Hundred Days, and no one could have been more reliable or efficient at the War Office than Davout. The biggest 'if' of all concerns Napoleon himself. Had he commanded according to the principles of clarity, speed, concentration and rapid manoeuvre, principles which he had so often adhered to formerly, the team of marshals and generals he *did* have at Waterloo might still have done the trick. Yet, 'after all,' he admits, 'I am only a man.'

Wellington's sentiments precisely. 'I ought to have someone behind me', he had said after Salamanca, when he triumphantly entered Cadiz, 'to remind me that I am but a man.' And again to Lady Salisbury in 1836 when wandering through the woods at Walmer: 'I feel I am but a man.' Perhaps so, but what a man! And whereas in the years following Waterloo, Napoleon is talking, Wellington is both talking and *doing*. While Napoleon endured six years of existence – one cannot call it more – at St Helena from 1815 to 1821, the Duke of Wellington was active in many fields – among them command of the Army of Occupation in France, membership of Lord Liverpool's Cabinet as Master General of the Ordnance, diplomacy at the Congress of Aix-la-Chapelle, and of course a favourite among the petticoats. We will look at them one by one. Wellington's victory at Waterloo, together with naval supremacy, enabled Britain further to pursue her traditional policy of striving to maintain a European balance of power, so that no single nation could dominate the Continent. After the twenty-year upheaval caused by Napoleon, there was a deep longing for peace. Yet there were influences at work designed to upset the peace, principally Liberalism, which, designed to produce the greatest good for the greatest number, was championed by constitutional government, and Nationalism, the right of each nation to control not just its own destiny but, as Napoleon had so sensationally demonstrated, the destinies of other less powerful nations too. In 1815 four powers were the arbiters of Europe – Russia, Austria, Prussia and Great Britain. Each took somewhat different views of these two influences. Alexander I of Russia was in theory liberal and benevolent, in practice harshly autocratic. Metternich had always been

[2] *Napoleon: The Last Phase*, Lord Rosebery.

and would always be implacably opposed to any form of Liberalism. To him all such ideas meant Revolution, and he was to succeed in keeping revolution more or less at bay in Austria for some thirty-odd years. Above all, the status quo must be maintained. Frederick William of Prussia also began by sympathizing with Liberalism, but soon turned away from it. Under the influence of Metternich, he became an Absolutist. For Great Britain, Castlereagh, Foreign Secretary from 1812 until his death in 1822, believed above all in the balance of power and favoured the sort of diplomacy which sprang from frequently conferring with the other great European states – hence the series of Congresses. Although Castlereagh was ultimately unsuccessful in reconciling the aims and attitudes of constitutional and autocratic countries, his realism in insisting that France must play an honourable and significant part in maintaining the balance of Europe ensured that there was no general European war involving all the Great Powers for a century. Eagerly and strongly supported by Wellington, Castlereagh was able to suppress the vindictiveness of the other three powers, who wanted to humiliate France. Happily the Army of Occupation was commanded by Wellington, who made sure that the Russians did not blow up the Bridge of Jena by the simple expedient of posting a British sentry on it. He also saw that an army of 150,000 was far too large and recommended its reduction.

Under his direction the British contingent set a splendid example of discipline and good behaviour. Their everyday conduct was quite unlike that of the Prussians, Russians and Austrians who arrogantly took all they wanted without paying for anything, who seemed to take pleasure in destroying and ravaging houses, farms and furniture, who played the Conquerors with their bullying, stealing and wanton destruction. The British redcoat was much milder, respecting property, paying for what he consumed, helping the Parisians, avoiding injury to the people and property. They even enjoyed the jokes made about them. And when it came to putting on a military display, they did it all with a minimum of orders, fuss or preparation. After three years, British troops were withdrawn from French territory, and Wellington was able to go home and enter the Cabinet as Master General of the Ordnance. Before we join him there, however, we will touch on his controversial position with regard to the execution of Marshal Ney, and his participation in the Congress of Aix-la-Chapelle.

Nothing could show the restored Bourbon régime and its adherents in a worse light than the trial, condemnation and death by firing squad of Marshal Ney. As A. G. Macdonnell has so splendidly described, the Household Corps, who at the time of the first Bourbon restoration had so elegantly lounged through the salons of Paris, snubbing Napoleon's marshals and generals, the veterans of twenty years' fighting and as many battlefields – these nobodies had taken no part in the defeat of Napoleon's army at Waterloo. They had left the actual fighting to the Prussians and the English with some Dutchmen and Hanoverians thrown in. 'In a word, the descendants of the great and ancient military houses of France had made cowardly fools of themselves and they knew it.' So the White Terror was howling for blood and at the top of the list in the so-called 'Royal Ordinances' was the name of the man who had promised to bring the Corsican usurper to Paris in an iron cage, but then had promptly gone over to him and commanded a large part of his army in Belgium, while King Louis and the other bolters had been scurrying about well away from the sound of cannon. Ney was arrested, and one of his fellow marshals, St Cyr, gave orders that he should be tried by court martial. Only two of the marshals stood by Ney – Moncey, who pleaded with the King himself that he should not be required to preside at such a court martial, and so persisted in his refusal that he was imprisoned, and Davout, who having forced an amnesty out of the Allied commanders before the second Peace of Paris, insisted that he would never have signed the amnesty had he not understood that it applied also to Ney. As it was, Ney was tried not by court martial, but at his own request, by the Chamber of Peers. During Ney's trial many appeals were made to the Duke of Wellington to inter- vene. But he did not. The three reasons for his not doing so have been explained by Elizabeth Longford in her incomparable biography of the Duke. First he could not speak solely for himself, being the representa- tive of the Allies; second it would not do for the King to be speaking, as it were, with the Duke of Wellington's voice. But most revealing of all is the third point as related by the Duke to Lord Alvanley. When Wellington approached Louis XVIII – that is in no sense connected with Ney – before Ney's arrest, he was surprised and angered at the King's cold-shouldering him – twice. It was during the consequent estrangement between them that Ney was executed, so Wellington reasoned that to have appealed to the King *then* would have been to ask a special favour for himself at a time when they were not on good terms. This he could not, or would not, do. The whole affair, however, gave Wellington the opportunity, when first it was suggested that some of the marshals had similarly shown their backs and second the King offered his apologies, to deliver the splendid rejoinder that it would not be the first time that the marshals had turned their backs on him. Soult, Masséna, Victor and Marmont had all done so in the Peninsula. It is distressing to recall how many of Ney's old comrades in arms voted for the death penalty. In December 1815 137 peers did so, including five marshals (Kellermann, Sérurier, Pérignon, Victor and Marmont) and fourteen generals, including some who had fought with Ney in Russia and whose lives had been saved by him. Most of the peers were of course from those ancient noble houses whose current scions had eschewed the battlefields and, as Macdonnell puts it, whose only experience of gunfire was that at Ney's firing party. Of course, the Bravest of the Brave died bravely, but when we reflect on what Ney had done and what those in his debt now did, we feel the force as never before of what Amiens sings to us in *As You Like It*. The winter wind across the steppes of Russia was, indeed, not so unkind to Ney as the ingratitude of his fellow commanders. The bitter sky in Russia during the retreat did not bite so nigh as benefits forgot, nor was the waters' sting as sharp as friend remembered not. Yet all that aside, while we may understand Wellington's reasons for not intervening, and may even acknowledge that the French discourtesy was perhaps designed to deter Wellington's intervention, still we know that *had* he intervened, Ney would not have been executed.

If the Ney affair could bring Wellington little comfort, there were other distractions and *affaires* which provided some consolation. There was no shortage of petticoats in both Brussels and Paris. While Napoleon on St Helena was able to enjoy the company of only two of his generals' wives – Albine de Montholon and Fanny Bertrand – Wellington had a wider field to choose from. There was Lady Frances Webster, to whom Wellington had written both just before and just after Waterloo, but although the newspapers made much of it, and the Duke undoubtedly liked pretty women – Frances had even inspired the admiration of Byron – the only action brought by Frances's husband, Captain James Wedderburn-Webster, was against the *St James's Chronicle*, an action which was handsomely won by the plaintiff. More in the heavyweight class was another friend of Wellington's – Madame de Staël – who shared with the Duke absolute opposition to Napoleon, and delighted him by her eccentricity, intellect and political enlightenment. Then there were Lady Caroline Lamb, Lady Shelley and Lady Jersey, and of course Harriet Arbuthnot, Mrs Marianne Patterson and Lady Charlotte Greville. The fact is that, unable to find either domestic happiness or intellectual stimulus in his Duchess, Wellington turned elsewhere both for romantic attachments – usually platonic – and satisfactory conversation. And the ladies, of course, adored him. Metternich himself told Lady Shelley that if he were a woman, he would love Wellington better than all the world.

Wellington had much to do with Metternich both at the Congress of Vienna and at subsequent Congresses. In an outstandingly perceptive essay on 'Wellington: The Diplomatist',[3] Harold Nicolson shows us how this remarkable man used his immense prestige and his innate sense of justice and moderation to ensure that after 1815 France was able to take her place once more among the Great Powers with dignity, economic strength and honour. While there were those who maintained that the Duke's diplomatic successes were in large measure attributable to his military achievements and powerful reputation and that, when representing the British government, he was always acting within precise instruction, not free to employ his own discretion or initiative, Nicolson points out that with the example of Castlereagh before him, Wellington understood only too well the principles which should be the proper guide for conducting relations between the Great Powers. It was essential, if further conflict were to be avoided, that these powers should act in unison and share the same broad objectives. For all his military fame, Wellington detested war, and strived throughout his political career for peace and order. 'He firmly upheld the axioms that particular interests should be subordinated to the general interest; that the acquiescence of the defeated countries could only be secured by moderation; that firmness and consistency must be accompanied by conciliation and flexibility, and that the essential aim of all sound diplomacy was not the display of astuteness, or the scoring of deft points, but the establishment of confidence.' Given these axioms – which the diplomats of today would do well to acknowledge and adhere to – and given also the Duke's ability

---

[3] *Wellingtonian Studies*, Gale & Polden, 1958.

to execute withdrawals when it was expedient to do so, but only in order to advance again later in order to attain an important objective, it would have been difficult, perhaps impossible, to produce anyone more likely to advance both Britain's and Europe's interests than himself. Having had great influence in bringing about the second restoration of Louis XVIII, not out of any noted respect for or approval of the King – indeed who could have that? – but simply because he saw it as a necessary measure for future stability, he further displayed his diplomatic skill and authority by persuading the King to reinstall both Talleyrand, the professional turncoat, and Fouché, the sinister tool of the Directory, the Terror and Napoleon Bonaparte, to their ministerial positions.

Wellington was further to demonstrate his diplomatic prowess at the Congress of Aix-la-Chapelle in the autumn of 1818. This conference of the Four Powers was attended by Alexander I, Frances II and Frederick William III with their Foreign Ministers, Capodistrias, Metternich and Hardenberg. Great Britain was represented by Castlereagh and Wellington, and Richelieu was present for France. One of the most important decisions taken was that the Army of Occupation should evacuate France by the end of November, and that this was possible owed much to Wellington's having aided France to pay the indemnity imposed on them because of the loan the House of Baring made to the French government at the Duke's behest. What is more, he scotched the idea put forward by Prussia, with support by Russia and Austria, that an international army of observation should be established at Brussels to act as a kind of European police force – to intervene anywhere. The alliance of the Four Powers – in order to check revolution in France – was, however, renewed. In general the conference was a triumphant success for Metternich, as the Alliance had been maintained and revolution had been checked. Metternich himself summed up his own objective by observing that the happiest state of affairs would be that there should be no change in the existing order of things. With a few hiccups here and there, he succeeded in maintaining the status quo for another thirty years. But it became clear at this conference that no government would or could subordinate the particular interest of its own country to the general interest of Europe.

Back in England after the Congress in December 1818, Wellington was appointed Master General of the Ordnance and a member of Liverpool's Cabinet. It cannot be said that he used his position to improve the lot of the ordinary soldier greatly. Of course, almost all considerations of the British Army's future after Waterloo were governed by money, and from its peak of prestige and competence in 1815, there followed a period of stagnation, economy and decline. The army administrative system was an absurd hotchpotch of divided responsibility. The Secretary for War was Palmerston. His precise duties were not clear, but being the man he was this imprecision did not prevent his interfering with others. In particular he was constantly in disagreement with the Commander-in-Chief, the Duke of York, who controlled appointments, discipline and promotion. The Master General of the Ordnance dealt with artillery, engineers, firearms, ammunition and greatcoats. The militia, volunteers and yeomanry all came under the Home Office, while transport, stores and provisions were supplied by the Treasury. Separate departments dealt with medical, pay, audit and clothing matters. All attempts to centralize control of these various functions were opposed by Wellington. Most surprising of all was that he did little to better the conditions under which the soldiers lived, particularly when we remember that while commanding troops in the field he had said how important it was 'to attend to the comfort of the soldier: let him be well clothed, sheltered and fed'. But later, as Commander-in-Chief of the Army, Wellington did see to it that soldiers were better housed and that barrack-room life was improved.

Early in 1820 George III died and Prinny at last became King. That year also saw the Cato Street conspiracy, in which the reformer Thistlewood[4] and his fellow conspirators planned to assassinate the entire Cabinet when they were to dine at the Grosvenor Square house of Lord Harrowby, Lord President of the Council. The plot was revealed by an informer and the conspirators were rounded up. Thistlewood himself and four other ringleaders were hanged. More excitement was to be had during the controversy as to whether George IV's wife, Caroline of Brunswick, should be allowed to become Queen. Wellington's part in negotiating with Brougham, Caroline's Whig adviser, and the government's introduction of a Bill to dissolve the King's marriage, resulted in the Duke's actually being hissed by an angry mob in Parliament Square and his almost being unhorsed, but Caroline's absurd and

---

[4] Thistlewood served both in the British Army and under Napoleon. 'I had rather kill that D—d villain Wellington than any of them,' he is said to have declared.

bizarre behaviour turned opinion against her. She died shortly after the King's Coronation on 19 July, at which Wellington as Lord High Constable rode a white Arab horse in Westminster Hall with the Earl Marshal and High Steward. Two months earlier another death had occurred. On 5 May 1821 Napoleon died at St Helena. Although some dismiss it as nonsense, according to Antommarchi, the Corsican anatomist who attended the Emperor, Napoleon, while on his death-bed, half-conscious and delirious, exclaimed: 'I shall meet my brave warriors in the Elysian fields, Kléber, Desaix, Bessières, Duroc, Murat, Masséna, Berthier.' Lord Rosebery comments that this is what Antommarchi considers Napoleon should have said, and we may add perhaps that it would have been fitting. There is more support for the report that Napoleon's last words were '*Tête d'armée*' and these too are fitting, for as Wellington himself told Stanhope fifteen years later: 'Napoleon was a *grand homme de guerre*, possibly the greatest that ever appeared at the head of a French army.' By a curious chance Wellington was in Paris when the news of Napoleon's death arrived and what is more was at the same reception, given by Madame Craufurd, as was Talleyrand. Talleyrand's reaction to the excited exclamation: '*What an event!*' was characteristically cynical and to the effect that it was not an event any more, only an item of news. But Elizabeth Longford comments that Talleyrand was wrong: 'For the piteous circumstances of the mighty Emperor's early dissolution under the twin blows of disease and confinement combined with his literary labour to clamp down on posterity a Napoleonic legend which only today is being dislodged.' Wellington's own instant response to the news, according to Madame Craufurd, was to observe that now he was the most successful general alive. A reminder of his Waterloo victory was given when later that year George IV insisted that Wellington should act as his guide to the battlefield. The two of them rode over it in September 1821. Afterwards the Duke reported that George took it all coolly, asking no questions and showing emotion only when Wellington pointed out where Anglesey's leg was buried, whereupon the King burst into tears. Although Wellington himself had expended his own tears immediately after the battle was over, he was seriously put out when he caught sight of the monument erected by the Dutch, the Lion Mound, and complained that they had spoiled his battlefield. Waterloo had been the last field of battle for both the Duke and the Emperor. Napoleon had now fought the last battle of all. Nor steel, nor poison, malice domestic, foreign levy, nothing could touch him further. After life's fitful fever, he slept well – a soldier's grave in a garden at the bottom of a ravine in St Helena, a place chosen by himself, if burial in France were refused. Within twenty years the Emperor would make a last journey – to Les Invalides, and we will accompany him on this journey later. By then Wellington would already have outlived his great rival by nineteen years, and would still have a dozen years to go. Towards the end of his long life, when he had been helped across Hyde Park Corner and thanked his benefactor, who protested that he had never even hoped to reach the day when he would have given assistance to 'the greatest man that ever lived', the Great Duke's retort was hardly courteous, but obviously in character: 'Don't be a damned fool!' We can hardly imagine Napoleon making a similar rejoinder in such circumstances.

One of the better literary efforts recounting events after the Emperor's death comes from William Hazlitt, who had been born nine years later than Napoleon and who also survived him by nine years. He tells us that the Emperor's bedroom became a funeral chamber, hung all in black. It was the purchase of this black cloth from the town that first made known to the island's inhabitants the fact of his death, for the dread Sir Hudson Lowe had been feeding them with false reports that 'General Buonaparte was doing well'. Napoleon's remarkably white corpse was lying on a camp bed covered by the blue cloak he had worn at Marengo. There was a crucifix on his breast and a sword by his left side. All members of the Emperor's suite were fittingly garbed in mourning.

After some hours those who had been waiting outside the house to view the Emperor's remains were admitted, led by officers of the 20th and 66th Foot. During the day of 7 May more of the troops and island's inhabitants, even women, came to pay their respects. The corpse was then laid in a coffin consisting first of a case of tin, Napoleon lying on white satin, a pillow under his head, and at his feet his hat, some eagles, French coins and plate engraved with his arms. When this part of the coffin had been firmly soldered and closed, it was placed in a second case of mahogany which in turn went into a third – of lead – itself enclosed by yet one more of mahogany – sealed and fastened with iron screws. Then the whole was covered by the Emperor's Marengo cloak. On the morning of the funeral, a fine one, all the island's dignitaries assembled at Longwood, the roads were lined by the people, solemn music was played by military bands, and at half the hour after noon, grenadiers carried the coffin through the garden to the hearse. It was placed there and covered by a pall of purple velvet, still with the Marengo cloak, the Emperor's household all in mourning.

Then there set forth from Longwood a solemn train. Led by the Abbé Vignali, Henri Bertrand, and the two doctors, Arnott and Antommarchi, the hearse set forth, its four horses led by grooms; an escort of twelve soldiers on either side flanked the hearse, together with Napoleon Bertrand and Marchand on foot; Count Bertrand and Count de Montholon rode immediately behind. Then came Countess Bertrand and her daughter Hortense in a light carriage drawn by two horses. The Emperor's own horse was led by his equerry, and was followed by marine officers and men, both mounted and on foot, officers of the staff, councillors of St Helena – finally General Coffin, the Marquis Montchenu, and the Governor himself, Sir Hudson Lowe. Bringing up the rear of this cortège came the island's inhabitants.

So the procession made its way to the burying place – greeted by the 2,500 soldiers of the garrison and bands playing mournful airs – while the troops followed on behind: dragoons, regiments of foot, volunteers and the royal artillery with fifteen guns. At Hut's Gate the hearse came to a halt, troops carried the coffin to the grave, everyone dismounted, the coffin was laid down by the tomb, prayers were offered by the Abbé Vignali, the coffin was lowered into the grave to salutes from the royal artillery and the Royal Navy's flagship, and a stone was lowered to close the grave. The people were eager to possess themselves of a branch or leaves of the trees shading the tomb. 'The tomb of the Emperor', concludes Hazlitt, 'is about a league from Longwood. It is of a quadrangular shape, wider at top than at bottom; the depth is about twelve feet. The coffin is fixed on two strong pieces of wood, and is detached in its whole circumference. The French were not allowed to mark the spot with a tomb-stone or with any inscription. The Governor opposed this, as if a tomb-stone or an inscription could tell the world more than they know already. Sir Hudson Lowe had committed Buonaparte to the ground; his task was ended; but he proceeded to ransack his effects with the same rage and jealousy as if he had been still alive, and refused the smallest trifle found among them, and that could be of no use to any one else, to the entreaties of his faithful followers.' If we did not know it well enough already, we would understand from this instance of malicious pettiness on Lowe's part what it is that Isabella means in *Measure for Measure* when she castigates mankind 'drest in little brief authority' for playing 'such fantastic tricks before high heaven, as make the angels weep'. Small wonder that Wellington had found himself ill disposed toward the idea that Sir Hudson Lowe should become a member of his staff before the Waterloo campaign.

CHAPTER 12

The Great Duke and Bonaparte Restored

I don't care a twopenny damn what becomes of the ashes of
Napoleon Bonaparte.

Attributed to Wellington

UNTIL the post-mortem which must follow, the game now
becomes somewhat one-sided. Between 1822 and 1852 the
Duke of Wellington played many parts. As a statesman he
represented his country at the Congress of Verona, continued as a
member of the Cabinet, fought a political duel with Canning and an
actual duel with Winchilsea, became Commander-in-Chief of the Army
briefly in 1827, Prime Minister, Chancellor of Oxford University,
Foreign Secretary, generally carried on the King's and the Queen's
Government, was Commander-in-Chief again, this time for ten years,
and all in all was such a Pillar of State (as Lemoinne put it) that very
little seemed to be done without his opinion being sought first. During
these same thirty years the Napoleonic legend grew apace; innumerable
memoirs of his campaigns, his rule, his years at St Helena appeared;
the Bourbons were finally kicked off the throne of France, which given
the stupidity of Charles X, Louis XVIII's brother, was hardly surprising;
Louis-Philippe reigned as King from 1830 until 1848, when further
revolution brought about the seizure of power by Louis Napoleon
(nephew of the great Emperor), who four years later in 1852, the year
in which Wellington died, was crowned Emperor of the French as Napoleon III. The Bonaparte dynasty had returned to power, but we will
look first at the Great Duke.

It was wholly characteristic of Wellington's insistence on telling the
truth that when in August 1822 Castlereagh was suffering from mental
derangement – the Foreign Secretary thought he was being blackmailed,

both for having been seen entering a brothel and for an 'unnatural' crime as well – it was he, the Duke, who straightforwardly warned his friend – Castlereagh in a state bordering on hysteria was pouring forth some tale of this fancied vice and blackmail – that he could not be in his right mind. 'Since *you* say so,' cried Castlereagh, 'it must be so.' Three days later Castlereagh committed suicide. An intriguing aspect of the whole affair concerned a great friend of both men, Harriet Arbuthnot. After warning Castlereagh of his condition, Wellington had written to Mrs Arbuthnot telling her of the great impression which the sight of a man of such sober mind in a state close to insanity had had upon him. Such a sight hardly reinforced confidence in the strength of the human mind. Yet one consequence of Castlereagh's death was to reinforce confidence between the Duke and Mrs Arbuthnot, who turned to him to satisfy her two great needs – friendship and involvement in the political affairs of the day. Having lost in Castlereagh an 'incomparable friend', she now turned to Wellington to 'fill the place of the friend I have lost'. Lady Longford stresses how greatly this change in her feelings affected his also, so that she became the favourite among all the many admirers of the Duke. Yet in spite of the Duke's ardent expressions of devotion – 'my thoughts and wishes are centred on you' – Lady Longford makes it clear that their friendship was platonic, for Harriet was 'a conventional and faithful wife'.

Castlereagh's successor as Foreign Secretary was George Canning, and it was Wellington's influence with the King, exerted simply because the Duke regarded Canning as the best man for the job, which made him so. Once more it was characteristic of Wellington that he put the public interest first. He had no liking for Canning, who, despite all his wit, brilliance, decisiveness and oratorical powers, was a distinctly uncomfortable, ungentlemanly and unclubbable colleague. But Wellington knew that to keep the government together and effectively to counter the opposition, Canning was necessary. It was a significant instance of the Duke's willingness to come down on one side or another of a crucial political matter and by doing so determine the outcome. It augured well for the future. His next mission was to attend the Congress of Verona, at a time when the main questions at issue were the revolts in Greece, Spain and Naples. Canning, like Castlereagh, was an advocate of the policy of non-intervention, but on arrival at Verona in October 1822, Wellington found that his efforts to prevent intervention in Spain were almost totally unsupported. Yet his mere presence at the Congress created infinite pleasure and had a most profound impact. Byron, never an ally or admirer, wrote later of Wellington's eagle beak from which he suspended the world, and another observer commented on the loftiness of his character and the grandeur of his position. Yet not all his prestige nor all his reasoning for peace could induce the other Great Powers to recede from their determination to invade Spain – ironically, it was a French army which did so in April 1823 – and restore to absolutism the King whom Napoleon had tricked out of his throne sixteen years earlier, Ferdinand VII. While at Verona Wellington actually entertained the former French Empress, Marie-Louise, playing cards with her and offering to make good his losses with *napoléons*. As usual Wellington discharged at Verona what he regarded as his duty. Small thanks he got for it. The broad result of Verona was the end of the Quintuple Alliance. France and England would henceforth pursue national policies, while the other Great Powers, Austria, Prussia and Russia, would continue to act together as the champions of Absolutism. It was once again characteristic of Wellington that he was not wholly satisfied with his own achievements at Verona, telling the King that someone abler might have produced better results, but at the same time making it plain how wholly improper he regarded the interference by one government in the affairs of another, and that civil war – which had been the issue in Spain – was not to be tolerated. Yet others contradicted his own modest view of his diplomacy. Canning, in spite of his deviousness in the House of Commons later, praised Wellington's stand against war, and Creevey looked upon the Duke as the 'only man who could keep those Royal imbeciles and villains in order'. He was to have another opportunity to practise his diplomatic skills before long, but before we accompany him to St Petersburg in 1826 – by which time Nicholas I would have succeeded Alexander I as Czar – we had better take a look at how the Napoleonic legend was getting on.

In his inquest into Napoleon's death Frank Richardson devotes his first chapter to the Napoleonic legend, whose rapid growth he calls the most amazing part of the whole amazing story. He confirms what others have claimed, that the 'chief architect and most industrious builder' of the legend was Napoleon himself, and that it all began at Lodi, where he personally directed an assault upon the bridge. As he later told Las Cases and Gourgaud at St Helena: 'Not until after Lodi did I feel that

I was destined to play a foremost part on our political stage, that kindled the spark of boundless ambition in me ... I felt the world spin away beneath me as if I was borne up into the air.' Legends, of course, are created by words, music and paintings, by the world of art, in short, and if ever there were a consummate artist with words, it was Napoleon himself. He had often claimed that one of the qualities required in a great commander was eloquence such as appeals to soldiers – and how often he had given rein to his own eloquence:

> Soldiers, here are your colours; these eagles will always serve you as rallying points; they will be wherever your Emperor judges it necessary for the defence of his throne and his people. You will swear to sacrifice your life to defend them, and to sustain them constantly by your courage on the road to victory. Do you swear?

Thus spoke the Emperor to his army on 5 December 1804 at a military parade on the Champs-de-Mars. He himself had made it clear that the influence of words over men was astounding. But in order 'to electrify the man' you had to 'speak to the soul'. Even during his last throw of the dice before disembarking after his flight from Elba, his way with words did not desert him. The promise he made that victory would advance at the charge, and that the eagle with the national colours would fly from spire to spire to the towers of Notre Dame, had the required effect. Ney himself was won over and commented later that this was how to talk to soldiers.

It was not long after Napoleon's death that the memoirs of those who had been at St Helena began to appear. And they were followed by the infinitely more valuable, inspiring, indeed immortal words of such men as Victor Hugo and Stendhal. It was the latter who made one of his fictional characters say: 'My present esteem for Napoleon is engendered by the scorn inspired in me by all that has followed him.' When we take a look at his successors on the throne – Louis XVIII, Charles X and even Louis-Philippe – we can hardly wonder at Stendhal, but before we do so, we may note the remarkable impact made by the revelations of Dr O'Meara, who had been the Longwood doctor from 1815 to 1818. His book, which appeared in 1822, was called *Napoleon in Exile or a Voice from St Helena*, and although it was dismissed by Lord Rosebery as worthless, even he admits that it created a great sensation. O'Meara served all masters – Napoleon himself, Hudson Lowe and the British government – but his book, which told of his conversations with the Emperor and Napoleon's persecution by Lowe, gave the reading public, both British and French, a portrait of Napoleon, ennobled by suffering and guiltless of countless ill deeds formerly ascribed to him, while Lowe's reputation was further and indelibly blackened.

More support for the Napoleonic legend was forthcoming in the following year, 1823, when Las Cases's *Mémorial* was published. Through Las Cases we hear Napoleon's own voice, indeed it was none other than Louis XVIII who, in his severe criticism of the *Mémorial*, testily observes that 'M. de Buonaparte has published his memoirs through the mediation of his chamberlain, Las Cases'. Yet although we all know that Napoleon was putting the record straight from his point of view, so that the legend would live on (he told Lowe that 500 years hence, Napoleon's name would shine over Europe, while Lowe's and Castlereagh's would be remembered only for their unjust, shameful conduct towards him – a shrewd enough comment in Lowe's case, although not in Castlereagh's), nevertheless some of Napoleon's sayings as recorded by Las Cases are remarkably prophetic and inspiring:

> Henceforth nothing can destroy or efface the great principles of our revolution. These great and beautiful truths must remain for ever, for we have laced them with gold and monuments, performed prodigies for their sake ... These principles will constitute the faith, religion and morality of all races, and, whatever men may say, that memorable era will be connected with me in person ... Whatever equality is possible to give, has been given the French by me.

On a less grandiloquent note, Napoleon recalls his contribution to order and justice in that his glory consists not in having won forty battles, but in the Code Civile and reports of the Council of State. He has presented France with new ideas which have taken root, and he predicts that there can be no going back. 'The Bourbons will not stay. After my death, there will be a reaction in my favour ...' No two Bourbon kings were better qualified to cause this reaction than Louis XVIII – who, Wellington noted on his way to Vienna and Verona in 1822, looked awful: 'His face is like a *scab*; all broke out and blotched' – and Charles X, described as 'a true *émigré* and a submissive bigot', who together with his right-wing supporters, the *ultras*, set his face against anything but reaction, who tried to erase from the people's minds any recollection of the Revolution and the Empire, and who was so unreceptive to any advice that when Wellington tried to reason with him, he simply retorted: '*N'en parlons plus, nous n'avons pas la même croyance.*' Wellington later compared Charles to James II. As if all this were not enough, literary giants like Byron and Goethe were singing the Emperor's praises, praises which were echoed by of all people that anti-royalist Chateaubriand, by Savary[1] and by Victor Hugo. Talleyrand, who had done so much to restore the Bourbons, saw when it was time for them to go. But when revolution came again, in July 1830, although there were cries of 'Long live Napoleon II', it was Louis-Philippe who became King of the French, the first and last genuinely constitutional monarch that France was ever to have. It would be another eighteen years before a Bonaparte was once more at the centre of affairs.

In that same year of 1830 Wellington stepped down from the highest political position open to him – that of Prime Minister. During the immediately preceding years Wellington had been serving his country with his customary zeal and in several different capacities. In 1826 he went off again on a diplomatic mission, this time to St Petersburg, in an effort to dissuade Russia from intervention in Greece's struggle for independence from Turkey.[2] The Czar Nicholas I, who had recently succeeded to the throne, while by no means enthusiastic about coming to the rescue of the Greeks, whom he looked upon as rebels, was not willing to give any assurance that he would not attack Turkey if Russia's interests required it. Wellington had never expected to achieve much with this mission, and indeed he was able to do no more than get agreement to an Anglo-Russian protocol for mediation between Greece and Turkey, by which Greece would become an autonomous state tributary to the Sultan. Additionally all Turks would leave Greece. Almost all

---

[1] Savary had been one of Napoleon's aides-de-camp and was later his Minister of Police.

[2] A cause for which Byron, the harsh critic of Castlereagh and Wellington, the champion of Napoleon, had given his life two years earlier. Some three months before his death in Greece he had completed these haunting lines:

> Seek out – less often sought than found –
> A soldier's grave, for thee the best;
> Then look around, and choose thy ground,
> And take thy rest.

the interested parties objected to this protocol, and it certainly prevented neither war nor intervention by some of the Great Powers. More particularly for Wellington it aggravated the growing disagreement between himself and Canning. Whereas Canning was a champion of countries like Greece and the South American colonies ('I called the New World into existence, to redress the balance of the Old'), not only for their own libertarian aspirations, but as a symbol of opposition to the Concert of Europe, Wellington took precisely the opposite stand, insisting that peace and security could be maintained only if intervention in the affairs of these lesser states were avoided. It was no surprise therefore that when Canning succeeded to the Premiership in April 1827, Wellington declined to serve in his administration. In doing so he was – temporarily – depriving himself of the position he most enjoyed, that of Commander-in-Chief of the Army, for in January of that year, on the death of the Duke of York, he had in addition to being Master General of the Ordnance succeeded the Duke as Commander-in-Chief. His comment on assuming this position was again simple and true: 'I am in my proper place, the place to which I was destined by my trade.' He did not keep it long, however, for Canning's becoming Prime Minister caused him to resign both offices. Yet he was back as Commander-in-Chief in August 1827 after Canning's death and during the short-lived Premiership of Goderich, whom George IV called a 'blubbering fool' and who was quite incapable of withstanding either the political turmoils of a crumbling government or the exciting international events which led to the battle of Navarino in October 1827, when Admiral Codrington in command of the combined British, French and Russian fleets destroyed the Turkish fleet in the bay of Navarino. George IV's sailor brother (and successor to the throne), William, sent a message to Codrington: 'Well done, Ned.' George himself awarded Codrington the Grand Cross of the Bath. Wellington was horrified and later called it an 'untoward event'. By this time Goderich had resigned and Wellington himself became Prime Minister in January 1828.

It was Disraeli who, apart from suggesting that Wellington had left his country a great legacy – the contemplation of his character – had some sharp things to say about the performance of Wellington as Prime Minister. He points out[3] that the Duke brought to this post immortal

---

[3] In *Sybil or The Two Nations*, first published in 1845.

fame. His public knowledge was wide; he knew well the sovereigns and leading statesmen of Europe; he possessed outstanding administrative talents – and yet, Disraeli continues, in spite of all this and other expectations that 'the Duke's government would only cease with the termination of his public career', Wellington failed, broke up his government, wrecked his party and annihilated his political position. Of course, Disraeli overstates the case, as was his custom, for in fact, although the Duke accepted the Premiership from a sense of duty – a duty which involved to his chagrin relinquishing command of the army – he had, as M. G. Brock has so eloquently emphasized,[4] 'a solid capacity for politics'. Brock points out that Wellington's integrity, courage and sheer drive were complemented by a practical turn of mind which could usually find sound solutions to concrete problems. Moreover, he knew a good deal about government already. His mastery of military matters was unchallenged, his familiarity with foreign affairs considerable, and unlike his conduct of campaigns in the field, when he kept the reins firmly in his own hands, he was able to delegate widely to his colleagues, particularly in areas, such as economic policy, where his experience was necessarily limited. In his conduct of government business, both in Cabinet and in the House of Lords, Wellington's patriotism, honesty, modesty and common sense were great allies for his management of affairs. Moreover, he was incapable of political intrigue. He treated his Cabinet rather as he had treated his staff when commanding the army. If they disagreed with his policy and plans, they were free to depart. That so great a man should be so affable and without a hint of arrogance and that he should be thinking always of the country's good first and foremost was as rare as it was admirable, and could not fail to have its effect on his colleagues. Greville, who was clerk to the Privy Council and a thoroughly clubbable man, while not always sympathetic to Wellington's political doings applauded the 'simplicity, gaiety, natural urbanity and good humour in him, which are marvellously captivating in so great a man'. All these qualities, together with his discipline, patience and perseverance, were of great assistance in dealing with George IV. The King was adept at avoiding tedious business and had infuriated or disintegrated previous Prime Ministers, but the Duke's rule of never interrupting the King when he was talking, allowing him

---

[4] 'Wellington: The Statesman', *Wellingtonian Studies*.

to tire himself out and then presenting his sovereign with the matter in hand, seemed to work time after time. 'Nobody', observed Wellington, 'can manage him but me.'

Patience and plain speaking may have prevailed with the sovereign. They were not sufficient for swaying opinion in parliamentary debate, for the Duke was no orator and knew it. His parliamentary tactics may have been effective, but, as he himself conceded, 'not being in the habit of addressing your Lordships, I should have been found, besides other disqualifications, incapable of ... defending the measures of the Government as they ought to be defended in this House.' The comments of others on his performance as a speaker in the House of Lords varied greatly. Greville recorded that the Duke made a clever speech on the Greek question; Disraeli admires his gruff down-to-earthness; Carlyle, while noting his humming and ha-ing, concedes that he does at least present some facts. But leaving aside his gift for words, it was as a practical man of business that he made his mark as Prime Minister. Creevey – whom we last met in Brussels after Waterloo – said two months after Wellington became Prime Minister that The Beau[5] is rising most rapidly in this respect. The proof of the pudding was there to be tasted – Catholic Emancipation[6] and the establishment of a police force (known both as Peelers and Bobbies after the Home Secretary, Robert Peel). But the issue of parliamentary reform was the great stumbling block. Wellington's shortcomings as both a politician and a Prime Minister might be summarized like this. First there was an unwillingness to face and accept unpalatable facts – in other words a tendency to 'make pictures' almost in the way that Napoleon had done, and to live in a world created by his own inclination and imagination. Secondly, having grown up in the shadow and terror of the French Revolution, he was wedded to the existing order of things and he closed his eyes to the new ideas and political aspirations of his own people; indeed he knew little of them – Disraeli was right in saying of him that he did not have much knowledge of England – nor, having hardly served at all in the House of Commons, did he have that politically instinctive awareness

---

[5] Wellington acquired this nickname in the Peninsula for his fastidious habits of dress and cleanliness.

[6] It was during the struggle for Emancipation that the duel was fought between Wellington and Winchilsea in Battersea Fields. The Duke fired wide and Winchilsea deloped.

of other Prime Ministers who were later in the House of Lords, like Liverpool, Grey or Melbourne. Then there was a sensitiveness to opposition, particularly the opposition of his own Tory aristocracy, which affected him and gave rise to an uncharacteristic irritability – not aided by his less than perfect health. The faulty treatment of his deafness in 1822 had had its effect: 'I have never been well,' he said nearly twenty years later, 'since that fellow poured liquid fire into my ear, and electricized not only the nerves of my ear, but all the adjacent parts, and the injury extended in all directions, sometimes to the head and then down to the stomach, then to the shoulders, and then back again to the head, and so on.' Being, as he was, ill informed about public opinion and unwilling to listen to warnings when they were given, he misjudged both the popular feeling of the country and the views of the moderate supporters of reform when he spoke so strongly against reform early in November 1830. It was therefore hardly surprising that the government was defeated in the House of Commons later that month, whereupon Wellington resigned.[7] He continued to oppose the Reform Bill, introduced by his successor as Prime Minister, Lord Grey - opposition which made him so unpopular that on 27 April 1831, when the Duchess was lying dead (she had died three days earlier) in Apsley House, the mob hurled stones through the plate-glass windows on the ground floor. In October of that year the mob repeated the treatment, but it was not because of such intimidation that Wellington finally withdrew his opposition to the Reform Bill in the House of Lords. It was for the sake of the King and the country, for anything, he believed, was better than revolution and civil war. As in his former military campaigns, he knew when to retreat and dared to do so. When he looked down on the reformed House of Commons, more than two-thirds of whose members were Whigs, he gave tongue to another expression which lives on today: 'I have never seen so many bad hats in my life.'

1832 was not only the year of the Reform Bill. In July of that year, Napoleon's son, formerly King of Rome, then Duke of Reichstadt, died

---

[7] By this time William IV had succeeded to the throne. George IV had died on 26 June, and Wellington's final pronouncement on him, kinder than his former description – 'the *worst* man that ever existed' – was 'the most extraordinary compound of talent, wit, buffoonery, obstinacy and good feeling – in short a medley of the most opposite qualities with a great preponderance of good – that I ever saw in any character in my life'.

in the palace of Schönbrunn, near Vienna. 'Endowed with every quality of mind and body' – so read the inscription in Latin on the lid of the sarcophagus – 'remarkable for the elegance of his figure, the great beauty of his features, the unusual grace of his language, for his studies and his literary work, he was attacked by phthisis in the flower of his age, and a tragic death carried him away . . .' Like Hamlet, he would no doubt have proved himself most royal, had he been put on. The former Empress, Marie-Louise, who was with her son when he died, wrote to Madame Mère with the sad news. Throughout France old emotions were stirred, the French newspapers were sympathetic – one, *Le Constitutionel,* even predicted that Reichstadt's heritage would fall to the man 'who can rally the mass of the people in the true interests of this country'. Who this man might be was clearly signalled by Metternich in a letter to the Austrian Ambassador in Paris, pointing out that there was such a thing as a Bonapartist succession, and that the young Louis Napoleon, son of the Emperor's brother, was already deeply committed to Bonapartist intrigues, and would certainly regard himself as the heir to that dynasty. Metternich required his ambassador in Paris to advise Louis-Philippe to pay attention to this person. The poets, of course, had their say, notably Heinrich Heine, who, making one of his many journeys, this one through Normandy, recorded that every cottage had in it a picture of Napoleon's son, and that the Grande Armée veterans wore a black armband. Victor Hugo too produced the sort of moving lines[8] which only he could.

It was in this year, 1832, that there was a general revival of Bonapartist sympathy. We may take as an instance what happened and was to happen concerning Napoleon's statue on the Vendôme column. It was in the previous year that the replacement of his statue on the column was authorized; in May 1832 people were laying flowers at the column to commemorate the Emperor's death; and in July 1833 the new statue, by Seuvre, depicting the Emperor in his celebrated grey overcoat, was unveiled in the presence of King Louis-Philippe himself, who actually

8 *Tous deux sont morts – Seigneur votre droite est terrible.*
Vous avez commencé par le maître invincible
Par l'homme triomphant;
Puis vous avez enfin complété l'ossuaire.
Dix ans vous ont suffi pour filer le suaire
Du père et de l'enfant.

doffed his cocked hat and cried out: '*Vive l'Empereur!*' Heine had written that a thousand cannons lay sleeping in Napoleon's name and in the column of the Place Vendôme – and if those thousand cannons were to wake one day, the Tuileries would tremble. It was not only in ceremonies of this sort that the Emperor's name was kept on people's lips. The theatre in Paris was dominated by plays about him, portraying him at Brienne, as an artillery lieutenant, at Schönbrunn, Berlin, St Helena, Wagram or Elba, or with Josephine at Malmaison. Even Alexandre Dumas wrote a play in six acts, which he was sure would be a success because of its title, *Napoleon Bonaparte*, even though he himself admitted that it was not good. Yet Reichstadt's death had weakened the Bonapartist cause, and not all the efforts of Napoleon's brother, Joseph, former King of Spain, nor of Jerome, who had fought so gallantly at Waterloo, nor the somewhat dangerous intrigues of Prince Louis Napoleon, had sufficient impact to turn France away from constitutional monarchy. Yet there were stirrings. In 1832 one of Napoleon's marshals, Soult, became President of the Council and his Minister of the Interior was Thiers, who was to play a key role in the further promotion of the Napoleonic legend. It was during Thiers' first Presidency of the Council in 1836 that Louis-Philippe inaugurated the Arc de Triomphe and dedicated part of a military museum at Versailles to the principal victories of Napoleon. It was all very well for the Bourbons to have talked of the Arc de Triomphe commemorating former glories of their own reigns or even the Republic, but as Gilbert Martineau stressed, 'the old men, the poets and soldiers associated it [the Arc de Triomphe] with the feats of the Emperor's armies'.

In the following year Thiers told Napoleon's brother Jerome that of all the Frenchmen of his day, he, Thiers, was one of those most attached to the glorious memory of Napoleon, and he worked tenaciously to secure the return of the Emperor's remains from St Helena to France. Thiers was again President of the Council from March to October 1840 and it was during this time – on 1 May, the name day of the King – that Louis-Philippe finally gave his agreement, telling Thiers: 'You wish to bring back Napoleon's remains to France. I consent. Come to an agreement on the subject with the British Government. We will send Joinville [Louis-Philippe's son] to St Helena.' Thiers thereupon wrote to the French Ambassador in London, Guizot, who in turn approached Palmerston, the Foreign Secretary, with suitably couched language:

'The King has very much at heart a desire that Napoleon's body should lie in France, in that soil he defended and made illustrious, and which respectfully shelters the mortal remains of so many thousands of his companions in arms, both leaders and soldiers, who like him devoted their lives to serving their country.' Palmerston was perfectly content to concede to France's request, since it did no damage to British interests – any issue which did met with violent opposition – and the whole process got under way, with the frigid approval of even the Duke of Wellington. During these years since his resignation as Prime Minister and with the Tory party largely out of office,[9] Wellington had been content to lead the opposition in the Lords, while Sir Robert Peel was the undisputed party chief. When Peel formed his second government in September 1841, Wellington was a Cabinet Minister without office. He also resumed the duties of Commander-in-Chief of the Army in 1842, an office he held until his death ten years later, and his acceptance of this position was, according to one of his descendants, the 7th Duke (father of the present Duke), 'the greatest mistake of his life . . .' for 'he was by then physically feeble and very deaf. Yet for the greater part of the year he would with difficulty mount his horse and ride through the adoring crowd to the Horse Guards. His dismounting was agonizing to watch, and once installed at his desk his day would be passed in a mixture of sleep and irritability.' We will return soon to his last period of army command, but first Napoleon must be embarked on his last journey.

Gilbert Martineau has told the story with unique authority and eloquence. The French Chamber of Deputies was informed by the Minister of the Interior, Rémusat, on 12 May 1840, that the King had instructed his son, the Prince de Joinville, to take his frigate to St Helena and bring back the Emperor Napoleon's mortal remains. The deputies' enthusiasm was unstinted and highly emotional. In June it was agreed by law that Les Invalides would be Napoleon's final resting place. With Joinville, in his frigate *La Belle Poule*, sailed two of the Emperor's former companions in exile – Bertrand and Gourgaud. Las Cases's son Emmanuel went too. Also on board was a splendid coffin, whose lead lining bore the inscription: 'Napoleon, Emperor and King, Died at

---

[9] Peel's first administration, in which Wellington was Foreign Secretary, lasted only four months – December 1834 to April 1835, when Melbourne became Prime Minister.

St Helena, May 5, 1821.' In company with another warship, *La Favorite* (in which Marchand, Napoleon's former valet, travelled), *La Belle Poule* departed from Toulon on 7 July 1840. They did not reach St Helena until early October and when the exhumation of Napoleon's remains took place on 15 October, the onlookers were astonished to see that instead of 'formless remains, only identifiable by some shreds of uniform, here was Napoleon covered in a sort of greyish mould but perfectly recognisable and apparently peacefully sleeping'. Marchand, the former valet, commented that the corpse resembled the Emperor more closely than the dead man of nearly twenty years before. His uniform – light cavalry of the Imperial Guard, white waistcoat, the Legion of Honour, breeches and boots – was well preserved, only the gold braid and decorations tarnished. But the body was exposed only for a few minutes, then resealed in the coffins. Martineau recorded that 'the three envelopes of 1821, tinplate, mahogany and lead, were screwed inside those of the sarcophagus' and that Napoleon was now 'in a sextuple coffin, proof against time and weather'. Soldiers carried the huge coffin to a waiting hearse, which was covered by an imperial cloak of purple, with 'N' at each corner and emblazoned with gold bees. The hearse was drawn by four horses with funereal trappings; there was an escort of the 91st Highlanders (Argyll and Sutherland) and men of the militia and the Royal Artillery. With the guns of the forts and the warships of both the Royal Navy and the French navy thundering out their salutes, the procession made its way to Jamestown and to the sea front, where the Prince de Joinville was waiting. There also awaiting the Emperor was a tricolour-decked launch into which the coffin was lowered, and so to *La Belle Poule* with a further, this time French, guard of honour, arms reversed. Next day there was a funeral Mass on *La Belle Poule* and, after prayers for the dead, the coffin was taken below to the mortuary chapel. On 18 October the mortal remains of the Emperor Napoleon began the journey from St Helena to Les Invalides. By the time *La Belle Poule* reached Cherbourg on 30 November, Thiers had fallen from power and Soult was again President of the Council; it was he who laid down that the final ceremony for Napoleon to enter Les Invalides would take place on 15 December. At Cherbourg the catafalque was transferred to *La Normandie* which made its way to Le Havre, where the first of numerous triumphant receptions took place – the prefect had notified the people that they were to pay 'the great man the last honours with dignified calm'. Near Rouen, the catafalque was again moved, this time to *La Dorade 3*, which could navigate the Seine. Escorted by a flotilla of similar vessels, *La Dorade 3* made its way through a specially constructed *arc de triomphe* at Rouen, along the route via Elbeuf, Les Andelys, Vernon and Mantes, with church bells pealing, drums beating, troops presenting arms and bands playing; at length it reached the bridge at Poissy on 12 December, to be greeted by more regular soldiers and the Garde Nationale. The following morning, a Sunday, Mass was celebrated and then on went the convoy, concluding its river voyage at Courbevoie, where the Emperor was again greeted by veteran soldiers of the Empire, by troops now serving and by a multitude of Parisians. To Courbevoie came Marshal Soult, hero of Austerlitz, who had told the Emperor on that December day thirty-five years previously that it would take him and his troops only twenty minutes to storm the Pratzen heights and so drive a wedge into the Austro-Russian armies to win the battle – to be rewarded that evening by the Emperor saying to him: 'Monsieur le Maréchal, you have covered yourself with glory.'

Then on the morning of 15 December, Napoleon's coffin was carried from *La Dorade 3* to the waiting hearse, a magnificent contraption, ten metres in height, with statues symbolizing the Emperor's past victories and all kinds of ornaments, flags, crowns, and precious stones. When the coffin itself had been placed in the under-carriage, the hearse moved off drawn by sixteen horses, cannonades boomed out from Neuilly and Les Invalides, and the bells of Notre Dame and other churches began to ring. Gilbert Martineau has given us a memorable picture of the cortège. With the National Guard lining the streets, the procession was led by the Seine gendarmerie, mounted municipal guardsmen, lancer squadrons, an infantry battalion, four mounted squadrons of the National Guard, and headed by Gérard – the very man who had vainly urged Marshal Grouchy to march to the sound of the guns at Waterloo, and who was now both a marshal himself and in command of the National Guard: it was a spectacle worthy of the Emperor in whose honour and memory it had been planned and executed. The hearse itself was escorted by Joinville and his sailors; the pall was carried by Bertrand, Molitor, Oudinot and Roussin. Members of the former Imperial Household were followed by veterans of Napoleon's Old Guard. Along the Champs-Elysées went this splendid array, watched among others by the widows of Marshals Ney and Suchet, with hurrahs for the Guard and for the Emperor Napoleon sounding in their ears. Thackeray was there – not only hearing cries of 'Down with the English' but himself noting that there must have been something great and good in Napoleon, something loving and kindly, that his name should be so cherished and that he should have gained such lasting affection. As the hearse passed under the Arc de Triomphe, there was a twenty-one-gun salute, and then on it went across the Place de la Concorde to the Esplanade, where 40,000 guests were seated, and so onwards still until it halted in front of Les Invalides. King Louis-Philippe and his Queen together with the court and ministers were in the chapel; when they were seated thirty sailors from *La Belle Poule* carried in the coffin, which was followed by General Bertrand. The King rose; stepping forward, his son the Prince de Joinville saluted and, according to *Le Moniteur*, spoke: 'Sire, I present you with the body of the Emperor Napoleon.' (Joinville's own recollection is that he did not speak but simply saluted.) The King received it in the name of France. Marshal Soult presented Louis-Philippe with a sword and the King duly gave it to Bertrand, charging him to place it on the Emperor's coffin. Gourgaud then placed the hat Napoleon had worn at Eylau on the coffin, and beside it the cross of the Legion of Honour. The service which followed went on for two hours, Mozart's *Requiem* sounding inappropriate to the ears of Berlioz. The Governor of Les Invalides, Marshal Moncey, who had been so loyal to both Napoleon and Ney, was there, having begged the doctors to keep him alive – he was eighty-six – until he could receive the Emperor. His plea was granted and Napoleon had at last been laid to rest in the beautiful city that he had made the centre of the world.

In that same year, 1840, the Duke of Wellington was beginning to be a favourite with his new sovereign Queen Victoria. Before long he would not only be once more a member of Peel's cabinet, but also resume his duties as Commander-in-Chief of the Army. We will not follow the intricacies of the last dozen years of his life, except to record his ceaseless activity – 'a costermonger's donkey is allowed some rest, but the Duke of Wellington never!' When Peel formed his second administration, he knew that he might rely upon the Duke, who had already made his position clear in another characteristically honest and conscientious expression of loyalty: 'The truth is that all I desire is to be as useful as possible to the Queen's service,' runs his letter to Peel several months before the Tory government took office, 'to do anything, go anywhere, and hold any office, or no office, as may be thought most desirable.' Wellington was a staunch supporter of Peel throughout his administration – even though 'rotten potatoes' (the failure of the Irish potato crop in 1845) put Peel 'in his damned fright' and the repeal of the Corn Laws followed. But it was command of the army that the Duke most relished and on the resignation of Lord Hill in August 1842 he got his wish. He resisted all change, but both kept the army in being and made sure it discharged its duties successfully.

Wellington's second stint as Commander-in-Chief of the Army was spent principally in opposing any kind of real change in its administration or for that matter the recruiting of its officers. He had always believed that the British Army's fine qualities owed most to the circumstances of its being officered by gentlemen, which ensured a degree not only of concord, but also of security. These officers would have such a stake in the continued order of things – constitutional, social and military – that they were unlikely to plump for drastic change, as soldiers of fortune might do. Wellington was therefore wholly wedded to the purchase of commissions, whose worst abuses had been removed by the Duke of York's reforms, as he believed that men of fortune and character in the army were best suited to uphold the well-being and safety of the country as well. Thus he felt that it was better to keep the army's leadership in the hands of sound, if amateurish gentlemen, than of mercenary professional players. Nor did he greatly change his views about the rank and file; although he amended his attitude to flogging later, it was ironic that three days after the battle of Waterloo, a debate in the House of Commons revealed the members' determination that flogging should continue, despite eloquent pleadings to the contrary. Why should the British soldier, opponents of the system asked, be liable to such ignominious torture when no other army was? Surely other methods of punishment could be devised than treating the soldier like a beast. But the counter-argument was that flogging was part and parcel of the British military system of voluntary enlistment (as opposed to European conscription) since those who did volunteer were men from the lowest classes. Indeed the conditions of service – being subject to military law, without legal rights, underpaid, sent off to battle anywhere, there to be killed or horribly mutilated, with no proper medical care and no pension on discharge – were such that no respectable Englishman, however patriotic he might be, was likely to volunteer, unless he were on the run either from the law or from a predatory female. Thus, given an army made up of ne'er-do-wells or those who enlisted for drink, the lash, so the argument went, was necessary to maintain discipline. It was a deterrent which Wellington long adhered to – even as late as 1836 he could not agree that the reforms in the Prussian army should be applied at home. Yet ten years later he acknowledged that flogging would sooner or later be abolished, and he expressed the hope that he would live to see the day.

Yet in spite of this reluctance to do away with flogging, Wellington did much to better the lot of the ordinary soldier – in particular to improve the appalling conditions of barrack life, by introducing proper ventilation, insisting on cleanliness, providing recreation and, most important, making sure that every soldier had his own bed. Although he did not share the enlightened zeal of Sir John Moore, who strove so hard to give his soldiers both self-respect and self-reliance, and insisted that his officers take upon themselves the well-being of the soldiers under their command, Wellington understood the importance of his troops' welfare and did what he thought proper to mitigate their hardships. Lady Longford makes a telling point when she writes that the Duke was devoted to the army 'as a disciplined body of men', as indeed they were to him – not, she adds, 'because he was *séduisant* in the way that people found Napoleon seductive, but for the trust he invited and never betrayed, for the guns he never lost and the armies he never threw away'.

Above all, he kept the army in being. Although he was sometimes accused of hiding it away in the Colonies, it must be remembered that during his time as Commander-in-Chief it had much to do. There were wars in India, Afghanistan, China and Burma, garrisons all over the world, and still the problem of unrest in Ireland and England itself. Of course, he was blamed for not instituting a proper reform of its administration, particularly when the shambles of the Crimean War brought to light its principal shortcomings. But his reasons for opposing such reforms were entirely comprehensible when we remember that they were largely constitutional. As Michael Howard put it: 'If the House of Commons had feared Army reform in the eighteenth century because it would increase the influence of the Crown, Wellington feared it no less in the nineteenth because it would increase the influence of the House of Commons.' Therefore he opposed the notion of the army's being subject to the control of the Secretary at War, for he could not conceive of any future Commander-in-Chief who would both enjoy the confidence of the officers and soldiers under his command, *and* be willing to be directed by a politician. To conserve things as they were, therefore, even though there were faults – for example the inadequate numbers of regular soldiers for the defence of the realm against invasion – was his great aim, and in this he succeeded. 'And why should he abandon it?' asks Michael Howard, as 'with the British Army, imperfect as it was, he had beaten the greatest captain the world had seen for nearly two thousand years'.

Apart from the threat of invasion it was an uneasy time at home for other reasons. Chartism was a menace to public order, and it was the Duke's particular responsibility to advise and prepare for the maintenance of order. Chartist demonstrations came to a head in April 1848, when the Duke mustered a force of 7,000 soldiers and some guns, but kept them well out of sight, so that not a redcoat was in evidence on the day of the great gathering at Kennington Common. Police and special constables were on parade. The potential outbreak of disorder did not materialize.

There were still plenty of petticoats about. To the Duke's great grief, Harriet Arbuthnot had died in 1834, but there were others. 'Apart from finding consolation in Lady Salisbury,' wrote Lady Longford, 'the Duke continued as before to be amused by the designs of ambitious girls.' Among them were Maria Tollemache (later wife of Lord Ailesbury), Mary Ann Jervis, Lord St Vincent's daughter, known as 'The Syren' because she sang beautifully, Anne Maria Jenkins, Lady Georgina Fane, and, of course, the redoubtable Angela Burdett-Coutts, whom we met briefly in the first chapter and who actually proposed marriage to the Duke in 1847, only to be gently dissuaded. In the following year, 1848, there was another French revolution, Louis-Philippe fled to England and Napoleon's nephew Prince Louis Napoleon (who had been a special constable at the Chartist gathering earlier that year) was elected President. Four years later, he would be crowned Napoleon III, Emperor of the French. The Bonapartist dynasty was to be given a second innings. But this second player would prove to be not a patch on the first. Yet much of contemporary opinion welcomed Louis Napoleon's assumption of power on the grounds that it would bring security with it. Even Wellington observed: 'France needs a Napoleon.' This was one of his last pronouncements about his great rival.

In 1852, the Duke of Wellington was at Walmer, and in September reiterated once more a phrase for which he will be gratefully remembered by every aspiring military commander. Visiting his old friends, the Crokers in Folkestone, he was teased by John Croker for not guessing how many hills there were between the station and their house. When Croker's wife looked puzzled, the Duke explained his meaning: 'All the business of war, and indeed all the business of life, is to endeavour to find out what you do not know by what you do; that is what I called guessing what was at the other side of the hill.' Eleven days later, on 14 September 1852, the Duke at last found out what was on the other side of the final hill. 'He was honest, brave, loyal and generous,' wrote G. R. St Aubyn. 'He was universally loved and respected. He walked with kings and kept the common touch. He was laden with honours and titles and wealth, he acquired widespread influence and wielded immense authority, yet nonetheless he survived that corruption which is so often the penalty of power. He was a great and good man, whose example was an inspiration to his contemporaries and when he died the whole nation mourned him.' The Duke of Wellington's funeral service and burial in St Paul's Cathedral on 18 November 1852 may not have been quite as grand as the Emperor Napoleon's final laying to rest at Les Invalides, but it was grand enough. They had been born in the same year. Now both were dead, Napoleon aged fifty-one, Wellington aged eighty-three. Which of them had played the more memorable innings?

CHAPTER 13

Legacy and Legend

Que de souvenirs! Que de regrets!
Lucien Bonaparte to Masséna, 1814

I N *The Prince* we find Machiavelli concluding that he who adapts his course of action to the nature of the times will succeed, while he who sets his course of action out of tune with the times will come to grief. Therein perhaps lies the essential difference between our two men. For whereas Wellington would always weigh the prevailing circumstances most carefully and then make plans to conform to them, Napoleon, having decided what he wanted circumstances to be, acted as though they were in fact so, even if they palpably were not. It was a difference of character which Victor Hugo identified as absolute regularity versus superhuman instinct. Wellington, observed Fortescue, was a St Vincent and not a Nelson.

A comparable distinction was made by Pieter van der Merwe in a letter to *The Times* (22 April 1993) whose principal subject was the matter of Trafalgar Day – he claims that to make it a public holiday would be more likely to foster Anglo-French relations than otherwise. In bringing Nelson into the discussion, he does a great service, for no examination of the characters of Napoleon and Wellington would be complete without looking also at Nelson – as earlier chapters here have tried to show. In answering the question as to why in this country 'Trafalgar still carries a popular emotional charge which the final victory, Waterloo, seems to have lost in Britain while remaining a considerable Napoleonic event to France,' van der Merwe says that 'it almost certainly revolves around the nature of charisma (Nelson and Napoleon) above and beyond exceptional generalship (Wellington).' This is a shrewd observation, for just as Napoleon totally outshone his generals, however brave and capable, and stood head and shoulders above his own relatives, so Nelson towered above his captains, his 'band of brothers'. Yet it was not just generalship that Wellington gave us. As Disraeli observed, there was also the contemplation of his character – a rich legacy indeed. Creevey put his finger on the Duke's great merit when he wrote: '. . . considering the impostors that most men in power are – the insufferable pretensions one meets in every Jack-in-office – the uniform frankness & simplicity of Wellington . . . coupled with the unparalleled situation he holds in the world for an English subject, make him to me the most interesting object I have ever seen in my life.' The Duke's legacy, however, was not even confined to his character. There are also his despatches, which being a model of accuracy, candour, industry and perseverance, illustrate his character perfectly. Disraeli called parts of these despatches the best reading he had ever come across, and even the Duke himself – the first man to eschew all form of humbug – was, on reading some of them over, 'surprised to find them so good – they are as good as I could write now. They show the same attention to detail – to the pursuit of all the means, however small, that could promote success.' In this last sentence he is summarizing his own special talent. Nothing was too much trouble for him.

In an essay about Wellington which appeared in the *Journal des Débats*, Lemoinne noted that 'in his multitudinous despatches, the word *glory* never occurs, but always the word *duty*'. Wellington's own view was, of course, that the means of obtaining glory – not that he ever sought it as such – was through the performance of duty, and as the Hon. G. R. St Aubyn has reminded us,[1] the path of duty was what Wellington trod; it was entirely fitting that on one of the entrances to Wellington College, the orphanage build at Crowthorn after his death for the sons of fallen officers to be educated for entry into the army, should be carved 'The Path of Duty'. But the mere introduction of the word 'glory' makes us think at once of both Napoleon and Nelson. We have seen that Wellington and Nelson, the two principal executors of British strategy against Napoleon, met but once, and that this meeting underlined the difference in their character. The one, aloof, austere, infinitely patient, tirelessly vigilant, an aristocrat, who, without being fired by inspirational genius,

---

[1] *Wellingtonian Studies*.

had made his way with slow perseverance and dedication to the service of his sovereign and fellow countrymen; the other vain, restless, intense, egotistic, paternal, his name still to this day the touchstone of naval excellence, who seemed to have an unrivalled instinct for sensing the feelings of the lower deck. Their horizons were widely different. Nelson was a sailor once and always – although his excursions into diplomacy had not been contemptible – and had he survived Trafalgar, we may suppose that he would have quitted public life, except for an occasional appearance in the House of Lords, and retired with his beloved Emma to Merton. Wellington's ultimate sphere of duty was much wider. Soldier, diplomat, statesman, and ultimately a kind of oracle, he was never and never could be out of harness. Yet they had some things in common – their ardent patriotism, their courage in battle, their simplicity, their unsatisfactory marriages, their diverting liaisons, and their holding and playing the aces of leadership. The four Nelsonian aces were imagination; the ability to inspire; confiding in subordinates and acknowledging their contribution to success; and above all, the offensive spirit. This last one was the kernel of the Nelson touch. The sheer nature of war at sea – control of a fleet being so much tighter than that of an army – made it much easier for Nelson to exploit all his aces. Wellington was less inclined to confide in his subordinates, but he never lacked the offensive spirit, even when conducting defensive battles, nor did his imagination in planning battles fail him, while his sheer soundness, reliability and habit of winning acted as the sort of inspiration which made his officers and men long for his presence on the battlefield. As for Napoleon – if anyone was a manifestation of the four aces to outshine Nelson himself, it was he. Napoleon was like Mark Antony:

> His legs bestrid the ocean; his rear'd arm
> Crested the world; his voice was propertied
> As all the tuned spheres, and that to friends;
> But when he meant to quail and shake the orb,
> He was as rattling thunder.

Napoleon's imagination in conceiving and executing the Italian campaign of 1796 defies comparison, as does the brilliant manoeuvring which led to the triumph of Austerlitz, and, despite initial mistakes, the whirlwind pursuit after Jena and Auerstädt. His confidence in subordinates was unlimited and his praise of their achievements unstinted. The devotion he inspired was as remarkable as anything in history and the offensive spirit never deserted him. Yet, unlike Wellington whose common sense was developed to the point of genius, Napoleon could not or would not see when it was time to call a halt. Imagination was all very well, but not when it ignored hard fact. Both Nelson and Wellington were able to take advantage of occasions when Napoleon allowed delusion to replace deduction.

On the one occasion that Nelson and Wellington met – in Castlereagh's ante-room, it will be remembered – Nelson at first disgusted Wellington with his boastfulness, although he soon changed his tune when he realized to whom he was talking. Not that Wellington disliked or disparaged the position of authority in which he eventually found himself. But again, it was a matter of plain recognition of circumstances. He did not deceive himself. People were bound to consult his opinion, just as they were bound to make calls on his time and on his purse, and that was that. With Nelson it was very different. 'Poor man,' said his old friend St Vincent, 'he is devoured with vanity, weakness and folly.' The fact is, however, that in contrast to the plain, reserved, at times even humble and disinterested man of duty that Wellington was, Nelson from the very beginning had something of the poet and the mystic in him. 'Nelson was the poet in action,' wrote Aubrey de Selincourt, 'in his grandest moments he ceased to belong to this world and entered a realm as visionary as Shelley's.' It is this explanation which helps us to understand why it was that, when he described the intended tactics of Trafalgar, the so-called Nelson touch, to his captains, they were overcome with emotion.[2] It was honour which predominated in Nelson's mind. He coveted honour in the way that both Hotspur and Prince Hal did. Indeed he misquoted from the Crispian speech, substituting the word 'glory' for 'honour'. But the acquisition of honour and glory was not the sole key to Nelson's character. He desired recognition as well. 'I am the child of opinion,' he wrote. So was Napoleon, and he did much to ensure opinion was on the right lines – first by creating his own legend, and then sustaining it.

Wellington despised such histrionics, and cared little or nothing for

---

[2] It also helps us to understand why in his study at Chartwell, Winston Churchill had busts of Nelson and Napoleon, but not of Wellington.

the opinion of others, although he liked to be asked by others for *his* opinion. Perhaps this quiet straightforwardness explains why it was that in France – despite all that Wellington did for that country after Waterloo, being sure, as he was, that France 'would never sleep on the pillow of shame' – it was Nelson who was admired, Wellington who was unpopular. Perhaps it is Napoleon who helps turn the key in this curious lock, for no sooner did he hear of Nelson's 'England expects . . .' signal at Trafalgar than he ordered a similar message to be inscribed in all French men-of-war. There is more to it, of course. What could have a greater appeal to the French than the poet in action, the perpetual seeker after glory, the man who, next to doing great things, loved to write of them? How could they resist a man of whom Thackeray was able to make Miss Crawley say in *Vanity Fair*: 'That was the most beautiful part of dear Lord Nelson's character. He went to the deuce for a woman. There *must* be good in a man who will do that.' Nelson had thwarted Napoleon time after time: at Aboukir, at Copenhagen, at Trafalgar. When there seemed to be no stopping Napoleon, the sailor had stepped on to the centre of the stage, and did not make his exit until the sea-power of France had been broken. Wellington's contribution was less dramatic, less sudden, but no less deadly. After the long Peninsular campaign, which drained the life-blood of the Grande Armée and enabled Britain's Continental allies once more effectively to take the field against the French Emperor, he had at last come face to face with the world's greatest general and done the unthinkable – defeated Napoleon in person.

'What is character,' demanded Henry James, 'but the determination of incident? What is incident but the illustration of character?' We may perhaps reinforce James's rhetoric in contemplating our two men. To appreciate the impact of Wellington's character upon incident we need look no further than at his military campaigns and political manoeuvrings. At the battle of Assaye in September 1803 we see those diverse traits in Wellington's character, not always associated with the Fabian general – desperate resolution, instant decision, calculated risk-taking, utter coolness in the thick of battle, and such tactical dexterity that with 7,000 men he overcame an enemy army of more than 50,000 infantry, countless cavalry and numerous guns, breaking the Mahratta power to such an extent that it was followed by mopping-up operations which brought peace to the Deccan. Here we see Wellesley, as he was then, determining incident in an encounter battle by his possession of 'a cool head, a quick eye and a stout heart' – Macaulay's recipe for the characteristics required for successful generalship. If Assaye was a splendid example of Wellington at his boldest, improvising best, we may now advance six or seven years and look at another side of his character which again determined incident – that side which encompassed infinite foresight, patience, preparation, discretion, administrative brilliance and strategic prudence. In October 1809, having seen off Soult at Oporto, and Victor at Talavera, but knowing that Napoleon's peace with Austria after Wagram would release further French troops for Spain, Wellesley gave orders for the construction in the greatest secrecy of the defensive Lines of Torres Vedras, so that when Masséna and Ney, having been checked at Bussaco, came up against these formidable defences, they reluctantly declined to attack them, starved throughout the winter and then conducted a disastrously punishing retreat. An incident infinitely damaging to the French position in Spain had been brought about by Wellesley's Fabianism. We might add that at Waterloo – the outcome of which determined not just Napoleon's fate but Europe's future – Wellington's own judgement, that had he not been there, it would not have done, must command general approbation. After Waterloo his magnanimity and his shrewd sense of maintaining balance were decisively influential in ensuring both the Bourbon restoration and terms with which France could be reconciled. Yet for all his belief in the old order and his instinctive dislike of radical change, when it came to such disruptive issues as Catholic emancipation, parliamentary reform and the Corn Laws, the strength of his character and the power of his influence were such that the future was shaped for the good of the country and its people. And only Wellington, as he himself claimed, could have insisted on George IV's seeing sense when that extraordinary monarch had to be brought up to the bit. As many have observed, Wellington possessed the advantage of common sense to the point of genius. When informed, for instance, that the ship in which he was sailing was about to founder, he exclaimed that he would not in that case remove his boots. Incidents of his generosity abound, as when his former Spanish liaison officer, General Alava, arrived in England impoverished and exiled from his own country; Wellington thereupon took him to Coutts Bank and told the manager to let Alava have what money he, Alava, thought it proper to draw for. Or as when Charles

Arbuthnot found him stuffing banknotes into an envelope to send to someone in need who seemed to have a claim on him. Or his habit of carrying with him a supply of gold sovereigns to give to old soldiers, formerly in his army, who accosted him in the street. Nor, in spite of his being dubbed the Iron Duke, was he hard-hearted – at Badajoz Picton found him in tears at the appalling losses suffered by his men, and after Waterloo his despatch was blotched with tears as he contemplated the loss of so many friends. Lieutenant-Colonel Sir William Verner, 7th Light Dragoons, was one of many to remember the Duke's kind heart on the occasion of his being ill and receiving a visit from the Duke, who sat at his bedside and talked. His sense of duty has been illustrated a hundred times already, but we may perhaps recall in particular his reaction to being offered command of a brigade after governing whole provinces in India – 'to serve with unhesitating zeal and cheerfulness' in any position that the King and the government thought fit to employ him. When, some ten years later, he was humbugged by Napoleon, there was no despondency or dismay, but simply the issue of clear, cool orders to concentrate the army at Quatre Bras. He even foresaw that Napoleon would not be stopped there and indicated the Waterloo position as the decisive battlefield, to which he unhesitatingly withdrew on hearing of Blücher's mauling at Ligny and retirement towards Wavre. Thus, incident illustrated Wellington's character.

As with the Duke so with the Emperor, but on an even more splendid canvas and in more strikingly dramatic a fashion. At Toulon the charismatic personality, irrefutable eloquence and tactical acuteness of a young artillery officer, Major Bonaparte, turned the tables on a royalist challenge to the Revolution and dismissed a powerful fleet of the Royal Navy. This brought his name to the attention of those Directors in power and, having blown away a further revolution with a whiff of grapeshot, he was given command of the Army in Italy. Now the extraordinary scope of his character was given the opportunity to astonish the world. He inherited the conscript armies of the French Revolution, armies whose rapidity of movement and independence from organized, regular supply enabled him to exploit the ruthless fervour of his soldiers and operate on wide fronts with formerly unknown flexibility and manoeuvrability, to which he added his own soaring vision, clarity of purpose, iron will-power and unity of direction over self-contained divisions of troops which were in their turn commanded by relatively young, yet astonishingly talented generals. By adhering to the principles of singleness of aim, concentration of force, lightning marches and massed fire-power, he overcame his enemies in battle after battle, creating as he did so a legend of genius and invincibility. We may take the Italian campaign of 1796 as a supreme instance of Napoleon's character determining incident. For the next ten years, as he drove his way to supreme power – despite a side-show in Egypt – his defensive wars against Austria (Marengo), Austria and Russia (Austerlitz), Prussia (Jena and Auerstädt), Russia again (Eylau and Friedland), with Napoleon in person commanding the Grande Armée, his own creation, there seemed to be no stopping him. As First Consul, then as Emperor, he imposed his character and will not only on his enemies but on his own people by completely and beneficially organizing the entire political, administrative, commercial and social structure of France. Here we see the most admirable side of Napoleon's character. It is when he starts on his aggressive wars, in Spain and in the Russian campaign of 1812, that the determination of incident turns sour. Even after his defeat at Leipzig, abdication and exile to Elba, the Emperor was not satisfied and his triumphant return from Elba to the Tuileries – the sheer bravado of the whole enterprise, his inviting soldiers to shoot their Emperor, flinging wide his greatcoat, his winning over Ney and the wild enthusiasm with which his veteran soldiers flooded back to his army – was surely a most exceptional instance of the power with which the personal magnetism of the man could overcome the longest odds against him and result in the spectacular and historic incidents crammed into what became known as the Hundred Days. Incident illustrated the many aspects of Napoleon's character, some genial, others less so. When Marie-Louise was having difficulty giving birth to the son Napoleon so ardently wanted, he told the doctors to save the mother first. Yet in shouting insults or threats at Talleyrand, he was grossly abusing his own power. His numerous acts of generosity to his family, his affection for his subordinates, such as pinching Marbot's ear when he was pleased with him, his affability to and concern for the inhabitants of Elba, his superhuman capacity for work, his touching tenderness towards Marie Walewska, his friendliness towards the crew of the *Bellerophon* – these are all admirable. But when he tells Metternich that he cares nothing for the lives of a million men, or talks of burying the world beneath the ruins of his throne, or declares that the Grande Armée has been

destroyed, but that his own health is excellent – we see the megalo-
maniac.

Napier dedicated his *History of the War in the Peninsula* to Wellington
'because I have served long enough under your command to know
why the soldiers of the Tenth Legion were attached to Caesar', while
Stendhal has one of his characters saying: 'Young General Bonaparte,
the conqueror of the bridge of Arcola, thrills me more than the finest
pages of Homer and Tasso.' What are we to make of two such remarkable men?

Incident, of course, not only illustrated character, but shaped it too,
and in the case of our two men shaped them for generalship. It cannot
be doubted that Napoleon was the greater general, commanding larger
armies, in more ambitious campaigns, entering most capitals of Europe
as a conqueror, dictating terms to hereditary monarchs and generally
ordering the affairs of a dozen nations. He mustered, directed and
triumphed with army after army, having what T. S. Eliot would have
called a habituation to war, just as Macbeth has a habituation to crime.
Misfortune, like success, as Metternich puts it, hurried Napoleon to
war. Wellington, on the other hand, loved peace, hated war; and unlike
Napoleon he commanded relatively small armies, seeing to tactical
details himself, riding up and down the line, taking a grip of and rec-
tifying the difficult moment or situation. Wellington looked on the true
object of battles as the peace of the world; Napoleon regarded them as
a means of extending his own power.

Of course, their apprenticeships were very different. The military
fiasco in the 1794–95 Low Countries campaign, when Wellington first
saw active service as a battalion and brigade commander, was to stamp
itself firmly on his mind. Not being responsible for what went wrong,
he was able to profit from it. He learned three things: first, that without
a clear plan of campaign together with the resources to execute it,
England might just as well keep her troops at home; secondly, that
sound administration was fundamental to offensive operations; thirdly,
that the British infantryman was steady under fire and resolute in
defence. And so in India he applied these lessons with great effect,
planning campaigns with meticulous care, then executing them, by personally directing his armies, winning battle after battle, negotiating with
wily potentates – so adding to his mastery of diplomacy, administration
and field command and, as Bryant puts it, creating 'order, trust, stability

and peace out of chaos and anarchy'. Then back at home, grasping the strategic potential of challenging French supremacy in Europe by exploiting Spanish and Portuguese resistance, he conducted a series of what he defined as defensive operations, meaning by this 'not that you should wait in any particular place till you shall be attacked, but that you should attack any party that may come within your reach'. And to the dismay of Soult, Victor, Marmont and Joseph Bonaparte he proceeded to do just this. He was, however, the first to recognize that it could not have been done without the favourable conditions provided by Spain itself, where intelligence, supplies and co-operation were assured for his own army, while the French were denied them and were constantly harassed by guerrillas. What is more, Wellington's conviction that the French tactical system was a false one against steady troops had been vindicated time after time, so that when he came up against the great Napoleon himself, his proven method of defence was once more triumphant.

How different had been Napoleon's own initiation into the art of command! At the age of twenty-four he virtually took charge of the battle for Toulon, saw the key to winning it, convinced everyone that he was right and then did it. Two years later he blew away a revolutionary mob, and got himself appointed to command the armies of Italy, so that, when still only twenty-six, General Bonaparte launched his army against the combined Austrian–Sardinian forces, and by a combination of deception, speed, untold energy and sheer inspiration, beat his enemies time and again, capturing huge sums of money, liberating Italy and threatening the very centre of the Habsburg Empire. He realized too that there was no limit to his future successes. The next venture was dazzling in its conception and initially dazzling in its execution, as Bonaparte descended on Egypt and conquered it, with the grandiose strategic notion of going on to India, linking up with Tippoo Sultan and establishing a great Empire of the East. Even Nelson's destruction of the French fleet did not dismay him. Returning to France, as he had promised he would when France was in need, he proceeded to make himself First Consul, confirmed his position at Marengo, and then advanced to overthrow all the great powers of Europe, making himself Emperor in the process. By 1808 all Europe lay at his feet, Austria and Prussia defeated, Russia an ally, the Iberian Peninsula in his grasp – only England defiant still. And this defiance was shortly to be manifested on land – there was never any doubt as to who was in charge at sea – by the very man whom Napoleon derogated as the Sepoy General.

The business of command has as its indispensable instruments the soldiers who do the fighting, and in their respective attitudes to these instruments is yet another illustration of contrast. Sir Charles Oman[3] criticized Wellington for never winning the affection of his men, even though he won their confidence. The reason for this deficiency, claimed Oman, was that far from feeling a personal interest in them, the Duke regarded his soldiers solely as tools to be kept in good repair. Yet when we look at this charge closely, we find it refuted time after time, not only by studying that surest of all sources, his own despatches, but by consulting the opinions of those who served under him. That they thought of him with respect and even affection is shown by referring simply to either Kincaid of the Rifle Brigade:

We anxiously longed for the return of Lord Wellington ... as we would rather see his long nose in the fight than a reinforcement of ten thousand men any day ... I'll venture to say that there was not a bosom in that army that did not beat more lightly, when it heard the joyful news of his arrival.

– or to Private Cooper, who tells us of his comrades asking: 'Whore's ar Arthur?' and adding 'Aw wish he wor here,' a sentiment totally shared by Cooper himself.[4] These reports hardly conjure up the picture of a cold, hard man who cared nothing for his soldiers. He may have used harsh words about their ill discipline whether in adversity or triumph, but we find him saying nonetheless: 'I know of no point more important than closely to attend to the comfort of the soldier: let him be well clothed, sheltered and fed. How should he fight, poor fellow! if he has, besides risking his life, to struggle with unnecessary hardships.' He goes further and condemns the authorities at home for making decisions 'as if men were sticks and stones'. Wellington's dislike of excessive emotion, his distaste for heroics and lack of sociability, his inordinate zeal in carrying out duties so prolonged and burdensome – these do much to

[3] 1860–1946. Professor of Modern History at Oxford. His works included *A History of the Peninsular War* and *The Art of War in the Sixteenth Century.*
[4] *Rough Notes of Seven Campaigns*, J. S. Cooper, 1869.

explain, although not to vindicate, some of the charges that he was indifferent to his soldiers as men.

A glance at Bonaparte reinforces the case. In spite of all his obsession with the grandeur of a nation in arms, his introduction of the Legion of Honour, marshals' batons in knapsacks, his utter dependence on the French soldier, his emotional eloquence, the habit of embracing his veterans and pulling their ears, Napoleon still found it possible cynically to boast that he had an income of 100,000 soldiers a year. Jules Maurel, like Lemoinne a contributor to the *Journal des Débats*, had this to say of the Emperor at Waterloo: 'Being accustomed, moreover, to consider soldiers in the light of machines, and not of men, he imagined that the Prussian army that had been beaten . . . would be paralysed for a long time. He was blind to the fact that the war for some years had assumed a new character; that the private soldiers were animated by violent passions; and that the English and Prussians in particular fought like men personally interested in the quarrel, and impelled by a fanatical love of honour.' It may be doubted in fact whether the British soldiers, like their commanders, gave much thought to honour. But they had a constitutional dislike of being worsted in a fight and they thought a good deal of their own regiments. The Prussians were more interested in revenge for past humiliations. The point, however, is that the allied soldiers were individuals to be reckoned with.

Nine years after Waterloo, Wellington told Chad[5] that Bonaparte did not care for the lives of his men, while 'we were obliged to husband them'. Maurel confirms this point when he writes of Wellington, 'Never did a commander show himself more caring of the lives of his soldiers, and never did a commander mitigate the labour, privations, and fatigues of his troops with more fatherly care: in fact, never did a general take more pains or care to secure the well-being and comfort of his army.' High praise indeed, and this from a Frenchman who was in no doubt about the greatness of Bonaparte. It shows that Wellington's care was not mere prudence. He always spared blood if he could, and when it had to be shed, as for instance at Badajoz and Waterloo, he shed it only with deep emotion. Napoleon, on the other hand – here we may reiterate the point – coupled the Grande Armée's destruction with his own good

---

[5] George William Chad, 1784–1849, Tory, member of the Diplomatic Service and friend of Wellington.

health and told Metternich that he was not much concerned with the lives of a million men.

One of the more curious and unjust comments about Wellington was made by that incomparably great historian of the British Army, Sir John Fortescue. In describing him as a patriot, whose whole career was one of duty, and in suggesting that Wellington was prouder of being an English gentleman than anything else, he is no doubt right. But when he goes on to say that he took over the British Army as an instrument to save England, and when he had done so 'threw the instrument aside without compunction, having no further use for it', he surely errs, for although the British government had no hesitation in reducing its armed forces after Waterloo for financial consideration, it was not Wellington who dismissed the army. Indeed, how could it be said of the man who toiled as Master General of the Ordnance and as Commander-in-Chief at the Horse Guards from 1819 to 1828, and again from 1842 almost until the day of his death, that he had no further use for the army? He may have resisted change or extra expenditure that he thought unnecess-ary. But, first and foremost, he kept the army in being and made sure it did its duty, as he himself always did. Fortescue recognized this when defining Wellington's true title to fame as 'the most industrious, the most patriotic, the most faithful, and the most single-hearted public servant that has ever toiled for the British nation'.

Another of Wellington's great qualities was his readiness to accept responsibility and blame. After his failure to take Burgos in 1813, and the army's consequent retreat and ill-discipline, although he may have said some harsh things, his integrity and candour were such that we find him writing: 'I see that a disposition already exists to blame the Government for the failure of the siege of Burgos. The Government had nothing to say to the siege; it was entirely my own act.' Or twenty-five years after Waterloo, when Stanhope tells us: 'The Duke lamented the loss of La Haye Sainte from the fault of the officer commanding there "who was the Prince of Orange"; but immediately correcting himself – "No – in fact it was my fault, for I ought to have looked into it myself."' Napoleon, on the other hand, puts the blame for his defeat at Waterloo on Grouchy, Soult, Vandamme and Ney.

In examining the difference in style and method of command between these two men, we must also bear in mind the matter of scale. Wellington was accustomed to commanding an army of at the most 70,000;

Napoleon directed armies of several hundred thousand – indeed in the Russian campaign the total was 650,000. But, of course, as Marmont observed: 'With 12,000 men one fights; with 30,000 one commands; but in great armies the commander is only a sort of Providence which can only intervene to ward off great accidents.' Both Wellington and Napoleon fought and commanded these smaller forces; only Napoleon directed great armies. It is particularly capricious of Napier, therefore, in pointing at both differences and similarities in their respective designs and achievements, to contend first – and correctly – that Wellington 'was less vast in his designs and less daring in their execution than the French emperor ... he displayed less rapidity and originality in his conception', and then to go on to say that their system of war was founded on the same principles: 'firm, tranquil and stubborn in resistance, vehement and obstinate in attack'. For Napoleon very rarely fought a battle of resistance, except after Leipzig. Nearly all his campaigns were those of sweeping manoeuvre, pulverizing bombardment, lightning assaults and grand outflanking movements. It was essentially Wellington who answers the description, and to some extent Napier acknowledges this when he goes on to suggest that in the exploitation of initial success, that is crowning victory with a blow of annihilation, 'the English general was far behind Napoleon'. He compares Wellington's technique with that of a battering ram, which strikes a heavy blow and makes an effective hole, but then stops, whereas Napoleon's battle was 'like the rush and irruption of a gigantic sea, which, descending from a mighty height, bursts through all obstacles and inundates the whole country to a great distance'. The pursuit and destruction of the Prussian army after Jena and Auerstädt in 1806 is perhaps the supreme example of the torrential Napoleonic battle of annihilation. Wellington was never in the position of having sufficient strength, reserves or cavalry to follow up a defeated army in this way. After Vimeiro, Salamanca and Vitoria, for instance, he had to be satisfied with a substantial victory and possession of the field, while obliged to forgo delivering the final *coup de grâce*. Even after Waterloo, he had to leave pursuit to the Prussians. Given, however, this great discrepancy in both scale and concept of operations, we must bear in mind that of the two Wellington was the one who never lost a battle.

Two more somewhat curious comments of Napier's were, first, that Napoleon was more inclined to operate by a flank than by a front attack than was Wellington; second, that Napoleon maintained his communications without extending them too much. Neither of these contentions stands up to serious examination. Although Napoleon's earlier campaigns in Italy were distinguished for rapid and paralysing manoeuvring and outflanking movements, his later tactics, for example in Spain, Austria, Russia and at Waterloo, were characterized more by a colossal blow at the centre of the enemy's forces, followed by an attempt to encircle the flanks. Borodino and Waterloo were frontal slogging matches. In Wellington's case, acknowledging that many of his battles were conducted in defensive positions, where flanks had to be secured rather than outmanoeuvred, when he did attack, at, say, Assaye, Oporto and Vitoria, he made admirable use of the flanks. On the other hand we must concede that in his final brilliant pouncing here and there in 1814, with the Allies advancing on Paris, Napoleon with 50,000 men did show the more ponderous Russians, Prussians and Austrians what could be done in his original, dazzling style, darting and striking everywhere and dismaying his enemy commanders into thinking that after all the Emperor was unbeatable. When it comes to lines of communication, it was Wellington who both in India and in the Peninsula made absolutely certain that, whether advancing or retiring, his communications were secure, his supply depots established and firm bases available, and in general matched his objectives to his resources. A striking instance of this technique was in moving his supply ships and their base to the north as he advanced towards France. By contrast, Napoleon took great risks by *not* securing his communications – witness his furious turning on Sir John Moore's army when it threatened his lines of communication from Spain back to France; or his neglect of such security in the Russian campaign. But then, of course, the whole strategic concept of the revolutionary armies' methods, which Napoleon exploited in his ultraprofessional way, was that they were *not* dependent on slow-moving and organized wagon-trains, but lived off the country in such a way that their speed and flexibility of movement were unlimited, and time after time would appear in front of, behind or to the flank of their opponents' more cumbersome forces. It worked very well for Napoleon while he adhered to those two great principles of war – singleness of aim and concentration of force. But failure to do so resulted in the strategically absurd and insupportable situation of stringing the Grande Armée out between Cadiz and Moscow. And once he multiplied his purpose in this way, he divided and dissipated his army.

Just as, in their conduct of war, we see Wellington's sound organiz-ation and practical husbandry of resources contrasted by Napoleon's grand schemes of conquest and prodigality with soldiers, so we observe also their wholly divergent attitudes to social and political order. 'Take but degree away,' warns Ulysses in *Troilus and Cressida*, 'untie that string, and hark! what discord follows.' In France degree had indeed been taken away, and it was one of Bonaparte's greatest and most admirable deeds that, while still First Consul, he set about the business of fusing the various factions of the nation, of whatever political, religious or social leanings, into one unified France – and at the same time, with almost sublime imaginative idealism, giving the country a system of administration in all fields of human endeavour and requirement, which would shackle accident and bolt up change. Bolting up change was very much Wellington's concern too, but what he wanted was not to create order out of political disorder, but rather to prevent disorder by main-taining the existing order of things. Only when it was clear that change was indispensable to good order would he give way. Then he would cheerfully let principles give way to patriotism. If he conceded some-thing, it was because the country's interests so demanded. He was always concerned to maintain intact those established institutions which he believed enabled England to keep up a barrier against the forces of revolution and anarchy, which had so disturbed Europe. What is more, as long as England preserved its stability, balance could be provided for the whole of Europe.

After the thunderbolt of Napoleon, Europe was in special need of balance. Wellington by his moderation did much to ensure that the roots of yet more turmoil were not sown by the Allies' dealings with France. It was notable that whereas Napoleon consistently misunderstood and underrated Wellington, Wellington was never in doubt about the genius of Napoleon. We have seen that Stanhope's *Conversations with Wellington* contains an interesting passage about the Duke's explanation of his uncharacteristically extravagant statement that Napoleon's presence on a battlefield made a difference of 40,000 men. He subsequently qualified this statement by writing that he should not be quoted as having said that Napoleon's presence was equivalent to a *reinforcement* of 40,000 men, however great the advantage of his being there may have been. As a '*grand homme de guerre*', perhaps the greatest ever to appear in command of a French army, Napoleon was also the sovereign and commander-in-chief of a nation totally geared to war, a nation moreover entirely subservient to his will; he was in a unique position to inspire supreme efforts by the entire army, whose soldiers were unified and inspired by the Emperor's presence, and who could win recognition and rewards from him. Nevertheless, Wellington concluded, his colourful figure of speech was a 'very loose way of talking'. Wellington paid further tribute to Napoleon when he observed after his battle against Masséna at Fuentes de Oñoro that the British would have been beaten if Boney had been there. He also said of Napoleon that there was no general in whose presence it would be more dangerous to make a false move. To cap it all, when asked who was the greatest general of his day, the Duke replied: 'In this age, in past ages, in *any* age, Napoleon.'

The Emperor was not so lavish with praise of Wellington. On the contrary, he had been thoroughly disparaging with talk of the Sepoy General, an emaciated leopard, and before Waterloo: '*C'est un mauvais général.*' Afterwards, according to Elizabeth Longford, Napoleon admitted during his voyage to St Helena that 'the Duke had everything he had' plus prudence. According to Dr William Warden, the senior surgeon aboard the *Northumberland*, however, when Napoleon was asked by him for his 'sentiments respecting the military character of the Duke of Wellington', the Emperor declined to answer. But Warden is generally regarded as an unreliable witness.

Perhaps the most memorable of all contemporary opinion of Duke and Emperor was that of another figure more or less equal to them both in fame and fortune – Lord Byron. Byron was in little doubt as to who was the greater man, although there were times when he was inclined to believe that he himself was greater than either. In 1816 we find the poet talking to his half-sister Augusta and his cousin Captain George Byron. Lord Byron is saying that he considers himself 'the greatest man existing', to which his cousin responds: 'Except Bonaparte,' only to receive the answer, 'God, I don't know that I do except even him.' Whatever we may think of Victor Hugo's calling Byron a greater man than Wellington, we may agree with another writer that Byron was, 'next to Napoleon, the only man in western Europe to command the attention of every intellectual he encountered, and almost everyone else he didn't.'[6] In his verse Byron has plenty to say about our two men. He

[6] *A Single Summer with L.B.*, Derek Marlowe, Jonathan Cape, 1969.

comes down firmly on Napoleon's side for, although he condemned Napoleon the despot, he admired and praised the liberator, and the Napoleonic Code.

> The Arbiter of others' fate
> A suppliant for his own.

and

> There sunk the greatest, nor the worst of men,
> Whose spirit antithetically mix't,
> One moment of the mightiest, and again
> On little objects with like firmness fix't.

He called Napoleon a 'glorious tyrant' and talks of his dominating 'by the power of Thought, the magic of the Mind'. He sees Napoleon's dynastic rivals as wolves, Napoleon himself as a lion. Toward Wellington Byron is less kind. When the Duke is at the Congress of Vienna:

> Proud Wellington, with eagle beak so curled,
> That nose, the hook where he suspends the world.

or

> Go dine from off the plate
> Presented by the Prince of the Brazils,
> And send the sentinel before your gate
> A slice or two from your luxurious meals;
> He fought, but has not dined so well of late.

This particular jibe fitted ill, for Wellington was notably modest in his eating habits – to the great disgust of General Alava, who, on his staff in the Peninsula, would dread the answer the Duke would invariably give to two questions: 'When would headquarters move and what would be for breakfast?' The answers were short but not sweet: 'Daylight' and 'Cold meat'. Byron is harsher when in 1821 on hearing of Napoleon's death, he writes: 'The Miscreant Wellington is the Cub of Fortune, but she will never lick him into shape: if he lives, he will be beaten – that's certain. Victory was never before wasted upon such an unprofitable soil, as this dunghill of Tyranny, whence nothing springs but Viper's eggs.' Nor should we underestimate the power of Byron's influence. Arthur Byrant notes that 'England was typified not by Castlereagh' (about whom Byron was even more bitingly unkind[7]) 'but by Byron', whose ardent embrace of liberal and nationalistic ideas, whose hatred of tyranny and love of freedom – all so wittily and eloquently expressed – had a profound and lasting effect on contemporary opinion.

Not only English literary giants lauded Napoleon. There were the French ones too. Stendhal scorns all who follow him, finds his frankness, good nature and boundless wit enchanting, and writes his *Mémoires sur Napoleon*, whose preface declares that the more that is known of the whole truth 'the greater Napoleon will become'. Victor Hugo called 18 Brumaire[8] the beginning not of slavery, but of the enchantment of all minds; in his poetry he was inspired by the astonishing character and achievements of Napoleon; in the poem *Lui* he writes:

> *Toujoirs lui! Lui partout! Ou brûlante, ou glacée*
> *Son image sans cesse ébranle ma pensée.*

When Hugo hears that the coffin being prepared to bring back the Emperor from St Helena will have the word NAPOLEON made in copper gilt, he cries out that only letters of gold will do. And Hugo also cajoles his companions to talk about the great man: 'It will do us good.' Alfred de Vigny in his *Servitude et grandeur – militaires* hero-worships the Emperor, and when St Beuve in 1811, at only six years old, for the only time saw Napoleon at a military review, it was an experience, wrote Harold Nicolson, 'which remained embedded in his memory for the remainder of his life . . . He found himself placed but a few yards from the Emperor and stared in fascination at his calm white face, at the quick movements of his small white hands . . . The news of Waterloo came to him when he was ten years old. He lay sobbing on his bed in

---

[7]   Posterity will ne'er survey,
A nobler grave than this
Here lie the bones of Castlereagh,
Stop, traveller, and . . .

[8] 18 Brumaire, 9 November 1799, was the day Bonaparte and his supporters removed the Directors from power. Two days later he was inaugurated as First Consul.

a darkened room. These Bonapartist emotions remained with him all his life.' So they did with the soldiers who served with him. The young cavalry *général de brigade*, Marbot, fought at Austerlitz, Jena, Eylau, in Spain, at Ratisbon, Essling, Wagram, in Russia and at Leipzig. He recorded these military adventures in his memoirs and his frequent encounters with Napoleon, whom he served so faithfully. Vyvyan Ferrers reports that his memoirs eventually found their way into the hands of the Emperor at St Helena, and that in his last will and testament Napoleon included a legacy of 10,000 francs to Colonel Marbot, charging him to continue with his writing 'for the glory of France, and to confound all turncoats and all evil-speakers, liars and slanderers'. Ferrers concludes his book by telling us that Marbot did not touch the 10,000 francs, but retained to the end what it was he had his whole life been striving for – 'the good opinion of the emperor Napoleon'. It was an attitude shared by countless thousands of veterans of his former Grande Armée.

It was, of course, to be expected that French soldiers would extol the genius of Napoleon. Less common was the praise of Prussians. Yet Clausewitz is one of the few soldier-historians to give Napoleon some good marks for the Russian campaign, regarded by most observers as a disastrous and ill-handled adventure. While he concedes that Napoleon may have been wrong in undertaking such an expedition in the first place – although the decision was comprehensible in that the French Emperor rightly regarded his position in Poland and Prussia as threatened by Alexander I – and while he also suggests that Napoleon may have been practising his old habit of deceiving himself in his calculations, yet, given that he was to settle matters with Russia, Clausewitz maintains that the Emperor set about achieving his object in the right way: that is, by a bold stroke which would astonish the Czar and bring about the peace that he, Napoleon, desired. The campaign did not fail, so runs Clausewitz's argument, because Napoleon advanced too fast or too far, but because what was regarded as the only means of bringing about victory – the seizure and occupation of Moscow, which should have brought with it the collapse of both Alexander's government and the support of the Russian people – itself failed. Thus in leading his army against the Russian forces, following up their withdrawal, and eventually bringing their main army to battle at Borodino, defeating, but not destroying them there and taking Moscow – in doing what he had so often done before in Italy, Austria, Prussia, even Spain – Napoleon was acting as he had previously acted in making himself master of Europe. 'He, therefore, who admires Buonaparte in all his earlier campaigns as the greatest of Generals, ought not to censure him in this instance.' Clausewitz goes on to argue that had Napoleon brought back across the Niemen 250,000 men, instead of 50,000 – which would have been possible in Clausewitz's view by arranging for the proper supply of the Grande Armée, by securing his line of withdrawal from Moscow, by not over-delaying this withdrawal, and by sounder tactics (Napoleon did not shine tactically at Borodino) – then although half the army would still have been lost, the scale of the catastrophe would have been greatly diminished. To which we might add – had Napoleon been in possession of an extra 200,000 men in 1813, the attitude and aspirations of Russia, Austria and Prussia might have been so altered that Leipzig would not have occurred at all. Such speculation brings us to the squandering of another 200,000 men in Spain.

While it is possible to comprehend Napoleon's hostility to Russia – a country which had after all indulged in numerous coalitions with other powers to bring France down, and whose Czar, after becoming Napoleon's friend and ally, had in the latter's view betrayed this friendship and alliance, and moreover whose armies constituted a permanent threat to the French Emperor's idea of what the future of Europe should be – Spain constituted no such threat. Indeed Spain was an ally, even allowing French troops passage through its territory in order to subdue Portugal, the ally of England. Only Napoleon's trickery and unjustified aggression turned Spain into an enemy – and an implacable one at that. What use would Portugal have been to England in a land war against the French, if France had kept Spain as an ally? But then, of course, without the war in Spain, we would have had no Viscount Wellington of Talavera, no Earl, Marquis or Duke of Wellington, no Lines of Torres Vedras, no battles of Salamanca or Vitoria, no crossing of the Bidassoa. It hardly bears thinking of.

We have noted that in his marvellous book about *Napoleon and his Marshals* A. G. Macdonnell is a little unfair to Wellington, saying that no general in history ever had such an easy task. 'Working on interior lines, with a mercenary army, in a country where every peasant and priest was at once an ally, a source of information, and an active assassin, with a constant flow of supplies from England, and with the complete command of the sea, the Duke of Wellington had the game in his hands, and yet it took him nearly six years to advance from Lisbon to the Pyrenees.' A refreshing view perhaps, but it is easy enough to fall under Napoleon's spell when writing a book about him. A little reflection, however, will not only put a very different complexion on Wellington's achievements, but will also show that Macdonnell misses the very purpose of Wellington's presence in the Peninsula in the first place and for the first years. It was not to advance to the Pyrenees at all. It was to defend Portugal and keep the French busy. We must allow Maurel to take up the story again – and perhaps forgive the hyperbole for the sake of the essence. He makes first the point that it was at a time when the Allies, one after another, had gone down like ninepins – Prussia at Jena and Auerstädt, Russia at Friedland, Austria at Ratisbon and Wagram – that Wellington hit upon his 'idea', his conception of how to strike a blow at Napoleon:

> Amidst this whirlwind of victories one man alone scanned the situation with a steady eye, and measured the whole depth of the chasm. Wellington was aware that fortune could not change sides at a leap . . . he saw at once that Napoleon was not to be beaten à la Napoleon – with his own weapons; that it was folly to stake all on one cast of the die, and to beard his colossal antagonist in his own stronghold; and that, before acquiring the art of gaining great victories, it was necessary to begin by learning to avoid defeats, and for a time to decline all engagements. This idea, simple enough in good sooth, was, as matters stood, a flash of genius. Men of the greatest ability, both in theory and practice, in the cabinet and on the field of battle, had groped about that idea for fifteen years without grasping it. All that Wellington did, said and thought from the first day that he held the supreme command, shows that he was under the sway of this master-idea; that he had a clearly defined system; that he had chalked out for himself a course to follow, and that he clasped it with all the tenacity of his race.

This explains what Wellington meant when he said that, whereas Napoleon's object was always to fight a great battle, his own object was on the contrary and in general to avoid fighting a great battle. It might, of course, be maintained that the idea was not Wellington's at all, but Sir John Moore's. In 1803 Moore foresaw the tactics which some years later were to defeat the French in battle and to destroy their lines of communication. His experience in the field and his tactical imagination inspired him to train the Light Brigade in initiative, manoeuvre and use of fire and movement in a way wholly superior to the French massed columns, and also enabled him to foresee the incalculable strategic potential of guerrilla warfare in the Peninsula. What Wellington did was to put theory into practice. Nothing explains his purpose more clearly than his own despatches: 'Our business is not to *fight* the French army, which we certainly cannot beat out of the Peninsula, but to give occupation to so large a portion of it as we can manage, and leave the war in Spain to the guerrillas,' or 'I shall continue to do the enemy all the mischief which the means at my own disposition will enable me,' or again 'With about 30,000 men in the Peninsula, we have now for five years given employment to at least 200,000 French.' He was convinced that without the presence of his army, neither the Portuguese nor the Spaniards could have resisted, and he was in no doubt that it was in the Peninsula that Great Britain's resources could most severely damage Napoleon. There its army would do ten times more to procure peace than ten armies would in Flanders. He had had his taste of failure and futility in Flanders already.[9] Wellington's task was clear – to waste Napoleon's army until he was strong enough to take the offensive.

Napoleon never understood the game in Spain, or what it was that Wellington was trying to do. He was quick enough to bring to battle any of his other adversaries. But except for his one lightning campaign in 1808, he never bothered to go to Spain himself. It was a side-show, which could safely be left to the marshals. It does not at first seem to have occurred to him that the marshals, far from co-operating in such a way that Wellington's tiny army would quickly have been sent back home, would put their own interests and ambitions first, and France's second. Only when Masséna was appointed to command the Army of Portugal was this particular failing overcome, and by then it was too late, for the Lines of Torres Vedras were complete. Never did Wellington display to more effect his foresight, a single-minded adherence to his *idea*, utter disregard for opinion, and ability to keep a secret, than in his defence of Portugal in 1810. It was wholly clear to him that he

---

[9] We may perhaps note that it was a taste of which Field-Marshal Haig and his fellow generals in the Great War were never to tire.

could only succeed in wearing out the French armies in the Peninsula if he began by conducting defensive campaigns, by refusing battle except on his terms, by keeping his army well in hand, and, although never risking all on a single throw, by attacking the French when he could do so with advantage. Yet the first years in Portugal and Spain were designed to lead up to assuming the offensive when he was ready and the time ripe. It was something that Napoleon did not understand. He looked on Wellington as a man of passive character, and did not see that he was a man of patience. Masséna, as we know, took one look at the Lines of Torres Vedras, gave tongue to some witticism about Wellington's not having built the mountains on which they were based, sat down doing nothing for months, starved and departed. It was the end of all efforts by the French to eject the British from Portugal.

Curiously enough it was at about this time that one of Wellington's rare references to glory appears in a letter. Having made earlier assessments in despatches to Lord Liverpool of what might happen in a thoroughly matter-of-fact way, suggesting that during the opening rounds of the contest there would be 'no brilliant events' and that he himself would be 'most confoundedly abused', he writes to a friend in 1811 – after Masséna's withdrawal and the appointment of Marmont in his place, and before Wellington undertook an advance into Spain – 'Hitherto, the only advantage that we have gained has been glory; but this is a real and solid advantage; for, strange to say, I have managed to hold all in check with the little British Army. I command an army unanimous in its spirit; I have a good understanding with my friends; and I think the whole world wishes me well.'

The world *did* wish him and his army well. It was not so much glory as reputation which they had gained. He had become 'that long-nosed b — who licks the French'. The Allies had found themselves a general. And it was at about this time, of course, that Napoleon began living in a world which Marmont described as being created by his own imagination. He not merely persisted in despatching instruction after instruction to the marshals in Spain, quite unrelated to the conditions or possibilities there, and in any case always arriving too late to have any relevance to the information on which he had based them; he not only failed to see that the winning of a battle by himself would not in the end produce the political hegemony he sought; he not only overlooked the dissatisfaction of the marshals, the disillusion of his allies, the war-weariness of France, and of the army itself; he made the terrible error too of failing to recognize in Wellington a soldier who would rival himself. This may have been one reason for his not returning to Spain. The ifs of history are endless, yet it is tempting to ask what would have been the outcome if, instead of setting out on the march to Moscow, Bonaparte had mustered his veterans and descended into Spain in 1812. It would have been impossible for Wellington to have withstood him. Napoleon chose instead the gigantic gamble of Moscow, and so Wellington was able to write to Charles Stuart: 'I am certain that if Buonaparte does not remove us from the Peninsula he must lower his tone with the world.' What a characteristically Wellingtonian understatement this last phrase is! Yet it touches the very issue of the day, for to Napoleon his tone with the world was all-important. No matter how many times the Emperors of Austria and Russia, the Kings of Prussia and even of England, were defeated in battle, they would retain their thrones, but a once-defeated Napoleon would quickly be shovelled off the stage. And although Napoleon was not personally defeated in Spain, Europe was slowly learning a lesson in the conduct of war there, which showed that if a country suited to guerrilla warfare, that is with the appropriate terrain and a people willing to wage it, is supported by a regular force of some outside power, and both are plentifully supplied with the sinews of war – arms, ammunition, food, forage and money[10] – so that the proper sort of coalition can be made between regular and irregular forces, this coalition is irresistible. It was this that Wellington had seen from the very beginning, inspired no doubt by the uprising in Spain, and making it plain in his memorandum to Castlereagh of 7 March 1809, that in his opinion Portugal could be defended whatever might occur in Spain, provided certain conditions were fulfilled. There would need to be a British army of at least 20,000 including 4,000 cavalry and also a reformed Portuguese army. To start with, moreover, the large French forces already in Spain would have to be kept busy by the Spaniards, whether by their regular forces or by guerrillas. Wellesley, as he was then, also laid it down as axiomatic that if such a course of

[10] Especially money which, as Farquhar put it, is the sinews of love as well as war – a point of view which Peterborough, a former Peninsular campaigner who filled his despatches with epigrams and acquired his intelligence from a string of mistresses, would have wholly endorsed.

action were adopted, everything to supply the army – arms, ammunition, clothing, accoutrements, flour, oats, ordnance, shoes for the soldiers – all would have to come from England. As always in such cases, Wellesley would state all the difficulties, explain how these might be overcome, make no rash promises about instant results, but plainly and sensibly state the strategic advantages together with the detailed administrative steps which such a plan of deploying troops in the Peninsula would respectively offer and demand. Castlereagh was not only convinced of the soundness of the advice Wellesley gave him but was equally certain that the proper man both to arrange the defence of Portugal and if fitting to co-operate with Spanish forces was Wellesley himself. So it turned out. Two years after putting his plan into operation, we find Wellington in a letter to Lord Bentinck both analysing what had by then happened and forecasting what was now to come: 'I have, however, long considered it probable that even *we* should witness a general resistance throughout Europe to the fraudulent and disgusting tyranny of Buona-parte, created by the example of what has happened in Spain and Portu-gal, and that *we* should be actors and advisers in these scenes . . . Those who embark in projects of this description should be made to understand that having once drawn the sword, they must not return it till they shall have completely accomplished their object[11] . . . when a nation determines to resist the authority and to shake off the government of Buonaparte, they must be prepared to risk all in a context which . . . has for its object to save all or nothing.'

Wellington was to live up to his own words. He had already shown his boldness at Salamanca, and in his final sortie from Portugal in 1813 he executed the shortest and most decisive of his offensive campaigns. It was, as it turned out, a masterly piece of timing, for it neutralized Napoleon's successes at Lützen and Bautzen, gave new life to the coalition and put Wellington in a position where, poised on the frontier of France, he could choose the opportune moment for its invasion. The initiative was in his hands, just as it was finally slipping from the hands of his great adversary. It was a nice turn of fortune also that arranged for Wellington to be in Vienna when Napoleon escaped from Elba. It did

---

[11] Wellington here is echoing Clarendon's point about John Hampden who in 1642 raised a regiment to dispute the divine right of Charles I. 'Without question,' wrote Clarendon, 'when he [Hampden] first drew the sword, he threw away the scabbard.'

not take that remarkable trio – Metternich, Talleyrand and Wellington – long to make up their minds what was to be done. Metternich, the cleverest of all the European diplomats, former lover of Napoleon's sister, Caroline, and chief conductor of the Congress, was as determined as Talleyrand – whose principal interests were those of France and of course himself – to ensure that Napoleon was not to be allowed a second innings, and it was clear to both, as it was to Castlereagh, that the employment of Wellington to achieve their aims would be indispensable.

Wellington got to Brussels on 4 April 1815, more than six weeks before his confrontation with Napoleon. Wellington was forty-six, Napoleon not quite. Each was about to fight his last battle. Wellington had by now conducted all types of military operation, defensive and offensive. Napoleon had at one time or another defeated every European army he had engaged except an English one,[12] and he saw no reason to alter his tactical ideas at this late stage. Wellington was essentially an infantry soldier, who had perfected the handling of his trump card, the fire-power of highly trained, disciplined infantry, enhanced by his skilful deployment of light infantry skirmishers (an inheritance from Moore) and his unfailingly sensible selection of ground. Napoleon was an artilleryman, who believed in his own genius for speed and manoeuvre, the devastating effect of massed artillery, the disruptive action of his *tirailleurs*, the irresistible power of his infantry columns, the invincibility of the Imperial Guard, and the torrent-like rush of his pursuing cavalry. If at Waterloo Wellington did not have enough of 'that article' – the British private soldier – together with Blücher's Prussians, the Allies between them had nearly twice as many soldiers as the French and more cavalry and guns. The whole thing from Napoleon's point of view depended on decisive concentration and timing, and on the very occasion when he should have been a tower of energy, speed and clarity, these qualities deserted him. Indeed the Emperor hardly took a personal grip of the battle at all – at least not until it was too late – whereas Wellington's cool and brilliant handling of the line was what won the time necessary for Blücher to bring his army into action and so clinch the affair. Waterloo was more than a battle lost and won. It was, for the time being anyway, a dynasty destroyed and an empire extinguished.

---

[12] Although he chased Sir John Moore's army in Spain in 1808/9, he returned to Paris before bringing the British to a general action, leaving it all to Soult.

'I shall always be a remarkable man,' declared Napoleon at St Helena – a view endorsed by most contemporary and later observers. In an appendix to his masterly *Napoleon*, Vincent Cronin gives us a valuable summary of the memoir-writers who knew Napoleon, pointing out that currying favour with the Bourbons was incompatible with publishing sympathetic accounts of the Emperor. Thus, Cronin explains, many of the recollections published between 1815 and 1830 are not to be trusted – including those of Claire de Rémusat, Josephine's lady-in-waiting, who became a protégé of Talleyrand's; Bourrienne, Napoleon's secretary, who was an embezzler and also a creature of Talleyrand; Barras, who never got over his resentment at being sacked by Napoleon; Talleyrand himself, of course; Marmont – we have already noted that the verb *raguser*, to betray, entered the French language because Marmont became Duke of Ragusa; the Duchesse d'Abrantès, spendthrift, opium addict and royalist; Chaptal, Napoleon's Minister of the Interior, who resigned office in 1804, abandoned the Emperor in March 1814, then accepted office during the Hundred Days, and before Waterloo described Napoleon as a hero who was unsurpassed in military or civil glory – yet who wrote his memoirs after Napoleon's fall to guarantee his re-entry into political life under the Bourbons. On the other hand, Cronin gives high marks for reliability to the reminiscences of Queen Hortense, Napoleon's step-daughter, wife of his brother Louis, and mother of Louis Napoleon. Similarly he finds the Emperor's brother Joseph's memoirs trustworthy, and those of Méneval, Marchand, Bertrand and Caulaincourt. What is the final picture we get from all their impressions and those of a thousand historians who have delivered their verdicts? That there have been so many pronouncements on this matter makes it no easier to choose among them. Yet the summing-up by Lord Rosebery, who knew what it was to play upon that instrument whose strings are the hearts of men, has much to commend it. He calls Napoleon the greatest of all soldiers because of his sheer speed of thought and movement, his inspiration of others, his grasp of infinite detail, his strategic vision and titanic achievements. 'The military genius of Napoleon,' he declares, 'in its results is unsurpassed.' But he goes on to point out that as an administrator too he had no rival, controlling a gigantic governmental machine by his astonishing memory, intellect and energy. Then as a legislator, he produced the Napoleonic Code which has survived a thousand natural shocks, is still the be-all and the end-all here, stretches out still on this bank and shoal of time to mould France's way of life. None of these great deeds would have been possible had it not been for Napoleon's truly iron constitution which supported his superhuman intellect. But Rosebery does not fail to discern the negative side of Napoleon's character. Despite his dazzling progress from military conquest to sovereign and ruler of Europe, there is still the inability to pause, to leave things alone, to consolidate. 'He arrived at the conclusion,' writes Rosebery, 'probably a just one, that his genius was as unfailing in the art of statesmanship as in the art of war, and that he was as much the first ruler as the first captain of the world.' In confirming his greatness, Rosebery concludes that Napoleon's coalition of intellect and energy has never been equalled. 'Under the fiercest glare of scrutiny he enlarged indefinitely the limits of human conception and human possibility. Till he had lived, no one could realize that there could be so stupendous a combination of military and civil genius, such comprehension of view united to such grasp of detail, such prodigious vitality of body and mind.'

Such extravagant language would hardly be fitting to describe Wellington, who would have rejected it anyway. For the Great Duke a more sober, commonsensical judgement fits the bill. It is provided by glancing at some of the contributions to *Wellingtonian Studies*, published in 1958. In writing of 'Wellington: The Man', the Hon. G. R. St. Aubyn pointed out that, for much of his life, the Duke was under the critical scrutiny of the public eye, and that constantly he not merely survived, but triumphed under the scrutiny. 'Even his bitterest rivals conceded that he always acted in the best interests of the country.' There are not many politicians or public figures of whom this can be said. Piers Mackay's portrait of 'Wellington: The General' shows him to have been a master of the battlefield, who was at his best commanding a small army which possessed steadiness, discipline and confidence, and which would conform to his orders. His great battles were won by the fire-power of his infantry and his own personal grip of the action. His courage, example and tactical instinct were both an inspiration and a recipe for victory. Never was Macaulay's definition of what made a general – 'a quick eye, a cool head and a stout heart' – more convincingly demonstrated. To which might be added, a substantial ration of common sense. Harold Nicolson, while acknowledging the mistakes made by 'Wellington: The Diplomatist', praises his striving always for peace and order. The Duke, he maintains, was looked upon in his diplomatic activities 'as an example of a man who was incapable of intrigue, who was moderate in all his dealings and who believed that confidence, which is based on credit, is the true aim of international intercourse and that the best negotiation is that conducted without ambition, stealth, duplicity or cunning'. Would that we had such a diplomatist in our midst today! In writing of 'Wellington: The Statesman', M. G. Brock reminds us that, although the Duke was instinctively opposed to interfering with established institutions, he came at last to see that the Reform Bill had to be passed, and by his sensible leadership of the Lords – both in allowing the Whigs of 1833 to 1841 to carry on the King's and then the Queen's government, and in ensuring the repeal of the Corn Laws during Peel's administration in 1846, on the grounds that the Lords should not oppose the Commons on a major issue – he did much to ensure what he so ardently believed in: the maintenance of good order. Indeed Walter Bagehot regarded Wellington's management of the House of Lords – so that it became 'a revising and suspending House' – as the Duke's sole claim to the name of a statesman. This is perhaps overstating the case, but, as Brock says, it 'remains perhaps his best claim'.

Let us take a last look at our two men before we come to a final comparison of them. We know that Wellington was 'a spare, well-knit, muscular man of medium height with long face and narrow jawbones, an aquiline patrician nose and firm chin, sunburnt complexion, close-cropped light brown hair already faintly streaked with grey, and clear blue eyes of a strange intensity. He had a quick abrupt way of speaking with a slight lisp, and save when roused by iniquity or gross dereliction of duty, a calm equable temper and good humour.'[13] This was how he looked on leaving India. Ten years later in 1815 after his fighting days were over, Wellington was, according to Elizabeth Longford, still in his prime, appearing to be 'taller than his 5 feet 9 inches, while his complexion was still as fresh as a young man's, his forehead romantic and his expression like a Roman hero's'. In this same year, 1815, we see Napoleon through the eyes of Captain Maitland on board the *Bellerophon*:

He was then a remarkably strong, well-built man, about five feet

[13] *The Great Duke*, Arthur Bryant.

seven inches high, his limbs particularly well formed, with a fine ankle and very small foot . . . His hands were also very small . . . His eyes light grey, teeth good; and when he smiled, the expression of his countenance was highly pleasing . . . His hair was of a very dark brown, nearly approaching to black, and though a little thin on the top and front, had not a grey hair amongst it. His complexion was a very uncommon one, being of a light sallow colour . . .

Maitland found his manners pleasing, his conversation lively; he promoted good humour and allowed his staff to be quite familiar, although their respect for him was clear. He had a great knack of impressing favourably those to whom he talked, especially by touching on subjects well known to those he was addressing.

It is perhaps no surprise therefore that Napoleon was so successful among the petticoats, although given his power and position, we may say he was surprisingly moderate. Vincent Cronin tells us that he loved women who were essentially feminine and passionate – Josephine most of all. Leaving Marie-Louise aside, there were Pauline Fourès in Cairo; Mademoiselle George and Giuseppina Grassini, actress and singer of the Paris stage; Madame Duchâtel and Madame Dénuelle, ladies of the court; a girl from Lyons called Emilie Pellapra; and, of course, Marie Walewska. None of these women meddled in politics or attempted to influence Napoleon's policy. It is to be noted that Wellington's taste was otherwise. Never indifferent to a pretty woman, he liked also to talk to them, particularly if they were intelligent and well informed. Their friendship and companionship were important to him. Lady Shelley (even though she overdid her enthusiastic hero-worship), Frances Webster, Harriet Arbuthnot, Madame de Staël, Marianne Patterson, Lady Charlotte Greville, Lady Salisbury, Miss Jenkins and, of course, Flashman's little Angie (Angela Burdett-Coutts) – these women made up for his unsatisfactory marriage. Elizabeth Longford stresses the point that Wellington was 'too much of a gentleman to boast of using women for pleasure . . . in the prime of life he settled for clever women'.

Napoleon accused Talleyrand of being *too* clever, and yet it may be, indeed has been, argued that it was Talleyrand and his fear of Napoleon, even when removed to Elba, which drove the Emperor to quit Elba, because of Talleyrand's demand at the Congress of Vienna that Napoleon be transported to the Azores or St Helena. In other words, as A. P.

Herbert put it, 'Napoleon did not break out of Elba – he was driven out.' Had the French government honoured the treaty of Fontainebleau with regard to money, had Marie-Louise joined her husband at Elba, had Talleyrand been less malignant, or Colonel Campbell more vigilant, had Royal Navy frigates blockaded the island properly, there would perhaps have been no escape, no Hundred Days, no Waterloo. A. P. Herbert concludes that no single person could be arraigned for the tragedy that ensued. Yet he adds this: 'The Emperor of Austria, if he had had more humanity: Louis XVIII, if he had had more sense and honesty: Marie-Louise, if she had had more faith and fortitude could have altered history and let one of the world's great men die peaceful and happy.' Before he did die on that other island, unhappy and restless, Napoleon wrote in his will: 'I have been defeated by the treachery of Marmont, Augereau, Talleyrand and Lafayette.'

The writings and sayings of Napoleon and Wellington, their maxims and aphorisms, will continue to be studied and enjoyed by countless readers. We may perhaps allow ourselves the luxury of recollecting a handful of them. First Napoleon: *'L'ambition et l'occupation des grandes places ne sont pas le bonheur et la satisfaction d'un grand homme, il les place dans l'opinion du monde, et dans l'estime de la postérité.'* To which we might add that in his own particular case, the Emperor both had his cake and ate it. The rewards of greatness were his as indeed were the praise and wonder of posterity. 'What will history say?' General Burgoyne was asked by his major in Shaw's *The Devil's Disciple*. Napoleon had already answered the question: *'Pour écrire l'histoire, il faut être plus qu'un homme, puisque l'écrivain qui tient le burin de cette grande justicière doit être dégagé de toute passion haineuse, de toute préoccupation d'intérêt ou de vanité.'* No one would dispute that Napoleon was more than a man, but whether he put aside all personal interests and vanities, or eschewed all feelings of spite when dictating his memoirs on St Helena, must be another question. His greatness will live in history, as too will his patriotism, for no matter how much we might mistake the glory Napoleon sought for France as glory he sought for himself, none of us would disagree with his assertion that: *'Rien n'exalte plus le courage et l'énergie d'un grand peuple que les dangers qu'il affronte pour conserver la sainte indépendance de la patrie.'* We may be sure that General de Gaulle was not unaware of this Napoleonic maxim when he made his great bid for the honour and freedom of France.

Beside such grandiloquence Wellington's pronouncements seem almost tame, certainly everyday. Lemoinne made it clear that it was necessary to quote Wellington in order to depict the man himself – 'he was so thoroughly honest, so plain, so straightforward, that what would have been with another scepticism or apostasy, was with him only virtue and disinterestedness.' Greville estimated that the Duke's greatness consisted in absolute simplicity, devoid of conceit, plus utter truthfulness and an enduring sense of duty. These elements of his character are illustrated when we find him writing: 'Field-Marshal, the Duke of Wellington regrets, &c., and begs to state that he generally minds his own business', or when he is said to have responded to a publisher's threat to reveal damaging evidence in Harriet Wilson's memoirs: 'Publish and be damned.' Or when asked by Lady Salisbury whether he did not sometimes lie awake with anxiety over political problems: 'No, I don't like lying awake – it does no good. I make a point never to lie awake . . .' Of course, we need to read his despatches and correspondence – a cool two and a half million words of them – to get to the heart of it, but we may perhaps recall the way in which he countered criticism of his soldiers' behaviour in Portugal as an example of his absolute honesty, both of feeling and of expression: 'If the British soldiers have committed, as all soldiers do commit, acts of misconduct, they have at least fought bravely for the country. They have, besides, recently shown that commiseration for the misfortune of the people of this country . . . Yet I have not heard that the Portuguese Government have expressed their approbation of this conduct . . . nor do I find that either their [his soldiers'] bravery in the field, or their humanity, or their generosity can induce those whom they are serving to look with indulgence at their failings, or to draw a veil over the faults of the few, in consideration of the military and other virtues of the many.'

And so we come to the ultimate comparison of our two men – Duke and Emperor. Perhaps one opinion will be sufficient for our purpose here, not only because it is so just, but because it is offered by one whose partiality – if it existed – would come down firmly on the side of Wellington. Elizabeth Longford concedes that 'Napoleon's total genius exerts a more powerful attraction on the world than Wellington's' – because of his poignantly tragic last years and because of his sheer grandeur. She adds that it is the dictatorial masters of the world that continue to capture our imagination rather than the truly deserving. Not only was Wellington less spectacular than Napoleon, he deliberately set out to be so – whereas, in Wellington's own words, Napoleon was not only 'a great man, but also a great actor'. Wellington, we might say, was unsurpassed as a gentleman, Napoleon supreme as a player – and for what stakes!

We are all familiar with the much-quoted saying of Bismarck's that 'political genius consisted in the ability to hear the distant hoofbeat of the horse of History – and then by a superhuman effort to leap and catch the horseman by the coat-tails'. Can there be any more striking illustration of such genius than Napoleon, who not only mounted the horse of History, but rode and guided it for the best part of two decades? It is true that he fell at the last fence but one, then miraculously remounted only to fall again at the last. But what a race! And what a finish! *'Voilà donc enfin le drame terminé,'* Lucien Bonaparte had written to Masséna in 1814. *'Tant de gloire perdue par la plus lâche fin. Bon Dieu! Que de souvenirs. Que de regrets.'* Wellington too had his memories and will always be remembered. Did he have regrets as well? When asked late in his life whether he could have wished to have done anything differently, he replied that he should have given more praise. His not having done so is perhaps explained by his never soliciting, indeed positively eschewing the praise of others. He too, like Nelson, but to a lesser degree, heard the horse of History's hoofbeats, and caught the horseman by his coat-tails both in India and in the Peninsula. He too rode it, but in a less dramatic and more pragmatic way than Napoleon. He mostly stayed in the saddle, yet as we have seen, was mistaken in deciding to remount in 1842. This talk of horses puts us in mind of a final and agreeable similarity between them: both Napoleon and Wellington loved horses. We have only to think of the Emperor's Marengo and the Duke's Copenhagen. How well, how boldly, how nobly, they carried their respective masters! The Napoleonic legend lives on, Wellington's legacy remains. We may perhaps leave the last word to Shakespeare, who in any case usually has it about all human activities, endeavours, thoughts, emotions or characteristics. In this case we need go no further than one play. Of Wellington we may observe that, despite all the fighting, his life was gentle (as became a gentleman); and the elements so mix'd in him that nature might stand up and say to all the world: 'This was a man.' For Napoleon, the great player, the gigantic gambler, the soaring eagle, there is a shorter tribute. He was a modern Caesar, and bestrode this narrow world like a Colossus. When we read or write of him today, he still does.

Bibliography

ANGLESEY, THE MARQUESS OF, *The Capel Letters, 1814–1817*, Cape, 1955.

AUDEN, W. H. AND KRONENBERGER, LOUIS (eds), *The Faber Book of Aphorisms*, Faber & Faber, 1962.

BAGEHOT, WALTER, *The English Constitution*, The World's Classics, OUP, 1928 (first pub. 1867).

BARNETT, CORRELLI, *Bonaparte*, George Allen & Unwin, 1978.

BLAKE, ROBERT, *Disraeli*, Eyre & Spottiswoode, 1966.

BRETT-JAMES, ANTHONY, *1812*, Macmillan, 1966.

BRYANT, SIR ARTHUR, *Freedom's Own Island*, Collins, 1986.

BRYANT, SIR ARTHUR, *The Years of Endurance*, Collins, 1942.

BRYANT, SIR ARTHUR, *Years of Victory*, Collins, 1944.

BRYANT, SIR ARTHUR, *The Age of Elegance*, Collins, 1950.

BRYANT, SIR ARTHUR, *The Great Duke*, Collins, 1971.

CECIL, DAVID, *Lord M*, Constable, 1954.

CHURCHILL, SIR WINSTON, *A History of the English-Speaking Peoples*, volumes III and IV, Cassell, 1957, 1958.

VON CLAUSEWITZ, CARL, *On War*, 3 volumes (tr. by Col. J. J. Graham), Routledge & Kegan Paul, 1949.

COOPER, DUFF, *Talleyrand*, Cape, 1932.

CRONIN, VINCENT, *Napoleon*, Collins, 1971.

DISRAELI, BENJAMIN, *Sybil or The Two Nations*, The World's Classics, OUP, 1926 (first pub. 1845).

EDWARDS, WILLIAM, *Notes on European History*, vol. IV, Rivingtons, 1937.

FERRERS, VYVYAN, *The Brigadier*, Art & Educational Publishers Ltd, 1948.

FORTESCUE, SIR JOHN, *A History of the British Army*, Macmillan, 1899–1930.

HAZLITT, WILLIAM, *Selected Essays*, The Nonesuch Press, 1934.

HEALEY, EDNA, *Lady Unknown, The Life of Angela Burdett-Coutts*, Sidgwick & Jackson, 1978.

HERBERT, A. P., *Why Waterloo?*, Methuen, 1952.

HIBBERT, CHRISTOPHER, *George IV, Prince of Wales*, Longman, 1971.

HOWARD, MICHAEL (ed), *Wellingtonian Studies*, Gale & Polden, 1958.

HOWARTH, DAVID, *A Near Run Thing*, Collins, 1968.

HUGO, VICTOR, *The Battle of Waterloo*, Haldeman-Julius Company.

KEEGAN, JOHN, *The Face of Battle*, Cape, 1976.

KEEGAN, JOHN, *The Mask of Command*, Cape, 1987.

LONGFORD, ELIZABETH, *Wellington: The Years of the Sword*, Weidenfeld & Nicolson, 1969.

LONGFORD, ELIZABETH, *Wellington: Pillar of State*, Weidenfeld & Nicolson, 1972.

LUDWIG, EMIL, *Napoleon*, Modern Library, New York, 1953.

MACAULAY, THOMAS BABINGTON, *Critical and Historical Essays*, Dent, 1907.

MACDONNELL, A. G., *Napoleon and his Marshals*, Macmillan, 1950.

MARCHAND, LESLIE A., *Byron: A Portrait*, John Murray, 1971.

MARTINEAU, GILBERT, *Napoleon's Last Journey*, John Murray, 1976.

MERCER, GENERAL CAVALIÉ, *Journal of the Waterloo Campaign*, Liverset Publishing, London, 1870.

NAPIER, SIR WILLIAM, *History of the War in the Peninsula*, Constable, 1992 (originally published by Thomas and William Boone, 1832).

NICOLSON, HAROLD, *Sainte-Beuve*, Constable, 1957.

NICOLSON, NIGEL, *Napoleon 1812*, Weidenfeld & Nicolson, 1985.

OMAN, SIR CHARLES, *A History of the Peninsular War*, OUP, 1902–31.

PETRIE, SIR CHARLES, *When Britain Saved Europe*, Eyre & Spottiswoode, 1941.

PLUMB, J. H., *The First Four Georges*, Batsford, 1956.

POCOCK, TOM, *Horatio Nelson*, Bodley Head, 1987.

READ, JAN, *War in the Peninsula*, Faber & Faber, 1977.

RICHARDSON, FRANK, *Napoleon's Death: An Inquest*, William Kimber, 1974.

RIDLEY, JASPER, *Lord Palmerston*, Constable, 1970.

ROSEBERY, LORD, *Napoleon: The Last Phase*, Arthur L. Humphreys, 1900.

ROTHENBERG, GUNTHER E., *The Art of Warfare in the Age of Napoleon*, Batsford, 1977.

SONTAG, SUSAN, *The Volcano Lover*, Cape, 1992.

STANHOPE, PHILIP HENRY, 5TH EARL OF, *Conversations with Wellington*, The World's Classics, Oxford, 1938 (first pub. 1888).

TOLSTOY, LEO, *War and Peace*, Penguin Books, 1957.
WATSON, J. STEVEN, *The Reign of George III, 1760–1815*, OUP, 1960.
WATSON, S. J., *Carnot*, Bodley Head, 1954.
WILLIAMSON, J. A., *The Evolution of England*, OUP, 1931.
WOODWARD, SIR LLEWELLYN, *The Age of Reform, 1815–1870*, OUP, 1962.

Index

Abercromby, General, Sir Ralph, 39, 66, 67, 77, 78
Aboukir, 58, 59, 61, 77, 274
Abrantes, 137
Abrantès, Duchesse d', 297
Acre, 23, 60, 61, 62
Adda, River, 46
Addington, Henry, 77, 79, 80, 81, 82, 83, 84, 96
Adige, River, 48, 49
Agueda, River, 147, 161
Ahmednuggur, 86, 87
Aix, 201
Aix-la-Chapelle, Congress of, 239, 240, 244
Ajaccio, 26
Alava, General, 275, 287
Alba Castle, 163
Alba de Tormes, 164
Albenga, 44
Albuera, battle of, 147
Alessandria, 44
Alexander I, Czar of Russia, and Third Coalition against France, 94–5, and battle of Austerlitz, 103, and treaty of Tilsit, 115, comment on Napoleon's character, 133, 148, and Napoleon's marriage, 142, and war with France, 150–1, 152, 157–8, 159, 160, 161, 171, 173, 289, alliance with Prussia, 178, suggests Bernadotte as successor to French throne, 198, and Congress of Vienna, 200, and Congress of Aix-la-Chapelle, 244, mentioned, 17, 186, 199, 211, 213, 239, 252
Alexandria, 57, 58, 59, 77, 78
Almarez, 157
Almeida, 143, 145, 146, 147
Alps, 35, 44, 192
Alvanley, Lord, 241
Alvinzi, General, 48, 49

Amiens, Peace of, 80, 81, 82, 85, 93
Ancona, 49
Andalusia, 142
Andréossi, Antoine François, 238
Anglesey, Marquess of *see* Paget, Lord Henry (later Earl of Uxbridge and Marquess of Anglesey)
Antommarchi, Dr, 246, 248
Antwerp, 139
Arbuthnot, Charles, 275–6
Arbuthnot, Mrs Harriet, 22, 112, 243, 251, 268, 300
Arcola, battle of, 48
Arcot, 87
Ardennes, 211
Argaum, 91
Arnott, Dr, 248
Aspern-Essling, 134, 221
Assaye, battle of, 17, 89–91, 274–5, 284
Astorga, 130
Auerstädt, battle of, 110, 111, 134, 272, 277, 283, 291
Augereau, Marshal, 14, 40, 41, 44, 47–8, 85, 94, 114, 189, 211, 301
Austerlitz, battle of, 15, 19, 24, 100, 101, 103, 107, 115, 134, 195, 221, 237, 264, 272, 277, 289

Bachelu, 220
Badajoz, 145, 146, 147, 154, 155, 156, 157, 158, 170, 276, 281
Bagehot, Walter, 18–19, 20, 24, 25, 37, 92, 102, 113, 126, 230, 299
Bagration, Peter Ivanovich, 159, 160, 166, 167, 169
Baird, Major-General David, 64, 65, 127, 128, 130
Balashov, 159, 160, 161
Bamberg, 213

309

Burrard, General Sir Harry, 120–1, 122, 125, 126
Bussaco, 143, 275
Byron, Captain George (cousin of Lord Byron), 286
Byron, Lord George Gordon, 61, 69, 194, 230, 242, 252, 255, 255n, 286–8

Cadibona Pass, 44
Cadiz, 33, 54, 74, 101, 117, 152, 177, 239, 284
Cairo, 58, 59, 60, 77, 300
Calcutta, 52, 62, 93
Calder, Admiral, 98
Campbell, Colin, 91
Campbell, Lady John, 213
Campbell, Colonel Neil, 194, 200, 201, 203, 205, 301
Campo Formio, Peace of, 50
Canning, George, 76, 115, 116, 119, 214, 250, 251, 252, 256
Cap d'Antibes, 205
Capel, Lady Caroline, 196, 211, 213
Capel, Maria ('Muzzy'), 196–7
Cape St Vincent, battle of, 53–4
Capodistrias, 244
Carlos, Don, de España, 164
Carlyle, Thomas, 258
Carnot, Lazare, 29–30, 35
Caroline of Brunswick, 245–6
Carrion de los Condes, 129
Carteaux, General, 35, 36
Castiglione, battle of, 14, 48
Castlereagh, Lord, and size of army, 109, in relation to Wellington, 120, 131, 137, 147, 203, 206, 250–1, 294, 295, 296, becomes Foreign Secretary, 147, wants workable settlement with France, 198, signs treaty of Paris, 198, at Congress of Vienna, 199, 200, policies, 240, at Congress of Aix-la-Chapelle, 244, mental derangement, 250–1, death, 251, Napoleon's view of, 254, Bryon's view of, 288, 288n, mentioned, 81, 93, 97, 214, 233, 234, 243
Catherine the Great, 50, 68
Caulaincourt, General Armand Augustin Louis Marquis de, 150, 150n, 152, 158, 166, 167, 169, 172, 174, 188, 198, 297
Cessac, de, 151
Ceva, 45
Chaboulon, Fleury de, 204
Chad, George William, 17, 281, 281n
Chambray, Marquis de, 174
Champaubert, 19, 193
Chandler, David, 216

Chaptal, 297
Charleroi, 211, 214, 215, 216, 219, 227
Charles IV, King of Spain, 117, 118
Charles X, King of France, 250, 253, 254–5
Charles XII, King of Sweden, 167, 167n
Charles XIII, King of Sweden, 151
Charles, Archduke of Austria, 66, 68, 103, 133, 134
Charles, Lieutenant Hippolyte, 51, 61, 69
Chateaubriand, François René de, 255
Château de Hougoumont see Hougoumont
Château-Thierry, 19, 193
Chatham, 33
Chatham, Earl of, 139
Chatham, Lord, 236
Châtillon-sur-Marne, 193
Chauvelin, François Claude de, 28
Cherasco, 45
Cherbourg, 202, 263
Chichagov, 172
Chitteldroog, 73
Churchill, Winston, 51, 273n
Cintra, Convention of, 125
Ciudad Rodrigo, 128, 135, 143, 145, 147, 152–4, 157, 170
Clary, Désirée, 39
Clausel, Bertrand, 163, 239
Clausewitz, Carl von, 289, 290
Clive, Robert, 52–3, 87
Clive, Lord (son of Robert Clive), 63
Close, Colonel, 64
Cockburn, Admiral Sir George, 233
Codrington, Admiral, 256
Coffin, General, 248
Coggan, Mrs, 93
Coimbra, 136, 143, 144
Colbert, General, 85
Colborne, Colonel, 153, 227
Cole, General Sir Lowry, 190
Collingwood, Lord, 54, 100–1
Como, 47
Constantinople, 55, 95
Cooper, Duff, 55–6, 178, 192–3, 234
Cooper, Private, 280
Copenhagen, 74, 79, 274
Corsica, 26, 42
Corunna, 78, 120, 128, 130, 131
Cotton, Admiral, 120
Cotton, General, 163, 164
Courbevoie, 264
Craufurd, Madame, 246
Craufurd, Major-General Robert, 130, 139, 143, 146, 153
Creevey, Thomas, 212, 212n, 228, 252, 258, 271

Mornington, Richard Wellesley, Lord
'Wellington's brother; Governor-General of
India; later Marquess of Wellesley), 54, 55,
62, 63, 64, 65, 85, 142
Mortier, Marshal, 68, 127, 158, 159, 164, 189,
211
Moscow, 74, 117, 148, 160, 161, 167, 169,
170, 171, 172, 174, 195, 237, 238, 284, 289,
290, 294
Mount Tabor, 61
Müffling, General, 215–6, 223
Munich, 76
Murat, Caroline (née Bonaparte) *see*
Bonaparte, Caroline
Murat, Joachim, as Napoleon's ADC, 39,
character, 41, at Aboukir, 61–2, and *coup
d-état*, 70, 71, in charge of cavalry, 85,
appointed Marshal, 94, at Spitz, 103,
becomes Grand Duke of Berg and Cleves,
105, and Pursuit of the Three Marshals,
111, at Eylau, 114, suppresses rising in
Madrid, 118, and intrigue against Napoleon,
130, at Danzig, 158, in Russia, 165, 167,
169, 175, at Leipzig, 189, and Napoleon's
return, 211, mentioned, 60, 102, 109, 110,
152, 178, 236, 238, 239, 246
Murillo, General, 19–20
Mysore, 55, 63, 72, 73, 74, 86

Nagpore, 86
Nangis, 19, 193
Napier, William, 118, 145, 156, 163, 229, 278,
283
Naples, 34, 49, 57, 65, 66, 95
Napoleon II, King of Rome, Duke of
Reichstadt (son of Napoleon), 210, 259–60,
261
Napoleon III, 250
Narbonne, Count, 157, 158
Navarino, battle of, 256
Neipperg, Count, 195, 201, 236
Nelson, Horatio, at Toulon, 33, 34, and Emma
Hamilton, 34–5, 57, 60, 65–6, 99, at battle
of Cape St Vincent, 53–4, searches for
French fleet, 56–8, at battle of the Nile,
59–60, and Northern League, 78–9, meets
Wellington, 93, 97–9, 273, and battle of
Trafalgar, 100–2, charisma, 270–1,
character, 273, compared with Wellington,
273, 274, mentioned, 23, 74, 80, 85, 96,
272, 279
Nesselrode, Count, 198, 199
Ney, Michel, as corps commander, 85,
appointed Marshal, 94, at Elchingen, 102, at
Jena, 110, at Friedland, 115, and plans for

advance into Spain, 127, at Salamanca, 143,
and Lines of Torres Vedras, 144, 275, in
Russia, 165, 167, 169, 170, 173, 175,
237–8, at Lützen, 179, at Leipzig, 189, and
abdication of Napoleon, 193, signs treaty of
Paris, 198, and Napoleon's return, 208–9,
253, 277, given responsibility by Napoleon,
210, 214, at Quatre Bras, 217, 221, 222,
230, at battle of Waterloo, 217, 219, 222,
223, 225, 226, 227, 229, 282, execution,
227n, 238, 240, 241–2, mentioned, 68, 100,
129, 178, 264, 265
Nice, 39, 40, 42, 68
Nicholas I, Czar of Russia, 252, 255
Nicolson, Harold, 243, 288, 298–9
Nicolson, Nigel, 173–4
Niemen, River, 115, 151–2, 158, 159, 160,
175, 237, 290
Nieuport, 35
Nile, battle of the, 59
Nivelle, battle of the, 192
Nivelles, 215, 216

Oder, River, 179, 187
Old Castile, 24, 128, 129, 182
Oman, Sir Charles, 129, 280
O'Meara, Dr, 253–4
Oporto, 120, 135, 136, 181, 275, 284
Orange, Prince of, 215, 216, 282
Orcha, 172, 173
Orrock, Colonel, 90
Ostend, 35
Oudinot, Marshal Nicolas Charles, 68, 103,
133, 165, 175, 178, 188, 189, 193, 264

Pack, Major-General Sir Denis, 224
Paget, Edward, 77, 130
Paget, Lord Henry (later Earl of Uxbridge and
Marquess of Anglesey), 67–8, 98, 127, 128,
130, 196, 212, 217, 222–3, 224, 227, 246
Pakenham, Edward, 24, 162, 163
Pakenham, Kitty (later Kitty Wellesley), 28,
37, 51, 93, 99–100, 111, 112, 196
Pakenham, Tom, 28
Palencia, 182
Palermo, 65
Palmerston, Henry John Temple, 3rd
Viscount, 245, 261, 262
Pamplona, 184, 189, 190, 191, 192
Papelotte, 227
Paris, 24, 27, 28, 34, 36, 39, 45, 51, 60, 61,
65, 69, 70, 83, 99, 113, 130, 158, 170, 174,
175, 176, 192, 193, 196, 197, 203, 204, 206,
208, 210, 212, 214, 228, 241, 242, 246, 260,
284, treaty of, 198